Lecture Notes in Artificial Intelligence   1147

Subseries of Lecture Notes in Computer Science
Edited by J. G. Carbonell and J. Siekmann

Lecture Notes in Computer Science

Edited by G. Goos, J. Hartmanis and J. van Leeuwen

Springer

Berlin
Heidelberg
New York
Barcelona
Budapest
Hong Kong
London
Milan
Paris
Santa Clara
Singapore
Tokyo

Laurent Miclet   Colin de la Higuera (Eds.)

Grammatical Inference: Learning Syntax from Sentences

Third International Colloquium, ICGI-96
Montpellier, France, September 25-27, 1996
Proceedings

Springer

Series Editors
Jaime G. Carbonell, Carnegie Mellon University, Pittsburgh, PA, USA
Jörg Siekmann, University of Saarland, Saarbrücken, Germany

Volume Editors

Laurent Miclet
École Nationale Supérieure de Science Appliquées et Technologie
6, rue de Kerampont, F-22305 Lannion Cedex, France
E-mail: miclet@enssat.fr

Colin de la Higuera
LIRMM, Département d'Informatique Fondamentale (DIF)
161 rue Ada, F-34392 Montpellier Cedex 5, France
E-mail: cdlh@lirmm.fr

Cataloging-in-Publication Data applied for

Die Deutsche Bibliothek - CIP-Einheitsaufnahme

Grammatical inference: learning syntax from sentences : third
international colloquium ; proceedings / ICGI 96, Montpellier,
France, September 25 - 27, 1996. Laurent Miclet ; Colin de la
Higuera (ed.). - Berlin ; Heidelberg ; New York ; Barcelona ;
Budapest ; Hong Kong ; London ; Milan ; Paris ; Santa Clara ;
Singapore ; Tokyo : Springer, 1996
  (Lecture notes in computer science ; Vol. 1147 : Lecture notes in
  artificial intelligence)
  ISBN 3-540-61778-7
NE: Miclet, Laurent [Hrsg.]; ICGI <3, 1996, Montpellier>; GT

CR Subject Classification (1991): I.2, F.4.2-3, I.5.1, I.5.4, J.5

ISBN 3-540-61778-7 Springer-Verlag Berlin Heidelberg New York

© Springer-Verlag Berlin Heidelberg 1996
Printed in Germany

Typesetting: Camera ready by author
SPIN 10513770   06/3142 – 5 4 3 2 1 0   Printed on acid-free paper

Preface

This book contains the two invited contributions and the twenty-five papers that were selected by the Scientific Committee for the International Colloquium on Grammatical Inference 1996 (ICGI '96), held in Montpellier, France, from the 25th to the 27th of September 1996.

Grammatical inference is a field with many facets: it can broadly be understood as a part of machine learning devoted to extracting syntactic structures from sentences. As such, it can be studied from several theoretical points of view, but also opens into a series of very promising applications.

The papers presented here show that a number of different mathematical and algorithmic tools can be applied to study grammatical inference: language theory, inductive inference, PAC-learning, statistical learning, neural networks. They also sample several application fields where such algorithms can be useful: natural language learning, speech recognition, automatic translation, pattern recognition, etc.

Grammatical inference is one of the few subproblems of machine learning that spans over almost all the research fields of this discipline. Since its practical applications are also of great variety and interest, it may be thought that its current blossoming will continue.

ICGI '96 is the third of a series initiated in 1993, at Essex University (U.K.), and continued in 1994, in Alicante (Spain). The papers of the latter have been edited as the volume "Grammatical Inference and Applications", LNAI 862 (Springer-Verlag), R. C. Carrasco and J. Oncina (Eds).

ICGI '96 has been possible thanks to the French Centre National de la Recherche Scientifique, the Région Languedoc-Roussillon, the Ministère Français des Affaires Étrangères, and the Universities of Montpellier 2 and Rennes 1. ICGI '96 also received support from the Special Interest Group in Natural Language Learning of the ACL.

September 1996

Laurent Miclet
Colin de la Higuera

Chairperson
Laurent Miclet

Organization
Colin de la Higuera

Scientific Committee
J. Berstel (University Paris 6, France)
M. Brent (J. Hopkins University, USA)
H. Bunke (University of Bern, Switzerland)
C. Cardie (Cornell University, USA)
W. Daelemans (KUB, Nederlands)
P. Dupont (FT-CNET, France)
O. Gascuel (LIRMM, France)
C. L. Giles (NEC Princeton, USA)
J. Gregor (University of Tennessee, USA)
J. P. Haton (CRIN-INRIA, France)
F. Jelinek (J. Hopkins University, USA)
T. Knuutila (University of Turku, Finland)
S. Lucas (University of Essex, England)
D. Luzeaux (ETCA, France)
D. Magerman (Renaissance Technology, USA)
E. Makinen (University of Tampere, Finland)
R. Mooney (University of Texas, USA)
G. Nagaraja (IIT Bombay, India)
J. Nicolas (IRISA, France)
J. Oncina, University of Alicante, Spain)
L. Pitt (University of Illinois, USA)
D. Powers (Flinders University, Australia)
Y. Sakakibara (Fujitsu Laboratories Ltd, Japan)
A. Stolcke (SRI International, Menlo Park, USA)
E. Vidal (Universidad Politecnica de Valencia, Spain)

Organization Committee
C. de la Higuera (LIRMM, France)
E. Ahronovitz (LIRMM, France)
A. Castellanos (Universidad Politecnica de Valencia, Spain)
P. Jappy (LIRMM, France)
R. Nock (LIRMM, France)
D. Pierre (LIRMM, France)
A. Preller (LIRMM, France)
J. M. Sempere (Universidad Politecnica de Valencia, Spain)
C. Zicler (LIRMM, France)

Table of Contents

Learning Grammatical Structure Using Statistical Decision-Trees*

David M. Magerman
magerman@rentec.com

Renaissance Technologies Corp.

Abstract. In this paper, I describe SPATTER, a statistical parser based on decision-tree learning techniques which avoids the difficulties of grammar development simply by having no grammar. Instead, the parser is driven by statistical pattern recognizers, in the form of decision trees, trained on correctly parsed sentences. This approach to grammatical inference results in a parser which constructs a complete parse for every sentence and achieves accuracy rates far better than any previously published result.

1 Introduction

Parsing a natural language sentence can be viewed as making a sequence of disambiguation decisions: determining the part-of-speech of the words, choosing between possible constituent structures, and selecting labels for the constituents. Traditionally, disambiguation problems in parsing have been addressed by enumerating possibilities and explicitly declaring knowledge which might aid the disambiguation process, i.e. writing a grammar. However, this approach has proved too brittle for most interesting natural language problems.

This work addresses the problem of automatically discovering the disambiguation criteria for all of the decisions made during the parsing process, given the set of possible features which can act as disambiguators. The candidate disambiguators are the words in the sentence, relationships among the words, and relationships among constituents already constructed in the parsing process.

Since most natural language rules are not absolute, the disambiguation criteria discovered in this work are never applied deterministically. Instead, all decisions are pursued non-deterministically according to the probability of each choice. These probabilities are estimated using statistical decision tree models. The probability of a complete parse tree (T) of a sentence (S) is the product of each decision (d_i) conditioned on all previous decisions:

$$P(T|S) = \prod_{d_i \in T} P(d_i|d_{i-1}d_{i-2}\ldots d_1 S).$$

---

* This paper discusses work performed at the IBM Speech Recognition Group under Frederick Jelinek and at the BBN Speech Recognition Group under John Makhoul.

Each decision sequence constructs a unique parse, and the parser selects the parse whose decision sequence yields the highest cumulative probability. By combining a stack decoder search with a breadth-first algorithm with probabilistic pruning, it is possible to identify the highest-probability parse for any sentence using a reasonable amount of memory and time.

The claim of this work is that statistics from a large corpus of parsed sentences combined with information-theoretic classification and training algorithms can produce an accurate natural language parser without the aid of a complicated knowledge base or grammar. This claim is justified by constructing a parser, called SPATTER (Statistical PATTErn Recognizer), based on very limited linguistic information, and comparing its performance to a state-of-the-art grammar-based parser on a common task.

One of the important points of this work is that statistical models of natural language should not be restricted to simple, context-insensitive models. In a problem like parsing, where long-distance lexical information is crucial to disambiguate interpretations accurately, local models like probabilistic context-free grammars are inadequate. This work illustrates that existing decision-tree technology can be used to construct and estimate models which selectively choose elements of the context which contribute to disambiguation decisions, and which have few enough parameters to be trained using existing resources.

The paper begins with a survey of recent work on grammatical inference. Next, I present an introduction to decision-tree modeling, defining a training algorithm for decision-trees and discussing specifically how decision-trees are used in this work. After that, I describe the algorithms developed for SPATTER, including the training and parsing procedures. Finally, I present some results of experiments comparing SPATTER with a grammarian's rule-based statistical parser, along with more recent results showing SPATTER applied to the Wall Street Journal domain.[2]

2 Recent Work in Grammar Induction

Over the past decade, the nature of work in grammar induction has largely been a function of the availability of parsed and unparsed corpora. For instance, Magerman and Marcus [15] explores the topic parsing without a grammar using mutual information statistics from a tagged corpus. Originally, the authors intended to do this work from a parsed corpus using supervised learning. But, at the time, no such corpus existed in the public domain. Thus, the earliest work on grammar induction involved either completely unsupervised learning, or, using the Tagged Brown Corpus, learning from a corpus tagged with syntactic parts-of-speech.

One approach to the grammar induction problem is to acquire a set of rewrite rules by some means and then assign probabilities to each rule, where the prob-

---

[2] Due to space limitations, many details have been omitted from this paper. For more details, see Magerman [13].

ability represents the likelihood that the rule will be used in the eventual derivation of the correct analysis of a given sentence.

The most common instance of this approach is the automatic acquisition of probabilistic context-free grammars (P-CFGs), described in Jelinek et al. [11]. A P-CFG is a context-free grammar with probabilities assigned to each production in the grammar, where the probability assigned to a production, $X \rightarrow Y_1 \ldots Y_n$, represents the probability that the non-terminal category X is rewritten as $Y_1 \ldots Y_n$ in the parse of a sentence. Black et al.[6], Kupiec [12], and Pereira and Schabes [16] have applied the inside-outside algorithm, a special case of the expectation-maximization algorithm for CFGs, to P-CFG estimation.

Other work has taken a similar approach to grammatical inference, but using different grammatical formalisms. For instance, Schabes and Waters[18] applies the P-CFG methodology to lexicalized tree-adjoining grammars (L-TAGs). Carroll and Charniak[9] uses a dependency grammar formalism. Both of these attempts improve over P-CFGs in their potential for modeling language by incorporating lexical information into the learning process.[3] However, neither approach has achieved significant improvements over the results of P-CFGs on broad-coverage parsing problems.

Given the amount of effort which has been put into grammatical inference and parsing research, an important question to ask is, why has there not been more progress? There are no easy answers to this question. But one way to pursue an answer is to find properties which are common among previous research and explore solutions which avoid these properties. The development of SPATTER was motivated by this strategy. In particular, the work on SPATTER is based on the following premises:

1. Grammars are too complex and detailed to develop manually for most interesting domains, and thus explicit grammars should be avoided.
2. Parsing models must rely heavily on lexical and contextual information to analyze sentences accurately.
3. Existing n-gram modeling techniques are inadequate for parsing models.

3 Decision-Tree Modeling

Much of the work in this paper depends on replacing human decision-making skills with automatic decision-making algorithms. The decisions under consideration involve identifying constituents and constituent labels in natural language sentences. Grammarians, the human decision-makers in parsing, solve this problem by enumerating the features of a sentence which affect the disambiguation decisions and indicating which parse to select based on the feature values. The grammarian is accomplishing two critical tasks: identifying the features which are relevant to each decision, and deciding which choice to select based on the values of the relevant features.

---

[3] [9] describes experiments which use statistics of part-of-speech co-occurrences, but the techniques described therein extend obviously to lexical co-occurrences.

Decision-tree classification algorithms account for both of these tasks, and they also accomplish a third task which grammarians classically find difficult. By assigning a probability distribution to the possible choices, decision trees provide a ranking system which not only specifies the order of preference for the possible choices, but also gives a measure of the relative likelihood that each choice is the one which should be selected.

3.1 What is a Statistical Decision Tree?

A decision tree asks questions about an event, where the particular question asked depends on the answers to previous questions, and where each question helps to reduce the uncertainty of what the correct choice or action is. More precisely, a *decision tree* is an n-ary branching tree in which questions are associated with each internal node, and a choice, or class, is associated with each leaf node. A *statistical* decision tree is distinguished from a decision tree in that it defines a conditional probability distribution on the set of possible choices.

Histories, Questions, and Futures There are three basic objects which describe a decision tree: histories, questions, and futures.

A *history* encodes all of the information deemed necessary to make the decision which the tree is asked to make. The content of a history depends on the application to which decision trees are being applied. In this work, a history consists of a partial parse tree, and it is represented as an array of n-ary branching trees with feature bundles at each node. Thus, the history includes any aspect of the trees in this array, including the syntactic and lexical information in the trees, the structure of the trees, the number of nodes in the trees, the co-occurrence of two tree nodes in some relationship to one another, etc.

While the set of histories represents the state space of the problem, the *questions,* and their possible answers, encode the heuristic knowledge about what is important about a history. Each internal node in a decision tree is associated with a question. The answers to these questions must be finite-valued, since each answer generates a new node in the decision tree.

A *future* refers to one of a set of possible choices which the decision tree can make. The set of choices is the *future vocabulary*. For a decision tree part-of-speech tagger in which the tree selects a part-of-speech tag for each word in a sentence, the future vocabulary is the tag set. Each leaf node of a decision tree is associated with an element from the future vocabulary, indicating which choice the decision tree recommends for events which reach that leaf.

In this parsing work, decision trees are applied to a number of different decision-making problems: assigning part-of-speech tags to words, assigning constituent labels, determining the constituent boundaries in a sentence, deciding the scope of conjunctions, and even selecting which decision to make next. Each of these decision-making tasks has its own definition of a history, i.e. its own set of feature questions, and its own future vocabulary. The algorithms which are described in the rest of this chapter illustrate how decision trees use distributional information from a corpus of events to decrease the uncertainty about the appropriate decision to make for each of these problems.

Binary Decision Trees Decision trees are defined above as n-ary branching trees, but the work described here discusses only binary decision trees, where only yes-no questions are considered.

The main reason for using binary decision trees is that allowing questions to have different numbers of answers complicates the decision tree growing algorithm. The trees are grown by selecting the question which contributes the most *information* to the decision, where information is defined in terms of entropy. It is difficult to compare the information provided by questions with different numbers of answers, since entropy considerations generally favor questions with more answers.

As an example of this, consider the case where histories come in four colors, red, blue, yellow, and magenta. The question set includes the following questions:

1. What is the color of the history?
2. Is the color either blue or red?
3. Is the color red?
4. Is the color magenta?

Question 1, with four values, provides the most information, and a decision tree growing algorithm would certainly select it over the other questions (Figure 1). The decision tree could effectively ask this question by asking a combination of binary questions 2, 3, and 4 (Figure 2); but, it would never choose this option over the single question.

Now, let's consider the situation where the only important feature of the history is whether the history is red or not. While question 3 achieves the same entropy reduction as question 1, question 1 divides the histories into four different classes when only two are necessary. This situation is referred to as *data fragmentation*. Since magenta histories and blue histories behave similarly, if there are very few (or no) magenta histories, then a decision tree which asks question 1 (Figure 1) will have more difficulty classifying the magenta history than one which asks question 3 (Figure 3).

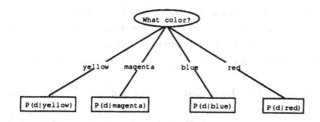

Fig. 1. A decision tree using n-ary questions.

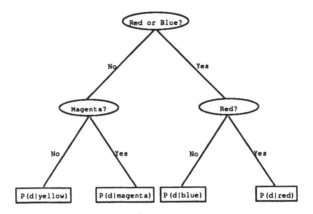

Fig. 2. A decision tree using only binary questions.

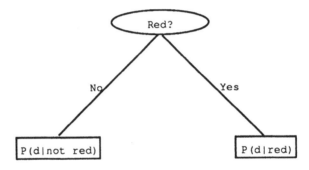

Fig. 3. Decision tree representing the red/not-red distinction. Here *d* is the random variable representing the shape of the object.

Another reason for considering only binary questions for decision trees is computational efficiency. During the growing algorithm, the histories at a node are sorted based on the answers to the question selected for that node. The case where there are only two possible answers is simpler to implement efficiently than the general case. Binary questions also speeds up the mathematical calculations, since loops which range over all possible answers to questions can be unraveled.

Recasting N-ary Questions as Binary Questions It is very difficult to pose all questions about a decision in binary terms. In the previous example, it would be counterproductive to expect a person to notice that blue, yellow, and magenta histories behave one way and red histories behave another in the training data.

An *n*-ary question can be recast as a sequence of binary questions by creating a binary classification tree (BCT) for the *answer vocabulary*, i.e. the set of answers to a given question. A BCT for the color questions in section 3.1 is shown in Figure 4. BCTs can be acquired using an unsupervised statistical clustering algorithm, as described in Brown et al.[8]; for smaller answer vocabularies, hand-generated BCTs are a viable alternative.

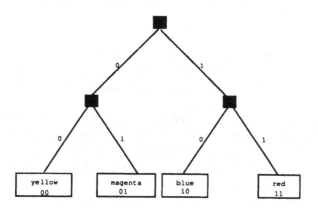

Fig. 4. A binary classification tree for the *color* vocabulary, along with its corresponding binary encoding.

The binary encoding of n-ary questions generates an implicit binary representation for the answer vocabularies, as is labeled in Figure 4, where each bit corresponds to a decision tree question. This interpretation offers two possible difficulties. First, since these questions are based on a hierarchical classification tree, the nth bit does not necessarily have much meaning without knowing the values of the first $n - 1$ bits. Also, if the BCT is unbalanced, the values in the shallower parts of the BCT will have fewer bits in their representations than those in the deeper parts. One could pad these shorter bit strings, but should they be padded with 0s or 1s?

Both of these problems are solved using principles of information theory. Since the children at a given node in the BCT are unordered, one can use a greedy algorithm to swap the order of the children to maximize the amount of information contained in each bit. This procedure is called *bit-flipping*. This makes the padding issue irrelevant, since regardless of which bit is initially assigned, it will be flipped if more information is gained by doing so.

Even without bit-flipping, whether or not questions should be asked out of order is not important. If a question is meaningless without knowing the answers to other questions first, the decision tree growing algorithm will detect this situation and ask only the meaningful questions. The exception to this is when there is very little data available to evaluate the relative value of questions, which happens in the later stages of the growing algorithm. *Overtraining* can occur at this point, where coincidences in the training data lead the algorithm to select questions which will be uninformative on new data. This is a general problem in decision trees, as well as in most inductive algorithms. It is addressed by applying a smoothing algorithm using a second set of training data.

3.2 Growing a Decision Tree

In this section, I present the maximum-likelihood (M-L) decision tree growing algorithm from Bahl et al.[1] and motivate the modifications made to the algorithm for this work.

Notation Let the random variables X and Y denote the history and future of the events being modeled by the decision tree. $\mathcal{X}$ is the set of possible X values and $\mathcal{Y}$ the set of possible Y values. Let C denote a corpus of examples of the form (x, y), where $x \in \mathcal{X}$ and $y \in \mathcal{Y}$.

A decision tree $\mathcal{D}$ assigns each history x to a leaf node, denoted by $l(x)$. $\mathcal{N}_\mathcal{D}$ is the set of nodes in a decision tree $\mathcal{D}$. $N_\mathcal{D}(x)$ denotes the set of nodes along the path from the root to $l(x)$, including $l(x)$. The ith ancestor of a node n is denoted by $a_i(n)$, where i is the length of the path from n to $a_i(n)$. Thus, the parent of a node is denoted by $a_1(n)$.

A node n can be interpreted as a subcorpus of a corpus C, where the sub-corpus is defined as the set of events in C which visit the node n on the path from the root to a leaf:

$$n = \{(x, y) \in C : n \in N_\mathcal{D}(x)\}. \tag{1}$$

A boolean question q_i is denoted by two sets Q_i^C and $\bar{Q}_i^C$, where

$$Q_i^C = \{(x, y) \in C : \text{the answer to question } q_i \text{ is yes for } x\} \tag{2}$$

and

$$\bar{Q}_i^C = \{(x, y) : (x, y) \notin Q_i^C\}. \tag{3}$$

$q_i(x)$ is true if the answer to q_i is yes for x, and $q_i(x)$ is false if the answer to q_i is no for x. The question $\bar{q}_i$ corresponds to the negation of question q_i.

The probability $\hat{p}_i^n(y|x)$ indicates the empirical conditional probability[4] that $Y = y$ given that $n \in N(x)$ and $q_i(x)$ is true:

$$\hat{p}_i^n(y|x) = \frac{|\{(x', y') \in Q_i^n : y' = y\}|}{|Q_i|}. \tag{4}$$

Likewise,

$$\bar{\hat{p}}_i^n(y|x) = \frac{|\{(x', y') \in \bar{Q}_i^n : y' = y\}|}{|\bar{Q}_i|}. \tag{5}$$

The Growing Algorithm The basic M-L decision tree growing algorithm is shown in Figure 5. The algorithm, starting with a set of questions $\{q_1, q_2, \ldots, q_m\}$ and a training corpus C, generates a decision tree which minimizes the expected conditional entropy of the training data.

---

[4] In general, $\hat{p}$ is used to refer to an emiprical probability distribution, i.e. a distribution estimated directly using the relative frequencies from a corpus. On the other hand, $\bar{p}$ refers to a smoothed distribution.

Begin with a single root node n and with a training corpus C.

1. If the y value is the same for all events in n, i.e.

$$\exists y_n \in \mathcal{Y} : \forall (x, y) \in n, y = y_n, \tag{6}$$

then n is a *pure* node. Designate n a leaf node and quit.

2. For each question q_i $(i = 1, 2, \ldots, m)$, calculate the average conditional entropy $\bar{H}_n(Y|q_i)$:

$$\bar{H}_n(Y|q_i) = \Pr\{(x, y) \in Q_i^n\} H(Y|q_i, n) + \Pr\{(x, y) \in \bar{Q}_i^n\} H(Y|\bar{q}_i, n) \tag{7}$$

$$= -\frac{|Q_i^n|}{|n|} \sum_{y \in \mathcal{Y}} \hat{p}^n(y|x \in Q_i^n) \log_2 \hat{p}^n(y|x \in Q_i^n) \tag{8}$$

$$-\frac{|\bar{Q}_i^n|}{|n|} \sum_{y \in \mathcal{Y}} \hat{p}^n(y|x \in \bar{Q}_i^n) \log_2 \hat{p}^n(y|x \in \bar{Q}_i^n) \tag{9}$$

$$\tag{10}$$

3. Determine the question q_k which leads to the lowest entropy:

$$k = \operatorname{argmin}_i \bar{H}_n(Y|q_i). \tag{11}$$

4. Calculate the reduction in entropy $R_n(k)$ achieved by asking question k at node n :

$$R_n(k) = H_n(Y) - \bar{H}_n(Y|q_i). \tag{12}$$

5. If $R_n(k) \leq R_{min}(n)$, then designate n a leaf node and quit.
6. Split node n based on q_k.
   (a) Assign question q_k to node n.
   (b) Create left and right children nodes n_l and n_r.
   (c) Assign nodes to n_l and n_r such that $C_{n_l} = Q_i^n$ and $C_{n_r} = \bar{Q}_i^n$.
   (d) Recursively apply this algorithm to n_l and n_r, removing q_k from the list of candidate questions.

Fig. 5. Maximum likelihood decision tree growing algorithm.

The main issue in applying a decision tree growing algorithm to a problem is to decide on an appropriate *stopping rule*. The stopping rule is the criterion by which the algorithm stops splitting a node.

Stopping rules are motivated by the fact that as the number of events at a node gets smaller, the decisions made based on the empirical distribution of these events become less accurate. This means that not only are the probability distributions at these nodes called into question, but also, since the conditional entropy values $\bar{H}_n(Y|q_i)$ are estimated empirically from the events at a node, the entire splitting process is suspect. Significant splits *might* occur using estimates from sparse data, but there is no way to determine the value of a split without validating the decision using more data. More likely, splits which occur based on fewer events will result in overtraining.

In the algorithm in Figure 5, the stopping rule dictates that a node should not be split if the entropy reduction $R_n(k)$ achieved by asking the best question q_k, is less than some minimum value $R_{min}(n)$. This minimum value can be a constant, but it also might be a function of the number of events at the node n. One heuristic to follow is that the fewer events at a node, the higher the $R_{min}(n)$ should be in order to consider the split statistically significant. One function used in experiments is the product of the number of events at a node and the entropy reduction achieved by the split, $|n| \cdot R_n(k)$. The units of this function are bit-events.

An alternative to a stopping rule is to grow the tree to completion and then prune nodes based on the significance of splits. For each node n, consider the node's children, n_l and n_r. If either node is not a leaf, apply the pruning algorithm recursively to the non-leaf child(ren). If both nodes are leaves after the pruning has been applied recursively, then prune the children of n if the split at n does not satisfy the stopping rule.

In this work, decision trees are grown using an $R_{min}(n)$ value of 0, i.e. decision trees are grown until none of the questions cause a reduction in entropy at a node. To avoid overtraining and to compensate for inaccurate probability estimates due to sparse data, an expectation-maximization smoothing algorithm is applied to the decision tree using a second training corpus.

3.3 Training a Decision Tree Model

The decision to grow trees to completion was made based on a previously un-published result comparing the test entropy of decision tree models using various combinations of growing algorithms, stopping rules, and training data set sizes.[5] The experiments were performed on the language modeling problem, predicting the class of the next word given the previous words in the sentence. The variations included: asking all of the questions in a predefined order vs. selecting the question order based on entropy reduction; growing the tree to completion vs. applying a chi-squared test with thresholds of 5, 10, and 15; and using different size training and smoothing sets. Regardless of the amount of training and smoothing data used, the best results were achieved by growing the tree to completion using entropy reduction as a question selection criterion. Different problems may exhibit different behaviors with regards to stopping rules, but in experiments involving applying a stopping rule to the parsing decision tree models, the trees grown to completion performed better on test data than those that were pruned.

The main reason the decision trees can be grown to completion without overtraining is that, after the model is grown, it is smoothed using a second, held-out training set. The smoothing procedure does not modify the structure of

---

[5] These experiments were performed during the summer of 1993 by members of the IBM Speech Recognition group, Peter F. Brown, Bob Mercer, Stephen Della Pietra, Vincent Della Pietra, Joshua Koppelman, and myself.

the decision tree or the questions asked at any of the nodes. Instead, it effectively adjusts the probability distributions at the leaves of the decision tree to maximize the probability of the held-out corpus.

If the leaf distributions were completely unconstrained during the smoothing procedure, then the best model it could find would simply be the M-L model determined by mapping each event in the held-out data to a leaf node and computing the relative frequency of the futures at each node. But this would result in overtraining on the smoothing data. To avoid this, the smoothing procedure uses the intuition behind stopping rules to uncover a model which, in a sense, statistically unsplits nodes which should not have been split.

Stopping rules dictate that, if there is not sufficient confidence that any question provides information about the future, then no question should be asked. Smoothing the model after growing eliminates the need for making such harsh and irreversible decisions. Each node n in the decision tree is assigned a parameter λ_n which loosely represents the confidence in the distribution at node n. The smoothed probability at a leaf, $\tilde{p}_n(y|x)$ is defined recursively as

$$\tilde{p}_n(y|x) = \lambda_n p_n(y|x) + (1 - \lambda_n)\tilde{p}_{a_1(n)}(y|x). \tag{13}$$

The smoothed probability of the root node is defined as:

$$\tilde{p}_{\text{root}}(y|x) = \lambda_n p_{\text{root}}(y|x) + (1 - \lambda_n)\frac{1}{|\mathcal{Y}|}. \tag{14}$$

If it turns out that a node n should not have been split, then the smoothing algorithm can assign $\lambda_{n_l} = \lambda_{n_r} = 0$, effectively pruning the children of n.

The Forward-Backward Algorithm for Decision Trees The Forward-Backward (F-B) algorithm [3] can be used to search for the optimal parameter settings for $\Lambda = \{\lambda_1, \lambda_2, \ldots, \lambda_m\}$. Given a held-out corpus C_h, the F-B algorithm computes the probability of C_h using Λ in the forward pass, and then computes the updated value vector Λ' in the backward pass.[6]

The algorithm starts by assuming some initial value for Λ. Consider the diagram in Figure 6 of a finite-state machine representing the path from a leaf node to the root. Imagine that a history x outputs its future y according to some distribution along the path from $l(x)$ to the root, or possibly it outputs its y according to the uniform distribution. Let $\alpha_n(x)$ represent the probability of starting at state $l(x)$ and visiting state n. Then

$$\alpha_n(x) = \begin{cases} \displaystyle\prod_{\substack{d \text{ along path from } n \text{ to } l(x)}} (1 - \lambda_d) & n \in N(x), n \neq l(x) \\ 1 & n = l(x) \\ 0 & n \notin N(x) \end{cases} \tag{15}$$

---

[6] This smoothing algorithm was first published in Lucassen's dissertation in 1983. It was also mentioned briefly in Bahl et al.[1].

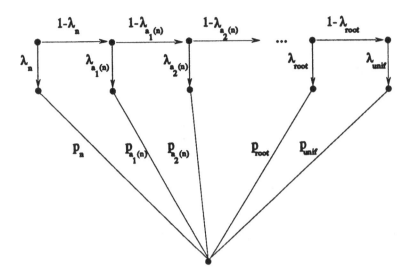

Fig. 6. Finite-state machine indicating the path for computing the forward probability in the Forward-Backward algorithm.

Let $\Pr_\Lambda(y, n|x)$ be the probability of generating y from state n on input x. Then

$$\Pr_\Lambda(y, n|x) = \alpha_n(x)\lambda_n p_n(y|x). \tag{16}$$

Now, let $\beta_n(y|x)$ be the probability that y was generated on input x from one of the states in $N(n)$. Then

$$\beta_n(y|x) = \lambda_n p_n(y|x) + (1 - \lambda_n)\beta_{a_1(n)}(y|x). \tag{17}$$

Let $\Pr_\Lambda^+(y, n|x)$ be the probability of visiting state n but outputting y from a state *other than* n. Then

$$\Pr_\Lambda^+(y, n|x) = \alpha_n(x)(1 - \lambda_n)\beta_{a_1(n)}(y|x). \tag{18}$$

Notice that $\beta_{l(x)}(y|x)$ is the probability of generating y on the input x.

Let $\Pr_\Lambda(n|x, y)$ be the probability of having generated y from n given that y was output. Let $\Pr_\Lambda^+(n|x, y)$ be the probability that x was generated by some state along the path from n to the root other than n. These are given by:

$$\Pr_\Lambda(n|x, y) = \frac{\Pr_\Lambda(y, n|x)}{\Pr_\Lambda(y|x)} = \frac{\alpha_n(x)\lambda_n p_n(y|x)}{\beta_{l(x)}(y|x)} \tag{19}$$

$$\Pr_\Lambda^+(n|x, y) = \frac{\Pr_\Lambda^+(y, n|x)}{\Pr_\Lambda(y|x)} = \frac{\alpha_n(x)(1 - \lambda_n)\beta_{a_1(n)}(y|x)}{\beta_{l(x)}(y|x)}. \tag{20}$$

$$\tag{21}$$

The F-B updates for the parameters are

$$\lambda'_n = \frac{\displaystyle\sum_{(x,y)\in C_h} \Pr_\Lambda(n|x,y)}{\displaystyle\sum_{(x,y)\in C_h} \Pr_\Lambda(n|x,y) + \sum_{(x,y)\in C_h} \Pr_\Lambda^+(n|x,y)}. \tag{22}$$

Bucketing λ's Generally, less data is used for smoothing a decision tree than for growing it. This is best, since the majority of the data should be used for determining the structure and leaf distributions of the tree. However, as a result, there is usually insufficient held-out data for estimating one parameter for each node in the decision tree.

A good rule of thumb is that at least 10 events are needed to estimate a parameter. However, since each event is contributing to a parameter at every node it visits on its path from the root to its leaf, this rule of thumb probably is insufficient. I have required at least 100 events to train each parameter.

Since there will not be 100 events visiting each node, it is necessary to *bucket* the λ's. The nodes are sorted by a primary key, usually the event count at the node, and any number of secondary keys, e.g. the event count at the node's parent, the entropy of the node, etc. Node buckets are created so that each bucket contains nodes whose event counts sum to at least 100. Starting with the node with fewest events, nodes are added to the first bucket until it fills up, i.e. until it contains at least 100 events. Then, a second bucket is filled until it contains 100 events, and so on. Instead of having a unique parameter for each node, all nodes in the same bucket have their parameters tied, i.e. they are constrained to have the same value.[7]

4 SPATTER Parsing

The SPATTER parsing algorithm is based on interpreting parsing as a statistical pattern recognition process. A parse tree for a sentence is constructed by starting with the sentence's words as leaves of a tree structure, and labeling and extending nodes these nodes until a single-rooted, labeled tree is constructed. This pattern recognition process is driven by the decision-tree models described in the previous section.

4.1 SPATTER Representation

A parse tree can be viewed as an n-ary branching tree, with each node in a tree labeled by either a non-terminal label or a part-of-speech label. If a parse tree is interpreted as a geometric pattern, a constituent is no more than a set of edges which meet at the same tree node. For instance, the noun phrase, "a brown cow," consists of an edge extending to the right from "a," an edge extending to the left from "cow," and an edge extending straight up from "brown".

---

[7] For historical reasons, this method is referred to as *the wall of bricks*.

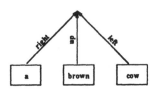

Fig. 7. Representation of constituent and labeling of extensions in SPATTER.

In SPATTER, a parse tree is encoded in terms of four elementary components, or *features*: words, tags, labels, and extensions. Each feature has a fixed vocabulary, with each element of a given feature vocabulary having a unique representation. The word feature can take on any value of any word. The tag feature can take on any value in the part-of-speech tag set. The label feature can take on any value in the non-terminal set. The extension can take on any of the following five values:

right - the node is the first child of a constituent;
left - the node is the last child of a constituent;
up - the node is neither the first nor the last child of a constituent;
unary - the node is a child of a unary constituent;
root - the node is the root of the tree.

For an n word sentence, a parse tree has n leaf nodes, where the word feature value of the ith leaf node is the ith word in the sentence. The word feature value of the internal nodes is intended to contain the lexical head of the node's constituent. A deterministic lookup table based on the label of the internal node and the labels of the children is used to approximate this linguistic notion.

The SPATTER representation of the sentence

```
(S (N Each_DD1 code_NN1
      (Tn used_VVN
          (P by_II (N the_AT PC_NN1))))
   (V is_VBZ listed_VVN))
```

is shown in Figure 8. The nodes are constructed bottom-up from left-to-right, with the constraint that no constituent node is constructed until all of its children have been constructed. The order in which the nodes of the example sentence are constructed is indicated in the figure.

4.2 Training SPATTER's models

SPATTER consists of three main decision-tree models: a part-of-speech tagging model, a node-extension model, and a node-labeling model.

Each of these decision-tree models are grown using the following questions, where X is one of word, tag, label, or extension, and Y is either left and right:

– What is the X at the current node?

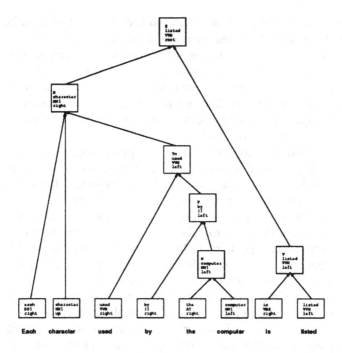

Fig. 8. Treebank analysis encoded using feature values.

- What is the X at the node to the Y?
- What is the X at the node two nodes to the Y?
- What is the X at the current node's first child from the Y?
- What is the X at the current node's second child from the Y?

For each of the nodes listed above, the decision tree could also ask about the number of children and span of the node. For the tagging model, the values of the previous two words and their tags are also asked, since they might differ from the head words of the previous two constituents.

The training algorithm proceeds as follows. The training corpus is divided into two sets, approximately 90% for tree growing and 10% for tree smoothing. For each parsed sentence in the tree growing corpus, the correct state sequence is traversed. Each state transition from s_i to s_{i+1} is an event; the history is made up of the answers to all of the questions at state s_i and the future is the value of the action taken from state s_i to state s_{i+1}. Each event is used as a training example for the decision-tree growing process for the appropriate feature's tree (e.g. each tagging event is used for growing the tagging tree, etc.). The decision-tree models are grown and smoothed using the algorithms described in section 3.

4.3 Parsing with SPATTER

The parsing procedure is a search for the highest probability parse tree. The probability of a parse is just the product of the probability of each of the actions made in constructing the parse, according to the decision-tree models.

Because of the size of the search space, (roughly $O(|T|^n|N|^n)$, where $|T|$ is the number of part-of-speech tags, n is the number of words in the sentence, and $|N|$ is the number of non-terminal labels), it is not possible to compute the probability of every parse. However, the specific search algorithm used is not very important, so long as there are no search errors. A search error occurs when the the highest probability parse found by the parser is not the highest probability parse in the space of all parses.

SPATTER's search procedure uses a two phase approach to identify the highest probability parse of a sentence. First, the parser uses a stack decoding algorithm to quickly find a complete parse for the sentence. Once the stack decoder has found a complete parse of reasonable probability ($> 10^{-5}$), it switches to a breadth-first mode to pursue all of the partial parses which have not been explored by the stack decoder. In this second mode, it can safely discard any partial parse which has a probability lower than the probability of the highest probability completed parse. Using these two search modes, SPATTER guarantees that it will find the highest probability parse. The only limitation of this search technique is that, for sentences which are modeled poorly, the search might exhaust the available memory before completing both phases. However, these search errors conveniently occur on sentences which SPATTER is likely to get wrong anyway, so there isn't much performance lossed due to the search errors. Experimentally, the search algorithm guarantees the highest probability parse is found for over 96% of the sentences parsed.

5 Experiment Results

In the absence of an NL system, SPATTER can be evaluated by comparing its top-ranking parse with the treebank analysis for each test sentence. The parser was applied to two different domains, IBM Computer Manuals and the Wall Street Journal.

5.1 IBM Computer Manuals

The first experiment uses the IBM Computer Manuals domain, which consists of sentences extracted from IBM computer manuals. The training and test sentences were annotated by the University of Lancaster. The Lancaster treebank uses 195 part-of-speech tags and 19 non-terminal labels. This treebank is described in great detail in Black et al.[5].

The main reason for applying SPATTER to this domain is that IBM had spent the previous ten years developing a rule-based, unification-style probabilistic context-free grammar for parsing this domain. The purpose of the experiment was to estimate SPATTER's ability to learn the syntax for this domain directly from a treebank, instead of depending on the interpretive expertise of a grammarian.

The parser was trained on the first 30,800 sentences from the Lancaster treebank. The test set included 1,473 new sentences, whose lengths range from 3 to 30 words, with a mean length of 13.7 words. These sentences are the same test sentences used in the experiments reported for IBM's parser in [5]. In [5], IBM's parser was evaluated using the 0-crossing-brackets measure, which represents the percentage of sentences for which none of the constituents in the parser's parse violates the constituent boundaries of any constituent in the correct parse. After over ten years of grammar development, the IBM parser achieved a 0-crossing-brackets score of 69%. On this same test set, SPATTER scored 76%.

5.2   Wall Street Journal

The experiment is intended to illustrate SPATTER's ability to accurately parse a highly-ambiguous, large-vocabulary domain. These experiments use the Wall Street Journal domain, as annotated in the Penn Treebank, version 2. The Penn Treebank uses 46 part-of-speech tags and 27 non-terminal labels.[8]

The WSJ portion of the Penn Treebank is divided into 25 sections, numbered 00 - 24. In these experiments, SPATTER was trained on sections 02 - 21, which contains approximately 40,000 sentences. The test results reported here are from section 00, which contains 1920 sentences.

The Penn Treebank is already tokenized and sentence detected by human annotators, and thus the test results reported here reflect this. SPATTER parses *word* sequences, not tag sequences. Furthermore, SPATTER does *not* simply pre-tag the sentences and use only the best tag sequence in parsing. Instead, it uses a probabilistic model to assign tags to the words, and considers all possible tag sequences according to the probability they are assigned by the model. No information about the legal tags for a word are extracted from the test corpus. In fact, no information other than the words is used from the test corpus.

For the sake of efficiency, only the sentences of 40 words or fewer are included in these experiments.[9] For this test set, SPATTER takes on average 12 seconds per sentence on an SGI R4400 with 160 megabytes of RAM.

To evaluate SPATTER's performance on this domain, I am using the PARSEVAL measures, as defined in Black et al.[4]:

Precision
$$\frac{\text{no. of correct constituents in SPATTER parse}}{\text{no. of constituents in SPATTER parse}}$$

Recall
$$\frac{\text{no. of correct constituents in SPATTER parse}}{\text{no. of constituents in treebank parse}}$$

---

[8] This treebank also contains coreference information, predicate-argument relations, and trace information indicating movement; however, none of this additional information was used in these parsing experiments.

[9] SPATTER returns a complete parse for all sentences of fewer then 50 words in the test set, but the sentences of 41 - 50 words required much more computation than the shorter sentences, and so they have been excluded.

Crossing Brackets no. of constituents which violate constituent boundaries with a constituent in the treebank parse.

The precision and recall measures do not consider constituent labels in their evaluation of a parse, since the treebank label set will not necessarily coincide with the labels used by a given grammar. Since SPATTER uses the same syntactic label set as the Penn Treebank, it makes sense to report labelled precision and labelled recall. These measures are computed by considering a constituent to be correct if and only if it's label matches the label in the treebank.

Table 1 shows the results of SPATTER evaluated against the Penn Treebank on the Wall Street Journal section 00.

Sent. Length Range	4-40	4-25	10-20
Comparisons	1759	1114	653
Avg. Sent. Length	22.3	16.8	15.6
Treebank Constituents	17.58	13.21	12.10
Parse Constituents	17.48	13.13	12.03
Tagging Accuracy	96.5%	96.6%	96.5%
Crossings Per Sentence	1.33	0.63	0.49
Sent. with 0 Crossings	55.4%	69.8%	73.8%
Sent. with 1 Crossing	69.2%	83.8%	86.8%
Sent. with 2 Crossings	80.2%	92.1%	95.1%
Precision	86.3%	89.8%	90.8%
Recall	85.8%	89.3%	90.3%
Labelled Precision	84.5%	88.1%	89.0%
Labelled Recall	84.0%	87.6%	88.5%

Table 1. Results from the WSJ Penn Treebank experiments.

Figures 10, 11, and 12 illustrate the performance of SPATTER as a function of sentence length. SPATTER's performance degrades slowly for sentences up to around 28 words, and performs more poorly and more erratically as sentences get longer. Figure 9 indicates the frequency of each sentence length in the test corpus.

6   Conclusion

This work illustrates the efficacy of using statistical decision-trees for acquiring models of grammatical structure. The learning technique described here deviates from previous work in grammar induction in that it does not learn an explicit grammar, but instead estimates probability distributions which help select the

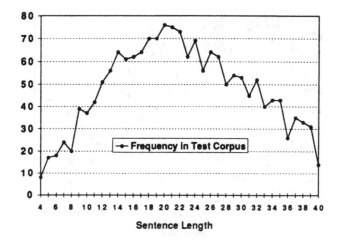

Fig. 9. Frequency in the test corpus as a function of sentence length for Wall Street Journal experiments.

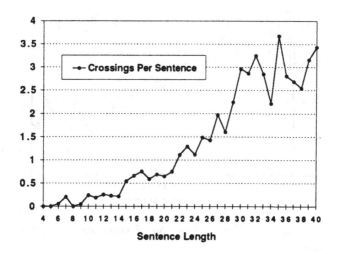

Fig. 10. Number of crossings per sentence as a function of sentence length for Wall Street Journal experiments.

most likely grammatical structure for a given input sentence. While the lack of an explicit grammar might make SPATTER unsatisfying to a grammarian, it proves to be extremely robust and accurate when applied to real-world parsing problems.

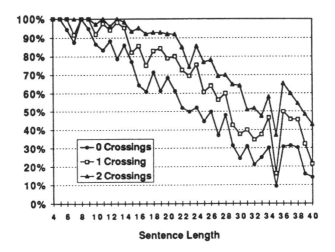

Fig. 11. Percentage of sentence with 0, 1, and 2 crossings as a function of sentence length for Wall Street Journal experiments.

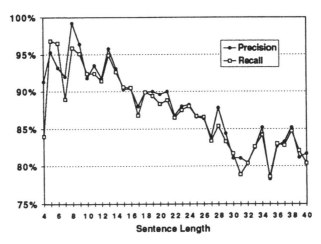

Fig. 12. Precision and recall as a function of sentence length for Wall Street Journal experiments.

References

1. L. R. Bahl, P. F. Brown, P. V. deSouza, and R. L. Mercer. 1989. A tree-based statistical language model for natural language speech recognition. *IEEE Transactions on Acoustics, Speech, and Signal Processing, Vol. 36, No. 7*, pages 1001–1008.

2. J. K. Baker. 1975. Stochastic modeling for automatic speech understanding. *Speech Recognition*, pages 521–542.

3. L. E. Baum. 1972. An inequality and associated maximization technique in statistical estimation of probabilistic functions of markov processes. *Inequalities, Vol. 3*, pages 1–8.

4. E. Black and et al. 1991. A procedure for quantitatively comparing the syntactic coverage of english grammars. *Proceedings of the February 1991 DARPA Speech and Natural Language Workshop*, pages 306–311.

5. E. Black, R. Garside, and G. Leech. 1993. *Statistically-driven computer grammars of english: the ibm/lancaster approach.* Rodopi, Atlanta, Georgia.

6. E. Black, J. Lafferty, and S. Roukos. 1992. Development and evaluation of a broad-coverage probabilistic grammar of english-language computer manuals. *Proceedings of the Association for Computational Linguistics, 1992.*

7. L. Breiman, J. H. Friedman, R. A. Olshen, and C. J. Stone. 1984. *Classification and Regression Trees.* Wadsworth and Brooks, Pacific Grove, California.

8. P. F. Brown, V. Della Pietra, P. V. deSouza, J. C. Lai, and R. L. Mercer. 1992. "Class-based n-gram models of natural language." *Computational Linguistics*, $18(4)$, pages 467–479.

9. G. Carroll and E. Charniak 1992. Learning probabilistic dependency grammars from labeled text. *Working Notes, Fall Symposium Series, AAAI*, pages 25–32.

10. F. Jelinek, J. Lafferty, D. M. Magerman, R. Mercer, A. Ratnaparkhi, and S. Roukos. 1994. Decision tree parsing using a hidden derivation model. *Proceedings of the 1994 Human Language Technology Workshop*, pages 272–277.

11. F. Jelinek, J. D. Lafferty, and R. L. Mercer. 1992. Basic methods of probabilistic context-free grammars. *Speech Recognition and Understanding: Recent Advances, Trends, and Applications. Proceedings of the NATO Advanced Study Institute*, pages 345–360.

12. J. Kupiec. 1991. A trellis-based algorithm for estimating the parameters of a hidden stochastic context-free grammar. *Proceedings of the February 1991 DARPA Speech and Natural Language Workshop*, pages 241–246, 1991.

13. D. M. Magerman. 1994. *Natural Language Parsing as Statistical Pattern Recognition.* Doctoral dissertation. Stanford University, Stanford, California.

14. D. M. Magerman. 1995. Statistical decision-tree models for parsing. *Proceedings of the Association for Computational Linguistics, 1995.*

15. D. M. Magerman and M. P. Marcus. 1990. Parsing a natural language using mutual information statistics. *Proceedings of AAAI-90.*

16. F. Pereira and Y. Schabes. 1992. Inside-outside reestimation from partially bracketed corpora. *Proceedings of the February 1992 DARPA Speech and Natural Language Workshop*, pages 122–127.

17. V. Pratt. 1973. A linguistics oriented programming language. *Proceedings of the Third International Joint Conference on Artificial Intelligence.*

18. Y. Schabes and R. Waters. 1993. Stochastic lexicalized context-free grammar. *Proceedings of the August 1993 International Workshop on Parsing Technologies.*

Inductive Inference from Positive Data: from Heuristic to Characterizing Methods

Timo Knuutila

University of Turku, Department of Computer Science
Lemminkäisenkatu 14 A, 20520 Turku, Finland
e-mail: `knuutila@cs.utu.fi`

Abstract. The practical work in the area of inductive inference of regular languages has to rely on incomplete positive data and thus to be content with approximative or heuristic solutions. We consider here the heuristic inference methods and present a formal approach — the *generalized quotient* — to them. Generalized quotients allows us to define clearly the heuristics used in these methods, and to examine from a firm basis relations between results produced by different heuristics. Although this approach gives us some tools to compare the results obtained via different heuristics, we are still not able to tell formally what is the concept we have derived. To overcome this problem we need *characterizing inference methods*, where the result of the inference process can always be given a formal description. A general framework based on *monotonic representation mappings* is constructed for building such methods.

1 Introduction

Valiant gave in his landmark article "A Theory of the Learnable" [Val84] requirements for all practical learning algorithms. Any successful 'learning machine' should fulfill the following requirements:

1. The machines can *provably* learn whole classes of concepts. Furthermore, these classes can be *characterized*.
2. The classes of concepts are *appropriate* and *non-trivial* for general-purpose knowledge.
3. The machines work in *polynomial time and space* with respect to the size of the information needed for learning.

In what follows, we restrict us on the families of regular languages. This is because they are almost the only languages that are both computationally tractable in what comes to their inference and yet general enough to represent many non-trivial real-life phenomena. Pattern languages [Ang80a, LW91] form another family of this kind.

1.1 Addition of additional information

It has been shown in many occasions that additional information (like membership queries) about the target concept or the class of target concepts greatly improves the learning power of inductive inference methods. However, in many cases the source of this additional information is the target language itself. Thus, most of the different ways to give additional information are concerned with playing a game with a black box containing the secret automaton. This differs from realistic inference situations, where the target language is totally unknown.

Henceforth, we would like to add to these requirements the following:

> The machine does not need additional information about the target concept.

Note that even the use of the simplest kind of additional information — negative examples — must rely on the existence of an *oracle* (human in practice). Supplying negative objects as sample data may seem as natural as supplying the positive ones, but it requires that someone or something knows *a priori* what the language does not contain – if this is the case, then we are either overloading some poor human or we already have a learning machine for the complement of our target concept (and our problem is solved).

All in all, the whole existence of even these simplest of oracles should be questioned. In simple pattern recognition problems we can surely tell bananas from apples, but if the target language is unknown, it may be impossible to tell whether an example is negative or not. Even if the classification (positive/negative) of the examples could be done by a human, the amount of negative examples is overwhelming: while there is an large amount of things that are apples, there is an even more larger amount of things that are not. Although the actual number of counterexamples that are actually needed in the process were tractable, it is unclear whether general methods exist for picking the counterexamples relevant to the learning from the set of all of them.

We cannot totally ban the use of additional information, however, because then we were not able to learn many interesting concept classes. This was shown already in 1967 by Gold [Gol67]. The uncomfortable truth given in Theorem 1.1 applies in particular to the class of regular languages.

Theorem 1.1 (Gold, 1967). *Let L be any infinite language and Fin the class of all finite languages. Then $Fin \cup L$ can not be inferred in the limit from text.*

Thus, in practice we have to use a bit relaxed version of our requirement:

> The additional information about the target concept should be *well-defined* and *logarithmic* with respect to the size of the information needed for learning.

The size requirement (actually a bound on the query complexity) evolves from practical learning situations, where the additional information is supplied by a human. We feel it hard to find any human patient enough to answer to a polynomial (or even linear) number of questions. One could argue that the oracle could also be a computer program or some physical apparatus, but if this were the case, then we already had a learning machine for the particular problem.

Note that our requirement allows the use of a constant amount of negative examples, which may sometimes be enough to give us the right direction in the search space.

1.2 The effect of polynomiality

If we are given an infinite amount of computational resources, there is much that can be learned. In particular, if our data source is an *informant*, we can learn in a *behaviorally correct* sense the class of recursively enumerable sets [CS83]. Setting any finite limit on our resources, however, causes a remarkable loss in the learning ability. For example, it is well-known that the only families that can be inferred in *finite time* are not very general (FIN-TXT and FIN-INF).

Consider then methods working with polynomially bound resources. Note first that the time complexity of an inference method cannot be defined solely in the terms of the size n of the concept to be learned, since the first example used in the learning process may be longer than $p(n)$ for some polynomial p. Note also that the property of being polynomial does not necessarily mean the same as practical [Just consider an algorithm running in time $O(n^{100})$] .

Here we know that even the most promising *approximative* approach, PAC-learning [Val84, HKLW88], learns regular languages in polynomial time only with additional information and/or with subclass restrictions. Actually, the problem of PAC-learning regular languages in polynomial time has been transformed into the inversion of the RSA encryption function in probabilistic polynomial time [KV89], which has no known solution.

1.3 Provability and characterizability

Many heuristic learning algorithms (see [BF72, GT78, Mic86], for example) unarguably perform efficiently enough for real-life purposes, but their results are hard if not impossible to describe. The situation has been even more obscure in the case of *tree languages* [GS84], where the inference methods (like [BF74, BF77, GET76, Lev81, FK84, Kam88]) often lack even the clear algorithmic description.

The criteria for the success of a heuristic method M are often very loose, too: it is only required that given a sample S, the hypothesis $H(M, S)$ must be consistent with S. The heuristic methods may contain one or more additional (integer) parameters, which are used to control the generality of the hypothesis. 'Good' heuristic methods controlled this way should produce results that grow or shrink monotonically with respect to the control arguments. In PAC-learning we can at least formally prove that we are such and such confident that our result is such and such correct.

Why are the results of many heuristic learning algorithms — or maybe we should speak of heuristic *generalization algorithms* — so hard to describe formally? In our opinion the reason is that their very basis, their generalization methods are too *ad hoc* to be given a formal treatment. We do not claim that they were totally useless because of this, but we should be able to do better.

Even if we give up the requirement about provably learning something we can characterize, we would at least like to say something on the *relation* between the results produced by different heuristics. This comparability of results was achieved with the concept of the *generalized quotient* [KS94].

If we are able to formally describe our result, we can entitle our method (heuristic or not) a *characterizing one*. Despite of Gold's theorem there exist many non-trivial concepts that can be learned with characterizing methods from positive data.

1.4 What can we do?

The aim of the discussion about the problems of practical learning was to give support to the claim that we are forced to use one or more items from the following list in any realistic learning application:

- heuristics;
- additional information; and
- approximations.

If we accept the restrictions on the use of additional information, then *subclass restrictions* form a very usable form of constant-size additional information, since they are typically of constant size. It is clear that even the subclass assumptions are heuristic in their essence. Actually, we have already made a heuristic decision by restricting ourselves to regular languages.

In what follows, we discuss in more detail the generalized quotient approach to the heuristic learning of regular languages and give a general framework for characterizing inference methods. The material is based on the earlier work of the author [Knu93a, Knu94] and collaboration with M. Steinby [KS94]. It should be noted that although the representation (for the sakes of simplicity) concentrates itself solely on the inference of string languages, all of the results have also been generalized to the case of tree languages. The interested reader is referred to [Knu93b, Knu93a, KS94] for details.

2 Preliminaries

In this section we define formally the concepts of *strings* and *string language automata* (a.k.a finite automata), show some of their main properties, and recall some important results on the learning from positive data.

2.1 Sets, relations and mappings

We present here some elementary concepts that can be just scanned for terminology and notation.

Let A be a finite set with n elements. Then the *cardinality* of A, denoted by $|A|$, is n. The *power set* of a set A, *i.e.* the set of all subsets of A, is denoted by $\mathfrak{p}A$.

Let A and B be sets and $\rho \subseteq A \times B$ a (binary) *relation* from A to B. The fact that $(a, b) \in \rho$ ($a \in A$, $b \in B$) is also expressed by writing $a \rho b$ or $a \equiv b$ (ρ). The opposite case is expressed by $a \not\equiv b$ (ρ). For any $a \in A$, we denote by $a\rho$ the set of elements of B that are in relation ρ with a, *i.e.* $a\rho = \{ b \in A \mid a \rho b \}$. The *converse* of ρ is the relation $\rho^{-1} = \{ (b, a) \mid a \rho b \}$. Obviously $b\rho^{-1} = \{ a \mid a \rho b \}$. Let $\rho \subseteq A \times B$ and $\tau \subseteq B \times C$ be relations. Then the *product* of ρ and τ is

$$\rho \circ \tau = \{ (a, c) \mid (\exists b \in B)\, a \rho b \tau c \}.$$

Next we consider relations on a set A, *i.e.* subsets of $A \times A$. As usual, we sometimes use the shorter form A^n for the Cartesian product $A \times A \times \cdots \times A$ of n copies of A ($n > 0$). These include the *diagonal relation* $1_A = \{ (a, a) \mid a \in A \}$, and the *universal relation* $\omega_A = A^2$. The *powers* ρ^n ($n \geq 0$) of a relation ρ are defined as $\rho^0 = 1_A$ and $\rho^{n+1} = \rho^n \circ \rho$ ($n \geq 0$). The relation ρ is called *reflexive* if $1_A \subseteq \rho$, *symmetric* if $\rho^{-1} \subseteq \rho$, and *transitive* if $\rho^2 \subseteq \rho$.

A relation on A is called an *equivalence relation* on A if it is reflexive, symmetric and transitive. The set of all equivalence relations on a set A is denoted by $\mathrm{Eq}(A)$. It is obvious that both $1_A \in \mathrm{Eq}(A)$ and $\omega_A \in \mathrm{Eq}(A)$.

Let $\rho \in \mathrm{Eq}(A)$. The *ρ-class* of an element a ($\in A$), is the set $a\rho$, which is often denoted by a/ρ, too. The *quotient set* or the *partition* of A with respect to ρ, is $A/\rho = \{ a\rho \mid a \in A \}$. If $\pi \in \mathrm{Eq}(A)$ and $\pi \subseteq \rho$, then the partition A/π is a *refinement* of A/ρ (each ρ-class is a union of some π-classes).

The cardinality of A/ρ is called the *index* of ρ; especially, if $|A/\rho|$ is finite, then ρ is said to have a *finite index*. For any subset H of A, H/ρ denotes $\{ a\rho \mid a \in H \}$. The equivalence ρ *saturates* the subset H, if H is the union of some ρ-classes. Hence, ρ saturates H iff $a\rho \in H/\rho$ implies $a\rho \subseteq H$.

A *mapping* or a *function* from a set A to a set B is a triple (A, B, φ), where $\varphi \subseteq A \times B$ is a relation such that for every $a \in A$ there exists exactly one $b \in B$ satisfying $a\varphi b$. We write the triple (A, B, φ) in the form $\varphi \colon A \to B$. If $a\varphi b$, then b is the *image* of a and a is a *preimage* of b. That b is an image of a is expressed by writing $b = a\varphi$, $b = \varphi(a)$, or $\varphi : a \mapsto b$; and that a is a preimage of b is written as $a \in b\varphi^{-1}$ or $a \in \varphi^{-1}(b)$. The notation $a = b\varphi^{-1}$ is justified when φ is bijective (see below).

The *composition* of two mappings $\varphi \colon A \to B$ and $\psi \colon B \to C$ is the mapping $\varphi\psi \colon A \to C$, where $\varphi\psi$ is the product of φ and ψ as relations. The *kernel* $\varphi\varphi^{-1}$ of a mapping $\varphi \colon A \to B$, also denoted by $\ker \varphi$, is an equivalence relation on A and $a_1 \equiv a_2$ ($\varphi\varphi^{-1}$) iff $a_1\varphi = a_2\varphi$ ($a_1, a_2 \in A$). Every $\rho \in \mathrm{Eq}(A)$ can be associated with the *natural mapping* $\rho^\natural \colon A \to A/\rho$, $a \mapsto a\rho$ ($a \in A$), such that the kernel of $\rho^\natural$ is ρ. A mapping $\varphi \colon A \to B$ is called *injective* if $\ker \varphi = 1_A$;

surjective (or *onto*) if $A\varphi = B$; and *bijective* if it is both injective and surjective. The natural mapping $\rho^{\natural}$ ($\rho \in \mathrm{Eq}(A)$) is always surjective.

2.2 String languages

We review here some basic concepts and facts from the theory of finite automata. The reader is requested to take a look at any standard textbook (like [Sal69, AU72, Eil74, Bra84]) for a more thorough treatment of the subject.

2.3 Strings

An *alphabet* is a finite nonempty set of *letters*, and in what follows, X always denotes an alphabet. A finite sequence of letters from an alphabet X is called a *string* over X. Consider a string w of the form $w = x_1 x_2 \ldots x_n$, where each $x_i \in X$. If $n = 0$, then w is the *empty string*, denoted by ϵ. The *length* of w, written as $\mathrm{lg}(w)$, is n. Especially, $\mathrm{lg}(\epsilon) = 0$. We denote by X^n the set of all strings of length n, by $X^{\leq n}$ the set of all strings of length n or less, and by $X^{<n}$ the set of all strings of strictly shorter than n, that is,

$$X^{\leq n} = \bigcup_{i=0}^{i=n} X^n \text{ and } X^{<n} = \bigcup_{i=0}^{i=n-1} X^n \quad (n > 0).$$

The set of all strings over X is denoted by X^*. A *language* over X, or an X-*language* is any subset of X^*.

From an algebraic point of view, X^* forms a monoid with identity ϵ under the operation of concatenation of strings. In what follows, we call the morphisms between the (free) monoids *morphisms of strings*, too. A mapping $\varphi: X^* \to Y^*$ is a morphism of strings iff it commutes with the catenation and preserves the identity ϵ; formally

$$\varphi\epsilon \quad = \epsilon,$$
$$\varphi(uw) = \varphi(u)\varphi(w) \quad (u, w \in X^*).$$

The sets of *prefixes*, *suffixes* and *subwords* of an individual string $w \in X^*$, $\mathrm{pref}(w)$, $\mathrm{suff}(w)$, and $\mathrm{subw}(w)$ respectively, are defined as follows:

$$\mathrm{pref}(w) = \{\, u \in X^* \mid (\exists v \in X^*)\ uv = w \,\};$$
$$\mathrm{suff}(w) = \{\, u \in X^* \mid (\exists v \in X^*)\ vu = w \,\};$$
$$\mathrm{subw}(w) = \{\, u \in X^* \mid (\exists v, v' \in X^*)\ vuv' = w \,\}.$$

The concepts just defined are generalized to sets of strings in the natural way. Suppose $L \subseteq X^*$ and $\varphi \in \{\mathrm{pref}, \mathrm{suff}, \mathrm{subw}\}$. Then $\mathrm{lg}(L) = \max\{\, \mathrm{lg}(w) \mid w \in L \,\}$ and $\varphi(L) = \bigcup_{w \in L} \varphi(w)$.[1]

---

[1] The concept $\mathrm{lg}(L)$ is well-defined only for finite sets L. However, it will not be used in any other context.

2.4 Recognizable string languages

The following definition gives an *automaton* that can be used to decide, whether a given string w belongs to certain language L or not.

Definition 2.1. An *automaton (Rabin–Scott recognizer)* $\mathfrak{A} = (A, X, \delta_{\mathfrak{A}}, a_0, A')$ consists of

1. a finite, nonempty set A of *states*,
2. the *input alphabet* X,
3. a *transition function* $\delta_{\mathfrak{A}} \colon A \times X \to A$,
4. an *initial state* $a_0 \in A$, and
5. a set $A' \subseteq A$ of *final states*.

The function $\delta_{\mathfrak{A}}$ is extended to a function $\hat{\delta}_{\mathfrak{A}} \colon A \times X^* \to A$ as follows:

$$\hat{\delta}_{\mathfrak{A}}(a, \epsilon) \ = a \qquad\qquad (a \in A),$$
$$\hat{\delta}_{\mathfrak{A}}(a, wx) = \delta_{\mathfrak{A}}(\hat{\delta}_{\mathfrak{A}}(a, w), x) \ (a \in A, w \in X^*, x \in X).$$

Definition 2.2. The *language recognized* by an automaton $\mathfrak{A}$ is defined as

$$L(\mathfrak{A}) = \{\, w \in X^* \mid \hat{\delta}_{\mathfrak{A}}(a_0, w) \in A' \,\}.$$

We will omit the cap from $\hat{\delta}_{\mathfrak{A}}$ in the sequel.

An X-language L is *recognizable* if there exists an automaton $\mathfrak{A}$ such that $L = L(\mathfrak{A})$. The set of all recognizable X-languages is denoted by $Rec(X)$. Two automata $\mathfrak{A}$ and $\mathfrak{B}$ are said to be *equivalent* iff $L(\mathfrak{A}) = L(\mathfrak{B})$.

2.5 Nondeterministic automata

We next extend the definition of an automaton to allow nondeterministic state transitions and a set of initial states.

Definition 2.3. A *nondeterministic (nd) automaton* $\mathfrak{A} = (A, X, \delta_{\mathfrak{A}}, A_0, A')$ consists of

1. a finite, nonempty set A of *states*,
2. the *input alphabet* X,
3. a (nd) *transition function* $\delta_{\mathfrak{A}} \colon (A \times X) \to \mathfrak{p}A$, [2]
4. a *set of initial states* $A_0 \in A$, and
5. a set $A' \subseteq A$ of *final states*.

The mapping $\delta_{\mathfrak{A}}$ is extended to $\mathfrak{p}A \times X$ in the natural way and then to a mapping $\hat{\delta}_{\mathfrak{A}} \colon \mathfrak{p}A \times X^* \to \mathfrak{p}A$ as follows:

$$\hat{\delta}_{\mathfrak{A}}(H, \epsilon) \ = H \qquad\qquad (H \in \mathfrak{p}A), \text{ and}$$
$$\hat{\delta}_{\mathfrak{A}}(H, wx) = \delta_{\mathfrak{A}}(\hat{\delta}_{\mathfrak{A}}(H, w), x) \ (H \in \mathfrak{p}A, w \in X^*, x \in X).$$

Informally speaking, $\hat{\delta}_{\mathfrak{A}}(H, w)$ is the set of states $\mathfrak{A}$ may reach under the input string w from at least one state in H.

---

[2] Alternatively, one could define $\delta_{\mathfrak{A}}$ as a subset of $A \times X \times A$.

Definition 2.4. The *language recognized* by an nd automaton $\mathfrak{A}$ is defined as

$$L(\mathfrak{A}) = \{\, w \mid \hat{\delta}_{\mathfrak{A}}(A_0, w) \cap A' \neq \emptyset \,\}.$$

It is obvious that every (deterministic) automaton can be interpreted as an nd automaton, where A_0 and the sets $\delta_{\mathfrak{A}}(a, x)$ are all singletons. We denote this nd interpretation of $\mathfrak{A}$ with $\mathfrak{A}^{\mathrm{nd}}$. On the other hand, every nd automaton can be transformed into the equivalent automaton, the *subset automaton* $\mathfrak{B} = (\mathfrak{p}A, X, \delta_{\mathfrak{B}}, A_0, A'')$, where $A'' = \{\, H \in \mathfrak{p}A \mid H \cap A' \neq \emptyset \,\}$. Thus, the deterministic and nondeterministic automata are able to recognize the same set of languages.

2.6 Congruences of string languages

Definition 2.5. An equivalence relation ρ on X^* is a *right congruence relation* of X^* if $u \rho v$ implies $uw \rho vw$ for all $u, v, w \in X^*$.

Every automaton $\mathfrak{A} = (A, X, \delta_{\mathfrak{A}}, a_0, A')$ defines a right congruence $\rho_{\mathfrak{A}}$ of the free monoid X^* as follows:

$$u \equiv v \ (\rho_{\mathfrak{A}}) \quad \text{iff} \quad \delta_{\mathfrak{A}}(a_0, u) = \delta_{\mathfrak{A}}(a_0, v) \quad (u, v \in X^*).$$

The index of $\rho_{\mathfrak{A}}$ is at most $|A|$ and

$$L(\mathfrak{A}) = \bigcup (\, u\rho_{\mathfrak{A}} \mid u \in X^*, \ \delta_{\mathfrak{A}}(a_0, u) \in A' \,).$$

Thus, every language in $Rec(X)$ is saturated by a right congruence of X^* of finite index.

Every X-language L can be recognized by the following *free automaton* of L,[3]

$$\mathfrak{F}_L = (X^*, X, \delta_{\mathfrak{F}_L}, \epsilon, L),$$

where $\delta_{\mathfrak{F}_L}(w, x) = wx$ for all $w \in X^*$ and $x \in X$. Since every regular language L is saturated by a right congruence ρ of X^* of finite index, we can define the following finite automaton

$$\mathfrak{F}_L/\rho = (X^*/\rho, X, \delta_{\mathfrak{F}_L/\rho}, \epsilon/\rho, L/\rho),$$

where ρ is such a congruence relation, and $\delta_{\mathfrak{F}_L/\rho}(w/\rho, x) = wx/\rho$ ($w \in X^*, x \in X$). It is straightforward to show that $\delta_{\mathfrak{F}_L/\rho}(\epsilon/\rho, w) = w/\rho$ for each $w \in X^*$, and therefore $L(\mathfrak{A}) = L$ and $L \in Rec(X)$.

The greatest congruence saturating a language $L \subseteq X^*$, denoted $\sim_L$ is called the *Nerode congruence of L*. It can be defined by the condition

$$u \sim_L v \quad \text{iff} \quad uw \in L \Leftrightarrow vw \in L$$

for all $w \in X^*$. The Nerode congruence can be defined also in some alternative ways, one of which is given below.

---

[3] The automaton $\mathfrak{F}_L$ has an infinite set of states. Although Definition 2.1 allows only finite state sets, it can be extended straightforwardly to handle this more general case.

Definition 2.6. The *left derivative* $w^{-1}L$ of a language L with respect to string $w \in X^*$ is defined by

$$w^{-1}L = \{\, v \in X^* \mid wv \in L \,\}.$$

Proposition 2.7. *Let* $L \subseteq X^*$ *and* $v, w \in X^*$. *Then* $v \sim_L w$ *iff* $v^{-1}L = w^{-1}L$.

2.7 Congruences, quotients and morphisms of automata

Let $\mathfrak{A} = (A, X, \delta_{\mathfrak{A}}, a_0, A')$. Two states a and b of $\mathfrak{A}$ are *equivalent*, which we express by writing $a \sim_{\mathfrak{A}} b$, if

$$(\forall w \in X^*)\, (\delta_{\mathfrak{A}}(a, w) \in A' \Leftrightarrow \delta_{\mathfrak{A}}(b, w) \in A').$$

The automaton is *reduced* if $a \sim_{\mathfrak{A}} b$ implies $a = b$, *i.e.* $\sim_{\mathfrak{A}} = 1_A$.

A relation $\rho \in \mathrm{Eq}(A)$ is a *congruence of* $\mathfrak{A}$ if

1. $a\,\rho\,b$ implies $\delta_{\mathfrak{A}}(a, x)\,\rho\,TransA(b, x)$ for all $a, b \in A$ and $x \in X$; and
2. ρ saturates A'.

We denote by $\mathrm{Con}(\mathfrak{A})$ the set of all congruences of $\mathfrak{A}$.

Proposition 2.8. *The relation* $\sim_{\mathfrak{A}}$ *is the greatest congruence of* $\mathfrak{A}$.

Definition 2.9. Let $\mathfrak{A} = (A, X, \delta_{\mathfrak{A}}, a_0, A')$ be an automaton and $\rho \in \mathrm{Con}(\mathfrak{A})$. The *quotient automaton* $\mathfrak{A}/\rho$ is defined as

$$\mathfrak{A}/\rho = (A/\rho, X, \delta', a_0/\rho, A'/\rho),$$

where $\delta'(a/\rho, x) = \delta_{\mathfrak{A}}(a, x)/\rho$.

Proposition 2.10. *Let* $\mathfrak{A}$ *be an automaton and* $\rho \in \mathrm{Con}(\mathfrak{A})$. *Then* $L(\mathfrak{A}) = L(\mathfrak{A}/\rho)$, *and in particular,* $L(\mathfrak{A}) = L(\mathfrak{A}/\sim_{\mathfrak{A}})$.

Definition 2.11. Let $\mathfrak{A} = (A, X, \delta_{\mathfrak{A}}, a_0, A')$ and $\mathfrak{B} = (B, X, \delta_{\mathfrak{B}}, b_0, B')$ be automata. A mapping $\varphi \colon A \to B$ is a *morphism* $\varphi \colon \mathfrak{A} \to \mathfrak{B}$ if

1. $\delta_{\mathfrak{A}}(a, x)\varphi = \delta_{\mathfrak{B}}(a\varphi, x)$ for all $a \in A$ and $x \in X$,
2. $a_0\varphi = b_0$, and
3. $B'\varphi^{-1} = A'$.

A morphism of two automata is an *epimorphism* if it is surjective, and an *isomorphism* if it is bijective. If φ is an epimorphism then $A'\varphi = B'$.

The following proposition shows that the relations between morphisms, quotients and congruences of automata are similar to their correspondents in algebra.

Proposition 2.12. *Let* $\mathfrak{A}$ *and* $\mathfrak{B}$ *be automata,* $\pi, \rho \in \mathrm{Con}(\mathfrak{A})$, *and* $\varphi \colon \mathfrak{A} \to \mathfrak{B}$ *a morphism. Then the following statements hold:*

1. $\ker \varphi \in \mathrm{Con}(\mathfrak{A})$;
2. *the natural mapping* $\rho^{\natural}$ *is an epimorphism* $\mathfrak{A} \to \mathfrak{A}/\rho$;
3. *if* φ *is an epimorphism, then* $\mathfrak{A}/\ker \varphi \cong \mathfrak{B}$;
4. *if* $\pi \subseteq \rho$, *then* $\mathfrak{A}/\rho$ *is an epimorphic image of* $\mathfrak{A}/\pi$; *and*
5. $L(\mathfrak{A}) = L(\mathfrak{B})$.

2.8 Inference from positive data

In the spirit of Theorem 1.1 it seems that the presence of negative examples is unavoidable if we want to — even ineffectively — infer any general language. Fortunately, Angluin [Ang80b] has stated a more constructive characterization of LIM-TXT and what is most important, the class of languages that can be inferred in the limit from text is not as trivial as Theorem 1.1 implies.

Theorem 2.13 (Angluin, 1980). *Let $\mathcal{L} = L_1, L_2, \ldots$ be an indexed class of languages (not necessarily recursive). Class $\mathcal{L}$ is in LIM-TXT if and only if there exists (for each alphabet X) an algorithm that on any input $i \geq 1$ enumerates a finite set of strings $T_i \subseteq L_i$ such that*

$$(\forall\, j \geq 1)\ (T_i \subseteq L_j\ \Rightarrow\ L_j \not\subseteq L_i).$$

The sets T_i in Theorem 2.13 are called *tell-tale sets* for languages L_i, since they tell each language L_i from any other language L_j $(i \neq j)$. Actually L_i is the smallest language in the family $\mathcal{L}$ containing the set T_i.

Corollary 2.14. *Let $\mathcal{L} = \{L_1, L_2, \ldots\}$ be a class of recursive languages. If $\mathcal{L}$ is in LIM-TXT, then there exists for every $i \geq 1$ a finite set $T_i \subseteq L_i$ such that*

$$(\forall\, j \geq 1)\ (T_i \subseteq L_j\ \Rightarrow\ L_j \not\subseteq L_i).$$

Corollary 2.15. *Let $\mathcal{L} = \{L_1, L_2, \ldots\}$ be a class of recursive languages such that for every nonempty finite set $T \subseteq X^*$, the cardinality of the set*

$$\{L \mid T \subseteq L,\ L \in \mathcal{L}\}$$

is finite. Then $\mathcal{L} \in$ LIM-TXT.

3 Heuristic inference methods

We shall introduce in Section 3.1 the concept of a *generalized quotient*, which allows us to form nondeterministic automata using equivalences of the free monoid X^* that are not necessarily congruences. After some general observations concerning such quotients and the corresponding languages we shall introduce a class of inference methods based on them. It was shown in [KS94] that the methods presented in [BF77, Lev81, FK84, Kam88] could all be seen as instances of this general scheme of algorithms.

Another common idea used for inferring a language is to merge states of some automaton of the sample set (*e.g.* [Ang82]). We shall generalize also this approach and compare it with the aforementioned monoid approach in Section 3.2. The main result of this comparison is that both approaches give (at least in theory) the same results.

3.1 Generalized quotient automata

We shall now consider nondeterministic automata obtained from equivalence relations that are not necessarily congruences. Then a few facts concerning the languages recognized by the corresponding nd automata are presented. The proofs of these facts can be derived from the results of [KS94], where they were presented for the case of tree languages.

Definition 3.1. Let $\mathfrak{A} = (A, X, \delta_{\mathfrak{A}}, A_0, A')$ and $\mathfrak{B} = (B, X, \delta_{\mathfrak{B}}, B_0, B')$ be nd automata. A mapping $\varphi: A \to B$ is a *morphism* of nd automata from $\mathfrak{A}$ to $\mathfrak{B}$, which we express by writing $\varphi: \mathfrak{A} \to \mathfrak{B}$, if $B'\varphi^{-1} = A'$, $\varphi(A_0) \subseteq B_0$ and

$$\varphi(\delta_{\mathfrak{A}}(a, x)) \subseteq \delta_{\mathfrak{B}}(\varphi(a), x))$$

for all $a \in A$ and $x \in X$. A morphism $\varphi: \mathfrak{A} \to \mathfrak{B}$ is called an *epimorphism* if it is surjective and all inclusions above are equalities. An *isomorphism* of nd algebras is a bijective epimorphism, and $\mathfrak{A}$ and $\mathfrak{B}$ are said to be *isomorphic* ($\mathfrak{A} \cong \mathfrak{B}$) if there is an isomorphism $\varphi: \mathfrak{A} \to \mathfrak{B}$.

Obviously, these concepts coincide with the usual ones when $\mathfrak{A}$ and $\mathfrak{B}$ are ordinary automata. The following lemma shows how the morphism properties extend on strings.

Lemma 3.2. *If $\varphi: \mathfrak{A} \to \mathfrak{B}$ is a morphism of nd automata, then $\varphi(\delta_{\mathfrak{A}}(A_0, w)) \subseteq \delta_{\mathfrak{B}}(B_0, w)$ for all $w \in X^*$. If φ is an epimorphism, then $\varphi(\delta_{\mathfrak{A}}(A_0, w)) = \delta_{\mathfrak{B}}(B_0, w)$.*

Proposition 3.3. *Let $\mathfrak{A} = (A, X, \delta_{\mathfrak{A}}, A_0, A')$ and $\mathfrak{B} = (B, X, \delta_{\mathfrak{B}}, B_0, B')$ be nd automata. If there is a morphism $\varphi: \mathfrak{A} \to \mathfrak{B}$, then $L(\mathfrak{A}) \subseteq L(\mathfrak{B})$. If φ is an epimorphism, then $L(\mathfrak{A}) = L(\mathfrak{B})$.*

If $\mathfrak{A} = (A, X, \delta_{\mathfrak{A}}, a_0, A')$ is an automaton and $\rho \in \mathrm{Eq}(A)$, the *generalized quotient automaton* or shortly the *ρ-quotient* $\mathfrak{A}{:}\rho$ is the nondeterministic automaton $(A/\rho, X, \delta_\rho, a_0/\rho, A'_\rho)$, where δ_ρ is defined so that

$$\delta_\rho(a/\rho, x) = \{\, \delta_{\mathfrak{A}}(b, x)/\rho \mid b \,\rho\, a \,\} \qquad (a \in A, x \in X)$$

and $A'_\rho = \{\, a/\rho \mid a \in A' \,\}$.

Since $\mathfrak{A}{:}1_A = \mathfrak{A}^{nd}$, every deterministic automaton can be regarded as its own generalized quotient. A generalized quotient $\mathfrak{A}{:}\rho$ is not always an epimorphic image of $\mathfrak{A}^{nd}$, but the following fact can be noted.

Lemma 3.4. *If $\mathfrak{A} = (A, X, \delta_{\mathfrak{A}}, a_0, A')$ and $\rho \in \mathrm{Eq}(A)$, then the natural mapping $\rho^{\natural}: A \to A/\rho$, $a \mapsto a/\rho$, is a morphism of nd automata from $\mathfrak{A}^{nd}$ to $\mathfrak{A}{:}\rho$. It is an epimorphism iff ρ is a congruence of $\mathfrak{A}$.*

The following more general result will also be of use.

Proposition 3.5. *Let* $\mathfrak{A} = (A, X, \delta_{\mathfrak{A}}, a_0, A')$ *be an automaton and* $\rho, \pi \in Eq(A)$. *If* $\rho \subseteq \pi$, *then there exists a morphism* $\varphi \colon \mathfrak{A}{:}\rho \to \mathfrak{A}{:}\pi$ *of nd automata.*

For any mapping $\varphi \colon A \to B$ and any $\rho \in Eq(B)$, we denote by ρ^{φ} the relation

$$\varphi \circ \rho \circ \varphi^{-1} = \{\, (a, a') \mid a, a' \in A, \ (a\varphi, a'\varphi) \in \rho \,\}.$$

The following lemma shows some properties of these relations ρ^{φ}.

Lemma 3.6. *Let* $\varphi \colon A \to B$ *be a mapping and* $\pi, \rho \in Eq(B)$. *Then*

1. $\rho^{\varphi} \in Eq(A)$,
2. $1_B{}^{\varphi} = \ker \varphi$,
3. $\rho \subseteq \pi$ *implies* $\rho^{\varphi} \subseteq \pi^{\varphi}$, *and*
4. $(\rho \cap \pi)^{\varphi} = \rho^{\varphi} \cap \pi^{\varphi}$.

We can now establish the connection between the generalized quotients of epimorphic automata.

Proposition 3.7. *Let* $\mathfrak{A} = (A, X, \delta_{\mathfrak{A}}, a_0, A')$ *and* $\mathfrak{B} = (B, X, \delta_{\mathfrak{B}}, b_0, B')$ *be automata,* $\varphi \colon \mathfrak{A} \to \mathfrak{B}$ *an epimorphism, and* $\rho \in Eq(B)$. *Then* $\mathfrak{A}{:}\rho^{\varphi} \cong \mathfrak{B}{:}\rho$.

Propositions 3.3 enables us to draw the main result concerning the generalized quotient automata.

Proposition 3.8. *Let* $\mathfrak{A} = (A, X, \delta_{\mathfrak{A}}, a_0, A')$ *be an automaton. If* $\rho, \pi \in Eq(A)$ *and* $\rho \subseteq \pi$, *then* $L(\mathfrak{A}{:}\rho) \subseteq L(\mathfrak{A}{:}\pi)$. *In particular,* $L(\mathfrak{A}) \subseteq L(\mathfrak{A}{:}\rho)$ *for any* $\rho \in Eq(A)$.

3.2 Generalized quotients and heuristic inference methods

A heuristic inference algorithm using free automata as a starting point involves a criterion for the equivalence of strings. Typically, this takes the form of a mapping

$$\Gamma \colon \mathfrak{p}X^* \times X^* \to V,$$

where V is some value set depending on the algorithm and the alphabet X. Given a sample S of strings, an equivalence ρ on X^* is defined by the condition

$$s \rho t \quad \text{iff} \quad \Gamma(S, s) = \Gamma(S, t) \qquad (s, t \in X^*).$$

Next, the generalized quotient $\mathfrak{F}_S{:}\rho$ is constructed and presented as the output of the algorithm.

As a rule, Γ should be defined so that for any S, $\sim_S \subseteq \rho$. This guarantees that the index of ρ is finite and, by Proposition 3.8 that

$$S = L(\mathfrak{F}_S/\sim_S) \subseteq L(\mathfrak{F}_S{:}\rho),$$

i.e. the hypotheses produced by the method are consistent with the given sample. Proposition 3.8 also confirms the intuitively obvious fact that a weakening of the condition Γ is likely to yield an enlarged inferred language; it leads to a greater equivalence relation.

Let us now consider the general pattern of algorithms based on an initial finite automaton. Such methods start with the construction of a finite connected automaton $\mathfrak{A}$ of the sample set S. Then an equivalence ρ of the state set of $\mathfrak{A}$ is defined following some criterion or by a stepwise construction. Finally, the generalized quotient $\mathfrak{A}{:}\rho$ is formed and returned as the output of the algorithm.

Again, Proposition 3.8 tells us that the inferred set $L(\mathfrak{A}{:}\rho)$ contains at least the sample S, and that if some other criterion gives an equivalence π such that $\rho \subseteq \pi$, then $L(\mathfrak{A}{:}\rho) \subseteq L(\mathfrak{A}{:}\pi)$. Usually the criterion for ρ-equivalence is such that all states equivalent in $\mathfrak{A}$ are also ρ-equivalent, i.e. $\sim_{\mathfrak{A}} \subseteq \rho$. If $\rho = \sim_{\mathfrak{A}}$, then the procedure yields simply the minimal automaton of the sample S.

Let us now compare the approaches with each other. The natural question is, whether all languages that may result from a given sample S using one approach, could always be obtained from S by using the other approach.

Suppose first that we used the second approach and started with a connected automaton $\mathfrak{A} = (A, X, \delta_{\mathfrak{A}}, a_0, A')$ of S and obtained an equivalence $\rho \in \mathrm{Eq}(A)$. Let $\varphi(w) = \delta(a_0, w)$ for all $w \in X^*$. Clearly φ is an epimorphism from X^* onto A. By Proposition 3.7 we get an equivalence ρ^φ on X^* such that $A{:}\rho \cong X^*{:}\rho^\varphi$ with

$$\psi \colon X^*{:}\rho^\varphi \to A{:}\rho, \quad a/\rho^\varphi \mapsto a\varphi/\rho$$

as an isomorphism. Moreover, $A'\varphi^{-1} = S$ implies that $S/\rho^\varphi = (A'/\rho)\psi^{-1}$. Hence, ψ is also an isomorphism between the nd automata $\mathfrak{F}_S{:}\rho^\varphi$ and $\mathfrak{A}{:}\rho$. This shows that any result that can be obtained using the second approach can, at least in principle, be obtained using the first approach, too.

It is rather obvious that the converse cannot be completely true if the construction of the initial automaton is fixed in advance. In fact, from a given finite $\mathfrak{A}$ one can get a finite number of generalized quotients and, hence, just a finite number of inferred languages. So let us state the question differently.

Suppose we have constructed a finite nd automaton $\mathfrak{F}_S{:}\rho = (X^*{:}\rho, S/\rho)$ using the first approach. If there is a congruence π of $\mathfrak{F}_S$ of finite index such that $\pi \subseteq \rho$, then we could get $\mathfrak{F}_S{:}\rho$ also starting from the finite automaton $\mathfrak{F}_S/\pi = (X^*/\pi, S/\pi)$. For this we define the equivalence τ on X^*/π by the condition

$$s/\pi \equiv t/\pi \ (\tau) \quad \text{iff} \quad s \equiv t \ (\rho) \qquad (s, t \in X^*).$$

It is easy to see that $\rho = \tau^\varphi$ when φ is the canonical epimorphism $t \mapsto t/\pi$ from X^* onto X^*/π. Proposition 3.7 gives now $(X^*/\pi){:}\tau \cong X^*{:}\rho$. Hence $\mathfrak{A}{:}\tau \cong \mathfrak{F}_S{:}\rho$ for $\mathfrak{A} = (X^*/\pi, A')$, where $A' = S/\pi$.

Similarly, one can show that from any given automaton $\mathfrak{A} = (A, X, \delta_{\mathfrak{A}}, a_0, A')$ of S one can infer the same language as one can infer from $\mathfrak{F}_S$ using some equivalence relation ρ on X^* such that $\ker \varphi \subseteq \rho$, where φ is defined as above.

3.3 Inference algorithms based on generalized quotients

In this section we consider formal schemes for inference algorithms using generalized quotient constructions. Presented in a mathematically formalized form such algorithms can be seen to differ from each other mainly in the criteria or methods used for forming the equivalence relation. Moreover, they can be divided into two main categories depending on whether the equivalence is defined on the set of strings or on the state set of an initial finite automaton. In the former case, the quotient automaton is obtained from the free automaton, and in the second case the finite initial automaton is used. We present the general schemes for both types of algorithms and make some comparisons between them.

Inference methods based on derivatives of the sample Many of the heuristic methods can be regarded as special implementations of the same general idea of approximating the Nerode congruence of the sample set by some equivalence relation among strings; the methods differ from each other in the way the equivalences are defined.

The alternative definition given by Proposition 2.7 suggests a general way to do this approximation. Instead of computing the full derivative sets $w^{-1}L$, one limits in some way the set of suffixes v to be taken into account. In an inference situation, where only a sample of the language is given, such approximations serve as heuristic rules for extrapolating beyond the sample: by assuming the syntactic equivalence of strings on such restricted grounds, strings sufficiently similar to the sample strings will also be counted into the inferred set. A prime example of this kind of a method is the algorithm due to Biermann and Feldman, where the length of the suffixes was bounded [BF72].

We next construct the required limitation by defining a *complexity measure* $\mu: X^* \to \mathbb{N}$ and restricting us only on the set of suffixes under some complexity $k \in \mathbb{N}$. The measure should, however, have a few simple properties to be useful.

Definition 3.9. A complexity measure $\mu: X^* \to \mathbb{N}$ is *reasonable* if

1. $\mu(v) \leq \mu(uv)$ for all $u, v \in X^*$, and
2. the languages $\{ w \in X^* \mid \mu(w) \leq k \}$ are effectively regular ($k \geq 0$).

For two reasonable complexity measures μ and ν, we write $\mu \leq \nu$ iff $\mu(w) \leq \nu(w)$ for all words w in X^*.

Condition (2) in the above definition means that there is an algorithm for constructing an automaton for any $\{ w \in X^* \mid \mu(w) \leq k \}$ ($k \geq 0$). Obviously, the length of a string, lg, is an RCM.

Definition 3.10 (Bounded derivative). Let $\mu: X^* \to \mathbb{N}$ be an RCM on X^* and let $k \in \mathbb{N}$. The (μ, k)-*bounded derivative* of a language L with respect to a string w is the set

$$w^{-1}L|(\mu, k) = \{ v \in X^* \mid wv \in L, \ \mu(v) \leq k \}.$$

Two strings s and t are (μ, k)-*equivalent* with respect to L, $s \equiv t \ (\theta(\mu, k; L))$ in symbols, if $s^{-1}L|(\mu, k) = t^{-1}L|(\mu, k)$.

It is clear that each $\theta(\mu, k; L)$ is an equivalence on X^*. The following lemma states a few more obvious facts.

Lemma 3.11. *For any language L, any RCMs μ and ν on X^*, and any natural numbers h and k, the following claims hold:*

1. $\sim_L \subseteq \theta(\mu, k; L)$;
2. *if $h \leq k$, then $\theta(\mu, h; L) \supseteq \theta(\mu, k; L)$;*
3. *if $\mu \leq \nu$, then $\theta(\mu, k; L) \subseteq \theta(\nu, k; L)$.*

Now we have a general scheme for defining a whole family of k-tail methods. Every choice of an RCM μ on X^* and any $k \geq 0$ yields an inference algorithm TAIL$[\mu, k](S)$ described in Figure 1. The language $L(\mathfrak{F}_S{:}\theta(\mu, k; S))$ inferred by the algorithm is denoted by TAIL$(\mu, k; S)$.

Algorithm TAIL$[\mu, k](S)$

Compute the set $\mathrm{pref}(S) = \{w_1, \ldots, w_n\}$
for each w in $\mathrm{pref}(S)$ **do**
       compute the set $w^{-1}S|(\mu, k)$
$\theta = 1_{X^*}.$
for $i = 1..(n-1)$ **do**
      for $j = (i+1)..n$ **do**
            if $w_i^{-1}S|(\mu, k) = w_j^{-1}S|(\mu, k)$ **then**
                $\theta = \theta \cup \{(w_i, w_j), (w_j, w_i)\}$

Construct and return $\mathfrak{F}_S{:}\theta$.

Figure 1. Algorithm family TAIL$[\mu, k]$

A few comments on these algorithms are in order. First, the number of strings in the set $\mathrm{pref}(S)$ is finite, and also each (μ, k)-bounded derivative to be computed is a finite set, which can be found by a finite number of comparisons. When computing the relation θ one should note that $w^{-1}S|(\mu, k) = \emptyset$ whenever $w \notin \mathrm{pref}(S)$. Hence these derivatives are not explicitly formed, and all of the complement set $X^* - \mathrm{pref}(S)$ is contained in one θ-class. However, it is to be noted that $w^{-1}S|(\mu, k)$ may be empty also when $w \in \mathrm{pref}(S)$.

From Lemma 3.11 and results of Section 3.1 we can infer the following proposition summing up our general knowledge about the TAIL-algorithms.

Proposition 3.12. *Let $\mu{:}X^* \to \mathbb{N}$ and $\nu{:}X^* \to \mathbb{N}$ be two RCMs for strings, $k \geq 0$, and S a finite sample. Then*

1. TAIL$(\mu, 0; S) \supseteq$ TAIL$(\mu, 1; S) \supseteq \ldots \supseteq S$,
2. *if $\mu \leq \nu$ then* TAIL$(\mu, k; S) \subseteq$ TAIL$(\nu, k; S)$, *and*
3. TAIL$(\mu, k; S) = S$ *if* $\max(\mu(v) \mid (\exists w \in \mathrm{pref}(S))\, v \in w^{-1}S) \leq k$.

3.4 State-merging methods: the string case

Let $\mathfrak{A} = (A, X, \delta_{\mathfrak{A}}, a_0, A')$ be an automaton of a finite sample S ($\subseteq X^*$). It is reasonable to assume that $\mathfrak{A}$ is connected. Merging all pairs of equivalent states does not change the language, but simply gives the minimal automaton $\mathfrak{A}/\sim_{\mathfrak{A}}$ of S. A general way to extend the sample is to somehow weaken the condition of equivalence (see Sec. 2.7) thus accepting lesser evidence for the equivalence of two states. This usually results in an equivalence $\rho \in \mathrm{Eq}(A)$ properly containing $\sim_{\mathfrak{A}}$. Hence, the generalized quotient $\mathfrak{A}:\rho$ is likely to yield a language properly including S. Of course, there should be at least some heuristic grounds for forming ρ. Let us consider a very general class of such algorithms.

3.5 Algorithm family MERGE

Assume that a language $U \subseteq X^*$, the *test set* is given. Then the condition for equivalence of states in automaton $\mathfrak{A}$ could be replaced by

$$(\forall w \in U) \quad (\delta_{\mathfrak{A}}(a, w) \in A' \Leftrightarrow \delta_{\mathfrak{A}}(b, w) \in A').$$

If we denote the set $\{w \in U \mid \delta_{\mathfrak{A}}(a, w) \in A'\}$ by $L(a, U)$, we can restate the above simply as $L(a, U) = L(b, U)$. Note that given $\mathfrak{A} = (A, X, \delta_{\mathfrak{A}}, a_0, A')$ and U, we can effectively construct an automaton for $L(a, U)$ ($a \in A$). In fact, these automata have not to be constructed explicitly because we can simulate the behavior of the automaton for $L(a, U)$ by driving the automaton $\mathfrak{A}$ with a as the start state and the automaton for U in parallel.

The test set U may depend on some adjustable parameters, and perhaps on the sample, too. A class of algorithms analogous to the TAIL-family is obtained if we let U depend on a complexity measure $\mu: X^* \to \mathbb{N}$ and a bound k ($\in \mathbb{N}$) so that $U = \{w \in X^* \mid \mu(w) \leq k\}$.

Given an RCM $\mu: X^* \to \mathbb{N}$, a value k in $\mathbb{N}$, and an algorithm $\mathcal{C}$ forming for every finite language S ($\subseteq X^*$) a connected automaton, we may formulate the algorithm of Figure 2. The fact that μ is an RCM guarantees that the construction of the test set U is effective. The language recognized by the result of the algorithm is denoted by $\mathrm{MERGE}(\mathcal{C}, \mu, k; S)$.

Lemma 3.13. *Let $\mu: X^* \to \mathbb{N}$ and $\nu: X^* \to \mathbb{N}$ be two RCMs, $\mathcal{C}$ an algorithm constructing connected automata for finite languages, S ($\subseteq X^*$) a finite sample, and $k \geq 0$. Then*

1. $\mathrm{MERGE}(\mathcal{C}, \mu, 0; S) \supseteq \mathrm{MERGE}(\mathcal{C}, \mu, 1; S) \supseteq \ldots \supseteq S$,
2. *if $\mu \leq \nu$, then $\mathrm{MERGE}(\mathcal{C}, \mu, k; S) \subseteq \mathrm{MERGE}(\mathcal{C}, \nu, k; S)$,*
3. $\mathrm{MERGE}(\mathcal{C}, \mu, k; S) = S$ *if $S \subseteq U$ for the U constructed in step (3) of the algorithm $\mathrm{MERGE}[\mathcal{C}, \mu, k]$.*

Algorithm MERGE$[C, \mu, k](S)$

$\mathfrak{A} = (A, X, \delta_{\mathfrak{A}}, a_0, A') = C(S)$.
$\rho = 1_A$.
$U = \{ w \in X^* \mid \mu(w) \leq k \}$.
Let $A = \{a_1, \ldots, a_n\}$
for $i = 1..(n-1)$ **do**
$\qquad$ for $j = (i+1)..n$ **do**
$\qquad\qquad$ **if** $L(a_i, U) = L(a_j, U)$ **then**
$\qquad\qquad\qquad$ $\rho = \rho \cup \{(a_i, a_j), (a_j, a_i)\}$

Construct and return $\mathfrak{A}{:}\rho$.

Figure 2. Algorithm family MERGE$[C, \mu, k]$

The role of the initial automaton

Lemma 3.14. *Let* $\mathfrak{A} = (A, X, \delta_{\mathfrak{A}}, a_0, A')$ *and* $\mathfrak{B} = (B, X, \delta_{\mathfrak{B}}, b_0, B')$ *be automata,* $\varphi\colon \mathfrak{A} \to \mathfrak{B}$ *an epimorphism of automata, and* L *a language over* X. *Define the equivalence relations* ρ *and* π *on* A *and* B, *respectively, by the conditions*

$a_1 \, \rho \, a_2$ *iff* $(\forall w \in L)$ $(\delta_{\mathfrak{A}}(a_1, w) \in A' \Leftrightarrow \delta_{\mathfrak{A}}(a_2, w) \in A')$ $\qquad (a_1, a_2 \in A),$ *and*
$b_1 \, \pi \, b_2$ *iff* $(\forall w \in L)$ $(\delta_{\mathfrak{B}}(b_1, w) \in B' \Leftrightarrow \delta_{\mathfrak{B}}(b_2, w) \in B')$ $\qquad (b_1, b_2 \in B).$

Then $\rho = \pi^{\varphi}$, $\mathfrak{A}{:}\rho \cong \mathfrak{B}{:}\pi$ *and* $L(\mathfrak{A}{:}\rho) = L(\mathfrak{B}{:}\pi)$.

Since the minimal automaton of any regular language L is an epimorphic image of any other connected automaton of L, Lemma 3.14 tells us that the language inferred by the MERGE-algorithm does not depend on the construction C of the initial automaton. This conclusion can be expressed as follows.

Proposition 3.15. *Let* $\mu\colon X^* \to \mathbb{N}$ *be an* RCM, $k \geq 0$, *and let* C *and* D *be any algorithms constructing connected automata for finite languages. Then for any finite sample* S $(\subseteq X^*)$, MERGE$(C, \mu, k; S) =$ MERGE$(D, \mu, k; S)$.

3.6   Pumping lemma method and generalized quotients

The pumping lemma expresses one of the most fundamental properties of regular languages, and it is a natural heuristic basis for inferring regular languages. For the use of the pumping lemma in the case of string languages the reader may consult [GT78] or [Mic86], for example. A demystified version of the tree case can be found from [KS94].

$\qquad$Here we shall consider an inference algorithm based on the pumping lemma as an example of the approach starting from an initial automaton, but not belonging to the family of MERGE-algorithms.

The pumping lemma can be used in several ways as a guideline for extrapolating from a given sample S. For example, one could decide that if $uw, uvw \in S$ for some u, v and w as in the pumping lemma, then the language to be inferred contains the whole set $\{ uv^k w \mid k \geq 0 \}$. The condition for including the set could be modified by requiring only that $uv^i w, uv^j w \in S$ for any two distinct values $i, j \geq 0$. On the other hand, one could also require that S contains more than two strings of the form $uv^i w$. Different strategies could also be adopted for handling cases where the sample strings exhibit several indications of pumping, possibly in overlapping parts. In the following inference algorithm we have set such issues aside and simply observe all pairs uw, uvw ($\in S$).

In order to interpret a pair uw, uvw in terms of the canonical automaton, we observe that in the proof of the pumping lemma the set $\{ uv^i w \mid i \geq 0 \}$ results from the fact that $\delta(a_0, uv) = \delta(a_0, u)$. This means that we should identify the states uv and u in the canonical automaton. Let θ be the equivalence on $A(S)$ generated by the relation

$$\rho = \{ (u, uv) \mid u, v \in X^*, v \neq \epsilon \ (\exists w \in X^*) \ uw, uvw \in S \}.$$

We can now formulate an inference algorithm using this equivalence for the construction of a generalized quotient of $\mathfrak{A}(S)$. The algorithm is shown in Figure 3. We denote the language inferred by the algorithm by $\text{PUMP}(S)$.

Algorithm $\text{PUMP}(S)$

Construct the canonical automaton $\mathfrak{A}(S)$.
Let $\text{pref}(S) = \{u_1, \ldots, u_n\}$.
$\rho = 1_{A(S)}$.
for $i = 1..n$ **do**
    $S_i = \{ w \mid u_i w \in S \}$.
    Let $S_i = \{w_1, \ldots, w_m\}$.
    for $j = 1..(m-1)$ **do**
        for $k = (j+1)..m$ **do**
            if $w_j = vw_k$ **or** $w_k = vw_j$ for some $v \neq \epsilon$ **then**
                $\rho = \rho \cup \{(u_i, u_i v)\}$

Construct the equivalence closure θ of ρ.
Construct and return as output the generalized quotient $\mathfrak{A}(S){:}\theta$.

Figure 3. Algorithm PUMP

The following observations are quite immediate.

Lemma 3.16. *For any finite sample $S \subseteq X^*$, the following hold:*

1. $S \subseteq \text{PUMP}(S)$.

2. If $uw, uvw \in S$, for some $u, v, w \in X^*$, $v \neq \epsilon$, then

$$\{ uv^i w \mid i \geq 0 \} \subseteq \text{PUMP}(S).$$

In order to be able to predict $\text{PUMP}(S)$ more precisely even if there are several pairs uw, uvw in S, one should probably restrict the use of the merging rule of PUMP. The computational work could also be reduced by restricting somehow the complexity of the pumped strings v.

4 Characterizing inference methods

When we are observing some arbitrary target languages, we do not necessarily know, what is the exact class of languages (the target class) they belong to. In the previous examples we have usually taken a large class (e.g. the regular languages) that surely contains all our targets. These classes are, however, too difficult to be learned even approximately from a practical amount of information. This difficulty originates from the large — infinite, or even uncountable — cardinality of these classes.

Many subclasses of regular languages can be inferred in the limit from positive examples. Moreover, the intermediate results of the inference process (results based on finite samples) are *characterizing* in the sense that they can be given a formal description. If we can make the assumption that our target languages (or at least a large part of them) belong to such a subclass, we can use more powerful inference methods than in the general case. Whether some assumption of this kind is justified or not is, of course, another question depending on the subclass chosen and on the nature of the targets. Among the restricted families considered in the literature are the *k-reversible* [Ang82, BG92], *terminal distinguishable* [RN87], *k-contextual* [Mug90], *k-testable* [GV90, YIK94], *Szilard languages* [Mäk90], *strictly deterministic* [TY92], *k-definite* and *reverse k-definite* [Knu93a] string languages. The author has generalized the inference of many of these subclasses to regular tree languages.

We define the concept of *characterizing inference* to mean that the result of a characterizing inference algorithm can be described formally. A more strict and often used definition is that the result can be shown to be the smallest language in a given subclass of languages that contains the given sample.

Another property worth to mention is the existence of *characteristic samples* of languages in a certain subclass $\mathcal{L}$. A set $S \subseteq L$ is characteristic for L if there is no $L' \in \mathcal{L}$ such that $S \subseteq L' \subset L$. If such a sample S exists and can be effectively constructed for each language in $\mathcal{L}$, then $\mathcal{L} \in LIM\text{-}TXT$, since S is naturally a tell-tale set for L (Thm. 2.13).

The inference methods presented in [Ang82], [RN87] and [Mug90] are based on the fact that obtaining more and more examples will eventually lead to a characterizing sample containing all the strings needed to define the language accurately. These samples are, however, rather complex and unintuitive, and the algorithms based on the utilization of the restrictions (like k-reversibility) on these languages do not seem to be generalizable to other families of languages.

It is our opinion that this complexity is due to the tight connection between the characterizing sample and the automaton of the language.

4.1 The k-testable string languages

The method proposed by Garciá and Vidal [GV90] for the *k-testable* languages [McN74, BS73, Zal72] has a more comprehensible basis: each language in this class is naturally associated with a 3-tuple of finite sets of strings. If $L \subseteq X^*$ is a k-testable language, then the L can be defined by three finite sets, $A, B \subseteq X^{<k}$ and $C \subseteq X^k$, as follows:

$$L = (AX^* \cap X^*B) - (X^*CX^*).$$

Informally, the words of L begin with a string from A, end with a string of B and do not contain as a substring any member of the set C. This leads to a natural interpretation of the sample S: $\mathrm{pref}(S) \cap X^{<k}$ gives us the set A, $\mathrm{suff}(S) \cap X^{<k}$ gives the set B, and $\mathrm{subw}(S, k)$ gives the set $X^k - C$. Thus, each sample generates a definition of a k-testable language; the inference algorithm has only to construct the corresponding automaton. This can be done effectively, since each 3-tuple (A, B, C) used in the definition of a k-testable language L can effectively used as the basis of the construction of the *associated automaton* recognizing L.

4.2 Class-specific hypothesis spaces

The criticism in the previous section was mainly due to the fact that the class of all automata is often too large in proportion to a given subclass of languages. If the family of target languages is restricted or even finite, why should we have such a non-restricted hypothesis space? As an example, the k-testable languages have a well-defined and finite hypothesis space $pX^{<k} \times pX^{<k} \times pX^k$ that, though large, certainly is more tractable than the class of all automata.

We define in this section an abstract inference model where the hypothesis space is not dependent on the automata but merely on the algebraic properties of the language family used.

4.3 Presentations and models

Let us first define the connection between language families and their abstract presentations. This definition bears a close connection to the original 'Goldian' inference model, where the hypothesis space was not bound to any particular objects like automata. We just require that the elements of the space can be used to represent the target languages.

Definition 4.1. Let $\mathcal{L}$ be a language family, $D_1, \ldots, D_n$ some sets $(n > 0)$, and $\mathbf{D} = D_1 \times \cdots \times D_n$. $\mathbf{D}$ is a *base*[4] of $\mathcal{L}$, and we write $\mathcal{L} = \lambda(\mathbf{D})$ if there exists

---

[4] The base $\mathbf{D}$ forms the hypothesis space of an inference method.

a surjective mapping $\lambda: \mathbf{D} \to \mathcal{L}$. Each member $M \in \mathbf{D}$ is a *presentation* of a language $L = \lambda(M) \in \mathcal{L}$. The function λ is called the *presentation mapping* between $\mathbf{D}$ and $\mathcal{L}$.

We have not fixed the domains of the sets D_i in order to keep Definition 4.1 as general as possible. It should be noted that λ is not necessarily injective; two different presentations may define the same language.

For example, the family of k-testable string languages, $\text{test}(k)$, has a base $\mathbf{D}(k) = \mathfrak{p}X^{<k} \times \mathfrak{p}X^{<k} \times \mathfrak{p}X^k$, since we can define a surjective mapping $\lambda: \mathbf{D}(k) \to \text{test}(k)$ by $(A, B, C) \mapsto (AX^* \cap X^*B) - (X^*CX^*)$ (for all $(A, B, C) \in \mathbf{D}(k)$).

4.4 An informal framework

The remarks concerning k-testable languages made in the previous section lead us to the following informal framework for the basis of inference. We assume that our target language L belongs to some family $\mathcal{L}$ of regular languages that can be defined in the sense of Definition 4.1.

1. Determine a set $\mathbf{D}$ and a surjective mapping λ such that $\mathcal{L} = \lambda(\mathbf{D})$.
2. Given a finite sample $S \subseteq L$, construct a presentation $\mu(S) \in \mathbf{D}$, as a hypothesis of a possible presentation M of L. This proposal is usually derived from the properties of $\mathbf{D}$ and λ. It can also be required that $S \subseteq \lambda(\mu(S))$, *i.e.* the hypothesis must be consistent with the sample.
3. Build the automaton for the language $\lambda(\mu(S))$.

The result is clearly a automaton of a language in $\mathcal{L}$ — thus the methods derived from the framework are class-preserving [JB81].

We can already now state the following obvious but important property of our framework.

Proposition 4.2. *Let $\mathcal{L} = \lambda(\mathbf{D})$ be a class of regular languages such that $\mathbf{D}$ is finite and λ can be calculated effectively. Then $\mathcal{L} \in LIM\text{-}TXT$.*

For example, since the base $\mathbf{D}(k)$ of the family of k-testable string languages is finite, $\text{test}(k) \in LIM\text{-}TXT$.

4.5 Monotonic presentation mappings

The practical value of our approach depends mainly on the 'goodness' of our proposal $\mu(S)$. Since λ is a mapping from the presentations M to the languages $\lambda(M)$, a choice from the set $\lambda^{-1}(S)$ seems to be the most natural. However, λ must be generalized to a mapping η in such a way that η^{-1} can be applied to all samples — not only to the languages in the current family $\mathcal{L}$. In order to formally do this generalization, we need first to consider some relations between λ and $\mathcal{L}$.

Definition 4.3. Let $\mathcal{L} = \lambda(\mathbf{D})$ with $\mathbf{D} = D_1 \times \cdots \times D_n$ be a presentation mapping between $\mathbf{D}$ and $\mathcal{L}$. For any i, $1 \leq i \leq n$, we call λ

1. *isotonic in the ith component* of $\mathbf{D}$ if $\lambda(M) \subseteq \lambda(N)$ whenever $M, N \in \mathbf{D}$ are such that $M = (M_1, \ldots, M_i, \ldots, M_n)$, $N = (M_1, \ldots, N_i, \ldots, M_n)$, and $M_i \subseteq N_i$; and

2. *antitonic in the ith component* of $\mathbf{D}$ if $\lambda(N) \subseteq \lambda(M)$ whenever $M, N \in \mathbf{D}$ are such that $M = (M_1, \ldots, M_i, \ldots, M_n)$, $N = (M_1, \ldots, N_i, \ldots, M_n)$, and $M_i \subseteq N_i$.

For any $M = (M_1, \ldots, M_i, \ldots, M_n), N = (M_1, \ldots, N_i, \ldots, M_n) \in \mathbf{D}$, we denote $M \leq_\lambda N$ if $M_i \subseteq N_i$ for each component i in which λ is isotonic, and $M_i \supseteq N_i$ for each component i in which λ is antitonic.

Definition 4.4. Let $\mathcal{L} = \lambda(\mathbf{D})$ and $\mathbf{D} = D_1 \times \cdots \times D_n$. Mapping λ is *monotonic* if it is either isotonic or antitonic in each component i $(1 \leq i \leq n)$ of $\mathbf{D}$.

Note 4.5. If λ is monotonic, then it follows from $M \leq_\lambda N$ that $\lambda(M) \subseteq \lambda(N)$ $(M, N \in \mathbf{D})$.

Let us consider the class $\text{test}(k)$, where $\text{test}(k) = \lambda(\mathbf{D}(k))$. Here λ is isotonic in components 1 and 2 and antitonic in component 3 of $\mathbf{D}(k)$. Thus, λ is monotonic.

Definition 4.6. Let $\mathcal{L} = \lambda(\mathbf{D}) \subseteq \mathfrak{p}X^*$. A function $\mu: \mathfrak{p}X^* \to \mathbf{D}$ is an *acceptable guess for* λ^{-1} if the following conditions hold.

1. $S \subseteq \lambda(\mu(S)))$ (consistency);
2. $L = \lambda(\mu(L))$ for all $L \in \mathcal{L}$ or alternatively $\mu(L) \in \lambda^{-1}(L)$, *i.e.* the guesses for the 'true members' of $\mathcal{L}$ are correct;
3. if $S \subseteq T$, then $\mu(S) \leq_\lambda \mu(T)$ (monotonicity).

Consider again the family $\text{test}(k)$ and the presentation mapping $\lambda: \mathbf{D}(k) \to \text{test}(k)$ introduced above. Let $\mu: \mathfrak{p}X^* \to \mathbf{D}(k)$ be defined by

$$
\begin{aligned}
S &\mapsto (A_k(S), B_k(S), C_k(S)), \text{ where} \\
A_k(S) &= \text{pref}(S) \cap X^{<k}, \\
B_k(S) &= \text{suff}(S) \cap X^{<k}, \text{ and} \\
C_k(S) &= X^k - \text{subw}(S, k).
\end{aligned}
$$

It is straightforward to show that μ is an acceptable guess of λ^{-1}.

The following proposition tells us that inference methods based on acceptable guesses are strong monotonic [Jan91, Wie91].

Proposition 4.7. Let $\lambda: \mathbf{D} \to \mathcal{L}$ be a monotonic presentation mapping and μ an acceptable guess of λ^{-1}. If $S \subseteq T$, then $\lambda(\mu(S)) \subseteq \lambda(\mu(T))$.

Proposition 4.8 below contains the important fact that $\lambda(\mu(S))$ is the smallest language in $\mathcal{L}$ containing S.

Proposition 4.8. *Let* $\lambda: D \to \mathcal{L}$ *(* $\mathcal{L} \subseteq pX^*$ *), be a monotonic presentation mapping, and let* μ *be an acceptable guess for* λ^{-1} *. For each* $S \subseteq X^*$ *, the language* $\lambda(\mu(S))$ *is the smallest language of* $\mathcal{L}$ *containing* S *.*

Together propositions 4.7 and 4.8 ensure that our guesses of an unknown language L become more and more accurate as the sample $S \subseteq L$ increases. Suppose that $L = \{w_1, w_2, \ldots\}$. If we denote $S_0 = \emptyset$ and $S_{i+1} = S_i \cup \{w_{i+1}\}$, then initially $\lambda(\mu(S_0)) \subseteq L$, and $\lambda(\mu(S_i)) \subseteq \lambda(\mu(S_{i+1}))$ for all $i \geq 0$. Now $\lambda(\mu(S_\infty)) = L$ for $S_\infty = \bigcup_{i \geq 0} S_i$ — which is exactly what 'inductive inference in the limit' means.

4.6 How to build a characterizing inference algorithm

The steps to follow are:

1. Determine a base for $\mathcal{L}$. This requires the definition of the surjective mapping λ between the presentations and $\mathcal{L}$. This is often already given in some form in the definition of $\mathcal{L}$.
2. Define an acceptable guess μ of λ^{-1}. The requirement $L = \lambda(\mu(L))$ (Definition 4.6), which can be transformed to the form $\mu(L) \in \lambda^{-1}(L)$ for each $L \in \mathcal{L}$, gives a natural basis for μ. Program the function μ.
3. Determine the connection between presentations and associated automata in such a way that given a presentation, the construction of a automaton can be done efficiently. Program the function REC that constructs a automaton from a presentation.
4. Your algorithm is REC($\mu(S)$).

Consider again the family test(k) and the construction of the automaton associated with a presentation $M = (A, B, C)$ of a sample S. The automaton $\mathfrak{A}_M = (A_M, X, \delta_M, a_0, A'_M)$ associated with M can be constructed as follows (0 is an auxiliary symbol not occurring in X):

$$
\begin{aligned}
A_M &= X^{<k} \cup (X^k - C) \cup \{0\}; \\
A'_M &= (X^* B \cap X^k) \cup (A X^* \cap X^* B \cap X^{<k}); \\
a_0 &= \epsilon; \\
\delta_M(w, x) &= \begin{cases} wx & \text{if } \lg(w) < k \text{ and } wx \in \text{pref}(A); \\ w'x & \text{if } \lg(w) = k, w = yw' \text{ and } w'x \notin C; \\ 0 & \text{otherwise } (x, y \in X). \end{cases}
\end{aligned}
$$

It was shown in [GV90] that this construction can be done in time $O(k|S| \log |S|)$. The implementation given in [Knu94] improves this to $O(k|S|)$.

5 Conclusion

Inductive inference can be studied at many levels. Much work has been done on the sole computability of various problems, and true implementations of pattern recognition tasks are of uttermost importance. Our aim has been to give both theoretical and algorithmic basis for the practical inductive inference of regular languages. The main idea in this work has been that we have to rely on incomplete positive data and only a small amount of additional information. If we accept this idea, we necessarily have to use heuristic or approximative inference methods, where the characterizability of results is currently the best we can strive for.

References

Ang80a.   D. Angluin. Finding patterns common to a set of strings. *Journal of Computer and System Sciences*, 21:46–62, 1980.

Ang80b.   D. Angluin. Inductive inference of formal languages from positive data. *Information and Control*, 45:117–135, 1980.

Ang82.   D. Angluin. Inference of reversible languages. *Journal of the ACM*, 29(3):741–765, July 1982.

AU72.   A. V. Aho and J. D. Ullman. *The Theory of Parsing, Translation, and Compiling*. Prentice-Hall, Englewood Cliffs, N.J., 1972.

BF72.   A. W. Biermann and J. A. Feldman. On the synthesis of finite state machines from samples of their behavior. *IEEE Transactions on Computers*, C-21:592–597, June 1972.

BF74.   B. K. Bhargava and K-S. Fu. Transformations and inference of tree grammars for syntactic pattern recognition. In *Proceedings of the 1974 IEEE International Conference on Systems, Man, and Cybernetics*, Dallas, Texas, 1974.

BF77.   J. M. Brayer and K-S. Fu. A note on the k-tail method of tree grammar inference. *IEEE Transactions on Systems, Man, and Cybernetics*, SMC-7:293–300, April 1977.

BG92.   A. Bonopera and B. Gaujal. Inference of reversible languages. *International Journal of Algebra and Computation*, 2(3):327–349, 1992.

Bra84.   Wilfried Brauer. *Automatentheorie*. B. G. Teubner, Stuttgart, 1984.

BS73.   J. A. Brzozowski and I. Simon. Characterizations of locally testable events. *Discrete Mathematics*, 4:243–271, 1973.

CS83.   J. Case and C. Smith. Comparison of identification criteria for machine inductive inference. *Theoretical Computer Science*, 25:193–220, 1983.

Eil74.   S. Eilenberg. *Automata, Languages and Machines*, volume A. Academic Press, New York, 1974.

ES76.   S. Eilenberg and M. P. Schützenberger. On pseudovarieties. *Adv. Math.*, pages 413–418, 1976.

FK84.   H. Fukuda and K. Kamata. Inference of tree automata from sample set of trees. *International Journal of Computer and Information Sciences*, 13(3):177–196, 1984.

GET76.   R. C. Gonzalez, J. J. Edwards, and M. G. Thomason. An algorithm for the inference of tree grammars. *International Journal of Computer and Information Sciences*, 5(2):145–164, 1976.

Gin66.   A. Ginzburg. About some properties of definite, reverse-definite and related automata. *IEEE Transactions on Electronic Computation*, EC-15:806–810, 1966.

Gol67.   E. M. Gold. Language identification in the limit. *Information and Control*, 10:447–474, 1967.

GS84.   F. Gécseg and M. Steinby. *Tree Automata*. Akadémiai Kiadó, Budapest, 1984.

GT78.   R. C. Gonzalez and M. G. Thomason. *Syntactic Pattern Recognition: An Introduction*. Addison-Wesley, Reading, MA, 1978.

GV90.   P. Garciá and E. Vidal. Inference of k-testable languages in the strict sense and application to syntactic pattern recognition. *IEEE Transactions on Pattern Analysis and Machine Intelligence*, PAMI-12(9):920–925, September 1990.

HKLW88.   D. Haussler, M. Kearns, N. Littlestone, and M. K. Warmuth. Equivalence of models for polynomial learnability. In Haussler and Pitt [HP88], pages 42–55.

HP88.   D. Haussler and L. Pitt, editors. *Proceedings of the 1st Workshop on Computational Learning Theory, 1988*. Morgan Kaufmann, San Mateo, CA, 1988.

Jan91.   K. P. Jantke. Monotonic and non-monotonic inductive inference. *New Generation Computing*, 8:349–360, 1991.

JB81.   K. P. Jantke and H. R. Beick. Combining postulates of naturalness in inductive inference. *Elektronische Informationsverarbeitung und Kybernetik*, 17:465–484, 1981.

JKTY93.   K. P. Jantke, S. Kobayashi, E. Tomita, and T. Yokomori, editors. *Proceedings of the 4th Workshop on Algorithmic Learning Theory, 1993, Tokyo*. Number 744 in Lecture Notes in Artificial Intelligence. Springer-Verlag, New York, 1993.

Kam88.   K. Kamata. Inference methods for tree automata from sample set of trees. In *Proceedings of the 1988 IEEE International Conference on Systems, Man, and Cybernetics*, pages 490–493, 1988.

Knu93a.   T. Knuutila. How to invent characterizable inference methods for regular languages. In Jantke et al. [JKTY93], pages 209–222.

Knu93b.   T. Knuutila. Inference of k-testable tree languages. In H. Bunke, editor, *Proceedings of the International Workshop on Structural and Syntactic Pattern Recognition, Bern, Switzerland, 1992*, pages 109–120. World Scientific, Singapore, 1993.

Knu94.   T. Knuutila. *On the Inductive Inference of Regular String and Tree Languages*. PhD thesis, Department of Computer Science, University of Turku, Turku, Finland, 1994.

KS94.   T. Knuutila and M. Steinby. Inference of tree languages from a finite samples: an algebraic approach. *Theoretical Computer Science*, 129:337–367, 1994.

KV89.   M. Kearns and L. G. Valiant. Cryptographic limitations on learning Boolean formulae and finite automata. In *Proceedings of the 21st Annual ACM STOC*, pages 433–444. Assoc. Comp. Mach., New York, 1989.

Lev81.   B. Levine. Derivatives of tree sets with applications to grammatical inference. *IEEE Transactions on Pattern Analysis and Machine Intelligence*, PAMI-3(3):285–293, May 1981.

LW91.   S. Lange and R. Wiehagen. Polynomial-time inference of arbitrary pattern languages. *New Generation Computing*, 8:361–370, 1991.

Mäk90.   E. Mäkinen. The grammatical inference problem for the Szilard languages of linear grammars. *Information Processing Letters*, 36:203–206, 1990.

McN74.   R. McNaughton. Algebraic decision procedures for local testability. *Math. Syst. Theor.*, 8:60–76, 1974.

Mic86.   L. Miclet. *Structural Methods in Pattern Recognition*. Springer-Verlag, New York, 1986.

Mug90.   S. Muggleton. *Inductive Acquisition of Expert Knowledge*. Addison-Wesley, Reading, MA, 1990.

Pin86.   J. E. Pin. *Varieties of Formal Languages*. North Oxford Academic, 1986.

RN87.   V. Radhakrishnan and G. Nagaraja. Inference of regular grammars via skeletons. *IEEE Transactions on Systems, Man, and Cybernetics*, SMC-17:982–992, 1987.

Sal69.   A. Salomaa. *Theory of Automata*. Pergamon Press, 1969.

Ste92.   M. Steinby. A theory of tree language varieties. In M. Nivat and A. Podelski, editors, *Tree Automata and Languages*, pages 57–81. Elsevier Science Publishers B.V., Amsterdam, 1992.

TY92.   N. Tanida and T. Yokomori. Polynomial-time identification of strictly regular languages in the limit. *IEICE Transactions on Information and Systems*, E75-D:125–132, 1992.

Val84.   L. G. Valiant. A theory of the learnable. *Communications of the ACM*, 27(11):1134–1142, 1984.

Wie91.   R. Wiehagen. A thesis in inductive inference. In J. Dix, K. P. Jantke, and P. H. Schmitt, editors, *Proceedings of the 2nd International Workshop on Nonmonotonic and Inductive Logic, 1991, Reinhardsbrunn Castle, Germany*, number 543 in Lecture Notes in Artificial Intelligence, pages 184–207. Springer-Verlag, New York, 1991.

YIK94.   T. Yokomori, N. Ishida, and S. Kobayashi. Learning local languages and its application to protein α-chain calculation. In *Proceedings of the 27th Hawaii International Conference on System Sciences*, pages 113–122. IEEE Computer Society Press, Los Alamitos, CA, 1994.

Zal72.   Y. Zalcstein. Locally testable languages. *Journal of Computer and System Sciences*, 6:151–167, 1972.

Unions of Identifiable Families of Languages [*]

Kalvis Apsītis[1], Rūsiņš Freivalds[2], Raimonds Simanovskis[2],
and Juris Smotrovs[2]

[1] Department of Computer Science, University of Maryland, College Park, MD 20742
USA, e-mail: kalvis@cs.umd.edu
[2] Institute of Mathematics and Computer Science, University of Latvia, Raiņa bulv.
29, Rīga, LV-1459, Latvia, e-mail: rusins@cclu.lv, raymond@dlb.bkc.lv,
smotrovs@cclu.lv

Abstract. This paper deals with the satisfiability of requirements put
on the identifiability of unions of language families. We consider identification in the limit from a text with bounds on mindchanges and anomalies. We show that, though these identification types are not closed under
the set union, some of them still have features that resemble closedness.
To formalize this, we generalize the notion of closedness. Then by establishing "how closed" these identification types are we solve the satisfiability problem.

1 Introduction

In this paper a problem in inductive inference of recursively enumerable languages is considered. Inductive inference as a term used for finding out an algorithm from sample computations was first used by E. M. Gold in [3]. Since then
many identification types have been introduced.

E. M. Gold in [3] proved that there are two families of languages that are
identifiable in the limit, while their union is not. Similar results were obtained
for other identification types. However, a further research shows that these non-
union theorems do not convey in full the structure of these identification types
in terms of unions of language families. Though not closed under union, these
types are not absolutely "open." For instance, if every union of three families
out of $\mathcal{L}_1, \mathcal{L}_2, \mathcal{L}_3, \mathcal{L}_4$ is identifiable in the limit, so is the union $\mathcal{L}_1 \cup \mathcal{L}_2 \cup \mathcal{L}_3 \cup \mathcal{L}_4$.
So not all the requirements put on the identifiability of the unions of families
are satisfiable. In the previous example, the requirement that $\mathcal{L}_1 \cup \mathcal{L}_2 \cup \mathcal{L}_3 \cup \mathcal{L}_4$
is not identifiable would be unsatisfiable.

The main intention of this paper is to uncover the closedness properties and
to find out which sets of requirements are satisfiable and which are not for the
identification in the limit from a text with bounds on mindchanges and anomalies. (For the identification of recursive functions, this problem was investigated

---

[*] The research of the last three authors was supported by Latvian Science Council
Grant No. 93.599. The research of the last two authors was supported by the "SWH
izglītībai, zinātnei un kultūrai" scholarship.

in [1, 8].) We deal with this problem by introducing a natural generalization of the notion of closedness. The identification type is called n-closed in case for every set of n families of languages: if all the unions of $n - 1$ of these families are identifiable, so is the union of all n families. It turns out that this notion is sufficient for establishing if the requirements are satisfiable. Interestingly, the n-closedness is related to team learning, a field that is intensively investigated at the moment.

We proceed as follows. Section 2 contains preliminaries. In Section 3 we define n-closedness and establish some properties of it. In Section 4 we reduce the problem of satisfiability of requirements to finding out, for which n the identification type is n-closed. In Section 6 we find these n for identification in the limit with bounds on mindchanges and anomalies. Before that, in Section 5 we point to the connection of n-closedness with team learning. Section 7 summarizes the results.

2 Preliminaries

2.1 Notation

Any recursion theoretic notation not explained below is from [7]. $\mathbb{N}$ denotes the set of natural numbers, $\{0, 1, 2, \ldots\}$. $*$ denotes "an arbitrary finite (natural) number." In inequalities $(\forall n \in \mathbb{N})[n < * < \infty]$. $\forall^\infty$ means "for all but finitely many;" $\exists^\infty$ means "there exist infinitely many." When applied to sets, $\subset$ denotes proper subset. $\langle x_1, x_2, \ldots, x_n \rangle$ denotes a Cantor number of $(x_1, x_2, \ldots, x_n)$.

We fix a Gödel numbering of the partial recursive functions of one argument and denote it by φ. The function computed by the program i we denote by φ_i. Its domain W_i is the recursively enumerable language accepted by φ_i. Letter $\mathcal{E}$ denotes the set of recursively enumerable languages. If a function f is undefined at point x, we write $f(x) \uparrow$; otherwise we write $f(x) \downarrow$.

For $L_1, L_2 \in \mathcal{E}, a \in \mathbb{N} \cup \{*\}$, by $L_1 =^a L_2$ we mean that $card((L_1 - L_2) \cup (L_2 - L_1)) \leq a$. These a differences between the languages are called *anomalies*.

We will consider finite and infinite sequences with values from $\mathbb{N} \cup \{\#\}$, where $\#$ means "no data." The length of a finite sequence σ is denoted by $|\sigma|$. For a sequence σ, the initial sequence of length n ($n \leq |\sigma|$ if σ is finite) is denoted by $\sigma[n]$. The *content* of a sequence σ is the set of natural numbers in the range of σ, denoted content(σ). An infinite sequence T is a text for a language L iff content(T) $= L$. $\sigma \subseteq \tau$ means that τ is an extension of σ; $\sigma \subset \tau$ means that τ is a proper extension of σ.

2.2 Identification

An *identification strategy* F is an algorithm that receives as input a finite sequence and it outputs either a natural number *(a hypothesis)* or the symbol $\perp$ in case it has no hypothesis to issue.

The sequence of outputs produced by F, when it receives larger and larger initial segments of a text for a language, should satisfy the requirements of the given identification type. In this paper we are interested in the identification in the limit [3] modified by restrictions on the number of mindchanges and anomalies. *A mindchange* is an event when $F(T[n])$ and $F(T[n+1])$ are different natural numbers.

Definition 1. [3, 2, 6] Let $a, b \in \mathbb{N} \cup \{*\}$. A strategy F *TxtEx$_b^a$-identifies* a language $L \in \mathcal{E}$ $(L \in \text{TxtEx}_b^a(F))$ iff for every text T for L:

1. $(\exists N)[(\forall n < N)[F(T[n]) = \bot] \wedge (\forall n \geq N)[F(T[n]) \in \mathbb{N}]]$;
2. $(\exists h)[(\forall^\infty n)[F(T[n]) = h] \wedge W_h =^a L]$;
3. the number of mindchanges made by F on T does not exceed b.

Definition 2. [3, 2, 6] A family of languages $\mathcal{L} \subseteq \mathcal{E}$ is *TxtEx$_b^a$-identifiable* $(\mathcal{L} \in \text{TxtEx}_b^a)$ iff $(\exists F)[\mathcal{L} \subseteq \text{TxtEx}_b^a(F)]$.

We sometimes omit the index a if $a = 0$ and b if $b = *$. Particularly, $\text{TxtEx} = \text{TxtEx}_*^0$.

The following basic relationship has been established between the defined identification types.

Theorem 3. [2, 6] $(\forall a, b, c, d \in \mathbb{N} \cup \{*\})[\text{TxtEx}_b^a \subseteq \text{TxtEx}_d^c \Leftrightarrow a \leq c \wedge b \leq d]$.

3 n-closedness

Here we establish the basic properties of n-closedness and connections with the defined identification types.

Definition 4. Let $\circ$ be an associative and commutative binary operation. A set S_1 is *n-closed in a set* S_2 $(n \geq 2)$ with respect to $\circ$ iff

$(\forall a_1, \ldots, a_n \in S_1)$
$[(\forall i \mid (1 \leq i \leq n))[a_1 \circ \ldots \circ a_{i-1} \circ a_{i+1} \circ \ldots \circ a_n \in S_1] \Rightarrow a_1 \circ \ldots \circ a_n \in S_2]$.

Definition 5. Let $\circ$ be an associative and commutative binary operation. A set S is *n-closed* $(n \geq 2)$ with respect to $\circ$ iff S is n-closed in S.

So "2-closed" is the same as "closed." In further the binary operation will be set union. The following statements concerning n-closedness can be easily proved.

Proposition 6. *If a set family S_1 is n-closed in a set family S_2, then $S_1 \subseteq S_2$.*

Proof. Suppose, $U \in S_1$. Define $U_1 = \ldots = U_n = U$. Since S_1 is n-closed in S_2, we get that $\bigcup_{j=1}^n U_j = U \in S_2$. □

Proposition 7. *If S_2 is n-closed in S_3, $S_1 \subseteq S_2$ and $S_3 \subseteq S_4$, then S_1 is n-closed in S_4.*

Proposition 8. *Let S_1 be n-closed in S_2 and satisfy the property $(\forall U \in S_1)$ $(\forall V \subsetneq U)$ $[V \in S_1]$. Then S_1 is m-closed in S_2 for all $m \geq n$.*

Proof. Suppose S_1 satisfies the conditions, $m \geq n$. Suppose some sets $U_1, \ldots, U_m$ satisfy the property $(\forall i \mid 1 \leq i \leq m)[\bigcup_{j=1, j \neq i}^{m} U_j \in S_1]$. Define $V_1 = U_1, \ldots, V_{n-1} = U_{n-1}$, $V_n = \bigcup_{j=n}^{m} U_j$. We have $V_n \in S_1$ because $V_n \subseteq \bigcup_{j=2}^{m} U_j \in S_1$, and $\bigcup_{j=1}^{n-1} V_j \in S_1$ because $\bigcup_{j=1}^{n-1} V_j \subseteq \bigcup_{j=1}^{m-1} U_j \in S_1$. Thus, $(\forall i \mid 1 \leq i \leq n)[\bigcup_{j=1, j \neq i}^{n} V_j \in S_1]$. Since S_1 is n-closed in S_2, $\bigcup_{j=1}^{n} V_j = \bigcup_{j=1}^{m} U_j \in S_2$. □

Note that the classes TxtEx_b^a satisfy the mentioned property, namely together with any language family TxtEx_b^a contains all its subfamilies. Proposition 8 shows that the n-closedness properties of these identification types can be characterized by the least n for which they are n-closed.

Definition 9. *Let a set family S_1 satisfy the property $(\forall U \in S_1)(\forall V \subseteq U)[V \in S_1]$. We say that n is the closedness degree of S_1 in superset S_2 ($n = \text{csdeg}(S_1, S_2)$) iff n is the smallest number such that S_1 is n-closed in S_2.*
  If such n does not exist, we define $\text{csdeg}(S_1, S_2) = \infty$.
  We shall call $\text{cdeg}(S) = \text{csdeg}(S, S)$ the closedness degree of S.

The next proposition will simplify the matters when we shall establish the closedness degrees in Section 6.

Proposition 10. *If $a_1 \leq a_2$, $b_1 \leq b_2$, $c_1 \leq c_2$ and $d_1 \leq d_2$, then*

$$\text{csdeg}(\text{TxtEx}_{b_2}^{a_2}, \text{TxtEx}_{d_1}^{c_1}) \geq \text{csdeg}(\text{TxtEx}_{b_1}^{a_1}, \text{TxtEx}_{d_2}^{c_2}).$$

Proof. It follows from Proposition 7 and Theorem 3. □

4   Satisfiability of Requirements

Suppose we are given a set of requirements on the identifiability or non-identifiability of every union of language families $\mathcal{L}_1, \mathcal{L}_2, \ldots, \mathcal{L}_k$. We want to distinguish between satisfiable and unsatisfiable requirements.

In this section we write vectors in boldface and their components in italics with indices.

Requirements can be conveniently expressed by means of the Boolean functions. The function $f(\mathbf{x})$, $\mathbf{x} \in \{0,1\}^k$, corresponds to the set of requirements "$\bigcup_{x_i=1} \mathcal{L}_i$ is identifiable" if $f(\mathbf{x}) = 0$, and "$\bigcup_{x_i=1} \mathcal{L}_i$ is not identifiable" if $f(\mathbf{x}) = 1$.

Definition 11. *For $a, b \in \mathbb{N} \cup \{*\}$, a Boolean function $f : \{0,1\}^k \to \{0,1\}$ is TxtEx_b^a-satisfiable iff*

$$(\exists \mathcal{L}_1, \ldots, \mathcal{L}_k \subseteq \mathcal{E})(\forall \mathbf{x} \in \{0,1\}^k)[\bigcup_{x_i=1} \mathcal{L}_i \in \text{TxtEx}_b^a \Leftrightarrow f(\mathbf{x}) = 0].$$

Now, which of the Boolean functions are satisfiable? First, the empty set should be considered as identifiable. Second, TxtEx_b^a have the property: if $\mathcal{L}_1 \in \text{TxtEx}_b^a$ and $\mathcal{L}_2 \subseteq \mathcal{L}_1$, then $\mathcal{L}_2 \in \text{TxtEx}_b^a$. So we demand that f is monotone. And, third, the closedness degree of TxtEx_b^a should be considered. The next definition combines these three restrictions.

Definition 12. [1] A Boolean function $f : \{0,1\}^k \to \{0,1\}$ is *n-convolutional* iff

1. $f(0) = 0$;
2. $(\forall \mathbf{x}, \mathbf{y} \in \{0,1\}^k)[\mathbf{x} \leq \mathbf{y} \Rightarrow f(\mathbf{x}) \leq f(\mathbf{y})]$ (monotonicity);
3. $(\forall \mathbf{x} \in \{0,1\}^k)(\forall i_1, \ldots, i_n \mid 1 \leq i_1 < i_2 < \ldots < i_n \leq k \land x_{i_1} = \ldots = x_{i_n} = 1)[(\forall r \mid 1 \leq r \leq n)[f(x_1, \ldots, x_{i_r-1}, 0, x_{i_r+1}, \ldots, x_k) = 0] \Rightarrow f(\mathbf{x}) = 0]$.

Theorem 13. *Let $a, b \in \mathbb{N} \cup \{*\}$. Suppose $\text{cdeg}(\text{TxtEx}_b^a) = n \in \mathbb{N}$. Then a Boolean function is TxtEx_b^a-satisfiable iff it is n-convolutional.*

Suppose $\text{cdeg}(\text{TxtEx}_b^a) = \infty$. Then a Boolean function f is TxtEx_b^a-satisfiable iff $f(0) = 0$ and f is monotone.

Proof. At first we prove that the condition is necessary. Suppose a function $f : \{0,1\}^k \to \{0,1\}$ is TxtEx_b^a-satisfiable. Let $\mathcal{L}_1, \ldots, \mathcal{L}_k$ be the families of languages that satisfy the corresponding requirements. Then, because of the mentioned properties of TxtEx_b^a, $f(0) = 0$ and f is monotone. Suppose $\text{cdeg}(\text{TxtEx}_b^a) = n \in \mathbb{N}$. Let $\mathbf{x}$ be an arbitrary vector from $\{0,1\}^k$. Let $i_1, \ldots i_n$ be such that $1 \leq i_1 < \ldots < i_n \leq k$ and $x_{i_1} = \ldots = x_{i_n} = 1$. We define $\mathbf{y}^j$, $1 \leq j \leq n$, to be such vectors that

1. $y_{i_j}^j = 1$,
2. $y_{i_r}^j = 0$ for $r \neq j$, $1 \leq r \leq n$,
3. $y_s^j = x_s$, for $s \in \{1, \ldots, k\} - \{i_1, \ldots, i_n\}$.

Let $\mathcal{U}_j$ be the union of $\mathcal{L}_1, \ldots, \mathcal{L}_k$ corresponding to the vector $\mathbf{y}^j$. Then the vectors $(x_1, \ldots, x_{i_r-1}, 0, x_{i_r+1}, \ldots, x_k)$, $1 \leq r \leq n$, correspond to the unions of $n-1$ families out of $\mathcal{U}_1, \ldots, \mathcal{U}_n$. If these are TxtEx_b^a-identifiable, so is $\bigcup_{j=1}^n \mathcal{U}_j$, because TxtEx_b^a is n-closed. Since $\bigcup_{j=1}^n \mathcal{U}_j$ corresponds to the vector $\mathbf{x}$, we have proved that f is n-convolutional.

Now, sufficiency.

Definition 14. A vector $\mathbf{x}$ is *a minimal 1-vector* for a Boolean function f iff $f(\mathbf{x}) = 1$ and $(\forall \mathbf{y} < \mathbf{x})[f(\mathbf{y}) = 0]$.

Let $\mathbf{x}^j$, $1 \leq j \leq t$, be all the minimal 1-vectors for f. Let n_j be the number of components in $\mathbf{x}^j$ that are equal to 1. Suppose that $\text{cdeg}(\text{TxtEx}_b^a) = n \in \mathbb{N}$ and f is n-convolutional. According to point 3 in the definition of n-convolutionality, $n_j < n$ for every $j \in \{1, \ldots, t\}$. Suppose $\text{cdeg}(\text{TxtEx}_b^a) = \infty$, $f(0) = 0$ and f is monotone. Then, trivially, every $n_j < \infty$.

So, in both cases TxtEx_b^a is not n_j-closed, $j \in \{1, \ldots, t\}$, and there are such families of languages $\mathcal{L}_1^j, \ldots, \mathcal{L}_{n_j}^j$ that every union of $n_j - 1$ out of them is identifiable, while $\bigcup_{i=1}^{n_j} \mathcal{L}_i^j$ is not.

Now we construct the families of languages $\mathcal{L}_1, \ldots, \mathcal{L}_k$ that satisfy the requirements given by f. Suppose $x_i^j = 1$ for some $1 \leq i \leq k$ and $1 \leq j \leq t$, and suppose x_i^j is the p-th component of $\mathbf{x}^j$ that is equal to 1. Then for every language $L \in \mathcal{L}_p^j$ we put the language $\{\langle 0, j \rangle\} \cup \{\langle 1, w \rangle \mid w \in L\}$ in $\mathcal{L}_i$. The family $\mathcal{L}_i$ contains all the langages generated by this rule for different values of j and no more.

Suppose $f(\mathbf{x}) = 1$. Then for some j, $\mathbf{x}^j \leq \mathbf{x}$, and the corresponding union contains the languages $\{\langle 0, j \rangle\} \cup \{\langle 1, w \rangle \mid w \in L\}$ for every L from $\bigcup_{i=1}^{n_j} \mathcal{L}_i^j \notin \mathrm{TxtEx}_b^a$, so it is unidentifiable.

Suppose $f(\mathbf{x}) = 0$. Now we construct a strategy F that identifies the corresponding union. F outputs $\bot$ until it receives $\langle 0, j \rangle$ for some j in the input. According to the monotonicity, there is such s that $x_s = 0$ and $x_s^j = 1$. Suppose x_s^j is the p-th component equal to 1 in $\mathbf{x}^j$. Then, extracting w from the inputs $\langle 1, w \rangle$, we get a text for a language that belongs to $\bigcup_{i=1, i \neq p}^{n_j} \mathcal{L}_i^j$ that is TxtEx_b^a-identifiable. So F can use the strategy that identifies this class. $\square$

The problem is reduced now to finding the closedness degrees for all the classes TxtEx_b^a.

5 Connection with Team Learning

At this moment we want to point to the connection of our results with team learning. It lets us use results from there and, vice versa, our results have conseque1ces in team learning.

Definition 15. $\mathcal{L} \subseteq \mathcal{E}$ is TxtEx_b^a-*identifiable by a team "k out of l"* ($\mathcal{L} \in [k, l]\mathrm{TxtEx}_b^a$, $1 \leq k \leq l$) iff there are l strategies such that every $L \in \mathcal{L}$ is identified by at least k of them.

Proposition 16. *Let* $a, b, c, d \in \mathbb{N} \cup \{*\}$, $n \in \mathbb{N}$, $n \geq 2$. *Then* TxtEx_b^a *is n-closed in* TxtEx_d^c *iff* $[n-1, n]\mathrm{TxtEx}_b^a \subseteq \mathrm{TxtEx}_d^c$.

Proof. Suppose TxtEx_b^a is n-closed in TxtEx_d^c. Suppose some family $\mathcal{L}$ is $[n-1, n]\mathrm{TxtEx}_b^a$-identified by a team $F_1, \ldots, F_n$. We define $\mathcal{L}_i = \{L \in \mathcal{L} \mid (\forall j \neq i)[L \in \mathrm{TxtEx}_b^a(F_j)]\}$. Clearly, $(\forall j \mid 1 \leq j \leq n)[\bigcup_{i=1, i \neq j}^n \mathcal{L}_i \subseteq \mathrm{TxtEx}_b^a(F_j)]$. Since TxtEx_b^a is n-closed in TxtEx_d^c, $\bigcup_{i=1}^n \mathcal{L}_i = \mathcal{L} \in \mathrm{TxtEx}_d^c$.

Now, suppose $[n-1, n]\mathrm{TxtEx}_b^a \subseteq \mathrm{TxtEx}_d^c$. Let $\mathcal{L}_1, \ldots, \mathcal{L}_n$ be such families that $(\forall j \mid 1 \leq j \leq n)[\bigcup_{i=1, i \neq j}^n \mathcal{L}_i \in \mathrm{TxtEx}_b^a]$. Let F_j be a strategy that TxtEx_b^a-identifies $\bigcup_{i=1, i \neq j}^n \mathcal{L}_i$. Then the team $F_1, \ldots, F_n$ $[n-1, n]\mathrm{TxtEx}_b^a$-identifies $\bigcup_{i=1}^n \mathcal{L}_i$. So $\bigcup_{i=1}^n \mathcal{L}_i \in \mathrm{TxtEx}_d^c$. Thus TxtEx_b^a is n-closed in TxtEx_d^c. $\square$

Corollary 17. *Let* $a, b, c, d \in \mathbb{N} \cup \{*\}$, $n \in \mathbb{N}$, $n \geq 2$. *Then* $\mathrm{csdeg}(\mathrm{TxtEx}_b^a, \mathrm{TxtEx}_d^c) = n$ *iff n is the minimal number for which* $[n-1, n]\mathrm{TxtEx}_b^a \subseteq \mathrm{TxtEx}_d^c$.

Corollary 18. *Let* $a, b \in \mathbb{N} \cup \{*\}$, $n \in \mathbb{N}$, $n \geq 2$. *Then* $\operatorname{cdeg}(\operatorname{TxtEx}_b^a) = n$ *iff* n *is the minimal number for which* $[n-1, n]\operatorname{TxtEx}_b^a = \operatorname{TxtEx}_b^a$. $\operatorname{cdeg}(\operatorname{TxtEx}_b^a) = \infty$ *iff for all* $n \in \mathbb{N}$: $\operatorname{TxtEx}_b^a \subset [n-1, n]\operatorname{TxtEx}_b^a$.

Current results in team learning of languages can be found in [4].

6 Closedness Degrees

In this section we find the closedness degrees for the identification types TxtEx_b^a.

Theorem 19.

$$(\forall b \in \mathbb{N})(\forall a, a' \in \mathbb{N} \cup \{*\} \mid a' \geq 2^{b+1}a)[\operatorname{csdeg}(\operatorname{TxtEx}_b^a, \operatorname{TxtEx}_b^{a'}) \leq 2^{b+2}].$$

Proof. It is sufficient to prove that TxtEx_b^a is 2^{b+2}-closed in $\operatorname{TxtEx}_b^{a'}$.

Let $\mathcal{L}_1, \mathcal{L}_2, \ldots, \mathcal{L}_{2^{b+2}} \subseteq \mathcal{E}$ be such families of languages that all the unions of $2^{b+2} - 1$ out of them are TxtEx_b^a-identifiable. Let $F_1, F_2, \ldots, F_{2^{b+2}}$ be the strategies that identify these unions. Now we construct a strategy F.

The strategy F redirects its input to the strategies F_i until $2^{b+2} - 1$ of them output a hypothesis. Such an event happens because every language $L \in \bigcup_{j=1}^{2^{b+2}} \mathcal{L}_j$ belongs to $2^{b+2} - 1$ of the unions of $2^{b+2} - 1$ families, thus at most one of the strategies F_i does not identify L.

Then F outputs h_0 that is based on these hypotheses. In further F outputs h_i, $1 \leq i \leq b$, iff it has output h_{i-1} and at least $2^{b+2-i} - 1$ of the strategies, on whose hypotheses was based h_{i-1}, output a new hypothesis. h_i is based on these hypotheses $h_i^1, \ldots, h_i^{2^{b+2-i}-1}$ in the following way: $x \in W_{h_i}$ iff at least 2^{b+1-i} of $W_{h_i^j}$, $1 \leq j \leq 2^{b+2-i} - 1$, contain x. h_0 is defined similarly.

It is easy to see that h_i can be a wrong TxtEx_b^*-hypothesis only if at least $2^{b+1-i} - 1$ of the strategies, on whose hypotheses h_i was based, output a new hypothesis. But in this case h_{i+1} is output. h_b, if output, is always a correct TxtEx_b^*-hypothesis, since it is based on the last allowed hypotheses of 3 strategies, at least 2 of which identify the language. So the last hypothesis h_{i_0} output by F is based on $2^{b+2-i_0} - 1$ hypotheses, 2^{b+1-i_0} of which are right TxtEx_b^a-hypotheses. h_{i_0} can have an anomaly only for the values at which at least one of these right hypotheses have an anomaly, that is at no more than $2^{b+1}a$ points. $\qquad \square$

Theorem 20. $(\forall b \in \mathbb{N})[\operatorname{csdeg}(\operatorname{TxtEx}_b, \operatorname{TxtEx}_b^*) > 2^{b+2} - 1].$

Proof. At first we construct an unidentifiable family $\mathcal{L} \subseteq \mathcal{E}$ by the diagonalization technique, and then we divide it into $2^{b+2} - 1$ subfamilies so that every union of $2^{b+2} - 2$ out of them is identifiable.

Let F be an arbitrary strategy. Using the fixed point theorem in Smullyan's form [9] we can construct functions φ_{n_i}, $1 \leq i \leq (2b+1) \cdot 2^{b+2} - 2b$, that use each others Gödel numbers as parameters. The algorithm below describes these functions.

- *Stage 0.*
  Let $k = 2^{b+2} - 2$. Put $\langle 1, 1, n_1 \rangle, \ldots, \langle k, 1, n_k \rangle$ in all the languages $W_{n_1}, \ldots,$ W_{n_k}. Let $r = 0$, $s = k$. Feed larger and larger initial segments of a text for the defined part of W_{n_1} to the strategy F. If F outputs a hypothesis on some segment σ_0, go to stage 1.
- *Stage i ($1 \le i \le b+1$).*
  Let $k = (k/2) - 1$. Put
  $$\langle r + k + 1 + j, i + 1, n_{s+j} \rangle \text{ for } 1 \le j \le k,$$
  $$\langle j, i, n_{s+k+j} \rangle \text{ for } 1 \le j \le r,$$
  $$\langle r + 2k + 2 + j, i, n_{s+r+k+j} \rangle \text{ for } 1 \le j \le 2^{b+2} - r - 2k - 3$$
  in $W_{n_{r+1}}, \ldots, W_{n_{r+k+1}}$. Make the languages $W_{n_{s+j}}, 1 \le j \le 2^{b+2} - k - 3$ to be equal to the defined part of $W_{n_{r+1}}$.
  Let $t = s + 2^{b+2} - k - 3$. Put
  $$\langle r + j, i + 1, n_{t+j} \rangle \text{ for } 1 \le j \le k,$$
  $$\langle j, i, n_{t+k+j} \rangle \text{ for } 1 \le j \le r,$$
  $$\langle r + 2k + 2 + j, i, n_{t+r+k+j} \rangle \text{ for } 1 \le j \le 2^{b+2} - r - 2k - 3$$
  in $W_{n_{r+k+2}}, \ldots, W_{n_{r+2k+2}}$. Put $\langle 0, w \rangle$ in these $k + 1$ languages for larger and larger values of w while in this stage. Make the languages $W_{n_{t+j}}, 1 \le j \le 2^{b+2} - k - 3$ to be equal to the defined part of $W_{n_{r+k+2}}$.
  The following applies only to the case $i \le b$. Take larger and larger extensions of σ_{i-1} that give texts for the languages $W_{n_{r+1}}$ and $W_{n_{r+k+2}}$ and give them as an input to F. If F makes a mindchange on the text for $W_{n_{r+1}}$, let $r = s$. If F makes a mindchange on the text for $W_{n_{r+k+2}}$, let $r = t$. In both cases let σ_i be the segment on which the new hypothesis is output, $s = t + 2^{b+2} - k - 3$, and go to stage $i + 1$.

Informally, the values $\langle j, \cdot, \cdot \rangle$, $1 \le j \le 2^{b+2} - 1$, constitute $2^{b+2} - 1$ arrays of hypotheses, proposed for the identifying strategies. $\langle j, i, h \rangle$ proposes h as the i-th hypothesis in the j-th array. $k = 2^{b+2-i} - 2$ is the number of $(i+1)$-th hypotheses put in the languages $W_{n_{r+1}}, \ldots, W_{n_{r+2k+2}}$ at the i-th stage. s is the number of indices n_j already used at the beginning of stage, while t is the corresponding number at the middle of the stage. r is used for the indices of the languages on whose text F makes a new hypothesis.

Suppose the process reached the stage i_0 and remained there. If $i_0 = 0$, F has not issued any hypothesis on a text for W_{n_1}, and we put W_{n_1} in $\mathcal{L}$. If $i_0 > 0$, the last hypothesis issued by F is invalid for at least one of the languages $W_{n_{r+1}}$ and $W_{n_{r+k+2}}$, because they differ in infinitely many values of kind $\langle 0, w \rangle$, and we put this language in $\mathcal{L}$. (Note that at the stage $b + 1$ the strategy F has already made b mindchanges.) So F does not TxtEx_b^*-identify $\mathcal{L}$.

We say that the j-th array is valid for a language L iff for $\langle j, i, h \rangle \in L$ with the largest i we have: $i \le b + 1$ and $L = W_h$. Note that, if the j-th array is valid for all languages in a family, then this family is TxtEx_b-identifiable, because the strategy can use the hypotheses contained by this array.

The only invalid array in $W_{n_{r+1}}$ is the $(r + 2k + 2)$-th. The only invalid array in $W_{n_{r+k+2}}$ is the $(r + k + 1)$-th. If $i_0 = 0$, the only invalid array in W_{n_1} is the $(k + 1)$-th. Let $\mathcal{L}_j$ contain those languages from $\mathcal{L}$ whose only invalid array is the j-th array $1 \leq j \leq 2^{b+2} - 1$. The l-th array is valid for all the languages in $\bigcup_{j=1, j \neq l}^{2^{b+2}-1} \mathcal{L}_j$, so the unions of $2^{b+2} - 2$ families are TxtEx$_b$-identifiable, while $\bigcup_{j=1}^{2^{b+2}-1} \mathcal{L}_j = \mathcal{L}$ is not TxtEx$_b^*$-identifiable. $\quad\square$

By using Proposition 10 we obtain from the last two theorems the closedness degrees of TxtEx$_b$ and TxtEx$_b^*$.

Corollary 21. $(\forall b \in \mathbb{N})[\mathrm{cdeg}(\mathrm{TxtEx}_b) = 2^{b+2}]$.

Corollary 22. $(\forall b \in \mathbb{N})[\mathrm{cdeg}(\mathrm{TxtEx}_b^*) = 2^{b+2}]$.

The next theorem is rather surprising. For similar classes EX$_b^a$ in the identification of recursive functions we have: csdeg(EX$_b^a$, EX$_{b'}^a$) = 2 for sufficiently large b' [8].

Theorem 23. $(\forall a \in \mathbb{N} \mid a \geq 1)[\mathrm{csdeg}(\mathrm{TxtEx}_0^a, \mathrm{TxtEx}^a) = \infty]$.

Proof. Let $k \in \mathbb{N}$, $k > 1$. We prove that TxtEx$_0^a$ is not k-closed in TxtEx^a. Similarly as in Theorem 20 we consider valid arrays for TxtEx$_0^a$-identification of a language. The family $\mathcal{L}_i$, $1 \leq i \leq k$ consists of the languages containing arrays $\langle j, \cdot, \cdot \rangle$, $1 \leq j \leq k$ such that the only invalid array among these is $\langle i, \cdot, \cdot \rangle$. (The valid arrays contain only one hypothesis, $\langle j, 1, h_j \rangle$.)

Then we use diagonalization over the strategies F and Smullyan's theorem to construct functions φ_{n_i} that use F and the Gödel numbers of themselves. The algorithm for φ_{n_i} is as follows.

- *Stage 0.*
  Put $\langle j, 1, n_j \rangle$, $1 \leq j \leq k$, in $W_{n_1}, \ldots, W_{n_k}$. Let $w = 0$. Simulate F on some text for W_{n_1}. If F outputs a hypothesis h_0 on some initial segment σ_0 of the text, then go to stage 1.
- *Stage r $(r \geq 1)$.*
  Let L_r denote the set of elements put in W_{n_1} before the start of stage r.
  - *Substage 0.*
    Put $\langle 0, j \rangle$, $w \leq j \leq w + a - 1$, in $W_{n_1}, \ldots, W_{n_{k-1}}$.
    Put $\langle 0, w + a \rangle$ in $W_{n_1}, \ldots, W_{n_{k-2}}$.
    Simulate F on such extensions of σ_{r-1} that give texts for all the languages $L_r \cup P$, where P is a non-empty subset of $\{\langle 0, j \rangle \mid w \leq j \leq w + a\}$.
    Simultaneously compute $\varphi_{h_{r-1}}(\langle 0, j \rangle)$ for $w \leq j \leq w + a$.
    Suppose F outputs a new hypothesis $h_r \neq h_{r-1}$ on a segment $\sigma_r \supset \sigma_{r-1}$. Then add $\langle 0, j \rangle$ for $w \leq j \leq w + a$ to W_{n_k}, and $\langle 0, w + a \rangle$ to $W_{n_{k-1}}$, let $w = w + a + 1$ and go to stage $r + 1$.
    Suppose $\varphi_{h_{r-1}}(\langle 0, j \rangle) \downarrow$ for all $j \in \{w, \ldots, w + a\}$. Then go to substage 1.
  - *Substage s $(1 \leq s \leq k - 3)$.*
    Put $\langle 0, w + a + s - 2 \rangle$ in $W_{n_{k-s+1}}, \ldots, W_{n_k}$.
    Put $\langle 0, w + a + s \rangle$ in $W_{n_1}, \ldots, W_{n_{k-s-2}}$.

Simulate F on such extensions of σ_{r-1} that give a text for $L_r \cup \{\langle 0, j\rangle \mid$ $(w+a-1 \leq j \leq w+a+s-2) \vee j = w+a+s\}$. Simultaneously compute $\varphi_{h_{r-1}}(\langle 0, w+a+s\rangle)$.

Suppose F outputs a new hypothesis $h_r \neq h_{r-1}$ on a segment $\sigma_r \supset \sigma_{r-1}$. Then add $\langle 0, j\rangle$ for $w \leq j \leq w+a+s$ to $W_{n_1}, \ldots, W_{n_k}$ (if necessary — all these values already have been added to some of these languages), let $w = w+a+s+1$ and go to stage $r+1$.

Suppose $\varphi_{h_{r-1}}(\langle 0, w+a+s\rangle) \downarrow$. Then go to substage $s+1$.

- *Substage $k-2$.*

Simulate F on such extensions of σ_{r-1} that give a text for $L_r \cup \{\langle 0, j\rangle \mid$ $w+a-1 \leq j \leq w+a+k-5\}$.

Suppose F outputs a new hypothesis $h_r \neq h_{r-1}$ on a segment $\sigma_r \supset \sigma_{r-1}$. Then add $\langle 0, j\rangle$ for $w \leq j \leq w+a+k-3$ to $W_{n_1}, \ldots, W_{n_k}$ (if necessary), let $w = w+a+k-2$ and go to stage $r+1$.

End of stage r.

Each of the stages deals with one hypothesis output by F. The language(s) on which F is simulated is/are chosen so that the current hypothesis have $a+1$ anomalies on it/them. There are two ways F can deal with this problem. First, it can change the current hypothesis. In this case all the differences between the current versions of languages W_{n_i} are cleared, and the algorithm goes to the next stage dealing with the new hypothesis. Second, the current hypothesis function can output a new value, so decreasing the number of anomalies. Then the algorithm goes to the next substage ensuring again $a+1$ anomalies. At substage $k-2$ the hypothesis function have no more such possibility.

So, either F makes infinitely many mindchanges, or its last hypothesis have at least $a+1$ anomalies. $\qquad \square$

Corollary 24. $(\forall a \in \mathbb{N} \mid a \geq 1)(\forall b \in \mathbb{N} \cup \{*\})[\text{cdeg}(\text{TxtEx}_b^a) = \infty]$.

The next three theorems are obtained from results in team learning (Theorems 17 and 20 in [4]) by applying to them Corollaries 17 and 18.

Theorem 25. $\text{csdeg}(\text{TxtEx}, \text{TxtEx}^*) > 3$.

Theorem 26. $\text{cdeg}(\text{TxtEx}) = 4$.

Theorem 27. $\text{cdeg}(\text{TxtEx}^*) = 4$.

7 Conclusion

Table 1 summarizes the obtained closedness degrees.

There are at least two directions for further research: (1) finding csdeg for an arbitrary pair $(\text{TxtEx}_b^a, \text{TxtEx}_d^c)$ that would help in deeper understanding of the interrelationships between the classes TxtEx_b^a, and (2) finding the cdeg values for other identification types, such as BC^a, Cons, Mon, $[k, l]\text{TxtEx}_b^a$, etc. Since the argument of Theorem 13 can be used for almost all identification types, it would be interesting to find a "natural" identification type for which it is not valid.

Table 1. Closedness degrees of $TxtEx_b^a$

$TxtEx_b^{a \rightarrow}$	0	1	...	*
0	4	∞	∞	4
1	8	∞	∞	8
...	...	∞	∞	...
n	2^{n+2}	∞	∞	2^{n+2}
...	...	∞	∞	...
*	4	∞	∞	4

References

1. K. Apsītis, R. Freivalds, M. Kriķis, R. Simanovskis, J. Smotrovs. Unions of identifiable classes of total recursive functions. *Lecture Notes in Artificial Intelligence*, vol. 642, pp. 99–107. Springer-Verlag, 1992.

2. J. Case and C. Lynes. Machine inductive inference and language identification. *Lecture Notes in Computer Science*, vol. 140, pp. 107–115, Springer-Verlag, 1982.

3. E. M. Gold. Language identification in the limit. *Information and Control*, vol. 10, pp. 447–474, 1967.

4. S. Jain and A. Sharma. On identification by teams and probabilistic machines. *Lecture Notes in Artificial Intelligence*, vol. 961, pp. 108–145, Springer-Verlag, 1995.

5. D. N. Osherson, M. Stob, S. Weinstein. *Systems That Learn*. The MIT Press, 1986.

6. D. Osherson and S. Weinstein. Criteria of language learning. *Information and Control*, vol. 52, pp. 123–138, 1982.

7. H. Rogers, Jr. *Theory of Recursive Functions and Effective Computability*. McGraw-Hill, New York, 1967.

8. J. Smotrovs. EX-identification of unions. In preparation, 1996.

9. R. Smullyan. *Theory of Formal Systems. Annals of Mathematical Studies*, vol. 47, Princeton, 1961.

Characteristic Sets for Polynomial Grammatical Inference

Colin DE LA HIGUERA[*],

*Département d'Informatique Fondamentale (DIF) LIRMM, 161 rue Ada,
34 392 Montpellier Cedex 5, France. Internet: delahiguera@lirmm.fr*

Abstract

When concerned about efficient grammatical inference two issues are relevant: the first one is to determine the quality of the result, and the second is to try to use polynomial time and space. A typical idea to deal with the first point is to say that an algorithm performs well if it identifies *in the limit* the correct language. The second point has led to debate about how to define polynomial time: the main definitions of polynomial inference have been proposed by Pitt and Angluin. We return in this paper to another definition proposed by Gold that requires a characteristic set of strings to exist for each grammar, and this set to be polynomial in the size of the grammar or automaton that is to be learnt, where the size of the sample is the sum of the lengths of all its words. The learning algorithm must also infer correctly as soon as the characteristic set is included in the data. We first show that this definition corresponds to a notion of teachability as defined by Goldman and Mathias. By adapting their teacher/learner model to grammatical Inference we prove that languages given by context-free grammars, simple deterministic grammars, linear grammars and non-deterministic finite automata are not polynomially identifiable from given data.

Keywords: exact identification, grammatical inference, polynomial learning.

1 Introduction and Related work

The problem of describing polynomial paradigms for learning has received much attention in the learning theory community. In his seminal paper Pitt (1989) discusses different possible ideas as to what polynomial complexity for the problem of exact identification of deterministic finite automata (DFA) should be. The model he analyses is Gold's classical model (1967): a presentation of the language is given, where strings appear with a label (+ if it is a positive instance, and - if it is a negative instance). A presentation is required to be complete, *i.e.* each example and counter-example appears at least once. In this model an algorithm is said to identify in the limit *iff* on input of any complete presentation of a language, the algorithm, at some point converges to a correct representation of the language. Pitt discards the

---

[*] This work has been performed while the author was visiting the Universidad Politecnica de Valencia, Spain.

possibility of time being polynomial in the size of the representation to be learnt, as we have no control over the presentation of the examples. It si possible that the very first example is too long. He also refuses polynomial update time (the complexity takes into account the sizes of the examples that have been seen so far) because the exhaustive search strategy can perform just that by an implementation where "when you have no time left, just delay the treatment of some examples for later". We note that to be able to use polynomial update time by Pitt's trick, the delaying of the treatment of the examples means that the algorithm has not inferred correctly, and at some point it has sufficient information to give the correct answer but does not.

Thus, Pitt proposes another measure of complexity: for an identification algorithm to be polynomial it must have polynomial update time, and also make a polynomial number of implicit errors (in the size of the automaton). An implicit error is made when the current hypothesis does not agree with a new example. This definition alas is shown (by Pitt) to be very restrictive, in the sense that even *DFA* do not comply with the conditions, so no superclasses of regular languages allow polynomial time inference.

Another model of learning has been proposed by Angluin (1987) and exhaustively studied since. The presentation of the language is not arbitrary, and can be somehow controlled by asking queries to an oracle. The two most important sorts of queries are the membership queries (a string is proposed to the oracle which returns its correct classification), and equivalence queries, where a representation is proposed to the oracle, which either accepts it as a correct representation of the language to be inferred, or returns a counter-example: a string from the symmetrical difference of the proposed language and the target one. This is known as the *MAT* model (minimally adequate teacher). With time complexity depending on the size of the automaton to be inferred and the length of the longest counter-example returned by the oracle, Angluin proves that *DFA* can be identified in polynomial time with membership queries and equivalence queries (to be exact the time complexity must hold at any point of the inference procedure). Angluin also proves that both these queries are necessary: neither membership queries alone, nor equivalence queries alone allow polynomial inference. Following Angluin's definitions further classes of grammars have been proven to be polynomially learnable with a *MAT* (Ishizaka 1989).

Both these models give main negative results, *i.e.* that even *DFA* can't be inferred in polynomial time (unless strong oracles are used). Nevertheless the need of applications in several fields (speech, pattern recognition, automatic translation...) has led to the construction of heuristics to solve the learning problems. The natural question that follows is whether these heuristics are necessary and what can be done in the (usual) case of learning from given data. When working in this framework an obvious parameter to the complexity of a learning algorithm is the size of the data where the size corresponds to the sum of the lengths of this data. We note that in the two models above, the argument justifying that the size of the target automaton can't be the only parameter is that we do not have enough control over the presentation (in the first case) or the oracle (in the second one) to avoid an unnecessarily long example to appear. This leads to the question: are such long examples really necessary for the identification process? Moreover, how judicious is it to talk of polynomial learning if the counter-examples returned by the oracle are of unreasonable length with respect to the concept to be learnt? By unreasonable we mean the usual polynomial barrier, and ask the question in another way: supposing the concept to be learnt is of size n, does the oracle have to return a counter-example of length larger than any fixed polynomial in n, or can it limit itself to returning a counter-example of reasonable size?

A theoretical framework to study these issues is provided by Gold (1978): he presented a model for identification from given data, where a sample of labelled strings $(S+, S-)$, with $S+$ a set of positive instances, and $S-$ a set of negative instances, is presented to the inference algorithm that must return a representation compatible with $(S+, S-)$. The further conditions are that for each language there exists a characteristic sample with which the algorithm returns a correct representation, and this must be monotonous in the sense that if correctly labelled examples are added to the characteristic set, then the algorithm infers the same language. These conditions insure identification, and it is easy to see that a class of representations is identifiable in the limit from given data if and only if it is identifiable in the limit from a complete presentation of examples. This model can be compared with the one refused by Pitt (1989): it consists in adding to the polynomial update time condition a second condition which is that as soon as all elements in the characteristic set have been presented, the algorithm must infer correctly; as in (Gold 1978) when this condition is met we will say that the class is *polynomially identifiable from given data*. Gold proved that deterministic finite automata are polynomially identifiable from given data. It must be noticed that in the same paper Gold proved the NP-completeness of the "Minimum Inferred Finite State Automaton" problem (is there a DFA with less than n states consistent with the data?); the results are not contradictory because a characteristic set is not just any set, and thus, in this special case the smallest automaton can be inferred in polynomial time. Further work in this model has contributed the following results: alternative algorithms have been proposed to infer DFA (Oncina & Garcia 1992), even linear grammars have been proven polynomially identifiable from given data (Takada 1988; Sempere & García 1994); these techniques have been extended to universal linear grammars in (Takada 1994). Following the same idea deterministic even linear grammars are inferable in the limit in polynomial time from positive examples only (Koshiba & al. 1995) and the same holds for total subsequential functions (Oncina & al. 1993). Algorithms provided in these papers have been implemented to deal with practical problems in the fields of speech (García & al. 1994), pattern recognition (García & Vidal 1990) or automatic translation (Castellanos & al. 1994). On the other hand no negative classes have been proposed for this model, and so the question as to whether the model is trivial remained open. This paper deals with proving that this is not so, and that many classes of grammars can not be inferred in the limit in polynomial time from given data.

The notion of characteristic sets leads in a natural way to the associated problem of teaching (Anthony & al. 1992, Wiehagen 1992): a teacher's goal is to help the learner (or the identification algorithm), by providing a good set of examples. Following Freivalds & al's general work on good examples (1989), different models of teaching have in recent years been proposed (Goldman & Kearns 1991, Jackson & Tomkins 1992). The approach that fits best to grammatical inference (from given data) is the one of Goldman & Mathias (1993): they define teachability of a class as the existence of a characteristic (to a learner) teaching set. We will prove that learnable in Gold's sense corresponds to teachable in Goldman & Mathias'.

Alternative models for teacher/learner couples have been presented; one main difference lies in the fact that in the above model the teacher will provide the examples for a specific learner, whereas (Goldman & Kearns 1991, Jackson & Tomkins 1992) want the teacher to be able to teach any consistent learner, *i.e.* any learner capable of returning a hypothesis compatible with the examples. A secondary result of this paper (Theorem 2) is that such a Universal Teacher does not exist for families of grammars fulfilling a reasonable condition; this condition holds for example for *DFA* and context-free grammars.

The following section contains the main definitions and results we need from formal languages theory. Section 3 deals with adapting the teacher/learner model for grammatical inference. The difficulties of this task are shown and some technical results given. In section 4 we prove that the following classes of representations do not admit polynomial identification from given data:

- Context-free grammars
- Linear grammars
- Simple deterministic grammars
- Non-deterministic finite automata.

2 Definitions

We only give here the main definitions from formal languages theory. For more details and proofs, the reader can refer to a textbook on the subject, for instance (Harrison 1978).

An *alphabet* is a finite non-empty set of distinct symbols. For a given alphabet Σ, the set of all finite strings of symbols from Σ is denoted by Σ^*. The empty string is denoted by λ. For a string w, $|w|$ denotes the length of w. A language L over Σ is a subset of Σ^*.

A *non-deterministic finite automaton (NFA)* is a 5-tuple $N=(Q, \Sigma, \delta, I, F)$ where Q is a finite set of states, Σ the alphabet, I and F two subsets of Q, denoting respectively the set of initial states and the set of final states of N, δ is the set of transitions, namely a subset of $Q \times \Sigma \to 2^Q$. We write $q' \in \delta(q, x)$ when there is a transition labelled by x from q to q'. An *NFA* N accepts a string w *iff* either $w=\lambda$ and $I \cap F \neq \varnothing$, or $w=x_1...x_j$ and there exists a sequence of states $q_0,..,q_j$ (possibly with repetitions) with $q_0 \in I$, $\forall i<j$ $q_{i+1} \in \delta(q_i, x_{i+1})$, and $q_j \in F$. When the set I contains a unique state and δ is functional, *i.e.* $\forall q \in Q$ $\forall x \in \Sigma$ $|\delta(q, x)| \leq 1$, the automaton is a *deterministic finite automaton (DFA)*. The *language* recognized by an automaton is the set of all strings accepted by the automaton. Two automata are *equivalent iff* they accept the same language.

A *context-free grammar* over Σ is a 4-tuple $G=(\Sigma, V, P, S_0)$ where Σ and V are alphabets (respectively of terminal symbols and of non-terminal symbols or variables), S_0 a special symbol in V called start symbol and P is a finite subset of $V \times (\Sigma \cup V)^*$ called set of productions or rules. A rule in this set is denoted by $S \rightarrow \alpha$ and has intended meaning: non-terminal symbol S rewrites into α. A derivation is a sequence $S_0 \Rightarrow_G w_1 \Rightarrow_G w_2 .... \Rightarrow_G w_n$ where w_{i+1} is obtained by substituting some occurrence of a non-terminal T in w_i by α when $(T \rightarrow \alpha) \in P$. The language generated by a context-free grammar G (denoted by $L(G)$) is the set of all words in Σ^* that can be obtained by derivation from S_0. A language is context-free *iff* there exists some context-free grammar generating it. Two context-free grammars are equivalent *iff* they generate the same language.

A context-free grammar $G=(\Sigma, V, P, S_0)$ is *linear* if all productions belong to $V \times (\Sigma^* \cup \Sigma^* V \Sigma^*)$. Thus, each rule has at most one non-terminal in its right-hand side.

The following classes shall be used in this paper :

DFA(Σ): the class of deterministic finite automata over alphabet Σ.
NFA(Σ): the class of non-deterministic finite automata over alphabet Σ.
CFG(Σ): the class of context-free grammars over alphabet Σ.
LIN(Σ): the class of linear grammars over alphabet Σ.

The size of the alphabet can be considered a constant, when working on some representation class $R(\Sigma)$.

When considering these classes the size of a representation (denoted $size(R)$) will be some reasonable quantity: it must be polynomial in the number of bits needed to encode a representation. The following sizes are typically correct (for a constant alphabet Σ):
For *DFA* and *NFA* the number of states. For *CFG*s and linear grammars the number of rules multiplied by the length of the longest rule.

We end this section with results concerning a specific problem on representations that is used in the sequel, and plays an important role for identification from given data:

The equivalence problem $EQ(R, \Sigma)$: For a class $R(\Sigma)$, are two given representations equivalent, *i.e.* do they represent the same language?

The following results are well known:

Theorem 1 (Garey & Johnson 1979, Harrison 1978)
$EQ(DFA, \Sigma) \in$ P.
$EQ(NFA, \Sigma)$ is co–NP-complete, even when $|\Sigma|=1$.
$EQ(CFG, \Sigma)$ is undecidable.
$EQ(LIN, \Sigma)$ is undecidable.

3 Teaching and Characteristic Sets

To take into account the fact that the length of the examples must depend polynomially on the size of the concept to be learnt we propose the following definition, which is just a generalisation of Gold's results (1978) and a natural restriction to the definition of polynomial update time (Pitt 1989).

> **Definition 1** A representation class R is polynomially identifiable from given data *iff* there exist two polynomials $p()$ and $q()$ and an algorithm A such that:
> 1) Given any sample $(S+, S-)$, of size m, A returns a representation R in R compatible with $(S+, S-)$ in $p(m)$ time.
> 2) for each representation R of size n, there exists a characteristic sample $(CS+, CS-)$ of size less than $q(n)$ for which, on data $(S+, S-)$, if $S+ \supseteq CS+$, $S- \supseteq CS-$, A returns a representation R' equivalent with R.

An algorithm fulfilling conditions 1 and 2 above is said to be a polynomial learner. With this definition Gold's 1978 result can be restated as follows:

> **Gold's theorem (1978)** *DFA* are polynomially identifiable from given data.

In fact his result is even stronger as for any *DFA* a characteristic set can also be computed in polynomial time (Oncina & García 1992).

Goldman & Mathias (1993) present a model for teaching and learning that takes into account the quantity of information a good teacher has to provide the learner with. The teaching session is described as follows, where to avoid collusion[1], a third element is introduced, namely the adversary who can complicate the learner's task by introducing extra examples :

1) The adversary selects a target function and gives it to the teacher.

2) The teacher computes a set of examples for the learner.

3) The adversary adds correctly labelled examples to this set, with the goal of causing the learner to fail.

4) On this augmented set the learner computes a function.

Goldman & Mathias prove that this model does not allow collusion, and define a class of functions as polynomially *T/L*-teachable *iff* both teacher and learner work in polynomial time, and if the learner always infers the intended function. Without the restrictive condition that the teachers computation takes polynomial time, the class is only semi-poly *T/L*-teachable.

It is obvious that this definition is related to the one of identification from given data, and from Gold's result it follows that *DFA* are semi-poly *T/L*-teachable. In fact

---

[1]collusion (or cheating) occurs when the teacher can pass information to the learner about the encoding of the concept and not the concept itself.

in this case a characteristic set can be computed in polynomial time (Oncina & García 1992) so the stronger result that *DFA* are polynomially *T/L*-teachable also holds.

It should be stressed that we have chosen here to adapt Goldman & Mathias' model for the case of grammatical inference by taking into account the length of the examples as a parameter. In their original setting this was unnecessary. When concerned with the inference of boolean functions all examples have the same size, the number of variables. In the framework of grammatical Inference the number of words is infinite, their length growing unbounded; thus, when considering the size of the teaching set the number of words alone is insufficient. A teacher that needs only a small number of examples, but some of them of excessive length will not allow the class to be called (semi-) polynomially teachable.

Formally:

> **Definition 2** A representation class R is semi-poly T/L teachable *iff* there exist 3 polynomials $p()$, $q()$, $r()$, a teacher T and a learner L, such that for any adversary *ADV* after the following teaching session:
>> 1) *ADV* selects a target representation R of size n in R and gives it to T.
>> 2) T computes a set of examples for L, with at most $p(n)$ examples, all of length at most $q(n)$.
>> 3) *ADV* adds correctly labelled examples to this set, with the goal of causing L to fail. Let m be the size of the completed set.
>> 4) On this augmented set L computes a representation R' in time less than $r(m)$.
>
> R and R' are equivalent.
>
> **Proposition 1** A class is polynomially identifiable from given data *iff* it is semi-poly T/L teachable.

The proof is straightforward and shall be only sketched. If a class is polynomially identifiable from given data, then for any target representation R, a polynomial characteristic set exists. This set meets the conditions to be the set of examples proposed by the teacher, and the monotony condition insures that no adversary can cause the learning algorithm to fail. Conversely the set of examples for L, with at most $p(n)$ examples, all of length at most $q(n)$ is a polynomial characteristic set. ◊

Thus, Goldman & Mathias' model is well adapted for grammatical inference. A natural question would be to consider other teaching models: a typical trend of research considers unspecialised teachers, that should be able to adapt to any learner. We limit the class of learners to be considered to consistent learners, those who always return a solution consistent with the data (as defined for instance in (Goldman & Kearns 1991)). We prove that a finite teacher does not exist in grammatical inference for consistent language learners, even when these are restricted to work in polynomial time. The proof is similar in many ways to the proof of lemma 1 in (Goldman & Kearns 1991); the difference is that the result here applies even when the learners work in polynomial time.

We first note that any learner fulfilling conditions of definition 1 is a consistent learner: it always returns a solution consistent with the data. Now take any class of language representations that contains all singleton languages (containing just one word) and the empty language, and that can be identified in polynomial time by given data by at least one algorithm A_{basic}. This is the case for instance of the regular languages, when represented by DFA. We define a family $\{A_k\}$ (for all integers k) of learning algorithms as follows:

> **Algorithm A_k**
> If $\{a^k\}$ is compatible with the sample then return $\{a^k\}$.
> Otherwise use algorithm A_{basic}.

It is straightforward to notice that each of these algorithms complies with the conditions of definition 1, so they are polynomial algorithms for identification, even if the complexity of each A_k grows with k.

> **Definition 3** Let R be a class of representations and P be a set of identification algorithms for R. R is *polynomially characterisable* for P *iff* any representation R in R admits a characteristic set polynomial in size(R), that allows any algorithm in P to identify it.

> **Theorem 2** Let R be any class of representations containing representations for all singleton languages (containing just one word) and the empty language. Let P be the set of all polynomial identification algorithms for R. R is not polynomially characterisable for P.

Proof: Suppose the target language is the empty set. Then to identify it an arbitrary learner A_k requires a^k as a negative instance. The number of learners is infinite, hence so is the size of the characteristic set. ◊

But the existence of such a universal teacher is not a necessary condition for polynomial identification to be possible. Next we give such a necessary condition:

> **Definition 4** A representation class R is polynomially characterisable *iff* there exist a polynomial $p()$, such that for each representation R of size n, there exists a characteristic sample $(CS+, CS-)$ of size less than $p(n)$ for which, if another non equivalent representation R' is compatible with $(CS+, CS-)$, then R is incompatible with the characteristic sample of R'.

Theorem 3 If R is polynomially identifiable from given data, then R is polynomially characterisable.

Proof[2]: If R is not polynomially characterisable, there are two non equivalent representations R_1 and R_2 that admit respective characteristic samples $(S+_1, S-_1)$, $(S+_2, S-_2)$. By compatibility $(S+_1 \cup S+_2, S-_1 \cup S-_2)$ would be accepted by R_1 and R_2. Hence any algorithm can only infer one of the representations.   ◊

In its negative form this provides us with a tool to prove that certain classes are not polynomially identifiable from given data.

4 Non Polynomially Identifiable Grammars

Theorem 4 $LIN(\Sigma)$, is not polynomially characterisable, for any alphabet Σ of size at least 2.

Proof: If equivalence is undecidable for a class R, then for every $p()$ and every n (sufficiently large) we can find two representations R_1 and R_2 of size bounded by n, representing different languages, and inseparable by any word of length smaller than $p(n)$. If not testing all strings up to that size would be a computable equivalence test of both representations. Thus, R is not polynomially characterisable. This, by theorem 1 applies to $LIN(\Sigma)$.   ◊

By class inclusion the above result extends to the class $CFG(\Sigma)$. Because of the undecidability of the equivalence problem (Theorem 1), restricting ourselves to computable normal forms (*e.g.* Chomsky, Greibach...)(Harrison 1978) does not help:

Corollary 1 For any alphabet Σ of size at least 2, the following classes are not polynomially characterisable:
- the class of context-free grammars in some computable normal form.
- the class of linear grammars in some computable normal form.

Even when the equivalence problem is decidable, if the separating words are too long, then inference cannot be obtained through characteristic samples of polynomial length. The class of simple deterministic grammars has been proven polynomially inferable (with queries) by Ishizaka (1989). A context-free grammar is simple deterministic (in 2-normal form) if the rules are of the following form:

$$S \to \alpha \text{ with } \alpha \in \Sigma \cup \Sigma V \cup \Sigma V^2,$$
$$\text{and if } A \to x\alpha \text{ and } A \to x\beta \text{ are productions, then } \alpha = \beta.$$

---

[2] This proof uses a similar technique to the proof of Theorem 1 in (Goldman & Mathias 1993), where unions of teaching sets are considered to prove that their method is not collusion.

Theorem 5 For any alphabet Σ, the class of simple deterministic grammars over Σ is not polynomially characterisable.

Proof: Take the following (indexed) simple deterministic grammar :
$G_k = <\{a\},\{S_0, S_1,.., S_k: \}, P, S_0 >,..,$
and $P = \{$ $S_i \rightarrow aS_{i+1}S_{i+1} \; \forall \; i{<}k$
  $S_n \rightarrow a$ $\}$
It follows that $L(G_k) = \{a^{2^{k+1}-1}\}$.
Thus, $L(G_k)$ cannot be separated from the empty language by any subset of words of polynomial length. And as above, the result follows. $\Diamond$

This result does not constitute a contradiction with Goldman & Mathias' theorem that "any class learnable in deterministic polynomial time using example-based queries is semi-poly T/L teachable" (Goldman & Mathias 1993). Indeed we have:
• Ishizaka has proven that simple deterministic grammars could be inferred in polynomial time with equivalence and membership queries (Ishizaka 1989).
• From Goldman & Mathias' result it follows that simple deterministic grammars are semi-poly T/L teachable.
• From proposition 1 it follows that semi-poly T/L teachable is equivalent to polynomially identifiable from given data.
• Theorem 5 states that simple deterministic grammars are not polynomially characterisable, hence not polynomially identifiable from given data.

The contradiction depends on the role of the length of examples and counter-examples. For Ishizaka, the oracle is independent, so the length of counter-examples is a parameter.
• Goldman & Mathias only consider boolean functions. The length is a constant.
• We believe this length must depend polynomially of the size of the target grammar.

These considerations explain that Goldman & Mathias' theorem is no longer true for the definition of teachability we have adapted to the case of grammatical inference. A second corollary of theorem 5 is that to infer a simple deterministic grammar with a *MAT* the length of the counter-examples to be expected can be bounded *a priori* by no polynomial.

Learning *NFA* is difficult, even with a *MAT* (see *e.g.* Yokomori 1993), this remains true for polynomial update time:

Theorem 6 If $P{\neq}NP$, for any alphabet Σ, the class $NFA(\Sigma)$ is not polynomially characterisable.

Proof: In the case where the input alphabet has only one letter, the equivalence problem is co-NP-complete (Garey & Johnson 1979). Thus, there is no polynomial $p()$ that given two NFA of size smaller than n can solve the equivalence problem by testing chains of length less than $p(n)$: if not the number of such chains is precisely $p(n)$, and the equivalence problem would be in P. Hence the result. $\Diamond$

Corollary 3 The following classes are not polynomially identifiable from given data:

$CFG(\Sigma)$, the class of context-free grammars over Σ, when $|\Sigma|>1$

$LIN(\Sigma)$, the class of linear grammars over Σ, when $|\Sigma|>1$

$SDG(\Sigma)$, the class of simple deterministic grammars over Σ

$NFA(\Sigma)$, the class of non-deterministic finite automata over Σ

The results follow by applying corollary 2 to the above results. The fourth result depends on the assumption P≠NP.

Conclusion

The framework of polynomial identification from given data has so far provided grammatical Inference with many positive results. This framework is implicitly defined in Gold's 1978 article, linked with Pitt's propositions (1989) and corresponds to Goldman & Mathias' teacher/learner model (1993) when the length of the examples is taken as a variable. A number of important classes are proven here not to be polynomially identifiable from given data. Nevertheless as this setting does not guarantee polynomial induction work remains to be done: in the positive cases (*DFA*...) how simple can the characteristic set be? As different algorithms will admit different characteristic sets, does this give us a quality measure of an identification algorithm (the smaller the characteristic set the better).

Acknowledgement

The author wishes to thank researchers from the Universidad Politecnica de Valencia for many fruitful discussions. He is more particularly indebted to Jose-Maria Sempere for ideas in theorem 2, and other important suggestions, and to Pierre Dupont for valuable comments on the manuscript.

Bibliography

Angluin, D. (1987). Queries and concept learning. *Machine Learning* **2**, 319-342.

Anthony, M., Brightwell, G., Cohen, D. & Shawe-Taylor, J. (1992). On exact specification by examples. *Proceedings of COLT* 92 (pp. 311-318). A.C.M.

Castellanos, A., Galiano I. & Vidal, E. (1994). Application of OSTIA to machine translation tasks. *Proceedings of the International Colloquium on Grammatical Inference ICGI*-94 (pp. 93-105). Lecture Notes in Artificial Intelligence **862**, Springer-Verlag.

Freivalds, R., Kinber, E.B. & Wiehagen, R. (1989). Inductive inference from good examples. *Proceedings of the International Workshop on Analogical and Inductive Inference* (pp. 1-17). Lecture Notes in Artificial Intelligence **397**, Springer-Verlag.

García, P., Segarra, E., Vidal, E. & Galiano, I. (1994). On the use of the morphic generator grammatical inference (MGGI) methodology in automatic speech recognition. *International Journal of Pattern Recognition and Artificial Intelligence* **4**, 667-685.

García, P. & Vidal, E. (1990). Inference of K-testable languages in the strict sense and applications to syntactic pattern recognition. *IEEE Transactions on Pattern Analysis and Machine Intelligence* **12** /9, 920-925.

Garey, M.R. & Johnson, D.S. (1979). Computers and intractability: a guide to the theory of NP-completeness. San Francisco: W.H. Freeman.

Gold, E.M. (1967). Language identification in the limit. *Inform.&Control.* **10**, 447-474.

Gold, E.M. (1978). Complexity of automaton identification from given data. *Information and Control* **37**, 302-320.

Goldman, S.A. & Kearns M.J. (1991). On the complexity of teaching. *Proceedings of COLT* 91 (pp. 303-314).

Goldman, S.A. & Mathias, H.D. (1993). Teaching a smarter learner. *Proceedings of COLT* 93 (pp. 67-76).

Harrison, M.A. (1978). Introduction to formal language theory. Reading: Addison-Wesley.

Ishizaka, I. (1989). Learning simple deterministic languages. *Proceedings of COLT* 89 (pp. 162-174). A.C.M.

Jackson, J. & Tomkins, A. (1992). A computational model of teaching. *Proceedings of COLT* 92 (pp. 319-326). A.C.M.

Koshiba, T., Mäkinen, E. & Takada, Y. (1995). Learning deterministic even linear languages from positive examples. *Proceedings of ALT '95*, Lecture Notes in Artificial Intelligence **997**, Springer-Verlag.

Oncina, J. & García, P. (1992) Inferring regular languages in polynomial time. *In Pattern Recognition and Image Analysis, World Scientific.*

Oncina, J., García, P. & Vidal E. (1993). Learning subsequential transducers for pattern recognition tasks. *IEEE Transactions on Pattern Analysis and Machine Intelligence* **15**, 448-458.

Pitt, L. (1989). Inductive inference, dfas and computational complexity. *Proceedings of the International Workshop on Analogical and Inductive Inference* (pp. 18-44). Lecture Notes in Artificial Intelligence **397**, Springer-Verlag.

Sempere, J.M. & García, P. (1994). A characterisation of even linear languages and its application to the learning problem.*Proceedings of the International Colloquium on Grammatical Inference ICGI*-94 (pp. 38-44). Lecture Notes in Artificial Intelligence **862**, Springer-Verlag.

Takada, Y. (1988). Grammatical inference for even linear languages based on control sets. *Information Processing Letters* **28**, 193-199.

Takada, Y. (1994). A hierarchy of language families learnable by regular language learners. *Proceedings of the International Colloquium on Grammatical Inference ICGI*-94 (pp. 16-24). Lecture Notes in Artificial Intelligence **862**, Springer-Verlag.

Wiehagen, R. (1992). From inductive inference to algorithmic learning theory. *Proceedings of ALT* 92, (pp 13-24). Lecture Notes in Artificial Intelligence **743**, Springer-Verlag.

Yokomori, T. (1993). Learning non-deterministic finite automata from queries and counterexamples. *Machine Intelligence* **13**. Furukawa, Michie & Muggleton eds., Oxford Univ. Press.

Query Learning of Subsequential Transducers

Juan Miguel Vilar*

Dpto. de Sistemas Informáticos y Computación
Universidad Politécnica de Valencia
Camino de Vera s/n
46071 Valencia(Spain)
E-mail: jvilar@dsic.upv.es

Abstract. An efficient (polynomial time) algorithm is presented for the problem of learning subsequential transducers given the ability to make two kind of queries; *translation queries*, where the translation of a given string is returned, and *equivalence queries*, that are answered either positively or with a counterexample. A probabilistic setting in which equivalence queries are substituted by a random sample oracle is also studied and the corresponding modifications to the algorithm presented.

1 Introduction

Subsequential transducers are a kind of finite state transducers [3] which have been used in practice for dealing with problems of automatic translation [6] and automatic learning of phonological rules [4]. They are can be identified in the limit, following the paradigm introduced by Gold [5], by means of the so-called Onward Subsequential Transducers Inference Algorithm (OSTIA) [7].

Angluin [1] presented an algorithm capable of learning deterministic finite state automata in polynomial time given the ability to make queries regarding the unknown automata. The model was that of a *Learner* trying to find a concept and a *Teacher* that knows that concept and is able to answer questions about it. In particular, two kind of queries were analyzed: *membership queries* and *equivalence queries*. A probabilistic setting was also presented in which equivalence queries were replaced by random sampling in a setting analogous to that of Valiant [8].

The main aim of this paper is to extend Angluin's results to subsequential transducers. In this case, the membership queries need to be modified in order to take into account the different nature of the functions defined. A natural modification is to use *translation queries*, in which the *Learner* is allowed to consult the translation of a string. The meaning of a counterexample is also changed, so that a counterexample will be a string that is not correctly translated by the hypothesis, together with its translation if it exists, or a signal indicating that the translation is not defined for it. The probabilistic setting is also examined and correspondingly modified by the case of the subsequential transducers.

---

* Supported by a grant of the Spanish *Ministerio de Educación y Ciencia*

2 Definitions and Notation

An alphabet X is a nonempty finite set of symbols. We use X^* to represent the free monoid of the strings over X. Given two strings $x, x' \in X^*$, the notation $|x|$ represents the number of elements of x, the concatenation of x and x' is written as xx'. With $x^{-1}x'$ (or $x'x^{-1}$) we denote the string resulting of eliminating from x' its prefix (or suffix) x. Given $S, F \subseteq X^*$ the set $S \cdot F$, or simply SF, represents the set of the concatenations of every string in S with every string in F, that is $S \cdot F = \{xy \in X^* \mid x \in S \wedge y \in F\}$. The set $S \oplus F$ is the set of the elements that are in one of S and F, but not in both. The symbol ϵ represents the empty string. When it is convenient we use a symbol and the string composed of only that symbol interchangeably. Given a set $S \subseteq X^*$ we use $\mathrm{Pref}(S)$ to represent the set of the prefixes of its strings, and $\mathrm{lcp}(S)$ to denote the *longest common prefix* of the strings in S, i.e. $\mathrm{lcp}(S) = x \Leftrightarrow x \in \mathrm{Pref}(S) \wedge \forall x' \in \mathrm{Pref}(S) : x' \in \mathrm{Pref}(\{x\})$. A set $S \subseteq X^*$ is said to be *prefix-closed* iff it contains the prefixes of all its strings, that is iff $\mathrm{Pref}(S) \subseteq S$. A *suffix-closed* set is defined analogously.

A *subsequential transducer* (SST for short) is defined as a tuple $H = (X, Y, Q, q_0, \pi, \delta, \lambda, \sigma)$, where X and Y are the input and output alphabet, Q is a finite set of states, $q_0 \in Q$ is the initial state, $\pi \in Y^*$ is the initial prefix[2], $\delta : Q \times X \to Q$ is the next-state function[3], $\lambda : Q \times X \to Y^*$ is the transition emission function, and $\sigma : Q \to Y^*$ is the state emission function.

The functions δ and λ can be easily extended to strings by defining:

$$\delta(q, \epsilon) = q \qquad\qquad \lambda(q, \epsilon) = \epsilon$$
$$\delta(q, ax) = \delta(\delta(q, a), x) \qquad \lambda(q, ax) = \lambda(q, a)\lambda(\delta(q, a), x)$$

where $q \in Q$, a is a symbol in X, and x is a string in X^*. With this, we can associate a function $|H| : X^* \to Y^*$ to every transducer H by defining $|H|(x)$ as:

$$|H|(x) = \pi\lambda(q_0, x)\sigma(\delta(q_0, x)),$$

that is, the concatenation of the initial prefix, the output of the translations that are followed from q_0 with x, and the output associated to the last state reached. $|H|$ is undefined if there is no path with the input symbols of x or if the state reached has no output associated to it. For instance, given the transducer in Fig. 1, the value of $|H|(aab)$ is 112122 and $|H|(baa)$ is undefined. The functions defined by the subsequential transducers are the *subsequential functions*.

A SST H is said to be *onward* iff

$$\forall x \in \mathrm{Pref}(\mathrm{Dom}\,|H|) : \pi\lambda(q_0, x) = \mathrm{lcp}\{|H|(xt) \mid xt \in \mathrm{Dom}(|H|)\}, \qquad (1)$$

where $\mathrm{Dom}(f)$ is the domain of the function f. This simply means that the output of every string is produced "as soon as possible". Every SST has a canonical representation in the form of an onward subsequential transducer that has a minimum number of states and is unique up to isomorphism [7].

---

[2] This is a slight difference with the definition given in [3], but both definitions are equivalent in the transductions they define and there is a polinomial time transformation from one into the other

[3] In this paper *function* means *partial function*

3 The Task

Our task is that of finding the canonical form of a SST corresponding to an unknown subsequential function $\tau : X^* \to Y^*$. We are allowed to consult two oracles. The first one answers what will be called *translation queries*; given a string $x \in X^*$, the oracle returns the value of $\tau(x)$ if it exists or a special value $\# \notin Y$ if it doesn't. The second oracle answers *equivalence queries*. The input for such a query is a SST H. If the function $|H|$ is the same as τ the output is *yes*. If the functions are different, the answer is *no* and a counterexample is given. The counterexample is a string $x \in X$ such that either $|H|(x) \cdot \neq \tau(x)$ or x is only in one of the domains of $|H|$ and τ. In case it exists, $\tau(x)$ is also returned.

Some considerations are in order before we go on. First, note that the translation query is a natural extension to the membership query used by Angluin in [1]. Note also that, as in the case of regular languages, it is possible to answer an equivalence query in time polynomial with the size of the automata. On the other hand, this kind of query cannot be answered by a Turing Machine in the case of rational relations because the equivalence problem for them is undecidable [3], so there is a limit in how much can be demanded from the oracle if we want it to be reasonable.

Other important question arises from the observation that a regular language can be interpreted as a subsequential transduction such that a string is translated into 1 if it belongs to the language and into 0 otherwise. This directly implies that the negative results for using only equivalence queries in [2] apply in our case, because the new type of queries does not provide any additional information.

4 Data Structure

The data collected during the execution of the algorithm will be stored in the form of a *table*, which is composed of the following elements:

- S, a prefix-closed set of strings of X^*.
- F, a suffix-closed set of strings of X^*.
- $l_F : S \to Y^* \cup \{\#\}$, a function that associates to each element $x \in S$ the lcp of the translations of the concatenations of x with those in F, that is[4],
  $l_F(x) = \mathrm{lcp}\{\tau(xf) \mid f \in F \wedge xf \in \mathrm{Dom}(\tau)\}$.
- $l_T : S \to Y^* \cup \{\#\}$, a function that associates to each element $x \in S$ the lcp of the translations of every string seen so far that begins with x, that is,
  $l_T(x) = \mathrm{lcp}\{\tau(xt) \mid xt \in (S \cup S \cdot X) \cdot F \cap \mathrm{Dom}(\tau)\}$.
- $T : (S \cup S \cdot X) \times F \to Y^* \cup \{\#\}$, a function that associates to each pair of elements $(s, f) \in S \times F$ the value $(l_F(s))^{-1}\tau(sf)$ if $sf \in \mathrm{Dom}(\tau)$ or the value $\#$ otherwise.

---

[4] We assume that $\mathrm{lcp}(\emptyset) = \#$

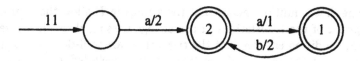

Fig. 1. Graphical representation of the transducer $H = (X, Y, Q, q_0, \pi, \delta, \lambda, \sigma)$, where $X = \{a, b\}$, $Y = \{1, 2\}$, $Q = \{A, B, C\}$, $q_0 = A$, $\pi = 11$, $\delta = \{(A, a, B), (B, a, C), (C, b, B)\}$, $\lambda = \{(A, a, 2), (B, a, 1), (C, b, 2)\}$, and $\sigma = \{(B, 1), (C, 1)\}$.

The intuitive interpretation of these elements is as follows. The elements in S will help in identifying the states, so that a state will be determined by a group of strings sharing certain characteristics. The strings in F, together with the corresponding values of T, are the ones that help in determining whether two strings in S lead to the same or different state. Using l_F and l_T we will be able to know when F is "large enough". In order to simplify the notation we will use $\hat{S}$ to represent the set $S \cup S \cdot X$.

Note that it is possible to recover from a table the information about a particular translation; given $s \in \hat{S}$ and $f \in F$, $\tau(sf) = l_F(s)T(s, f)$.

5 Building a hypothesis

From a table it is possible to construct a SST, which will be used by the algorithm as hypothesis for the oracle. In this section we present this construction, but before that, some preliminary considerations are in order.

5.1 Prerequisites

Given a string $s \in \hat{S}$, define row(s) by the function $r : F \to Y^* \cup \{\#\}$ for which $r(f) = T(s, f)$. We say that a string $s \in \hat{S}$ is *alive* iff $\exists f \in F \mid T(s, f) \neq \#$. Define the set alive($S$) = $\{s \in S \mid s$ is alive$\}$.

A table (S, F, T, l_F, l_T) is said to be *closed* iff

$$\forall s \in S, a \in X : \exists s' \in S \mid \text{row}(sa) = \text{row}(s'). \qquad (2)$$

The intuitive interpretation of this is that a table is closed if for every hypotesized state and every symbol we are able to find a destination for the arc in question.

A table (S, F, T, l_F, l_T) is said to be *consistent* iff given any two strings $s_1, s_2 \in S$ such that row(s_1) = row(s_2) and any symbol $a \in X$ the following conditions are met:

$$l_F(s_1) = l_T(s_1) \qquad (3)$$

$$\text{row}(s_1 a) = \text{row}(s_2 a) \qquad (4)$$

$$s_1 a \in \text{alive}(\hat{S}) \implies (l_F(s_1))^{-1} l_F(s_1 a) = (l_F(s_2))^{-1} l_F(s_2 a) \qquad (5)$$

The first condition means that the strings in F allow the characterization of the prefix of the translations of the strings passing through a given state. The second condition ensures that the transitions are well-defined. Finally, the third ensures that the output of the transitions is well-defined. It may be the case that the first two conditions are true and the third false A condition for (5) to be true is given in the following lemma[5]:

Lemma 1. *If T is a closed table in which conditions (3) and (4) hold, and for every $a \in X$, whenever $s_1 a$ is alive, there exists $af \in F$ such that $T(s_1, af) \neq \#$, then condition (5) holds.*

Before presenting the construction of the hypothesis, we give a couple of lemmas regarding the properties of alive strings.

Lemma 2. *Let T be a table and $s \in \hat{S}$. Then s is alive iff $l_F(s) \neq \#$.*

Lemma 3. *Let T be a consistent table and suppose $sa \in \hat{S}$ is alive. Then s is alive.*

5.2 Construction of the hypothesis

Given a closed and consistent table T it is possible to construct a hypothesis $\mathcal{H}(T)$ as follows[6]:

- $Q = \{\text{row}(s) \mid s \in \text{alive}(S)\} \cup \{\text{row}(\lambda)\}$.
- $q_0 = \text{row}(\lambda)$.
- $\pi = \begin{cases} l_F(\lambda) & \text{if } l_F(\lambda) \neq \#, \\ \lambda & \text{otherwise.} \end{cases}$
- $\delta(\text{row}(s), a) = \text{row}(sa)$ if $sa \in \text{alive}(\hat{S})$.
- $\lambda(\text{row}(s), a) = (l_F(s))^{-1} l_F(sa)$ if $sa \in \text{alive}(\hat{S})$.
- $\sigma = \{(\text{row}(s), T(s, \lambda)) \mid T(s, \lambda) \neq \#\}$.

To prove that $\mathcal{H}(T)$ is well-defined, it suffices to show that the definitions of δ and λ are correct. As T is closed and consistent, for each s and a, whenever sa is alive, it will be possible to define the corresponding values of $\delta(s, a)$ and $\lambda(s, a)$. Moreover, they will be unique, i.e. if $\text{row}(s_1) = \text{row}(s_2)$ then $\text{row}(s_1 a) = \text{row}(s_2 a)$ and $(l_F(s_1))^{-1} l_F(s_1 a) = (l_F(s_2))^{-1} l_F(s_2 a)$. An example of a table and the associated transducer can be seen in Fig. 2.

5.3 Properties

The essential property of the hypotheses constructed in this manner is that they are the smallest (up to isomorphism) that are compatible with the observed pairs. This is proved with the help of a series of lemmas. To alleviate the notation, in the following we assume that the table T consists of (S, F, T, l_F, l_T) and its associated hypothesis has the elements $(X, Y, Q, q_0, \pi, \delta, \lambda, \sigma)$. The elements of other SSTs will be marked with their names.

---

[5] The proofs of the lemmas are in appendix A.

[6] The definition of the function σ is specified by means of the set of input-output pairs.

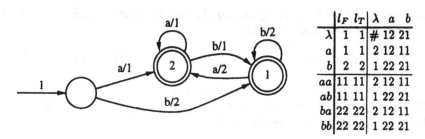

	l_F	l_T	λ	a	b
λ	1	1	#	12	21
a	1	1	2	12	11
b	2	2	1	22	21
aa	11	11	2	12	11
ab	11	11	1	22	21
ba	22	22	2	12	11
bb	22	22	1	22	21

Fig. 2. An example of a closed an consistent table and the associated transducer. Tables are represented with $S \cup S \cdot X$ in the vertical axis, S separated by a line from $S \cdot X$ and F in the horizontal axis, following l_F and l_T.

Lemma 4. *If $\mathcal{T}$ is a closed consistent table and $\mathcal{H}(\mathcal{T})$ is its associated SST, then for every alive string $s \in S$:*

$$\delta(q_0, s) = \text{row}(s) \qquad \pi\lambda(q_0, s) = l_F(s)$$

Corollary 5. $H(\mathcal{T})$ *is onward.*

Lemma 6. *In a closed consistent table, if $T(s, f) \neq \#$ and $s' \in S$ is such that $\delta(\text{row}(s), f) = \text{row}(s')$, then*

$$\forall s \in S, f \in F : T(s, f) = \lambda(\text{row}(s), f)T(s', \epsilon) \tag{6}$$

and if $T(s, f) = \#$ either $\delta(\text{row}(s), f)$ is not defined or $T(\delta(s, f), \epsilon) = \#$.

Now, we prove that the hypothesis defined from the table are "well-behaved", that is, that

$$|\mathcal{H}(\mathcal{T})| (sf) = \begin{cases} l_F(s)T(s, f) & \text{if } T(s, f) \neq \# \\ \# & \text{if } T(s, f) = \# \end{cases} \tag{7}$$

which means that they are compatible with the data seen so far.

Theorem 7. *If $\mathcal{T}$ is a closed consistent table, then the corresponding hypothesis $\mathcal{H}(\mathcal{T})$ is compatible with $\mathcal{T}$.*

Proof. Let $s \in S$ and $f \in F$. If $T(s, f) \neq \#$, let s' be a string with $\text{row}(s') = \delta(\text{row}(s), f)$. Then, using lemmas 4 and 6

$$l_F(s)T(s, f) = \pi\lambda(q_0, s)T(s, f) = \pi\lambda(q_0, s)\lambda(\text{row}(s), f)T(s', \epsilon)$$
$$= \pi\lambda(q_0, sf)\sigma(\delta(q_0, sf))$$

And in case $T(s, f) = \#$, the second part of lemma 6 can be applied, so either $\delta(q_0, sf)$ is undefined or $\sigma(\delta(q_0, sf))$ does not exist, in either case the theorem holds. $\square$

The following lemmas will be used in proving that, the transducer defined above is the minimum, up to isomorphism, that is compatible with the data in the table.

Lemma 8. *Let* $L(X, Y, Q_L, q_0^L, \pi_L, \delta_L, \lambda_L, \sigma_L)$ *be an onward SST compatible with a closed consistent table* $\mathcal{T}$. *Then:*

$$\forall s, s' \in S : \delta_L(q_0^L, s) = \delta_L(q_0^L, s') \implies \text{row}(s) = \text{row}(s'). \qquad (8)$$

Corollary 9. *If* $\mathcal{T}$ *is a closed consistent table and* L *is an onward SST compatible with* $\mathcal{T}$, *the number of states in* L *is greater than or equal to the number of diferent values of* $\text{row}(s)$ *with* s *alive.*

Lemma 10. *If* L *is an onward SST compatible with a closed consistent table* $\mathcal{T}$, *and with the same number of states as* $\mathcal{H}(\mathcal{T})$:

$$\forall s \in \text{alive}(S) : l_F(s) = \pi_L \lambda_L(q_0^L, s).$$

Now we are ready to prove the result.

Theorem 11. *If* $\mathcal{T}$ *is a closed consistent table, then* $\mathcal{H}(T)$ *is the minimum onward SST compatible with it, up to isomorphism.*

Proof. We know that if L is another SST compatible with $\mathcal{T}$ it will have at least as many states as $\mathcal{H}(\mathcal{T})$. Suppose then that it has the same number of states. Define now the correspondence[7] $\phi : Q \to Q_L$ as $\phi(\text{row}(s)) = \delta_L(q_0^L, s)$. First we prove that ϕ is well defined. Suppose there were strings s and s' such that $\delta_L(q_0^L, s) \neq \delta_L(q_0^L, s')$ and $\text{row}(s) = \text{row}(s')$, then there should be another s'' such that $\text{row}(s'') \neq \text{row}(s)$ and $\delta_L(q_0^L, s'')$ equals $\delta_L(q_0^L, s)$ or $\delta_L(q_0^L, s')$ (or else there would be a different number of states in L and $\mathcal{H}(\mathcal{T})$). Both equalities violate lemma 8. To see that ϕ is injective note that by lemma 8 we cannot have two strings s and s' such that $\delta_L(q_0^L, s) = \delta_L(q_0^L, s')$ and $\text{row}(s) \neq \text{row}(s')$.

Using lemma 10, we have that $\pi_L = \pi_L \lambda(q_0, \epsilon) = l_F(\epsilon) = \pi$ so the prefixes are equal. Now, $\phi(\text{row}(\epsilon)) = \delta(q_0^L, \epsilon) = q_0^L$, so the initial state is mapped onto the initial state. Let s' be the string in $\text{alive}(S)$ such that $\text{row}(s') = \text{row}(sa)$ for an alive string $sa \in \hat{S}$. Then $\phi(\delta(\text{row}(s), a)) = \phi(\text{row}(sa)) = \phi(\text{row}(s_1)) = \delta_L(q_0, s_1)$ and $\delta_L(\phi(\text{row}(s)), a) = \delta_L(\delta_L(q_0^L, s), a) = \delta_L(q_0^L, sa)$ which is equal to $\delta_L(q_0^L, s_1)$, so transitions are maintained. With respect to λ we have

$$\lambda_L(\phi(\text{row}(s)), a) = \lambda_L(\delta_L(q_0^L, s), a) = \left(\pi_L \lambda_L(q_0^L, s)\right)^{-1} \pi_L \lambda_L(q_0^L, sa)$$
$$= (l_F(s))^{-1} l_F(sa) = \lambda(\text{row}(s), a)$$

by direct application of lemma 10. So, λ is preserved. Finally, if $s \in S$ is such that $s \in \text{Dom}(\tau)$, we have:

$$\sigma_L(\phi(\text{row}(s))) = \sigma_L(\delta_L(q_0, s)) = \left(\pi_L \lambda_L(q_0^L, s)\right)^{-1} \tau(s)$$
$$= (l_F(s))^{-1} \tau(s) = T(s, \lambda) = \sigma(\text{row}(s)),$$

again by using lemma 10. □

---

[7] We use the subindex L to mark the elements of L

1. Construct an initial table using $S := \{\epsilon\}$ and $F := \{\epsilon\}$, and extend it with translation queries.
2. **Repeat** the following until the answer to an equivalence query is *yes*
   2.1. **While** T is not closed or consistent do the following:
      2.1.1. **If** $\exists s \mid l_F(s) \neq l_T(s)$, find a string p such that $sp \in \hat{S} \cdot F$ and $l_F(s)$ is not a prefix of $\tau(sp)$. Add p and its suffixes to F, extend T using translation queries. Restart the while loop.
      2.1.2. **If** $\exists s_1, s_2 \in S, a \in X \mid \mathrm{row}(s_1) = \mathrm{row}(s_2) \wedge \mathrm{row}(s_1a) \neq \mathrm{row}(s_2a)$, find a string $f \in F$ such that $T(s_1a, f) \neq T(s_2a, f)$. Add af to F, extend T using translation queries. Restart the while loop.
      2.1.3. **If** $\exists s_1, s_2 \in S, a \in X \mid \mathrm{row}(s_1) = \mathrm{row}(s_2) \wedge (l_F(s_1))^{-1} l_F(s_1a) \neq (l_F(s_2))^{-1} l_F(s_2a)$, find a string $f \in F$ such that $\tau(s_1p) \neq \#$, add p and its suffixes to F, extend T using translation queries. Restart the while loop.
      2.1.4. **If** T is not closed, find a string $s \in S$ and a symbol $a \in X$ such that $\forall s' \in S, \mathrm{row}(sa) \neq \mathrm{row}(s')$. Add sa to S, extend T using translation queries. Restart the while loop.
   2.2. Build the hypothesis $H = \mathcal{H}(T)$ and use an equivalence query for it.
   2.3. **If** the answer is *yes* end the process and return H, **else** add the counterexample and its prefixes to S and extend T using translation queries.

Fig. 3. Algorithm for learning subsequential transducers with translation and equivalence queries.

6 The algorithm

So far the basic elements for the learning algorithm have been presented. The idea is to use the translation queries in order to obtain a table that is both closed and consistent. From this table a hypothesis is built and passed for an equivalence query. If the answer is positive we are done. If not, the counterexample is added to the table and new queries are done as necessary until a new closed consistent table is obtained. The cycle is repeated until a correct hypothesis is found.

The algorithm can be seen in Fig. 3. Extending T simply means doing the necessary queries to have all the values of $T(s, f)$ with $s \in S$ and $f \in F$.

To illustrate the algorithm, we present in Fig. 4 an example of execution.

6.1 Termination and Cost

Note that the cost of the algorithm depends on two factors, the size of the target automaton and the length of the counterexamples provided. The automaton can be represented in space linear with the number of states plus the number of arcs, times the maximum output string in an arc or a state.

Due to the condition for the termination of the algorithm, it is obvious that if it terminates, the returned value is correct. It remains to prove that it really ends, and that it does it in a polynomial amount of time. Note that after adding a counterexample to S and obtaining another closed consistent table, the number

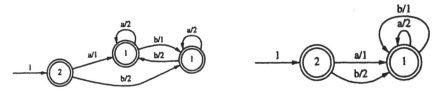

(a) The target SST. (b) The first hypothesis.

	l_F	l_T	ϵ
ϵ	12	1	ϵ
a	111	111	ϵ
b	121	121	ϵ

	l_F	l_T	ϵ	a
ϵ	1	1	2	11
a	11	11	1	21
b	12	12	1	21

	l_F	l_T	ϵ	a
ϵ	1	1	2	11
a	11	11	1	21
b	12	12	1	21
aa	112	112	1	21
ab	111	111	1	21

(c) First table. It is not consistent because $l_F(\epsilon) \neq l_T(\epsilon)$, a is added to F.

(d) Second table. It is not closed because there is no row in S equal to row(a), a is added to S.

(e) Third table. It is closed and consistent, so a hypothesis is made.

	l_F	l_T	ϵ	a
ϵ	1	1	2	11
a	11	11	1	21
b	12	12	1	21
bb	122	122	1	21
aa	112	112	1	21
ab	111	111	1	21
ba	122	122	1	21
bba	1222	1222	1	21
bbb	1221	1221	1	21

	l_F	l_T	ϵ	a	b
ϵ	1	1	2	11	21
a	11	11	1	21	11
b	12	12	1	21	21
bb	122	122	1	21	11
aa	112	112	1	21	11
ab	111	111	1	21	21
ba	122	122	1	21	21
bba	1222	1222	1	21	11
bbb	1221	1221	1	21	11

(f) The table after the counterexample $(bb, 1221)$ is received. It is not consistent, because $row(a) = row(b)$ but $(l_F(a))^{-1} l_F(ab) \neq (l_F(b))^{-1} l_F(bb)$, b is added to F.

(g) Final table. It is closed, consistent, and its corresponding hypothesis agrees with the target.

Fig. 4. An example run of the algorithm.

of different values for row(s) is increased at least by one. That and the Theorem 11 limit the total number of equivalence queries (and hence, the number of iterations of the outer loop) to the number of states of the target automaton.

Now let us analyze what may happen inside the inner while loop. For the step 2.1.1, note that the value of $l_F(s)$ decreases each time a new string is added to F and its original length is a linear function of the length of the strings sf. So the number of times this step can be executed is polynomial in the length of the maximum counterexample returned and the size of the unknown automaton. Regarding step 2.1.2, note that each time a new value is added to F the number of different rows in S is increased, so the total number this step is executed is again bounded by the number of states of the target automaton. The same argument applies to step 2.1.4. Step 2.1.3 will be executed at most once for each value of $row(s)$. So the total cost of the algorithm is polynomial in time. The total size of the table is clearly polynomial with the length of the counterexamples provided and the number of translation queries made by the algorithm (the length of the translations of an SST is linear with the corresponding input).

7 Use of a Probabilistic Oracle

In this section we extend the results of Angluin concerning the use of a random sampling oracle. As noted in [1], those results do not depend on the domain being the regular sets. In our case though, a different version of the concept of error must be provided.

In the stochastic setting, it is assumed that there exists a probability distribution over the set X^*. This distribution may be unknown to the learner. Use $Pr(x)$ to denote the probability assigned by the distribution to x. The learner is allowed to make two kind of queries, *translation queries* as before, and *sampling queries*. In this case, the query has no input and returns a string x drawn according to the distribution and the same response that would give a translation query for that string. Different queries are assumed to be statistically independent.

The probability of error of a hypothesis can be defined with the help of the set

$$\mathcal{E}(\tau, H) = \{x \in \text{Dom}(\tau) \cap \text{Dom}(|H|) \mid \tau(x) \neq |H|\,(x)\} \cup \text{Dom}(\tau) \oplus \text{Dom}(|H|).$$

Then we say that a hypothesis H is an ϵ-*approximation* of τ iff:

$$\sum_{x \in \mathcal{E}(\tau, H)} Pr(x) \leq \epsilon.$$

The aim of the learner is to obtain an ϵ-approximation with a probability higher than $1 - \delta$, using a number of queries polynomial in the size of the target automaton, in $1/\epsilon$ and in $1/\delta$. This can be accomplished by modifying the algorithm in Fig. 3 so that the ith equivalence query is replaced by $\lceil r_i \rceil$ queries. If any of them gives a string x that serves as a counterexample for the hypothesis, the algorithm proceeds like if it were a negative answer to an equivalence query. If all the samples agree with the hypothesis, this is assumed to be correct and it is returned as result of the execution. An adequate value for r_i is[8]

$$r_i = \frac{1}{\epsilon}\left(\log \frac{1}{\delta} + i \log 2\right).$$

And using the same proof as Angluin we arrive to the following:

Theorem 12. *If n is the number of states in the minimum onward SST for the unknown subsequential function τ, then the algorithm terminates after $O(n + (1/\epsilon)(n \log(1/\delta) + n^2))$ sampling queries and the probability that the result is an ϵ-approximation of τ is at least δ.*

---

[8] We use log for the natural logarithm.

References

1. D. ANGLUIN: "Learning Regular Sets from Queries and Counterexamples". *Information and Computation*, Vol. 75, pp. 87–106, 1987.
2. D. ANGLUIN: "Negative Results for Equivalence Queries". *Machine Learning*, Vol. 5, pp. 121–150, 1990.
3. J. BERSTEL: *Transductions and Context-Free Languages*. Teubner, Stuttgart. 1979.
4. D. GILDEA, D. JURAFSKY "Automatic Induction of Finite State Transducers for Simple Phonological Rules". ICSI. Technical Report, TR-94-052, 1994.
5. E. M. GOLD: "Language Identification in the Limit". *Information and Control*, Vol. 10, pp. 447–474, 1967.
6. V.M. JIMÉNEZ, A. CASTELLANOS, E. VIDAL, J. ONCINA: "Some Results with a Trainable Speech Translation and Understanding System". *Proceedings of the ICASSP-95*.
7. J. ONCINA, P. GARCÍA, E. VIDAL: "Learning Subsequential Transducers for Pattern Recognition Interpretation Tasks". *IEEE Transactions on PAMI*, Vol. 15, No. 5, pp. 448–458, 1993.
8. L.G. VALIANT: "A theory of the Learnable", *Communications of the ACM*, Vol. 27, pp.1134–1142, 1984.

Appendix

A   Proofs of the lemmas

Proof. (Lemma 1). The values of $T(s_1, af)$ and $T(s_1a, f)$ are $(l_F(s_1))^{-1} \tau(s_1af)$ and $(l_F(s_1a))^{-1} \tau(s_1af)$, respectively. Then $T(s_1, af)(T(s_1a, f))^{-1}$ is equal to $(l_F(s_1))^{-1} l_F(s_1a)$. Using condition (4) we have that $T(s_1, af)(T(s_1a, f))^{-1}$ equals $T(s_2, af)(T(s_2a, f))^{-1}$ so $(l_F(s_1))^{-1} l_F(s_1a) = (l_F(s_2))^{-1} l_F(s_2a)$. □

Proof. (Lemma 2). Suppose s is alive and let $f \in F$ be a string such that $T(s, f) \neq \#$ then $l_F(s)$ is the lcp of a set than includes at least $\tau(sf)$, so it is not $\#$. On the other hand, if $l_F(s)$ is not $\#$, there must be at least one f in F such that $\tau(sf)$ is defined, so s is alive. □

Proof. (Lemma 3). By lemma 2, $l_F(sa)$ is not $\#$. As $l_T(s)$ is a prefix of $l_F(sa)$, it is not $\#$. Finally, as $\mathcal{T}$ is consistent, $l_F(s) = l_T(s)$, so s is alive. □

Proof. (Lemma 4). We will prove the result by induction. If there is no alive string, the result is trivial. If there is at least one alive string then ϵ will be alive by lemma 3, and for it the proposition is clearly true. Now consider the case of an alive string with the form sa. By lemma 3, s is alive, so the result is true for it. And for sa, we have:

$$\delta(q_0, sa) = \delta(\delta(q_0, s), a) = \delta(\text{row}(s), a) = \text{row}(sa)$$
$$\pi\lambda(q_0, sa) = \pi\lambda(q_0, s)\lambda(\delta(q_0, s), a) = l_F(s)\lambda(\text{row}(s), a)$$
$$= l_F(s)(l_F(s))^{-1}l_F(sa) = l_F(sa),$$

which completes the proof. □

Proof. (Lemma 6). First suppose $T(s, f) \neq \#$. The result can be proved by induction on f. For $f = \epsilon$ it is trivial. Suppose it is true for a certain f, and let us analyze the case af (induction must go "backwards" because F is suffix-closed). Let s' be an element of S such that $\text{row}(s') = \text{row}(sa)$. Then

$$T(s, af) = \lambda(\text{row}(s), a)T(sa, f) = \lambda(\text{row}(s), a)T(s', f)$$
$$= \lambda(\text{row}(s), a)\lambda(\text{row}(s'), f)T(s'', \epsilon) = \lambda(\text{row}(s), af)T(s'', \epsilon)$$

where the induction hypothesis is used by letting s'' be such that $\text{row}(s'') = \delta(\text{row}(s'), f) = \delta(\text{row}(s), af)$. If $T(s, af) = \#$, there are two possibilities. If sa is not alive, $\delta(\text{row}(s), af)$ is not defined. If sa is alive then $\delta(\text{row}(s), af) = \delta(\text{row}(sa), f)$ with $T(sa, f) = \#$ and induction applies. $\quad\square$

Proof. (Lemma 8). Let s and s' be strings such that $\delta_L(q_0^L, s) = \delta_L(q_0^L, s')$. Now consider the translations of the form $|L|(sf)$ with $f \in F$. They can be written as:

$$|L|(sf) = \pi_L\lambda_L(q_0^L, s) \overbrace{\lambda_L(\delta_L(q_0^L, s), f)\sigma_L(\delta_L(\delta_L(q_0^L, s), f))}^{t(f)} = \pi_L\lambda_L(q_0^L, s)t(f),$$

where $t(f)$ is a shortcut for $\lambda_L(\delta_L(q_0^L, s), f)\sigma_L(\delta_L(\delta_L(q_0^L, s), f))$, and $t'(f)$ is analogously defined for the translations of $s'f$. By hypothesis, $\delta_L(q_0^L, s) = \delta_L(q_0^L, s')$, hence $t'(f) = t(f)$ for all $f \in F$. As L is compatible with the table we have

$$l_F(s)T(s, f) = \pi_L\lambda_L(q_0^L, s)t(f).$$

As L is onward, $\pi_L\lambda_L(q_0^L, s)$ must be a prefix of $L_F(s)$, which implies that $T(s, f)$ is a suffix of $t(f)$. Let l be the value $l = \text{lcp}\{t(f)|f \in F, T(s, f) \neq \#\}$. It is clear that $T(s, f) = lt(f)$ for every value of f such that $T(s, f) \neq \#$. Using the same reasoning with s' we arrive at $T(s', f) = lt'(f) = lt(f)$, wich implies that $T(s', f) = T(s, f)$ for the values of f such that both $T(s, f)$ and $T(s, f')$ are different from $\#$. But there cannot be a value of f making one of them equal to $\#$ and the other different, because then L would not be compatible with T. Then $\text{row}(s) = \text{row}(s')$. $\quad\square$

Proof. (Lemma 10). Let $B = \{t \in X^* \mid \exists s \in \text{alive}(S) : l_F(s) \notin \text{Pref}(|H|(st))\}$. Note that this set would not be empty if the proposition were false, and in any case $B \cap F = \emptyset$. Consider the smallest element of B in lexicographic order and let it be[9] at, where a is a symbol of X. Now consider one of the strings $s \in \text{alive}(S)$ such that $l_F(s) \notin \text{Pref}\{|H|(sat)\}$. Let q be the state $\delta_L(q_0^L, sa)$. As $\mathcal{H}(T)$ and L have the same number of states, there must be an alive string $s' \in \text{alive} S$ such that $\delta(q_0, s') = q$. And by construction of at we have that $l_F(s') = \pi_L\lambda(q_0, s')$. As T is closed and consistent, there must be an $f \in F$ such that $T(s', f) \neq \#$, and then $l_F(s)$ included in its computation the value of $\tau(saf)$ that means that the influence of $\lambda_L(q, a)$ in the computation of $l_F(s)$ was noted when considering the value of $\tau(saf)$, which is a contradiction. $\quad\square$

---

[9] Note that it can not be ϵ because $\epsilon \in F$

Lexical Categorization: Fitting Template Grammars by Incremental MDL Optimization

Michael R. Brent and Timothy A. Cartwright

Department of Cognitive Science, Johns Hopkins University
3400 North Charles St., Baltimore, MD 21218, USA.

1   Introduction

To acquire his or her native language, a child must learn the grammatical categories of individual words. Suppose, counterfactually, that infants were born knowing everything there is to know about their language *except* which words belong to which categories. How could they infer the categories of words? An obvious solution is that they could parse the sentences they hear according to the innate grammar, and then read the categories of words off the pre-terminals of the parse tree. Clearly, though, knowing the grammar is not enough—in general, there is no way to parse a sentence without already knowing a lot about the syntactic properties of individual word types. The child's problem is made even worse by the fact that it cannot be born knowing the entire grammar up to categories, since languages vary, at least to some degree, in their grammars.

Previous attempts to devise unsupervised categorization algorithms for natural language have employed hierarchical cluster analysis [5, 6, 7, 10, 12]. In general, they involve characterizing the local environments in which a word occurs in the input as a vector in a high-dimensional space. For example, Redington, Finch, and Chater [12] computed the relative frequency with which each of the 150 most common words occurred immediately to the left of the target word, immediately to its right, two words to its left, and two words to its right. This resulted in a 600-element vector characterizing the local environments in which the target word tends to occur. A hierarchical cluster analysis was then performed on the points in this vector space. Other researchers have proposed other ways of obtaining the initial vectors. For example, Elman [5] trained a simple recurrent net to predict the next word. He then froze the weights, presented each word to the net again, and used the activations on the hidden layer as the vector for each word.

The use of algorithms based on hierarchical cluster analysis has provided intuitively convincing evidence that information about the syntactic categories of words is reflected in their local co-occurrence statistics. However, most of these algorithms were not intended as models of how young children categorize words. Further, this approach is fundamentally ill-suited to modeling human language acquisition. First, they do not produce discrete categorizations, but rather hierarchies of thousands of nested clusters. Although children may have some knowledge of this form, the generally accepted theory is that speakers of a language have discrete categorizations. One reason for this theory is that speakers can, in many cases, make discrete grammaticality judgments. For example, any native speaker of English knows beyond the shadow of a doubt that "John threw the cat" is grammatical, while "John catted the threw" is not (unless these sounds are interpreted as novel technical terms with unknown meanings). Second, clustering is done off-line—adjacency statistics are collected for an entire corpus before the words are clustered. It is conceivable that some incremental version of cluster analysis could be devised, but such an effort would be far from straightforward. Third, the environments in which an ambiguous word occurs will be a mixture of those that result from its different categories. For example, *saw* is both a noun and a verb, so it can occur in "John likes to saw", "John forged a saw", and even "John saw a saw". The standard cluster analysis approach has no way to determine that *saw* belongs to two categories. Instead, *saw* would appear to be unlike words such as *cat*, which are unambiguous nouns, and unlike words such as *destroyed*, which are unambiguous verbs. In fact, however, *saw* is extremely like both *cat* and *destroyed*, in that *saw* can appear in almost any position where either of the other two can appear. Finally, there is an enormous data sparsity problem. For example, Redington, Finch, and Chater [12] clustered only words that occurred 100 times or more in their natural language corpus. Elman performed an artificial language experiment in which the expected frequency of each lexical item in the input was approximately 6,000.

In this paper, we present an algorithm for learning to group together words that have the same grammatical category, using as evidence only the sequences of words in a sample of sentences. This algorithm is not strictly memoryless or on-line, but it is incremental, in the sense that it takes only one pass through the input, processes only one sentence at a time, and discards most (though not all) of the information from each sentence before processing the next one. The algorithm begins without any language-specific information, and outputs a discrete category symbol, or *tag*, for every word token in the input. The algorithm can handle categorial ambiguity—that is, it can put a single word type into multiple categories. Finally, it can sometimes categorize a word based on a single occurrence of that word in the input (although it does not always do so). We present experiments showing that this algorithm performs extremely well in categorizing words from two artificial languages generated, one of which displays lexical ambiguity. We then present experiments showing that this algorithm is useful for categorizing words in transcripts of spontaneous child-directed English, although its performance is far from perfect.

Our algorithm attempts to fit a particular kind of formal grammar, called a *template grammar*, to the input, and categorizes the input in the process. A template grammar is a finite set of category symbols (preterminals), a mapping from category symbols to finite sets of words (terminals), and a finite set of templates. A template is a finite string of category symbols. Sentences are generated from such a grammar by selecting a template and replacing each category symbol in the template with a word in the corresponding category. For example, let A-F be category symbols. Then the five templates

$$ABC\ DEF\ ABCD\ EAFB\ DCEF, \qquad (1)$$

together with the following assignment of terminals to categories,

$$
\begin{array}{ll}
A: a1\ a2\ a3\ a4\ ae5 & D: d1\ d2\ d3\ d4\ bd5 \\
B: b1\ b2\ b3\ b4\ bd5 & E: e1\ e2\ e3\ e4\ ae5 \\
C: c1\ c2\ c3\ c4\ cf5 & F: f1\ f2\ f3\ f4\ cf5
\end{array}
\tag{2}
$$

constitutes a template grammar that generates such sentences as

$$
\begin{array}{ll}
a2\ b1\ \ cf5 & a4\ b3\ \ c1\ d2 \\
d4\ ae5\ cf5 & e1\ ae5\ f1\ bd5
\end{array}
$$

Although human languages cannot be completely characterized by template grammars, the process of fitting a template grammar to a sample of natural language can still produce an adequate categorization. The resulting grammar is only a poor approximation to the true one, but it is good enough for categorization.

We treat template-grammar fitting as an optimization problem, and describe an incremental algorithm that searches for an approximately optimal grammar. The objective function to be optimized was derived by a Minimum Description Length (MDL) analysis [2, 3, 4, 8, 11, 13, 14] of the problem of fitting a template grammar. In the next section we describe the objective function and the search algorithm. In the following section, we present a quantitative analysis of the algorithm's performance in learning the categories of the artificial template grammar described above. In the final section, we analyze the algorithm's ability to categorize words in transcripts of spontaneous child-directed English.

2 The algorithm

Our algorithm is defined in terms of a global optimization problem, over the entire set of input sentences. Although the algorithm itself is incremental, it is best to define the global objective function independent of any particular algorithm. The optimization is over all possible assignments of category symbols to word tokens in the input. Another way of thinking of a token categorization is as a tagging of the input sample with arbitrary category symbols. For example, each word token could be in a category by itself, or all word tokens could be in the same category. This tagging determines the template of each input sentence—it is simply the string of category symbols assigned to the words of the sentence. Thus, such a token categorization constitutes a both a template grammar and a "parsing" or "derivation" of the input sentences in terms of that grammar.

The objective function to be minimized depends on a number of variables whose values are determined by the token categorization. These variables are listed in Table 1. In presenting the objective function, we use the term *group* to refer to the putative categories induced by a hypothesized token categorization, reserving the term *category* for the true categories or, sometimes, the final output. The objective function itself is dominated by four entropy-times-length terms

n	number of word types in the input
g	number of distinct groups in the tagged input
o	number of groups containing only one type
t	number of templates in the categorized input
GROUPS[i]	number of groups that word type i is in
GFREQ[j]	number of occurrences of group j in the template set
FREQ[i, j]	number of tokens of type i in group j
TFREQ[k]	number of occurrences of template k
TLEN[k]	length (in category symbols) of template k

Table 1. The state variables that are used to compute the objective function for a given token categorization (tagging) of an input sample.

that result from Huffman coding various sequences in the representational system used for the MDL analysis. We now define shorthand notation for these:

$$w = \sum_{i=1}^{n} \text{GROUPS}[i]$$

$$H(\text{GROUPS}[*]) = -\sum_{i=1}^{n} \frac{\text{GROUPS}[i]}{w} \log\left(\frac{\text{GROUPS}[i]}{w}\right)$$

Thus, w is the total number of group/type pairs, and $H(\text{GROUPS}[*])$ is the entropy, over all word types, of their relative group counts.

$$G = \sum_{j=1}^{g} \text{GFREQ}[j]$$

$$H(\text{GFREQ}[*]) = -\sum_{j=1}^{g} \frac{\text{GFREQ}[j]}{G} \log\left(\frac{\text{GFREQ}[j]}{G}\right)$$

Thus, G is the total length of all the templates in the grammar, measured in group symbols, and $H(\text{GFREQ}[*])$ is the entropy, over all group symbols, of their relative frequencies in the template set.

$$m_j = \sum_{i=1}^{n} \text{FREQ}[i, j]$$

$$H(\text{FREQ}[*, j]) = -\sum_{i=1}^{n} \frac{\text{FREQ}[i, j]}{m_j} \log\left(\frac{\text{FREQ}[i, j]}{m_j}\right)$$

Thus, m_j is the number tokens tagged with the symbol for group j, and $H(\text{FREQ}[*, j])$ is the entropy, over all group symbols, of their relative frequencies in the tagged input.

$$T = \sum_{k=1}^{t} \text{TFREQ}[k]$$

$$H(\text{TFREQ}[*]) = -\sum_{k=1}^{t} \frac{\text{TFREQ}[k]}{T} \log\left(\frac{\text{TFREQ}[k]}{T}\right)$$

Thus, T is the number of input utterances (and hence template instances). $H(\text{TFREQ}[*])$ is the entropy, over all templates, of their relative frequencies in the input.

Using this notation, the function to be minimized is:

$$wH(\text{GROUPS}[*]) + GH(\text{GFREQ}[*]) + \sum_{j=1}^{g} m_j H(\text{FREQ}[*, j]) + TH(\text{TFREQ}[*])$$

$$+t \log \max_k \text{TLEN}[k] + g - o + 2(n + w + t)$$

Unfortunately, space does not permit going into the mathematical justification for this formula.

Now let us consider algorithms for optimizing the token categorization of a particular set of example sentences. The most straightforward way to guarantee finding the global minimum would be to enumerate all possible token categorizations of the input. However, this is wildly impractical, even for extremely short inputs, and further would not provide an algorithm that children could use to continually refine their categorization as new input sentences become available. Instead, we propose an incremental algorithm. After each sentence is processed, the algorithm maintains a current hypothesis about the set of templates used to generate the input so far, the number of times each template has occurred, the set of word types in each category, and the number of tokens of each type that in each category. As each sentence comes in, each of the word tokens in it is assigned a new category that has no other members. The algorithm then processes the sentence as follows. It considers all pairs of categories, of which at least one is the category of some word in current input utterance. If the value of the objective function is reduced by merging any such pair into a single category, then it merges the pair that reduces the value of the objective function most. This step is repeated until the objective function can no longer be reduced by merging such pairs. Then the current sentence is discarded and the next one is read in.

3   Experiments

An obvious first step in determining the effectiveness of this algorithm was to see how well it performed on input that was in fact generated by a template grammar. Our reasoning was that if the algorithm performed moderately well on natural language but poorly on template languages, its performance on natural language would be a mystery. If it performed moderately well on natural language and even better on template languages, that would support our prediction that template grammars constitute a useful zeroth-order approximation to the grammars of natural languages. If it performed poorly on natural language but very well on template languages, that would suggest that our grammar-fitting techniques are on target, but that a more sophisticated class of grammars is needed for modeling natural language, or else that some other sources of information are needed.

3.1 Artificial Grammars

To test performance on template languages we generated samples using the five templates in (1) and two versions of the lexicon in (2). For the first experiment we used a subset of the lexicon that omitted the ambiguous lexical items $ae5$, $bd5$, and $cf5$. Obviously, the implementation treated each lexical item as an atomic symbol and did not make use of its string representation. This unambiguous template grammar generates 896 distinct sentences. We generated each sentences of each input sample by selecting one of the five templates with uniform probability and then replacing each category symbol with one the four lexical items in in the named category with uniform probability.

In pilot experiments we determined that the algorithm always learne the correct categorization exactly, and did so with fairly small input samples. Thus, we set out to determine empirically how performance varied as a function of sample size. We devised a system of scoring performance based on the fact that the output of the algorithm is a token categorization—in other words, a tagged corpus, and that the only meaning of the tags is that words with the same tag belong to the same category. For each pair of word tokens in the input sample, we scored a true positive when they correctly received the same tag, a false positive when they incorrectly received the same tag, and a false negative when they incorrectly received distinct tags. These were then converted to precision and recall scores, where precision is true positives divided by all positives, and recall is true positives divided by the number of pairs that should have received the same tag. Given samples of the unambiguous grammar, the program produced no false positives, so its precision was always perfect. The results for recall are shown in Table 2, where each cell shows the average over 100 randomly generated samples. By 30 sentences of input, which can include at most 3.4% of the 896 possible sentences (if there happen to be no repetitions), the average recall was nearly 90%. By 35 sentences ($< 4\%$) the average recall was nearly 100%, and by 40 sentences ($< 4.5\%$) the correct token categorization had been found for every one of 100 randomly generated input samples.

The next step was to see how well the algorithm could handle a much harder problem—categorizing input from an ambiguous template grammar. For this purpose we used the entire lexicon in (2), including the ambiguous lexical items $ae5$, $bd5$, and $cf5$. In order to perform this task, the algorithm had to tag some of the tokens of type $ae5$ with category A, and some with category E, and the right tokens had to receive the right tags. Pilot experiments suggested that the algorithm would sometimes conflate two categories that shared a lexical item—for example, it would conflate A and E into a single group. Further, these

Sample size	Recall	(SD)
10	29.2	(8.2)
15	32.6	(10.9)
20	41.7	(14.8)
25	65.9	(24.3)
30	86.5	(21.8)
35	98.9	(5.8)
40	100.0	(0)

Table 2. Recall as a function of the number of sentences in the input sample, sentences generated from the unambiguous subset of the lexicon in (2). Averages over 100 samples, with standard deviations in parentheses.

errors seemed to occur when two sentences containing the same ambiguous item generated from different categories occurred very early in the input. Thinking that these errors might result from poor behavior of the objective function at boundary conditions, we set out to see how performance would be affected by the amount of unambiguous input preceding the first ambiguous input. To do this, we generated 100 samples of 85 sentences each from the full, ambiguous lexicon. The ambiguous word types had the same expected frequencies as all the other word types (they were half as likely to be generated from each of two different categories). We also generated 100 samples of 40 sentences each from the unambiguous subset of the lexicon. Finally, we ran the algorithm on each of the ambiguous samples alone, and also on another 100 ambiguous samples with a 40-sentence unambiguous prefix. The results are shown in Table 3. The recall is good

	Precision	Recall
No Prefix	63.7 (10.62)	97.4 (2.61)
Prefix	98.0 (1.49)	98.0 (1.40)

Table 3. Precision and recall on samples generated from the ambiguous lexicon, with and without a 40-sentence prefix generated from the unambiguous subset of the lexicon. Averages over 100 randomly generated samples, with standard deviations in parentheses.

in both conditions, and does not differ significantly between conditions. That is because conflation errors are reflected in precision, not in recall. The precision is moderate when there is no prefix, but has a high variance. This reflects the fact that anywhere from zero to three conflation errors can occur, with the mean being about one. Each conflation error reduces the precision greatly. In addition, there can be sporadic mistagging errors for ambiguous tokens even when their categories are not conflated, but these only reduce the precision a little. In the prefix condition, precision was very good and significantly better than in the no prefix condition. All errors appear to result from mistagging rather than category conflation.

These two experiments suggest that our algorithm performs surprisingly well on template languages, and can discover lexical ambiguity so long as it is not too common at the very beginning of the input sample.

3.2 Natural Langauge

Since our initial experiments suggested that the proposed categorization strategy is effective for artificial languages generated by template grammars, we set out to determine whether it is useful for categorizing words in spontaneous, child-directed English. Because most words in the input corpora occurred only a few times, we did not expect high recall. Indeed, most of the existing algorithms do not even attempt to categorize words with so few occurrences. We did not expect precision to be perfect either. One reason is that our algorithm sometimes does go out on a limb to categorize words that have occured only a few times. Another is that template grammars are expressively weak, and therefore looking at natural language through the lens of template grammars is likely to lead to some erroneous conflations. To determine whether our algorithm is potentially useful, we compared its performance to that of randomly permuting the correct tagging.

Method Programs. The implementation of our algorithm was the same as the one used on the artificial language experiments, except that declarative, imperative, and interrogative sentences were maintained separately in the list of templates (see Inputs below). The permutation program started with each word token being tagged with its correct category (see Scoring Standard below). This resulted in a tagging that was guaranteed to have the correct number of categories and the correct number of tokens in each category. It is important to note that this is not a zero-knowledge baseline—the correct number of categories and the correct number of tokens in each category is extremely useful information that is not available to our algorithm.

Inputs. Both programs were run on edited transcripts of spontaneous, child-directed English. The inputs were the first-session orthographic transcripts made by Bernstein-Ratner [1] and were obtained from the CHILDES database [9]. The speakers were nine mothers speaking freely to their 13- to 21-month-old children (mean = 18 months); the children ranged in linguistic sophistication from being prelinguistic to producing multi-word utterances.

The original transcripts were edited to make them as internally consistent as possible. In order for the program to group together tokens of the same type, it must know when two tokens belong to the same type. Thus, transcripts were primarily edited to eliminate spelling variations within types. For example, the original orthographic forms da+da, dada, and daddy were all considered tokens of the type daddy. Furthermore, there were many contraction-like forms in the original, such as w(oul)dja, wouldja, and wouldya. Due to the difficulty of knowing which contractions are perceived as single words versus multiple ones, we decided to spell out all contractions. Thus, all three forms above became would you.

Sentence breaks were taken to occur wherever a period (.), comma (,), exclamation mark (!), or question mark (?) occurred (see MacWhinney, 1995, for details of the CHAT file encoding standard). Pauses, marked in the orthographic transcripts by a hash-mark (#), were treated as sentence terminators, except when they clearly interrupted a complete sentence; other obviously incorrect sentence divisions were fixed. All quoted material was replaced by the symbol QUOTE in the main clause, then the quoted material occurred next as though it were a separate sentence.

Once delimited, each sentence was classified as being declarative, imperative, or interrogative. The point of this classification is that different sentence classes have different distributions of their constituents (at least in English); since our system works by finding distributional similarities, it is important to distinguish the classes.

Non-words were removed wherever they occurred. Sentences consisting of the repetition of just one word type, including all single-word sentences, were also removed because they contain little or no distributional information.

The resulting input files contained 172–384 sentences (mean = 244) and 662–1,553 word tokens (mean = 994).

Scoring. A scoring standard was created by labeling each word token in the inputs with one of the following grammatical category labels: *noun, verb, copula, auxiliary/modal, adjective, preposition, determiner, adverb, conjunction, interjection*, and the inflection morpheme *to*. If a word type was used in more than one category, each token was categorized according to its own environment. The tagged Brown corpus served as an authority in resolving questions about the proper category of a token. Precision and recall were computed as in the artificial language experiments.

Results and Discussion The scores are shown in Table 4. All scores are aver-

	Precision	Recall
Permutation	22.8 (2.01)	22.8 (2.01)
Template	85.3 (9.43)	17.8 (6.05)

Table 4. Precision and recall averaged over nine corpora of child-directed speech, with standard deviations in parentheses.

ages over the nine inputs. Precision was significantly greater for our algorithm than for permutation (t(8) = 21.81, p ¡ .0001). Recall was significantly lower for our algorithm than for permutation (t(8) = 2.88, p = .02).

Clearly, our algorithm outperformed the permutation algorithm. Permutation had slightly greater recall because it had the advantage of knowing that there are only a few categories, whereas our algorithm is more cautious about grouping words together, so it ends up with many categories. But the accuracy of our algorithm is much, much greater than that of permuting the correct labels. Indeed, our algorithm is accurate enough to suggest that, with some further tuning and perhaps a little help from semantics, it could go a long way toward explaining children's ultimate success at categorization.

The output for one of the nine corpora is shown below. Specifically, all groups containing multiple word types are shown, in order of the number of types they contain, with token frequencies in parenthesis.

> smile (2), ball (1), balloon (1), bunny (2), kitty (1), boy (4), house (1),
> phone (5), doggy (10), telephone (2), block (9)
> this (19), that (36), it (39), alice (5), him (4)
> feed (4), get (13), feel (3), do (12)
> open (2), take (4), pull (2)
> on (7), in (6), one (1)
> right (2), away (6), okay (1)
> out (5), up (4)
> want (14), say (14)
> the (34), a (33)
> what (43), who (2)
> touch (3), tickle (2)
> daddy (8), good (5)
> sorry (6), lonesome (1)
> your (7), alice's (1)
> sit (1), fall (1)
> go (5), are (9)
> to (20), QUOTE (13)

With the exception of *one*, *QUOTE*, *away*, and *good*, these groups seem to be nearly perfect. Further, the presence of frequency one words indicates that the algorithm is capable of correctly classifying words based on a single occurrence. In addition to the multi-word groups shown above, there were 121 groups containing tokens of just a single word type, of which 53% contained only one token, 22% contained two tokens, 16% contained three to five tokens, and only 9% contained six or more tokens. Tokens in single-type groups can be interpreted as "uncategorized", although this interpretation falls outside the formalism itself.

References

1. N. Bernstein-Ratner. The phonology of parent child speech. In K. Nelson and A. van Kleeck, editors, *Children's Language: Vol. 6.* Erlbaum, Hillsdale, NJ, 1987.
2. Michael R. Brent and Timothy A. Cartwright. Distributional regularity and phonotactic constraints are useful for segmentation. In press, 1996.

3. T. Mark Ellison. Learning vowel harmony. In Walter Daelmans and David Powers, editors, *Background and Experiments in Machine Learning of Natural Language: Proceedings of the 1st* SHOE *Workshop*. Institute for Language Technology and Artificial Intelligence, Katholieke Universiteit, Brabant, Holland, 1992.

4. T. Mark Ellison. *The Machine Learning of Phonological Structure*. Cambridge University Press, Cambridge, 1996. In press.

5. Jeffrey Elman. Finding structure in time. *Cognitive Science*, 14:179–211, 1990.

6. Steven Finch and Nick Chater. Bootstrapping syntactic categories using statistical methods. In Walter Daelmans and David Powers, editors, *Background and Experiments in Machine Learning of Natural Language: Proceedings of the 1st* SHOE *Workshop*. Institute for Language Technology and Artificial Intelligence, Katholieke Universiteit, Brabant, Holland, 1992.

7. G. R. Kiss. Grammatical word classes: A learning process and its simulation. *Psychology of Learning and Motivation*, 7:1–41, 1973.

8. Ming Li and Paul M. B. Vitányi. *An Introduction to Kolmogorov Complexity and Its Applications*. Springer Verlag, New York, 1993.

9. Brian MacWhinney and Catherine Snow. The child language data exchange system. *Journal of Child Language*, 12:271–296, 1985.

10. Toby H. Mintz, Elissa E. Newport, and Thomas G. Bever. Distributional regularities of grammatical categories in speech to infants. In J. Beckman, editor, *Proceedings of the North East Linguistics Society 25, Vol. 2*, Amherst, MA, 1995. GLSA.

11. J. Ross Quinlan and Ronald L. Rivest. Inferring decision trees using the minimum description length principle. *Information and Computation*, 80:227–248, 1989.

12. Martin Redington, Steven Finch, and Nick Chater. Distributional information and the acquisition of linguistic categories: A statistical approach. In *Proceedings of the Fifteenth Annual Conference of the Cognitive Science Society*, pages 848–853, 1993.

13. Jorma Rissanen. *Stochastic Complexity in Statistical Inquiry*. World Scientific Publishing, Teaneck, NJ, 1989.

14. Andreas Stolcke and Stephen Omohundro. Inducing probabilistic grammars by Bayesian model merging. In Rafael C. Carrasco and José Oncina, editors, *Grammatical Inference and Applications. Proceedings Second International Colloquium*, volume 862 of *Lecture Notes in Artificial Intelligence*, pages 106–118, Alicante, Spain, 1994. Springer Verlag.

Selection Criteria for Word Trigger Pairs in Language Modeling

Christoph Tillmann and Hermann Ney

Lehrstuhl für Informatik VI, RWTH Aachen – University of Technology
D-52056 Aachen, Germany
{tillmann,ney}@informatik.rwth-aachen.de

Abstract. In this paper, we study selection criteria for the use of word trigger pairs in statistical language modeling. A word trigger pair is defined as a long-distance word pair. To select the most significant trigger pairs, we need suitable criteria which are the topics of this paper. We extend a baseline language model by a single word trigger pair and use the perplexity of this extended language model as selection criterion. This extension is applied to all possible trigger pairs, the number of which is the square of the vocabulary size. When a unigram language model is applied as baseline model, this approach produces the mutual information criterion used in [7, 11]. The more interesting case is to use this criterion in the context of a more powerful model such as a bigram/trigram model with a cache. We study different variants of including word trigger pairs into such a language model. This approach produced better word trigger pairs than the conventional mutual information criterion. When used on the Wall Street Journal corpus, the trigger pairs selected reduced the perplexity of a trigram/cache language model from 138 to 128 for a 5-million word training set and from 92 to 87 for a 38-million word training set.

1 Introduction

In speech recognition, the most widely used and successful language model is the so-called N-gram model, e.g. a bigram or trigram model, where the dependency of the word under consideration is limited to the immediate predecessor words. However, it is clear that some sort of long-distance dependencies exist as well. The main goal in this paper is to include long-distance dependencies into the language model by means of so-called "trigger pairs" [7, 8, 11]. We restrict ourselves to trigger pairs where both the triggered and the triggering events are single words (as opposed to word phrases). Unlike the approach presented in [1, 7], where the trigger pairs are selected on the basis of a mutual information criterion, the selection criterion presented in this paper is directly the perplexity improvement obtained by extending the baseline language model by a single trigger pair. What makes the selection criteria for word pair triggers interesting in general, is the following broader view: Given a baseline language model how can we improve this model by including additional types of dependencies?

For the selection criterion, we consider two new variants. In the first variant, we directly combine trigger pairs with a given baseline model using a backing-off scheme [6]. When using a unigram language model as baseline model, this approach produces the mutual information criterion used in [7, 8, 11]. The second variant we study is based on the idea that word trigger pairs should be used only in those cases where the probabilities of the baseline model are not already high. In the context of a bigram/cache language model, this idea amounts to exploiting word trigger dependencies only when neither the cache component nor the bigram component of the language model are 'active'.

The organization of this paper is as follows. Section 2 covers the mathematical models of the three selection criteria presented in this paper. In Section 3 we present the experimental results. We give and discuss examples of trigger pairs, which were obtained by the different selection criteria. The identity of these examples significantly varies for the different selection criteria. In the last section, perplexity results are reported for the combination of word trigger pairs with a trigram/cache language model on a text corpus from the Wall Street Journal task. As might be expected, the experimental results depend heavily on the criterion used to select the word triggers; in particular, the third variant of the trigger selection criteria developed in the next section gives better results than the conventional mutual information criterion used in [7, 8, 11].

2 Selection Criteria for Trigger Pairs

The goal of this paper is to reduce the perplexity of a given baseline language model by means of word trigger pairs. Typically, the baseline language model is a trigram/cache model. For a vocabulary of size V, there are V^2 possible word trigger pairs. The basic approach to selecting the best trigger pairs is as follows. We consider the possible word trigger pairs one by one and extend the baseline language model by the word trigger pair under consideration. Then for each word trigger pair, we compute the perplexity improvement on a training corpus and select the best trigger pairs. A similar idea is applied in [2] to the so-called feature selection in the maximum entropy framework. In this section, we develop the basic framework for the extension of a baseline language model with a single word trigger pair. There are three variants of how we select the word triggers. Therefore, we distinguish three types of selection criteria and word trigger pairs: *high level triggers*, *unigram level triggers* and *low level triggers*.

2.1 High Level Triggers

The baseline language model we use in the following is denoted by $p(w|h)$, where w is the word whose probability is to be predicted for the given history h. Here, the word history consists of the last M, say 200, words. To denote a specific word trigger pair, we use the symbol $a \rightarrow b$, where a is the *triggering* word and b is the *triggered* word. In order to combine a trigger pair $a \rightarrow b$ with the baseline language model $p(w|h)$, we define the extended model $p_{ab}(w|h)$:

$$
p_{ab}(w|h) = \begin{cases}
q(b|a) & \text{if } a \in h \text{ and } w = b \\[2mm]
[1 - q(b|a)] \cdot \dfrac{p(w|h)}{\sum\limits_{w' \neq b} p(w'|h)} & \text{if } a \in h \text{ and } w \neq b \\[4mm]
q(b|\overline{a}) & \text{if } a \notin h \text{ and } w = b \\[2mm]
[1 - q(b|\overline{a})] \cdot \dfrac{p(w|h)}{\sum\limits_{w' \neq b} p(w'|h)} & \text{if } a \notin h \text{ and } w \neq b\,,
\end{cases}
\tag{1}
$$

where $q(b|a)$ and $q(b|\overline{a})$ are two interaction parameters of the word trigger pair $a \rightarrow b$. For symmetry reasons, we have introduced a special interaction parameter $q(b|\overline{a})$, when a has not been seen in the history. The unknown parameters $q(b|a)$ and $q(b|\overline{a})$ will be estimated later by maximum likelihood, which is equivalent to the criterion of minimum perplexity. In the above definition, the interaction parameters of the word trigger pair are applied at the highest level, i.e. they have priority over the baseline language model. To distinguish this selection criterion from the criteria to be studied later, we refer to these trigger pairs as *high level triggers*.

We consider the difference between the log-perplexity F_{ab} of the extended model $p_{ab}(w|h)$ and the log-perplexity F_0 of the baseline model $p(w|h)$ on a corpus $w_1, ..., w_n, ..., w_N$:

$$
\begin{aligned}
F_{ab} - F_0 &= \sum_{n=1}^{N} \log \frac{p_{ab}(w_n|h_n)}{p(w_n|h_n)} \\
&= \sum_{h} \Big[N(a; h, b) \log \frac{q(b|a)}{p(b|h)} + N(a; h, \overline{b}) \log \frac{1 - q(b|a)}{1 - p(b|h)} \\
&\quad + N(\overline{a}; h, b) \log \frac{q(b|\overline{a})}{p(b|h)} + N(\overline{a}; h, \overline{b}) \log \frac{1 - q(b|\overline{a})}{1 - p(b|h)} \Big],
\end{aligned}
\tag{2}
$$

where the counts $N(.;.,.)$ are defined in a natural way. E.g. the count $N(a; h, b)$ is the number of occurrences that the word b was observed for the history h and the word a appeared at least once in the history. To further rewrite the perplexity improvement $F_{ab} - F_0$, we introduce another set of counts that is independent of the history h:

$$
N(a; b) = \sum_{n : a \in h_n, b = w_n} 1
\tag{3}
$$

$$
N(a; \overline{b}) = \sum_{n : a \in h_n, b \neq w_n} 1
$$

$$
N(\overline{a}; b) = \sum_{n : a \notin h_n, b = w_n} 1
$$

$$
N(\overline{a}; \overline{b}) = \sum_{n : a \notin h_n, b \neq w_n} 1\,.
$$

Using these count definitions, we obtain after some elementary manipulations:

$$
\begin{aligned}
F_{ab} - F_0 = \quad & N(a;b)\log q(b|a) + N(a;\bar{b})\log[1 - q(b|a)] \\
& + N(\bar{a};b)\log q(b|\bar{a}) + N(\bar{a};\bar{b})\log[1 - q(b|\bar{a})] \\
& - S(b)
\end{aligned} \tag{4}
$$

where $S(b)$ depends only on the baseline language model $p(w|h)$ and is defined as:

$$
S(b) = \sum_{n=1}^{N} \delta(w_n, b)\log\frac{p(b|h_n)}{1 - p(b|h_n)} + \sum_{n=1}^{N}\log[1 - p(b|h_n)] \quad , \tag{5}
$$

where $\delta(x,y)$ is the usual Kronecker delta. Here, for the sake of clarity, we point out the notation: the symbol $p(b|h_n)$ denotes the probability of word b following the history h_n although it typically never occurred at position n in the training corpus. It is interesting to note that $S(b)$ is independent of the triggering word a. From the representation given by Eq. (4), we can derive the conclusions:

– The maximum-likelihood estimates of the interaction parameters $q(b|a)$ and $q(b|\bar{a})$ are obtained by taking the derivates of Eq. (4) and equating them to zero:

$$
q(b|a) = \frac{N(a,b)}{N(a,b) + N(a,\bar{b})} \tag{6}
$$

$$
q(b|\bar{a}) = \frac{N(\bar{a},b)}{N(\bar{a},b) + N(\bar{a},\bar{b})}, \tag{7}
$$

– If we fix a triggered word b and consider its triggering words a_i, $i = 1, 2, , ,,$ the ranking of the a_i does not depend in any way on the baseline language model.

Implementation. The practical problem of computing the perplexity improvement as given by Eq. (4) is the second sum in Eq. (5). To manage this computational problem, we use a sampling approach, i.e. we take every 20-th position in the training corpus to estimate this sum. We tested this sampling approximation for 200 words (having different unigram probabilities) and found the approximation error to be typically smaller than 5%. To calculate the perplexity improvement for all trigger pairs $a \rightarrow b$, we compute beforehand both the counts in Eq. (3) and the quantity $S(b)$ for each triggered word b (by sampling). Then we compute the perplexity improvements on the training corpus for each possible trigger pair $a \rightarrow b$.

2.2 Unigram Level Triggers

Choosing a unigram model $p(w)$ as baseline model $p(w|h)$, we obtain:

$$
\begin{aligned}
F_{ab} - F_0 = {} & N(a;b)\log\frac{q(b|a)}{p(b)} \;+\; N(a;\bar{b})\log\frac{1-q(b|a)}{1-p(b)} \\
& + N(\bar{a};b)\log\frac{q(b|\bar{a})}{p(b)} \;+\; N(\bar{a};\bar{b})\log\frac{1-q(b|\bar{a})}{1-p(b)}
\end{aligned}
\tag{8}
$$

Identifying the probability $p(a;b)$ with the relative frequency $N(a;b)/N$ and similarly for the other joint events $(a;\bar{b}), (\bar{a};b), (\bar{a};\bar{b})$, we obtain exactly the mutual information criterion as suggested in [7, 11]. In other words, this criterion is simply the improvement on the log-perplexity of a unigram model using the above backing-off model for the trigger pair $a \rightarrow b$. The trigger pairs selected by this criterion are called *unigram level triggers*.

2.3 Low Level Triggers

The high level model defined by Eq.(1) might have a drawback due to the following observation. If $w_n \neq b$ for a trigger pair $a \rightarrow b$, the baseline language model is always discounted by a factor $[1 - q(b|a)]$ or $[1 - q(b|\bar{a})]$ in the model defined by Eq. (1), which may hurt in terms of perplexity. As confirmed by the experimental results, there is another approach to combining a trigger pair into a baseline language model. The idea is to use the trigger pair $a \rightarrow b$ only in positions h_n where the baseline language model provides a poor probability. To give a quantitative formulation, we assume a linear interpolation of a unigram distribution $\beta(w)$ and a specific language model $p_S(w|h)$, e.g. an unsmoothed trigram/cache model. For the baseline language model $p(w|h)$, we have then the form:

$$
p(w|h) = (1 - \lambda) \cdot p_S(w|h) + \lambda \cdot \beta(w).
$$

To incorporate a trigger pair $a \rightarrow b$ into the baseline language model, we replace the unigram distribution $\beta(w)$ by a new quasi-unigram distribution $\beta_{ab}(w)$, which is defined in a similar fashion as Eq.(1). The extended language model $p_{ab}(w|h)$ is then given by linear interpolation:

$$
p_{ab}(w|h) = (1 - \lambda) \cdot p_S(w|h) + \lambda \cdot \beta_{ab}(w|h) \quad .
$$

As expressed by this equation, the trigger pairs are incorporated into the baseline model at the lowest possible level, namely at the level of the unigram distribution. Therefore these trigger pairs will be referred to as *low level triggers*.

Using a probability threshold p_0, we define the set of words whose probability can be affected by the trigger model for a given history h:

$$
V(h) = \{ w : p_S(w|h) > p_0 \} \quad .
$$

As expressed by this equation, for the difference $F_{ab} - F_0$ in the log-likelihoods, we use the approximation:

$$F_{ab} - F_0 = \sum_{n=1}^{N} \log \frac{p_{ab}(w_n|h_n)}{p(w_n|h_n)} \qquad (9)$$

$$= \left[\sum_{n:\, w_n \notin V(h_n)} + \sum_{n:\, w_n \in V(h_n)} \right] \log \frac{p_{ab}(w_n|h_n)}{p(w_n|h_n)}$$

$$\cong \sum_{n:\, w_n \notin V(h_n)} \log \frac{p_{ab}(w_n|h_n)}{p(w_n|h_n)}$$

$$\cong \sum_{n:\, w_n \notin V(h_n)} \log \frac{\beta_{ab}(w_n|h_n)}{\beta(w_n)}.$$

This approximation amounts to reducing the training corpus by considering only positions n with $w_n \notin V(h_n)$. Then the set of these positions can be processed as in the case of the unigram level triggers. In particular, the trigger interaction parameters $q(b|a)$ and $q(b|\bar{a})$ are estimated on the reduced corpus, too. In informal experiments, we found that the quality of the selection criterion could be improved by computing $\beta(w)$ also only on the reduced corpus of all words $w_n \notin V(h_n)$ rather than the whole corpus.

3 Experimental Results

The experimental tests were performed on the the Wall Street Journal (WSJ) task [10] for a vocabulary size of $V = 20000$. We computed trigger pairs for the three selection criteria introduced before:

A: unigram level selection criterion in Eq. (8)
B: high level selection criterion in Eq. (1)
C: low level selection criterion in Eq. (9).

For the baseline language model, there were three training corpora with sizes of 1, 5 and 38 million running words. Unlike the baseline language models, the word trigger pairs were *always* selected from the 38-million word training corpus. In the first part of this section, we present samples of the selected trigger pairs for the three selection criteria. These samples were chosen because we deemed them typical of the three criteria. In the second part, we present perplexity results for the combination of trigger pairs with a baseline language model.

3.1 Examples of Trigger Pairs

As stated before, for a vocabulary size of V words, there are V^2 possible word trigger pairs. Only trigger pairs that were observed at least 3 times in the training corpus were used to calculate the perplexity improvement using the different

Table 1. Best word trigger pairs along with perplexity improvement (ΔPP) for the three selection criteria A, B and C (self triggers and same-root triggers excluded).

	Rank	ΔPP	a	b	$N(a,b)$	$N(a,\overline{b})$	$N(\overline{a},b)$	$N(\overline{a},\overline{b})$
A	3	-2.22	the	a	839783	31263065	6175	3901023
	4	-2.21	a	share	15107	33430899	39833	2524207
	5	-1.75	in	nineteen	72010	33119066	54615	2764355
	11	-1.45	point	dollars	174009	14577007	66658	21192372
	12	-1.44	of	the	1793280	31921904	246783	2048079
	13	-1.41	the	company	75945	32026903	58876	3848322
	14	-1.29	the	U.	49630	32053218	47096	3860102
	16	-1.22	a	the	1985329	31460677	54734	2509306
	17	-1.17	the	of	767430	31335418	197787	3709411
	18	-1.10	percent	point	149707	12327082	92944	23440313
	19	-1.06	to	be	112112	33569246	44121	2284567
	20	-1.03	the	S.	80343	32022505	50732	3856466
	26	-0.96	the	company's	4693	32098155	19640	3887558
	27	-0.95	rose	point	65694	3275140	176957	32492255
	28	-0.95	in	the	1778846	31412230	261217	2557753
	29	-0.94	dollars	million	128117	16221255	42062	19618612
	32	-0.90	the	to	895618	31207230	36689	3870509
	33	-0.89	nine	point	122853	9678103	119798	26089292
	37	-0.86	dollars	cents	53792	16295580	4828	19655846
B	18	-0.0103	Texaco	Pennzoil	1423	294204	433	35713986
	19	-0.0102	Pennzoil	Texaco	1911	152412	2312	35853411
	30	-0.0074	Fe	Santa	1111	95276	1379	35912280
	34	-0.0071	distillers	Guinness	835	79004	802	35929405
	38	-0.0064	Am	Pan	1241	346056	975	35661774
	41	-0.0062	Campeau	Federated	844	134468	542	35874192
	45	-0.0061	Cola	Coca	807	144817	634	35863788
	64	-0.0051	oil	Opec	2274	2138246	221	33869305
	72	-0.0048	Federated	Campeau	941	129385	856	35878864
	107	-0.0039	multiples	negotiable	367	54612	86	35954981
	130	-0.0035	Geller	Lord	494	26838	652	35982062
	131	-0.0035	Beazer	Koppers	262	25132	131	35984521
	137	-0.0034	soviet	Moscow	1712	1173777	663	34833894
	163	-0.0031	rales	Interco	243	22795	147	35986861
	165	-0.0031	Eddie	crazy	478	67269	565	35941734
	171	-0.0030	Arabia	Saudi	802	147960	1145	35860139
	181	-0.0029	Warner	Borg	345	204029	132	35805540
	182	-0.0029	Shield	Robins	731	104266	517	35904532
	190	-0.0028	Robins	Dalkon	295	80880	40	35928831
	192	-0.0028	Shoreham	Lilco	247	29555	146	35980098
C	1	-0.00371	neither	nor	411	28775	567	1853529
	14	-0.00109	tip	iceberg	55	4944	4	1878279
	15	-0.00107	soviet	Moscow's	119	80652	26	1802485
	26	-0.00101	named	succeeds	147	63692	164	1819279
	27	-0.00100	Iraq	Baghdad	74	13766	45	1869397
	33	-0.00093	Eastman	Kodak's	49	3919	16	1879298
	40	-0.00090	Eastman	photographic	55	3913	61	1879253
	43	-0.00089	Carbide	Danbury	51	3350	46	1879835
	50	-0.00088	Eurodollar	syndication	60	3758	139	1879325
	55	-0.00086	filed	alleges	103	52441	80	1830658
	57	-0.00085	asked	replied	120	67419	110	1815633
	60	-0.00085	Kodak	photographic	57	6367	59	1876799
	68	-0.00083	motor	Ford's	74	25221	47	1857940
	71	-0.00083	South	Pretoria	87	71047	18	1812130
	75	-0.00080	Iran	Baghdad	80	42050	39	1841113
	76	-0.00080	occupational	Osha	40	3011	12	1880219
	80	-0.00079	soviet	Moscow	100	80671	45	1802466
	81	-0.00079	machines	Armonk	68	29004	28	1854182
	86	-0.00077	Peabody	Kidder's	49	8388	22	1874823

criteria. For the unigram level triggers and the low level triggers, the calculation of all possible trigger pairs took a maximum of 6 hours (on a R4000 SGI workstation). For the high level triggers, the computation time was dominated by the time for calculating $S(b)$ in Eq. (5) using the sampling approximation; typically it took 48 hours when every 20th position was sampled.

Table 1 shows the best trigger pairs for each of the three selection criteria. In each case, it was found that the word trigger pairs were dominated by the self-triggers and the so-called same-root triggers. A trigger pair $a \rightarrow b$ is a self-trigger pair if $a = b$, i.e. it is equivalent to the cache effect. Same-root triggers are trigger pairs $a \rightarrow b$, where the two words a and b differ only by an ending s-character, e.g. the possessive and plural forms for nouns. To single out the really interesting word trigger pairs, the self-triggers and same-root triggers were removed. To illustrate the effect of these self-triggers and same-root triggers, the first column of Table 1 shows the rank of each trigger pair within the original list. The second column presents the perplexity improvement ΔPP of the extended model over the baseline model. In addition, Table 1 gives the four counts defined in Eq. (3), where, of course, for the low level selection criterion, only the reduced corpus (resulting in 1.8 million positions) was used. For these experiments, the baseline model was a bigram/cache model [9], where the bigram component and the cache component were linearly interpolated using a cache with a weight of 0.1. Table 2 gives another representation of the best trigger pairs. For a chosen set of triggering words a, Table 2 shows the best triggered words b. The words b are ordered by decreasing perplexity improvement. For each of the three selection criteria, the trigger pairs were taken from a list of the best 500 000 trigger pairs. We now discuss the two new selection criteria in more detail.

High Level Triggers. All in all, the results for the high level triggers were less satisfactory than for the low level triggers, but there are some interesting facts to note. There are asymmetries as for the trigger pair "Fe $\rightarrow$ Santa", which has a high ranking position. The inverse trigger pair "Santa $\rightarrow$ Fe" did not get a high ranking, because "Fe" is already well predicted by the bigram model in the case of predecessor word "Santa". In Table 1, the high level triggers shown consist of proper names only; all of these trigger pairs seem reasonable considering the financial domain of the WSJ corpus. However, the situation is different when looking at Table 2. Here, some of the high level triggers (i.e. criterion B) are more difficult to understand. An interesting fact to notice for high level triggers is that only 3000 out of V^2 possible trigger pairs were able to improve a given bigram/cache model as expressed by Eq. (9).

Low Level Triggers. In both Tables 1 and 2, the low level trigger pairs yield the best overall result of the three selection criteria. Some words produce very interesting trigger pairs, e.g. the triggering words "asked" and "says" in Table 2. These verbs mostly trigger verbs again, which even have the same tense. Additional interesting examples are the triggering words "airlines" and "Ford" in Table 2, where the triggered words are airlines or car models produced by the

Table 2. List of best triggered words b for some triggering words a for the selection criteria A, B and C.

a	b
asked	A: point replied Mr. I he percent asked one seven eight B: Deltona Prism Benequity Taiyo Ropak Genesis Quintessential Envirodyne target's Teamster C: replied answered responded refused replies responses reply yes request requesting
airlines	A: airlines airline air passenger fares carriers traffic flights miles continental B: Delta's Northwest's Maxsaver Transtar Swissair Primark United's Motown Airbus's Cathay C: American's passengers Airlines' Eastern's United's hubs fares Northwest's carriers flights
buy	A: buy shares stock dollars company price offer million share stake B: Sheller Deltona Motown Northview Barren Philipp Selkirk Oshkosh Radnor Bumble C: repurchased Landover purchases repurchases Kohlberg repurchase Southland's undervalued
concerto	A: orchestra concerto music symphony piano violin philharmonic ballet composer concert B: Mozart violin Bach poignant C: strings orchestra violin score Mozart pianist recordings keyboard listen variations
Ford	A: Ford Ford's cars auto Chrysler car G. Jaguar models M. B: Ford Ford's Edsel ambulances Dearborn Jaguar Bronco Mustang Jaguar's Sheller C: Ford's Dearborn Bronco Taurus Escort Chrysler's Tempo Mustang Thunderbird subcompact
love	A: her love she point his I said dollars percent You B: Genex polly soothing boyish pathetic authenticity quaint Horace chalk Domino's C: beautifully passion sweet sexy romantic hero pop lovers pale wit
Microsoft	A: Microsoft software Lotus computer Microsoft's Apple computers personal O. one B: Microsoft Microsoft's Borland Ashton Lotus's Adobe Oracle Redmond Novell Bausch C: Microsoft's Redmond Apple's Borland spreadsheets Ashton Lotus's database spreadsheet
says	A: says said point million dollars adds seven he five one B: Benham Barren accredited Philipp Panasonic Radnor Deltona kids' Battelle Motown C: concedes explains adds agrees recalls asks insists acknowledges asserts predicts

"Ford" company. The corresponding unigram level triggers look worse for the same verbs, but for some nouns as triggering words, the triggered words seem to be more general. In addition, we emphasize the following results for the low level triggers:

- Among the best low level triggers are nouns that trigger their possessives, while self triggers do not occur at all.

- In another experiment, we found that very much the same low level triggers were obtained by the following criterion: only those corpus positions n were used where the count of the bigram (w_{n-1}, w_n) was exactly 1 and where w_n was not in the cache, i.e. in the history h_n.

- If we confine the history to the current sentence, we get trigger pairs related to grammatical structure, e.g. "I → myself", "We → ourselves". These results can be compared to the link grammar results in [4], where long-distant word pairs (and triples) are used to find the lexicalized grammar rules.

As the experimental tests reported in the following will show, the low level triggers were also able to improve the perplexity of a trigger/cache baseline model.

3.2 Perplexity Results

In this subsection, we present perplexity results for the trigger pairs. The trigger pairs were selected as described in the preceding subsection and were used to extend a baseline language model, which was a trigram/cache model. We used the following model to incorporate the selected trigger pairs into a full language model and to define an extended language model $p_E(w_n|h_n)$:

$$p_E(w_n|h_n) = (1 - \lambda_1 - \lambda_2) \cdot p_S(w_n|h_n) + \lambda_1 \cdot p_C(w_n|h_n) + \lambda_2 \cdot p_T(w_n|h_n) \quad ,$$

where the history $h_n = w_{n-M}^{n-1}$ consists of the M predecessor words of w_n. The cache model $p_C(w_n|w_{n-M}^{n-1})$ is defined as:

$$p_C(w_n|w_{n-M}^{n-1}) = \frac{1}{M} \sum_{m=1}^{M} \delta(w_n|w_{n-m}) \quad ,$$

with $\delta(w, v) = 1$ if and only if $w = v$. The trigger model $p_T(w_n|h_n)$ is defined as:

$$p_T(w_n|w_{n-M}^{n-1}) = \frac{1}{M} \sum_{m=1}^{M} \alpha(w_n|w_{n-m}) \quad .$$

The $\alpha(b|a)$ are obtained by renormalization:

$$\alpha(b|a) = \frac{q(b|a)}{\sum_{b'} q(b'|a)},$$

where the interaction parameters $q(b|a)$ are the maximum likelihood estimates given by Eq. (7). In the experiments, the history h was defined to start with the most recent article delimiter.

The baseline trigram model was a backing-off model described in [9]. Although the interpolation parameters λ_i in Eq. (10) could be trained by the EM procedure [3, 5], they were adjusted by trial and error in informal experiments. For the different extended language models, the perplexity was computed on a test corpus of 325 000 words from the WSJ task.

In a first experiment, we tried to improve a unigram model with the unigram level triggers and with the low level triggers. The unigram model was trained

Table 3. Perplexity results for the extension of a unigram language model (5-million training words) with three different components: low level triggers, unigram triggers and cache.

model	5 Mio
unigram	1027
+ low level triggers	960
+ unigram level triggers	860
+ cache	750

Table 4. Perplexity results for the combination of trigger pairs with a trigram/cache language model (1, 5 and 38 million training words).

model	Number of Triggers	1 Mio	5 Mio	38 Mio
trigram with no cache		252	168	105
trigram/cache		197	138	92
+ unigram level triggers	1500000	191	135	91
+ low level triggers	500000	182	130	88
+ low level triggers	1500000	180	128	87

on the 5-million corpus. We used the 500 000 best trigger pairs for the low level and unigram level selection criterion. The resulting perplexities are presented in Table 3. The unigram level triggers improve the perplexity to a much higher extent than the low level triggers as can be expected from the corresponding selection criteria.

In a second experiment, the baseline language was a trigram/cache model which was extended by different sets of trigger pairs. The perplexity results are given in Table 4. For comparison purposes, the effect of the cache component in the baseline model was studied, too. Thus the Table 4 shows the perplexities for the following conditions: trigram with no cache, trigram/cache and its extensions using a set of 1.5 million unigram level trigger pairs, a set of 0.5 million low level trigger pairs and a set of 1.5 million low level trigger pairs. By far the best results were obtained for the low level trigger pairs. Increasing the number of low level trigger pairs from 0.5 million to 1.5 million improves the perplexity only slightly.

As expected, the combination of the low level trigger pairs produced the best perplexity improvement using the model defined in Eq. (10). The problem with all the selection criteria presented is that the combination of the selected trigger pairs into one global language model is not captured by any of the criteria. However, the low level criterion provides a better approximation to the use of the trigger pairs in Eq. (10). As opposed to the low level triggers, the high level triggers were never found to result in perplexity improvements because the selection criterion as defined by Eq.(1) is not consistent with the extended model defined in Eq. (10).

4 Summary

In this paper, we considered the problem of selecting word trigger pairs for language modeling. Instead of using some more or less arbitrary ad-hoc selection criterion, we presented a new method for finding word trigger pairs: given a baseline language model to start with, we extend it by including one word trigger pair at a time and compute the perplexity improvement of this extended model over the baseline model. This perplexity improvement is used to select the most important word trigger pairs. For the special case that the baseline language model is a unigram model, this new method results in the well-known mutual information criterion. The more interesting case is that the trigger pair under consideration is integrated at a lower level of the baseline language model, which leads to the so-called low level selection criterion. In the experimental tests, we found the following results:

1. The low level selection criterion produced intuitively better word trigger pairs than the usual mutual information criterion.
2. When combined with a full baseline language model, namely a trigram/cache model, the low level triggers reduced the perplexity from 138 to 128 for the 5-million training set and from 92 to 87 for the 38-million training set. In comparison, when using the conventional mutual information criterion, the perplexity improvements were significantly smaller.

References

1. L.R. Bahl, F. Jelinek, R.L. Mercer and A. Nadas. "Next Word Statistical Predictor". *IBM Techn. Disclosure Bulletin*, 27(7A), pp. 3941–3942, 1984.
2. A. Berger, S. Della Pietra and V. Della Pietra. "A Maximum Entropy Approach to Natural Language Processing". In *Computational Linguistics*, Vol. 22, No. 1, pp. 39-71, March 1996.
3. A.P. Dempster, N.M. Laird and D.B. Rubin. "Maximum Likelihood from Incomplete Data via the EM Algorithm". In *Journal of the Royal Statistical Society*, Vol. 39, No. 1, pp. 1-38, 1977.
4. S. Della Pietra, V. Della Pietra, J. Gillett, J. Lafferty, H. Printz and L. Ures. "Inference and Estimation of a Long-Range Trigram Model". In *Lecture Notes in Artificial Intelligence*, Grammatical Inference and Applications, ICGI-94, Alicante, Spain, Springer-Verlag, pp. 78–92, September 1994.
5. F. Jelinek. "Self-Organized Language Modeling for Speech Recognition". In *Readings in Speech Recognition*, A. Waibel and K.F. Lee (eds.), pp. 450–506, Morgan-Kaufmann, 1991.
6. S.M. Katz. "Estimation of Probabilities from Sparse Data for the Language Model Component of a Speech Recognizer". In *IEEE Trans. on Acoustics, Speech and Signal Processing*, Vol. 35, pp. 400–401, March 1987.
7. R. Lau, R. Rosenfeld and S. Roukos. "Trigger-Based Language Models: A Maximum Entropy Approach". In *Proc. IEEE Int. Conf. on Acoustics, Speech and Signal Processing*, Minnesota, MN, pp. II 45–48, April 1993.
8. R. Lau, R. Rosenfeld and S. Roukos. "Adaptive Language Modeling Using the Maximum Entropy Approach". In *Proceedings of the ARPA Human Language Technology Workshop*, pp. 108-113, Morgan–Kaufmann, March 1993.
9. H. Ney, M. Generet and F. Wessel. "Extensions of Absolute Discounting for Language Modeling". In *Fourth European Conference on Speech Communication and Technology*, pp. 1245–1248, Madrid, September 1995.
10. D.B. Paul and J.B. Baker. "The Design for the Wall Street Journal-based CSR Corpus". In *Proceedings of the DARPA SLS Workshop*, pp. 357–361, February 1992.
11. R. Rosenfeld. "Adaptive Statistical Language Modeling: A Maximum Entropy Approach". *Ph.D. thesis*, School of Computer Science, Carnegie Mellon University, Pittsburgh, PA, CMU–CS–94–138, 1994.

Clustering of Sequences Using a Minimum Grammar Complexity Criterion

Ana L. N. Fred

Instituto Superior Técnico, Lisboa, Portugal
IST-Torre Norte, Av. Rovisco Pais,1096 Lisboa Codex PORTUGAL
Email: eanafred@beta.ist.utl.pt

Abstract. The problem of cluster analysis of syntactic patterns is addressed. A new clustering method is proposed based on a minimum grammar complexity criterion. Grammars, describing the structure of patterns, are used as kernel functions in a hierarchical agglomerative clustering algorithm, taking a ratio of decrease in grammar complexity as criterion for cluster association. Cluster analysis of a set of contour images is performed to illustrate the proposed approach.

1 Introduction

In structural pattern recognition, patterns are represented in symbolic form, such as strings and trees, and recognition methods are based on symbol matching or on models that treat symbol patterns as sentences from an artificial language. These methods seek relevant modeling and discriminating information in terms of structural relationships inherent in a pattern. The formalism of grammars [1, 2, 3] is very powerful as, not only it describes these structural relationships in terms of productions, and can be used for language generation, as it also provides a mechanism for recognition by means of parsing algorithms [4, 5, 6]. Another common approach to structural pattern analysis consists of string matching, based on string edit operations – insertion, deletion and substitution – to which costs are associated [1, 7, 8, 9].

Clustering of syntactic patterns consists of an unsupervised association of data based on the similarity of their structures and primitives. Clustering algorithms for syntactic pattern analysis found in the literature are extensions of conventional clustering methods [11, 12] by introducing distance measures between strings. References [1, 13] present sentence-to-sentence clustering procedures based on the comparison of a candidate string with sentences in previously formed clusters (clustering based on a nearest-neighbor rule) or with cluster center strings (cluster center technique). String edit operations are there used to determine the distance between strings. A similarity measure between strings based on the search of common subpatterns by means of Solomonoff's coding is proposed in [10]. This coding method is explored in a clustering scheme to associate strings that share structural information, adopting a minimum description length type criterion. Grammatical inference and error-correcting parsing are combined in a clustering procedure described in [1, 14]. The basic idea is to characterize cluster structure in terms of a grammar inferred from cluster data. Using the distance between a sentence and the language generated by a cluster grammar, by means of error-correcting parsing, new strings are added to previously formed clusters or proposed to form new clusters as a result of the comparison of this distance measure with a threshold. String edit operations are once again assumed for the computation of distances between strings and languages in this nearest-neighbor based method.

In this paper a new approach to clustering of syntactic patterns is proposed. The underlying idea is that, if two patterns exhibit a similar structure, then their joint description in terms of a common grammar will be smaller than the combination of the descriptions of the individual elements. The new algorithm is essentially a hierarchical agglomerative clustering method that combines grammatical inference, to characterize cluster structure, with a minimum grammar complexity criterion, to cluster formation.

Section 2 describes the proposed method. The approach is illustrated in section 3 in cluster analysis of contour images.

2 Clustering of Syntactic Patterns

Consider the examples of patterns in figure 1-I and their corresponding string descriptions according to the coding scheme in 1-II. By straightforward application of string edit operations, different length samples of the same pattern (such as (a) and (b)) would be given a non-null distance; depending on the costs assigned to the several edit operations and on the lengths of the strings, higher similarity would be found between equal length strings with distinct patterns than between variable size repetitions of a given pattern. On the other hand, similarity measures based on the identification of common subpatterns in which order dependency is not taken into account are not able to discriminate between patterns such as the ones in figure 1 (e) and (f).

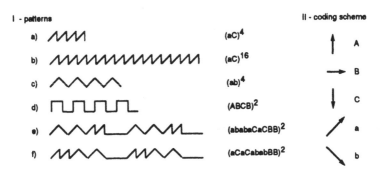

Fig. 1. I - Repetitive patterns and corresponding string descriptions. Superscripts indicate the number of repetitions of the substrings inside parentesis. II - coding scheme

In the following a hybrid approach, combining grammatical inference with a minimum grammar complexity criterion for the association of structural patterns, is proposed. The underlying idea for string clustering is that, if sequences exhibit a similar structure, then their joint description will be more compact than the combination of the descriptions of the individual elements. Grammars are then used to describe patterns structure and grammar complexity is taken as a measure of compactness of the description. The similarity of both structures and primitives of patterns is thus translated into a shared set of grammar productions and therefore into a reduction in grammar complexity. The similarity between structural patterns is determined as a ratio of decrease in grammar complexity, as described in section 2.1.

The new algorithm is essentially an agglomerative type clustering method that combines grammatical inference, to characterize cluster structure, with a minimum grammar complexity criterion to cluster formation.

2.1 Minimum Grammar Complexity Criterion

Let $G = (V_N, V_T, R, \sigma)$ be a context-free grammar, where V_N represents the set of nonterminal symbols, V_T is the set of terminal symbols, σ is the start symbol and R is the set of productions, written in the form:

$$
\begin{aligned}
A_1 &\rightarrow \alpha_{11} \mid \ldots \mid \alpha_{1l_1} \\
&\vdots \\
A_r &\rightarrow \alpha_{r1} \mid \ldots \mid \alpha_{rl_r}
\end{aligned}
\tag{1}
$$

Let α be a grammatical sentence, $\alpha \in (V_N \cup V_T)^*$, of length n, in which the symbols $A_1, A_2, \ldots, A_m$ appear $k_1, k_2, \ldots, k_m$ times, respectively. The complexity of the sentence, $C(\alpha)$, is given by [15, 16]:

$$
C(\alpha) = (n+1)log(n+1) - \sum_{i=1}^{m} k_i log k_i
\tag{2}
$$

One defines the complexity of grammar G, $C(G)$, as

$$
C(G) = \sum_{i=1}^{r} \sum_{j=1}^{l} C(\alpha_{ij})
\tag{3}
$$

This expression can be seen as a non stochastic version of the measure described in [15, 16] for the complexity of stochastic grammars.

When two strings have a common structure, the grammars inferred from each will share a set of productions. If a common grammar is inferred from the two strings, this grammar will have less productions than the sum of the productions of the grammars inferred from the individual strings, exhibiting lower complexity. The extension of this minimum grammar complexity concept to clusters of strings is straightforward, by associating a grammar with each data set. Given two clusters C_1 and C_2, one defines the *ratio of decrease in grammar complexity*, $RDGC(C_1, C_2)$, as

$$RDGC(C_1, C_2) = \frac{C(G_{C_1}) + C(G_{C_2}) - C(G_{C_1,C_2})}{min\{C(G_{C_1}), C(G_{C_2})\}} \qquad (4)$$

with G_{C_i} representing the grammar inferred from the data in cluster C_i, and $C(.)$ is the grammar complexity. This ratio can be seen as a measure of similarity between string patterns and corresponds to the minimum grammar complexity criterion for the clustering of patterns. This measure has the following properties:

$$
\begin{aligned}
&RDGC(C_1, C_2) = RDGC(C_2, C_1) \\
&RDGC(C_1, C_2) = 1 \quad if \ C_1 \subseteq C_2 \ or \ C_1 \supseteq C_2 \\
&RDGC(C_1, C_2) = 0 \quad if \ G_{C_1} \ and \ G_{C_2} \ have \ no \ common \ rules \\
&0 \le RDGC(C_1, C_2) \le 1 \quad \forall C_1, C_2
\end{aligned} \qquad (5)
$$

The actual values of the $RDGC$ depend on the grammars that model string sets and therefore on the underlying grammatical inference algorithm used. Table 1 shows a few examples of strings and their $RDGC$ measure when using Crespi Reghizzi's method [15].

String	RDGC
$(dfg)^n$	0
$(cba)^n$	0
$(abc)^p(cba)^q$	0.59
$(abc)^n$	1.0

Table 1. $RDGC$ when associating the string $(abc)^2$ with the string on the left column of the table. Values on column 2 correspond to applying Crespi Reghizzi's method for grammatical inference (no *a priori* information being used except for left/right precedence in the string).

2.2 The Clustering Procedure

The clustering algorithm starts by forming a cluster with each string, to which a grammar is associated. Then, iteratively, among the possible associations of cluster pairs, the one exhibiting the highest reduction ratio in grammar complexity is selected and compared with a threshold th. If this ratio is greater than th, the two clusters will be joined; the algorithm ends when no further improvements in grammar complexity, with respect to the threshold th, is achieved.

Clustering Algorithm

Input: A set of strings $X = \{x_1, x_2, \ldots, x_n\}$ and a threshold th.

Output: A partition of X into m clusters $C_1, C_2, \ldots, C_m$ and their grammar representations $G_{C_1}, G_{C_2}, \ldots, G_{C_m}$.

Steps:

1. Assign x_i to C_i, $i = 1, \ldots, n$ and infer a grammar G_{C_i} for each cluster. Let $m = n$.

2. Among the m^2 possible associations of two clusters, C_i, C_j, select the one that produces the highest ratio of decrease in grammar complexity ($RDGC$), as given by expression 4. If the improvement is greater than the threshold th, then associate these clusters, set their grammatical description as the grammar inferred from the joint set of data G_{C_i, C_j} and decrease m by one; otherwise stop returning the clusters found.

A design parameter, th, is present in the algorithm. It can be derived in a supervised fashion from a set of pattern samples with known classifications ($th < min(RGCD(C_i, C_j)$ such that the $C_k, K = 1, \ldots$ are in accordance with the training data) or can be obtained based on some stopping criterion (for instance an *a priori* known number of clusters).

3 Clustering of Contour Images

In this section the proposed clustering method is applied to the analysis of contour images.

Figure 2 shows the shapes under analysis and their labels. They consist of three star type contours (labels (0), (3) and (4)), a square shape (contour (5) and its scaled version (6)) and three types of arrows (patterns (7) through (14)). Contours (1), (2), (9) and (12) were added as noisy versions of the shapes.

3.1 Coding of Contours in String Description

Each contour was decomposed into line segments of fixed length and the angle between successive segments was coded using the 16-characters alphabet in figure 3 (b). A string description is obtained by concatenating the symbols associated with each segment by starting at an initial position on the contour (lowest left point) and moving counter-clockwise. Figure 3 illustrates the coding method for the contour (4). The string descriptions thus obtained correspond to using the first difference of a 16-directional chain code [17], with the 16 difference values being mapped into alphabetic symbols. Table 2 presents the string descriptions of the patterns of figure 2.

3.2 Cluster Analysis

The clustering algorithm presented in the previous section was applied to the set of strings describing the contour patterns. Crespi-Reghizzi's method [15, 16] was

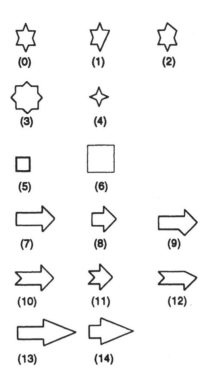

(0) (1) (2)

(3) (4)

(5) (6)

(7) (8) (9)

(10) (11) (12)

(13) (14)

Fig. 2. Contours and respective labels.

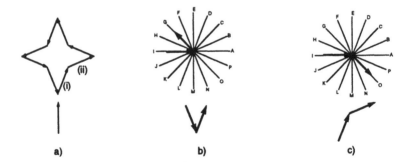

a) b) c)

Fig. 3. Obtaining contour's string description. The initial position for the contour is indicated by the arrow ↑. The code for the first segment in (a) – (i) – is obtained by alining the segment preceding it with the horizontal line in the coding scheme, as shown in (b), and by reading the symbol pointed by the segment to be coded. Segment (i) will therefore be coded as "G". In (c) the same procedure is repeated for segment (ii). The resulting code is: "GOGOGOGO".

Pattern	String Description
0	GNFOFNGNFOFN
1	GAAFNGNFOFN
2	GNFODENFOFN
3	EOEOEOEOEOEOEOEOEO
4	GOGOGOGO
5	EAEAEAEA
6	EAAEAAEAAEAA
7	EAAAMGAEAGMAAAEA
8	EAMGAEAGMAEA
9	EAAOEAEAGMAAAEA
10	GAAAMGAEAGMAAAGM
11	GAMGAEAGMAGM
12	GAAAMGAFABAAAGM
13	EAAAFAAGAAFMAAAEA
14	EAFAAGAAFMAEA

Table 2. Contour's string descriptions.

used to infer cluster grammars. Structural samples were formed from the string descriptions by imposing a left-right precedence on the symbols representing line segments. For instance, the string

$$GNFOFNGNFOFN$$

has associated the structural sample

$$[G[N[F[O[F[N[G[N[F[O[F[N]]]]]]]]]]]],$$

where the parenthesis "[" and "]" indicate symbol precedence.

Figure 4 summarizes the results obtained when running the algorithm with a zero threshold and tracing the clusters formation (in step 2 of the clustering algorithm, output the indexes of the clusters joined and the corresponding ratio of decrease in grammar complexity). A diagram of the clusters formed is depicted on the left of the figure. Arcs link merged clusters and coordinate values indicate the ratio of decrease in grammar complexity thus obtained. The order by which clusters were built, with the associated ratio of decrease in grammar complexity, are indicated on the right of the figure.

As can be seen, the ratio of decrease in grammar complexity when grouping non-noisy versions of the same shape is 1 (for patterns 7-8, 10-11 and 13-14) or close to one (5-6 are grouped for threshold values less than or equal to 0.99999994). Lowering the threshold to 0.66 leads to the formation of 8 clusters, with the noisy patterns (8) and (1) being included in the corresponding shape clusters. By progressively lowering the threshold, less clusters are obtained, with an intermediate level with one cluster formed by the arrows and square patterns, another with the six edge star and its noisy versions and two other groups

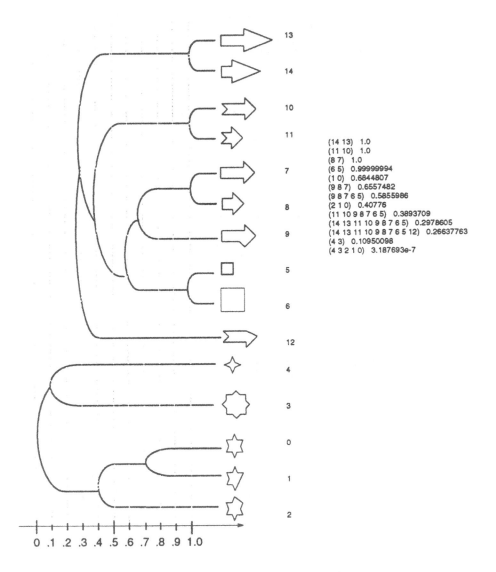

Fig. 4. Results of clustering. Values inside parentesis on the rigth side of the figure indicate the indexes of the patterns grouped into a cluster; the value that follows it corresponds to the associated RDGC.

with the remaining star shaped patterns. For extremely low thresholds (less than 3.188e-7) two clusters are obtained, separating the stars from the arrow and the square shapes.

4 Conclusions

A new clustering method for syntactic patterns was proposed. Grammars, describing the structure of patterns, were used as kernel functions in a hierarchical agglomerative clustering algorithm, taking a ratio of decrease in grammar complexity as criterion for cluster formation. Cluster analysis of a set of contour images was performed to illustrate the proposed approach. The good results obtained in preliminary tests encourage future work on the subject, namely in what concerns cluster order selection criteria and a deeper evaluation of the method for pattern analysis and classification purposes.

References

1. K. S. Fu. Syntactic pattern recognition. In *Handbook of Pattern Recognition and Image Processing*, chapter 4, pages 85–117. Academic Press, 1986.
2. Michael G. Thomason. Syntactic pattern recognition: Stochastic languages. In *Handbook of Pattern Recognition and Image Processing*, chapter 5, pages 119–142. Academic Press, 1986.
3. R. N. Moll, M. A. Arbib and A. J. Kfoury, *An Introduction to Formal Language Theory*. Springer Verlag, 1988.
4. A. V. Aho and J. D. Ullman. *The Theory of Parsing, Translation and Compiling*, volume I. Englewood Cliffs, New Jersey, 1972.
5. A. L. N. Fred and J. M. N. Leitão. Improving sentence recognition in stochastic context-free grammars. In *Proc, of the Int'l Conference on Acoustics, Speech and Signal Processing, ICASSP-93*, pages 9–12, August 1994.
6. A. L. N. Fred and J. M. N. Leitão. Parsing in attributed context-free grammars: application to automatic sleep analysis. In *Proc, of the Int'l Conference on Acoustics, Speech and Signal Processing, ICASSP-96*, May 1996.
7. H. Bunke, String matching for structural pattern recognition, in *Syntactic and Structural Pattern Recognition, Theory and Applications*, H. Bunke and A. Sanfeliu (Eds.), World Scientific, pp 119–144, 1990.
8. H. Bunke, Recent advance in string matching, in *Advances in Structural and Syntactic Pattern Recognition*, H. Bunke (Ed.), World Scientific, pp 107–116, 1992.
9. R. L. Kashiap and B. J. Oommen. String correction using probabilistic models. *Pattern Recog. Letters*, pp 147–154, 1984
10. A. L. N. Fred and J. M. N. Leitão. A minimum code length technique for clustering of syntactic patterns. In *Proc, of the 13th IAPR Int'l Conference on Pattern Recognition*, Vienna, August 1996.
11. R. Duda and P. E. Hart, *Pattern Classification and Scene Analysis*, John Wiley and Sons, 1973.
12. A. K. Jain and R. C. Dubes. *Algorithms for Clustering Data*. Prentice Hall, Englewood Cliffs, 1988.

13. S. Y. Lu and K. S. Fu. A Sentence-to-Sentence Clustering Procedure for Pattern Analysis. *IEEE Trans. Systems Man Cybernetics*, SMC-8, 5, pp 381–389, 1978.
14. K. S. fu and S. Y. Lu, A clustering procedure for syntactic patterns, *IEEE Trans. Systems, Man Cybernetics*, SMC-7, No. 7, 537-541, 1977.
15. K. S. Fu and T. L. Booth. Grammatical inference: introduction and survey - part I and II. *IEEE Trans. Pattern Anal. and Machine Intell.*, PAMI-8, pp 343–359, 1986.
16. L. Miclet, Grammatical inference. In *Syntactic and Structural Pattern Recognition - Theory and Applications*, Scientific Publishing, pp 237–290, 1990.
17. R. Gonzalez and R. E. Woods, *Digital Image Processing*, Addison-Wesley, 1992.

A Note on Grammatical Inference of Slender Context-free Languages *

Yuji Takada[1] and Taishin Y. Nishida[2]

[1] Netmedia Lab., Fujitsu Laboratories Ltd.,
2-2-1 Momochihama, Sawara-ku, Fukuoka 814, Japan
yuji@flab.fujitsu.co.jp
[2] Faculty of Engineering, Toyama Prefectural University,
Kosugi-machi, Toyama 939-03, Japan
nishida@pu-toyama.ac.jp

Abstract. In this paper, we consider the grammatical inference problem of slender context-free languages from the point of view of cryptosystems. We show that the inference problem of slender context-free languages is not hard, and therefore, the languages have some weakness as cryptosystems. Then, we propose a hierarchical construction of families of slender languages by using some type of linear grammars and slender context-free languages. This makes the grammatical inference problem of those families harder, and therefore, the cryptosystems using our method become safer.

1 Introduction

Arising from formal language theoretic study of the classic Richelieu cryptosystem (hiding the message by shuffling it with some garbage text) in [1], in a recent series of papers [10, 9, 5, 12, 8], one investigated the family of slender languages. A language L is said to be k-thin if the cardinality of the set of all strings with length n is bounded by a constant positive integer k for every $n \geq 0$. A language is slender if it is k-thin for some positive integer k.

Such languages are useful in the cryptographic frame described in [1] in the key management. In order to rediscover the message from ciphertext, a key of the same length with the ciphertext must be used. If the set of keys is a slender language then only its grammar must be known by the legal receiver; by checking all the at most k strings of a given length, the receiver can find the correct key and decrypt. Further details can be found in [1].

In such a situation, the study of grammatical inference plays an important role; if an enemy finds an efficient grammatical inference method for slender languages then he can attack such cryptosystems easily. If a grammar which generates keys is identified then all ciphertexts can be decrypted by the enemy.

* The second author was supported by the Foundation for the Promotion of Higher Education in Toyama Prefecture.

In this paper, we consider the grammatical inference problem of slender languages. We shall show that the inference problem of slender context-free languages is not hard, that is, there is a method to identify the family of slender context-free languages efficiently. Then, we shall show one way to make the systems stronger; we shall propose a hierarchical construction of families of slender languages by using some type of linear grammars and slender context-free languages. This makes the grammatical inference problem of those families harder. Thus, the cryptosystems using our method become safer.

2 Preliminaries

We generally follow the notations and definitions of [4]. Let Σ denote an alphabet and Σ^* denote the set of all strings over Σ including the empty string λ. $lg(w)$ denotes the length of a string w. A *language* over Σ is a subset of Σ^*. We denote by $\mathcal{CFL}$ the family of context-free languages and by $\mathcal{CS}$ the family of context sensitive languages.

Let L be a language. We denote by $N(L, n)$ the number of strings of length n in L, that is,

$$N(L, n) = card(\{w \in L \mid lg(w) = n\}),$$

where $card(S)$ denotes the cardinality of the set S. For any integer $k \geq 1$, L is called *k-thin* if, for some integer n_0,

$$N(L, n) \leq k \quad \text{whenever } n \geq n_0.$$

A language is called *slender* if it is k-thin for some integer k, and is called *thin* if it is 1-thin.

A language L is said to be a *union of paired loops* (UPL) if, for some integer $k \geq 1$ and strings u_i, v_i, w_i, x_i, y_i, $1 \leq i \leq k$,

$$L = \bigcup_{i=1}^{k} \{u_i v_i^n w_i x_i^n y_i \mid n \geq 0\}.$$

Theorem 1 (Păun and Salomaa [10], Ilie [5], Raz [12]). *A language L is slender context-free if and only if L is a UPL language.*

A *linear grammar* is a quadruple $G = (N, \Sigma, P, S)$. N is a finite set of *nonterminals*. P is a finite set of *productions*; each production in P is of the form

$$\pi_n : A \rightarrow uBv \quad \text{or} \quad \pi_t : A \rightarrow w,$$

where $A, B \in N$, $u, v, w \in \Sigma^*$. π_n and π_t are labels of productions; we assume that each production is labeled by a unique label symbol and therefore uniquely referable with its label. S is a special nonterminal called the *start symbol*. We assume $N \cap \Sigma = \emptyset$ and denote $N \cup \Sigma$ by V. For two linear grammars $G_1 =$

(N_1, Σ, P_1, S) and $G_2 = (N_2, \Sigma, P_2, S)$, $G_1 \cup G_2$ denotes the linear grammar $G_1 \cup G_2 = (N_1 \cup N_2, \Sigma, P_1 \cup P_2, S)$.

Let $G = (N, \Sigma, P, S)$ be a linear grammar. We write $x \xRightarrow{\pi}_G y$ to mean that y is derived from x using the production π. Let $x_0, x_1, \ldots, x_n$ be strings over V. If

$$x_0 \xRightarrow{\pi_1}_G x_1, \; x_1 \xRightarrow{\pi_2}_G x_2, \; \ldots, \; x_{n-1} \xRightarrow{\pi_n}_G x_n,$$

then we denote $x_0 \xRightarrow{\alpha}_G x_n$, where $\alpha = \pi_1 \pi_2 \cdots \pi_n$, which is called a *derivation from x_0 to x_n with the associate string α in G*. The *language generated by G* is the set

$$L(G) = \{w \mid S \xRightarrow{\alpha}_G w \text{ and } w \in \Sigma^*\}$$

and the *Szilard language of G* is the set

$$Sz(G) = \{\alpha \mid S \xRightarrow{\alpha}_G w \text{ and } w \in \Sigma^*\}.$$

A *linear language* is the language generated by a linear grammar.

We note that every UPL language, and therefore, every slender context-free language, is a linear language.

Definition 2. Let $G = (N, \Sigma, P, S)$ be a linear grammar. A subset C of P^* is said to be a *control set on G* and

$$L(G, C) = \{w \in \Sigma^* \mid S \xRightarrow{\alpha}_G w \text{ and } \alpha \in C\}$$

is called the *language generated by G with the control set C*.

3 Inferring Slender Context-free Languages

In this section, we shall show that the grammatical inference of slender context-free languages is not a hard problem. This reveals a weakness of slender context-free languages as cryptosystems.

Proposition 3. *The family of slender context-free languages is not identifiable in the limit from positive examples only.*

Proof. Every finite language is a UPL language thus a slender context-free language. The language Σ^* is an infinite UPL language. Hence, the proposition follows from [2]. □

For a string s, $T(s)$ denotes the set of 5-tuples $\{(u, v, w, x, y) \mid s = uvwxy\}$. We note that if $lg(s) = n$ then the cardinality of $T(s)$ is bounded by $O(n^4)$. For each element $(u, v, w, x, y) \in T(s)$, $G(u, v, w, x, y) = (N, \Sigma, P, (\lambda, \lambda, \lambda, \lambda, \lambda))$ denotes the linear grammar such that $N = \{(\lambda, \lambda, \lambda, \lambda, \lambda), (u, v, w, x, y)\}$ and

$$P = \{(\lambda, \lambda, \lambda, \lambda, \lambda) \to u(u, v, w, x, y)y,$$
$$(u, v, w, x, y) \to v(u, v, w, x, y)x, (u, v, w, x, y) \to w\}$$

Clearly, $L(G(u, v, w, x, y)) = \{uv^n wx^n y \mid n \geq 0\}$.

Given a string s, the algorithm PL outputs the linear grammar

$$\bigcup_{(u,v,w,x,y) \in T(s)} G(u, v, w, x, y)$$

in the obvious way. Since the cardinality of $T(s)$ is bounded by $O(n^4)$, the time complexity of PL is bounded by $O(n^4)$, where $n = lg(s)$. For any string s, we denote by $G(PL(s))$ the linear grammar that is the output of the algorithm PL for the input s. Then, for the set S of strings, $G(PL(S))$ denotes the linear grammar $\bigcup_{s \in S} G(PL(s))$.

Definition 4. Let L be a slender context-free language. A *characteristic sample of L* is a finite set of strings

$$CS(L) = \{u_1 v_1 w_1 x_1 y_1, u_2 v_2 w_2 x_2 y_2, \ldots, u_k v_k w_k x_k y_k\}$$

such that $L = \bigcup_{i=1}^{k} \{u_i v_i^n w_i x_i^n y_i \mid n \geq 0\}$.

Lemma 5. *Every slender context-free language has a characteristic sample.*

Proof. Let L be a slender context-free language. By Theorem 1, L can be denoted by

$$L = \bigcup_{i=1}^{k} \{u_i v_i^n w_i x_i^n y_i \mid n \geq 0\}$$

for some integer $k \geq 1$. Then

$$CS(L) = \{u_1 v_1 w_1 x_1 y_1, u_2 v_2 w_2 x_2 y_2, \ldots, u_k v_k w_k x_k y_k\}$$

is a characteristic sample of L. $\qquad\square$

Lemma 6. *Let L be a slender context-free language and $CS(L)$ be a characteristic sample of L. Then $L \subset L(G(PL(CS(L))))$.*

Proof. The construction of the algorithm PL ensures that, for each element $u_i v_i w_i x_i y_i \in CS(L)$, PL outputs a linear grammar $G(PL(u_i v_i w_i x_i y_i))$ such that

$$\{u_i v_i^n w_i x_i^n y_i \mid n \geq 0\} \subset G(PL(u_i v_i w_i x_i y_i)).$$

Hence, the lemma follows. $\qquad\square$

Now we show the learnability of slender context-free languages. Our criterion for successful learning is "identification in the limit" and the efficiency is measured by "updating time" ([11]).

Theorem 7. *The family of slender context-free languages is identifiable in the limit from positive and negative examples with polynomial update time.*

Proof. We consider the following procedure.

1. Let $G_0 = (\{(\lambda, \lambda, \lambda, \lambda, \lambda)\}, \Sigma, \emptyset, (\lambda, \lambda, \lambda, \lambda, \lambda))$ and $i = 0$.
2. Read an input example s. If s is a positive example such that $s \notin L(G_i)$ then let $G_{i+1} = G_i \cup G(\mathsf{PL}(s))$. If s is a negative example such that $s \in L(G_i)$ then remove any production π such that $(\lambda, \lambda, \lambda, \lambda, \lambda) \xRightarrow[G_i]{\alpha\pi\beta} s$ from P and let G_{i+1} be the updated grammar. Otherwise, let $G_{i+1} = G_i$.
3. Set i to $i + 1$ and repeat the above procedure.

Let L be a target slender context-free language. Eventually, this procedure feeds all elements of the characteristic sample of L. Since this procedure removes only the productions that generates negative examples, by Lemma 6 there exists some i such that $L \subset L(G_i)$. Then, for any $j \geq 1$, G_{i+j} is never augmented. Eventually, this procedure feeds all negative examples and the procedure removes all unnecessary productions. Hence, the procedure identifies L in the limit.

For any positive example s with length n, the number of nonterminals and productions augmented by the procedure is bounded by $O(n^4)$. For any negative example, the number of nonterminals and productions removed by the procedure is bounded by the size of conjecture, which is bounded by a polynomial of the size of all input positive examples. Therefore, the update time is bounded by a polynomial of the size of all input examples. □

4 A Hierarchy of Slender Languages

From the point of view of cryptosystems, the results in the previous section means that if a number of secret keys enough to include a characteristic sample are revealed then the grammar which generates keys may be also revealed easily by the simple method. Especially, Lemma 6 means that negative examples are not necessary for this purpose.

In this section, we show a way to make the systems more complicated so that the simple method introduced in the previous section does not work efficiently.

A linear grammar G is called *derivation-even* if, for any two derivations $S \xRightarrow[G]{\alpha_1} w_1$ and $S \xRightarrow[G]{\alpha_2} w_2$, $lg(w_1) = lg(w_2)$ implies $lg(\alpha_1) = lg(\alpha_2)$. We note that w_1 and w_2 may be the same string.

Lemma 8. *Let G be a derivation-even linear grammar and C a k-thin context-free language. Then $L(G, C)$ is a k-thin language.*

Proof. For each integer n, let $A(G, n)$ denote the set

$$A(G, n) = \{\alpha \mid S \xRightarrow[G]{\alpha} w \text{ and } lg(w) = n\}.$$

Since G is derivation-even, all associate strings in $A(G, n)$ have the same length. Then, since C is k-thin, $A(G, n) \cap C$ has at most k number of elements, and therefore, for each n, $N(L(G, C), n)$ is bounded by k. Hence, $L(G, C)$ is k-thin. □

Let G_{de} be a collection of derivation-even linear grammars. We denote by $\mathcal{SCFL}$ the family of slender context-free languages. Then, for any integer $i \geq 1$, we inductively define the family $\mathcal{SL}_i$ of languages as

$$\mathcal{SL}_1 = \mathcal{SCFL}$$
$$\mathcal{SL}_i = \{L(G,C) \,|\, G \in G_{de} \text{ and } C \in \mathcal{SL}_{i-1}\}.$$

Proposition 9. *For any integer $i \geq 1$, every language in $\mathcal{SL}_i$ is slender.*

Proof. We prove this by induction on i. $\mathcal{SL}_1$ is the family of slender context-free languages and this ensures the base of induction. Suppose that the assertion holds for $i \geq 1$. Let G be a linear grammar in G_{de} and C a language in $\mathcal{SL}_i$. Then, by Lemma 8, $L(G,C)$ is slender. $\qquad\square$

Lemma 10. $\mathcal{SL}_i \subseteq \mathcal{SL}_{i+1}$ *for each integer $i \geq 1$.*

Proof. Let $C \in \mathcal{SL}_i$ and let Σ be the alphabet of C. Then we denote by $C\#$ the set $\{w\# \,|\, w \in C\}$, where $\#$ is a new symbol not in Σ. Since it is easy to verify that $\mathcal{SL}_i$ is closed under concatenation by a finite set, we have $C\# \in \mathcal{SL}_i$. Let $G = (\{S\}, \Sigma, P, S)$ be the linear grammar where

$$P = \{a : S \to aS \,|\, a \in \Sigma\} \cup \{\# : S \to \lambda\}.$$

Clearly G is derivation-even. Then $C = L(G,C)$ is in $\mathcal{SL}_{i+1}$. $\qquad\square$

Khabbaz [6] has shown the following hierarchy. Let $\mathbf{G}$ be a collection of all linear grammars. Then, for any integer $i \geq 1$, the family $\mathcal{L}_i$ of languages is inductively defined as

$$\mathcal{L}_1 = \mathcal{CFL}$$
$$\mathcal{L}_i = \{L(G,C) \,|\, G \in \mathbf{G} \text{ and } C \in \mathcal{L}_{i-1}\}.$$

Theorem 11 (Khabbaz). $\mathcal{L}_1 \subset \mathcal{L}_2 \subset \cdots \subset \mathcal{CS}$.

Obviously, for any integer $i \geq 1$, $\mathcal{SL}_i \subseteq \mathcal{L}_i$. Hence, we have the following.

Lemma 12. $\mathcal{SL}_i \subseteq \mathcal{CS}$ *for each integer $i \geq 1$.*

Definition 13. For each integer $i \geq 1$, let

$$L_i = \{b_1 a^n b_2 a^n \cdots a^n b_{2^i+1} \,|\, n \geq 0\}.$$

That is,

$$L_1 = \{b_1 a^n b_2 a^n b_3 \,|\, n \geq 0\},$$
$$L_2 = \{b_1 a^n b_2 a^n b_3 a^n b_4 a^n b_5 \,|\, n \geq 0\},$$
$$L_3 = \{b_1 a^n b_2 a^n b_3 a^n b_4 a^n b_5 a^n b_6 a^n b_7 a^n b_8 a^n b_9 \,|\, n \geq 0\},$$

$$\vdots \quad \vdots$$

Lemma 14. $L_i \in S\mathcal{L}_i$ *for each integer $i \geq 1$.*

Proof. Let $G_1 = (\{S, A\}, \Sigma_1, P_1, S)$ be a linear grammar where

$$\Sigma_1 = \{a, b_1, b_2, b_3\}$$

$$P_1 = \{S \rightarrow b_1 A b_3, A \rightarrow aAs, A \rightarrow b_2\}.$$

Clearly $L_1 = L(G_1) = \{b_1 a^n b_2 a^n b_3 \mid n \geq 0\}$.
 Let $G_i = (\{S\}, \Sigma_i, P_i, S)$ be a linear grammar where

$$\Sigma_i = \{a, b_1, b_2, \ldots, b_{2^i+1}\}$$

$$P_i \supset \quad \{b_j : S \rightarrow b_j S b_{2^i+2-j} \mid 1 \leq j \leq 2^{i-1}\}$$
$$\cup \{b_{2^{i-1}+1} : S \rightarrow b_{2^{i-1}+1}\}$$
$$\cup \{a : S \rightarrow aSa\}.$$

Obviously, each G_i is derivation-even.
 Inductively assume that $L_j \in S\mathcal{L}_j$ for any integer $j \geq 1$. Then it is easy to verify that $L(G_j, L_j) = L_{j+1}$. Hence $L_{j+1} \in S\mathcal{L}_{j+1}$. □

The following lemma is obtained by modifying the result in [6].

Lemma 15. *For each integer $i \geq 1$, if $L \in S\mathcal{L}_i$, there exist positive integers p, q depending on L such that if $z \in L$ and $lg(z) > p$ then*

$$z = \prod_{j=1}^{2^{i-1}} u_j v_j w_j x_j y_j, \quad \prod_{j=1}^{2^{i-1}} v_j x_j \neq \lambda, \quad lg(\prod_{j=1}^{2^{i-1}} v_j w_j x_j) < q,$$

and for any integer $n \geq 0$

$$z_n = \prod_{j=1}^{2^{i-1}} u_j v_j^n w_j x_j^n y_j$$

is an element of L, where $\prod$ denotes concatenation.

Theorem 16. $S\mathcal{L}_1 \subset S\mathcal{L}_2 \subset \cdots \subset C\mathcal{S}$.

Proof. Lemmas 10 and 12 establish the inclusions. It remains to show that these are proper.
 Let $L_p = \{a^p \mid p \text{ is a prime}\}$. It is known that $L_p \in C\mathcal{S}$. By Lemma 15 and the argument being the same as that used in showing L_p is not context-free with the use of the pumping lemma for the context-free family, $L_p \notin S\mathcal{L}_i$ for each integer $i \geq 0$.
 We shall show that $L_i \notin S\mathcal{L}_{i-1}$ for any integer $i \geq 1$. By Lemma 15, if $L_i \in S\mathcal{L}_{i-1}$ then we can pump nontrivially within 2^{i-1} bounded segments. By choosing n large enough, we can force each of these bounded segments to be contained within a substring of the form $ab_j a$. Hence at most $2^{i-1} + 1$ number of b_j's can be involved, thus affecting at most 2^{i-1} number of a^n's. Since we have 2^i

number of a^n's, some a^n's will not be changed. Thus we arrive at a contradiction because we can pump nonempty segments within some a^n's while leaving others unchanged, thereby introducing strings not in L_i. This shows $L_i \notin \mathcal{SL}_{i-1}$ and, with Lemma 14, completes the proof of the theorem. □

The inference method introduced in the previous section also works for the hierarchy in Theorem 16. First, we guess a positive integer k big enough so that $\mathcal{SL}_k$ may include the target language. When any positive example s not covered by the current conjecture is given, we construct the set of $(5 \times 2^{j-1})$-tuples $T(s, j)$ for each integer j $(1 \leq j \leq k)$

$$T(s,j) = \{(u_1, v_1, w_1, x_1, y_1, \ldots, u_{2^{j-1}}, v_{2^{j-1}}, w_{2^{j-1}}, x_{2^{j-1}}, y_{2^{j-1}}) \mid$$
$$s = u_1 v_1 w_1 x_1 y_1 \cdots u_{2^{j-1}} v_{2^{j-1}} w_{2^{j-1}} x_{2^{j-1}} y_{2^{j-1}} \}.$$

Then, for each element $(u_1, v_1, w_1, x_1, y_1, \ldots, u_{2^{j-1}}, v_{2^{j-1}}, w_{2^{j-1}}, x_{2^{j-1}}, y_{2^{j-1}}) \in T(s, j)$, we construct all linear grammars which have the productions of the form

$$A \rightarrow u_1 B y_{2^{j-1}}, A \rightarrow v_1 B x_{2^{j-1}}, A \rightarrow w_1 B w_{2^{j-1}}, A \rightarrow x_1 B v_{2^{j-1}}, A \rightarrow y_1 B u_{2^{j-1}},$$
$$\vdots$$

Obviously, this algorithm constructs a huge number of conjectures; if we consider k as a parameter then the number of conjectures is bounded by $O(2^{k-1})$. As in the previous case, positive examples are enough to find a conjecture which includes the target language. However, such a conjecture may have a huge number of incorrect keys which may lead to incorrect decryptions. Thus, from the point of view of cryptosystems, this hierarchical approach is much safer than the use of slender context-free languages only.

5 Concluding Remarks

We have shown that the family of slender context-free languages can be identified in the limit with polynomial update time. This reveals a weakness of slender context-free languages as cryptosystems. As one of ways to make the systems stronger, we have proposed a hierarchical construction of families of slender languages by using derivation-even linear grammars and slender context-free languages.

In using our method, one must be careful to chose the collection of linear grammars. As we have shown in [13] and [7], if the collection of linear grammars is exactly the collection of *even linear grammars*, then the grammatical inference problem becomes easier; the problem is reduced to the problem for regular languages. However, the method in [13] may not work for the hierarchy in this paper. In near future, we will show this.

References

1. M. Andraşiu, G. Păun, J. Dassow, and A. Salomaa. Language-theoretic problems arising from Richelieu cryptosystems. *Theoretical Comput. Sci.*, 116:339–357, 1993.
2. D. Angluin. Inductive inference of formal languages from positive data. *Information and Control*, 45:117–135, 1980.
3. J. Dassow and G. Păun. *Regulated Rewriting in Formal Language Theory*, volume 18 of *EATCS Monographs on Theoretical Computer Science*. Springer-Verlag, Berlin, 1989.
4. M. A. Harrison. *Introduction to Formal Language Theory*. Addison-Wesley, Reading, Massachusetts, 1978.
5. L. Ilie. On a conjecture about slender context-free languages. *Theoretical Comput. Sci.*, 132(1-2):427–434, 1994.
6. N. A. Khabbaz. A geometric hierarchy of languages. *Journal of Computer and System Sciences*, 8:142–157, 1974.
7. T. Koshiba, E. Mäkinen, and Y. Takada. Learning deterministic even linear languages from positive examples. To appear in *Theoretical Computer Science*.
8. T. Y. Nishida and A. Salomaa. Slender 0l languages. *Theoretical Comput. Sci.*, 158(1-2):161–176, 1996.
9. G. Păun and A. Salomaa. Closure properties of slender languages. *Theoretical Comput. Sci.*, 120, 1993.
10. G. Păun and A. Salomaa. Thin and slender languages. *Discrete Applied Mathematics*, 61(3):257–270, 1995.
11. L. Pitt. Inductive inference, DFAs, and computational complexity. In K. P. Jantke, editor, *Proceedings of 2nd Workshop on Analogical and Inductive Inference, Lecture Notes in Artificial Intelligence, 397*, pages 18–44. Springer-Verlag, 1989.
12. D. Raz. On slender context-free languages. In *STACS'95, Lecture Notes in Computer Science*, volume 900, pages 445–454. Springer-Verlag, 1995.
13. Y. Takada. A hierarchy of language families learnable by regular language learning. *Information and Computation*, 123(1):138–145, 1995.

Learning Linear Grammars from Structural Information *

Jose M. Sempere and Antonio Fos

Departamento de Sistemas Informáticos y Computación
Universidad Politécnica de Valencia, Valencia, SPAIN.
email:jsempere@dsic.upv.es

Abstract. Linear language class is a subclass of context-free language class. In this paper, we propose an algorithm to learn linear languages from structural information of their strings. We compare our algorithm with other adapted algorithm from Radhakrishnan and Nagaraja [RN1]. The proposed method and the adapted algorithm are heuristic techniques for the learning tasks, and they are useful when only positive structural data is available.

1 Introduction

In this paper we present a method to infer linear grammars from positive structural examples (*grammar skeletons*). The method that we propose is inspired in a previous work by Radhakrishnan and Nagaraja [RN1]. In their work, Radhakrishnan and Nagaraja proposed an algorithm to infer even linear grammars [AP1] from grammar skeletons under the grammatical inference paradigm [An1]. Learning of even linear grammars has been carried out by other methods from positive and negative strings as in [SG1, Ta1], while learning of context-free grammars has been carried out from skeletons and tree automaton [Ga1, RG1, Sa1]. Learning of linear grammars has not been carried out from string because of the linear grammar ambiguity problem. Anyway, we can apply the methods proposed in [Ga1, Sa1] to learn directly linear languages as context-free grammars. What we propose in this paper is to learn linear languages as linear grammars. So, we can obtain linear time parsers to carry out the test phase in opposite to those obtained in [Ga1, Sa1].

2 Basic definitions and notation

In the first place, we are going to provide several definitions which help us to understand the inference methods. The definitions of formal language theory have been obtained from [HU1, Sa2].

Definition 1. Given a grammar G=(E_A,E_T,P,S), we will say that it is a linear grammar if every production in P follows one of the forms

---

* Work partially supported by the Spanish CICYT under grant TIC-1026/92-CO2

- $A \rightarrow vBw$, where $A, B \in E_A$ and $v, w \in E_T^*$
- $A \rightarrow x$, where $A \in E_A$ and $x \in E_T^*$

It is clear that, for every linear grammar, we can obtain an equivalent grammar with its productions in the following forms

- $A \rightarrow aB$, where $A, B \in E_A$ and $a \in E_T$
- $A \rightarrow Ba$, where $A, B \in E_A$ and $a \in E_T$
- $A \rightarrow a$, where $A \in E_A$ and $a \in E_T \cup \{\lambda\}$

From now on, we will deal with linear grammars in the latter form.

Definition 2. Given a grammar G and a string $w \in \mathrm{L}(G)$, we define a *skeleton* for the string w in the grammar G as a derivation tree for the string, where the internal nodes of the tree appear without labels.

In Figure 1 you can see a skeleton for the string *aaabb* of the following grammar

- $S \rightarrow aA$
- $A \rightarrow Sb \mid aA \mid b$

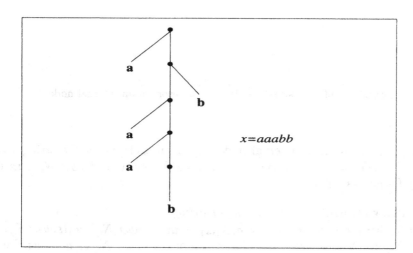

Fig. 1. An example of a skeleton for the string *x=aaabb*.

Definition 3. Given a string w, we denote by *Ter(w)* the set of symbols that appear in the string w.

In what follows, we are going to define several concepts that can distinguish every internal node in the skeleton from the others. So, we suppose that the internal nodes of the skeleton are ordered, and every node is denoted by N_{ij}. For every internal node, we can associate the pair $< x, y >$ or the singleton $< x >$ depending on the number of sons that the node has. If it has two sons then we associate to it the pair, otherwise the singleton. It is obvious that every internal node has two sons or only one. In Figure 2 we can see the different situations that can be held. If the node has a single son, then it is a terminal symbol and we associate to the internal node the singleton $< a >$, where a is the terminal symbol label, otherwise the node has two sons, that is, a terminal symbol and other internal node, and we associate to the node the pair $< N_{ij+1}, a >$ or $< a, N_{ij+1} >$ depending on the location of the terminal symbol label a.

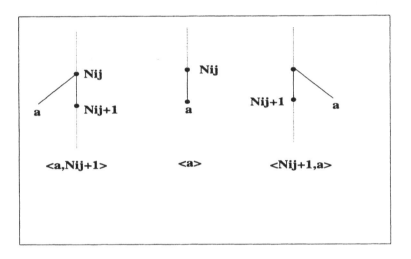

Fig. 2. Different situations for the succesors of an internal node.

Definition 4. Given an internal node N_{ij} of an skeleton for the string x, we define the left substring of the node, and we denote it by $lsubst(N_{ij})$, as the string formed as follows

1. Initially $lsubst(N_{ij}) = \lambda$ (*the empty string*).
2. If N_{ij} has the associated pair $< a, N_{ij+1} >$, then $lsubst(N_{ij})=a(lsubst(N_{ij+1}))$.
3. If N_{ij} has the associated singleton $< a >$ or the pair $< N_{ij+1}, a >$ then finish.

Definition 5. Given an internal node N_{ij} of an skeleton for the string x, we define the right substring of the node, and we denote it by $rsubst(N_{ij})$, as the string formed as follows

1. Initially $rsubst(N_{ij}) = \lambda$ (*the empty string*).
2. If N_{ij} has the associated pair $< N_{ij+1}, a >$, then $rsubst(N_{ij})=(rsubst(N_{ij+1}))a$.

3. If N_{ij} has the associated singleton $< a >$ or the pair $< a, N_{ij+1} >$ then finish.

We denote by $\mid x \mid$ the length of the string x.

Definition 6. For every internal node N_{ij} of an skeleton for the string x, we define the set of left successors of the node, and we denote it by $lsucc(N_{ij})$ as follows

- Initially $lsucc(N_{ij}) = \oslash$ (*the empty set*).
- If N_{ij} has the associated pair $< a, N_{ij+1} >$ then $lsucc(N_{ij}) = \{N_{ij+1}\} \cup lsucc(N_{ij+1})$.
- If N_{ij} has the associated singleton $< a >$ or the pair $< N_{ij+1}, a >$ then finish.

Definition 7. For every internal node N_{ij} of an skeleton for the string x, we define the set of right successors of the node, and we denote it by $rsucc(N_{ij})$ as follows

- Initially $rsucc(N_{ij}) = \oslash$ (*the empty set*).
- If N_{ij} has the associated pair $< N_{ij+1}, a >$ then $rsucc(N_{ij}) = \{N_{ij+1}\} \cup rsucc(N_{ij+1})$.
- If N_{ij} has the associated singleton $< a >$ or the pair $< a, N_{ij+1} >$ then finish.

From the definitions above, we can give a more global definition by summarizing the left and the right substring into the context of the string.

Definition 8. Given an internal node N_{ij} of an skeleton for the string x such that $\forall 1 \leq k < j \ N_{ij} \notin lsucc(N_{ik}) \cup rsucc(N_{ik})$, we define the context of the node and we denote it by $context(N_{ij})$ as follows

- If the node has the associated pair $< N_{ij+1}, a >$, then the context is defined by the tuple $context(N_{ij}) = < Right, rsubst(N_{ij}), Ter(rsubst(N_{ij})) >$.
- If the node has the associated pair $< a, N_{ij+1} >$, then the context is defined by the tuple $context(N_{ij}) = < Left, lsubst(N_{ij}), Ter(lsubst(N_{ij})) >$.
- If the node has associated the singleton $< a >$, then the context is defined by the tuple $context(N_{ij}) = < Final, a, \{a\} >$.

Finally, we can define the *projection functions* π_i of a tuple $(x_1, x_2, \ldots, x_n)$ as $\pi_j((x_1, x_2, \ldots, x_n)) = x_j$.

3 An adaptation of a previous algorithm

Our first approach to learn linear grammars has been done by adapting Radhakrishnan and Nagaraja's algorithm [RN1]. The adaptation has been quite easy, given that, from the linear skeletons we can obtain even linear ones, by creating new right or left sons of an internal node. We have labeled these new nodes with the special symbol $*$. In figure 3, we can see an example of the transformation applied to the original skeleton.

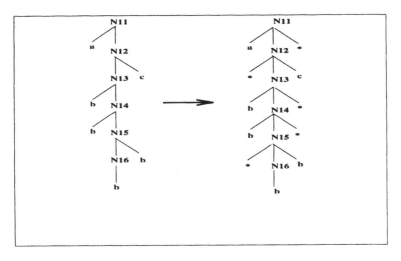

Fig. 3. Skeleton transformation for the adapted algorithm.

From this transformation, the application of the algorithm is made directly. After applying the algorithm, we can obtain an even linear grammar with an special terminal symbol $*$, which can be deleted in order to obtain a linear grammar. Let us see an example of how to apply the learning algorithm.

Taking the following target linear grammar

$$S \to aB \qquad B \to Cc \qquad C \to bD$$
$$D \to bE \mid bC \qquad E \to Fb \qquad F \to b \mid c$$

The input sample is the set $\{(a((b(b((b)b)))c)), (a((b(b(b(b((c)b)))))c))\}$, which after be adapted to become even linear strings is $\{a*bb*bb**c*, a*bbbb*cb****c*\}$

Then we can calculate all the sets defined in the algorithm [RN1]

$N_{11} =< \lambda, \lambda, (a, b, c) >$	$NS_1 = \{N_{11}, N_{21}\}$	$S_1 = \{abbbc, abbbbcbc\}$
$N_{12} =< a, \lambda, (b, c) >$	$NS_2 = \{N_{12}, N_{22}\}$	$S_2 = \{bbbc, bbbbcbc\}$
$N_{13} =< a, c, (b) >$	$NS_3 = \{N_{13}\}$	$S_3 = \{bbb\}$
$N_{14} =< ab, c, (b) >$	$NS_4 = \{N_{14}\}$	$S_4 = \{bb\}$
$N_{15} =< ab, bc, (b) >$	$NS_5 = \{N_{15}\}$	$S_5 = \{b\}$
$N_{21} =< \lambda, \lambda, (a, b, c) >$	$NS_6 = \{N_{23}\}$	$S_6 = \{bbbbcb\}$
$N_{22} =< a, \lambda, (b, c) >$	$NS_7 = \{N_{24}\}$	$S_7 = \{bbbcb\}$
$N_{23} =< a, c, (b, c) >$	$NS_8 = \{N_{25}\}$	$S_8 = \{bbcb\}$
$N_{24} =< ab, c, (b, c) >$	$NS_9 = \{N_{26}\}$	$S_9 = \{bcb\}$
$N_{25} =< abb, c, (b, c) >$	$NS_{10} = \{N_{27}\}$	$S_{10} = \{cb\}$
$N_{26} =< abbb, c, (b, c) >$	$NS_{11} = \{N_{28}\}$	$S_{11} = \{c\}$
$N_{27} =< abbbb, c, (b, c) >$		
$N_{28} =< abbbb, bc, (b, c) >$		

After this process, the inferred even linear grammar obtained by the algorithm is the following one

$$
\begin{array}{llll}
1 \rightarrow a2* & 4 \rightarrow *5b & 7 \rightarrow b8* & 10 \rightarrow 11b* \\
2 \rightarrow *3c \mid *6c & 5 \rightarrow b & 8 \rightarrow b9* & 11 \rightarrow c \\
3 \rightarrow b4* & 6 \rightarrow b7* & 9 \rightarrow b10*
\end{array}
$$

and, by deleting the special terminal symbol $*$, we obtain the linear grammar

$$
\begin{array}{llll}
1 \rightarrow a2 & 4 \rightarrow 5b & 7 \rightarrow b8 & 10 \rightarrow 11b \\
2 \rightarrow 3c \mid 6c & 5 \rightarrow b & 8 \rightarrow b9 & 11 \rightarrow c \\
3 \rightarrow b4 & 6 \rightarrow b7 & 9 \rightarrow b10
\end{array}
$$

4   An algorithm to learn linear grammars

In what follows, we are going to propose another algorithm to obtain linear grammars from positive structural examples. The algorithm is inspired in that proposed by Radhakrishnan and Nagaraja in [RN1], in the sense that we use a similar notation and concepts like in their work. The basic idea is to observe similar context nodes, to label them with the same nonterminal symbol and to construct the grammar from the labeled skeletons or derivation trees.

- **Input** A non empty positive sample of skeletons S^+.
- **Output** A linear grammar that generalize the sample.
- **Method**
  - **STEP 1** To enumerate the internal nodes of every skeleton according to the following notation. For the j-th skeleton, to start to enumerate every skeleton by levels from the root to the last level $N_{j1}, N_{j2}, \ldots$
  - **STEP 2** To calculate the context of every node N_{ij} according to definition 8.
  - **STEP 3** To define a relation between nodes $\equiv$ as follows $N_{ij} \equiv N_{pq}$ iff $\pi_1(context(N_{ij})) = \pi_1(context(N_{pq}))$ and $\pi_3(context(N_{ij})) = \pi_3(context(N_{pq}))$ With the defined relation, to form the classes of nodes NS_k by enumerating the classes for $k = 1, 2, \ldots$. The nodes without context do not belong to any class.

(Creation of nonterminal symbols of the grammar)
$\forall NS_k$ **do**

  - **STEP 4** If $\forall N_{ij} \in NS_k \; \pi_1(context(N_{ij})) = Final$ then $N_{ij} = A_{k,0}$.
  - **STEP 5** If NS_k only contains a single node N_{ij}, with $\mid \pi_2(context(N_{ij})) \mid = m$ then $N_{ij+p} = A_{k,p} \forall 0 \le p \le m - 1$.
  - **STEP 6** If NS_k contains more than one node then
    - **STEP 6.1** To select N_{ij} such that $\mid \pi_2(context(N_{ij})) \mid = m$ is minimal. Then $N_{ij+p} = A_{k,p} \forall 0 \le p \le m - 1$.
    - **STEP 6.2** To eliminate the node N_{ij} of STEP 6.1 from the set NS_k. If NS_k is a singleton then go to STEP 6.3, else go to STEP 6.1.
    - **STEP 6.3** Take the only node N_{ij} of the set NS_k with $\mid \pi_2(context(N_{ij})) \mid = n$ and take the value m of STEP 6.1. If $n \le m$ then $N_{ij+p} = A_{k,p} \forall 0 \le p \le n - 1$, else $N_{ij+p} = A_{k,(p\|m)} \; \forall 0 \le p \le n - 1$ (where $p\|m$ denotes p module m).
  - **STEP 7** To rename the labels of all the skeleton roots as S, which will be the axiom of the grammar.
  - **STEP 8** To build a linear grammar as result of the derivation trees constructed by putting labels to the nodes. If the skeleton for the empty string belongs to S^+ then to add the production $S \rightarrow \lambda$ to the set P.

An example.

Taking the following target linear grammar

$S \rightarrow aB$ $B \rightarrow Cc$ $C \rightarrow bD$

$D \rightarrow bE \mid bC$ $E \rightarrow Fb$ $F \rightarrow b \mid c$

The input sample is the set $\{(a((b(b((b)b)))c)), (a((b(b(b(b((c)b)))))c))\}$ of figure 4.

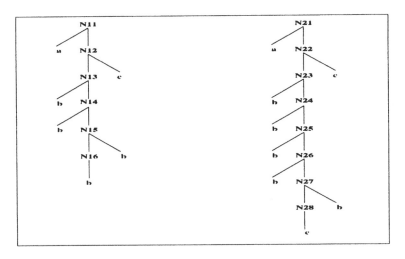

Fig. 4. Input sample for the proposed algorithm.

We can calculate the contexts of every node in the following way

$$
\begin{array}{lll}
N_{11} =< Left, a, \{a\} > & N_{22} =< Right, c, \{c\} > & NS_1 = \{N_{11}, N_{21}\} \\
N_{12} =< Right, c, \{c\} > & N_{23} =< Left, bbbb, \{b\}) > & NS_2 = \{N_{12}, N_{22}\} \\
N_{13} =< Left, bb, \{b\} > & N_{27} =< Right, b, \{b\} > & NS_3 = \{N_{13}, N_{23}\} \\
N_{15} =< Right, b, \{b\} > & N_{28} =< Final, c, \{c\} > & NS_4 = \{N_{15}, N_{27}\} \\
N_{16} =< Final, b, \{b\} > & & NS_5 = \{N_{16}\} \\
N_{21} =< Left, a, \{a\} > & & NS_6 = \{N_{28}\}
\end{array}
$$

After this process, the inferred linear grammar obtained by the algorithm is the following one

$S \rightarrow aA_{2,0}$ $A_{3,1} \rightarrow bA_{4,0} \mid bA_{3,0}$ $A_{6,0} \rightarrow c$

$A_{2,0} \rightarrow A_{3,0}c$ $A_{4,0} \rightarrow A_{5,0}b \mid A_{6,0}b$

$A_{3,0} \rightarrow bA_{3,1}$ $A_{5,0} \rightarrow b$

5   Acknowledgements

We would like to thank Professor G. Nagaraja's interest and all the mail that we have interchanged about this work. We would like to thank Dr. Pedro García's original contribution to the transformation of linear skeletons to even linear skeletons.

References

[AP1]   Amar, V., Putzolu, G.: On a Family of Linear Grammars. Information and Control **7** (1964) 283-291.

[An1]   Angluin, D., Smith, C.: Inductive Inference : Theory and Methods. Computing Surveys **15** No. 3 (1983) 237-269.

[Ga1]   García, P.: Learning K-Testable Tree Sets from positive data. Technical Report DSIC-II/46/93. Universidad Politécnica de Valencia. (1993)

[HU1]   Hopcroft, J., Ullman, J.: Introduction to Automata Theory, Languages and Computation. Addison-Wesley Publishing Company. (1979)

[RN1]   Radhakrishnan, V., Nagaraja, G.: Inference of Even Linear Grammars and its Application to Picture Description Languages. Pattern Recognition **21** No. 1 (1988) 55-62.

[RG1]   Ruiz, J., García, P.: The Algorithms RT and k-TTI : A First Comparison. Lecture Notes in Artificial Intelligence. Proceedings of the Second International Colloquium on Grammatical Inference ICGI94. Ed. Springer-Verlag. (1994) 180-188.

[Sa1]   Sakakibara, Y.: Efficient Learning of Context-Free Grammars from Positive Structural Examples. Information and Computation **97** (1992) 23-60.

[Sa2]   Salomaa, A.: Formal Languages. Academic Press. (1973)

[SG1]   Sempere, J., P. García, P.: A Characterization of Even Linear Languages and its Application to the Learning Problem. Lecture Notes in Artificial Intelligence. Proceedings of the Second International Colloquium on Grammatical Inference ICGI94. Ed. Springer-Verlag. (1994) 38-44.

[Ta1]   Takada, Y.: Grammatical Inference of Even Linear Languages based on Control Sets. Information Processing Letters **28** No.4 (1988) 193-199.

Learning of Context-Sensitive Language Acceptors Through Regular Inference and Constraint Induction

René Alquézar[1], Alberto Sanfeliu[2] and Jordi Cueva[3]

[1] Dept. LSI, Universitat Politècnica de Catalunya (UPC),
Diagonal 647, 8a, 08028 Barcelona, Spain
[2] Institut de Robòtica i Informàtica Industrial, UPC-CSIC, Barcelona
[3] Institut de Cibernètica, UPC, Barcelona
alquezar@lsi.upc.es, sanfeliu@ic.upc.es, cueva@ic.upc.es

Abstract. Recently, Augmented Regular Expressions (AREs) have been proposed as a formalism to describe and recognize a non-trivial class of context-sensitive languages (CSLs), that covers planar shapes with symmetries [1, 2]. AREs augment the expressive power of Regular Expressions (REs) by including a set of constraints, that involve the number of instances in a string of the operands of the star operations of an RE. A general method to infer AREs from string examples has been reported [2] that is based on a regular grammatical inference (RGI) step followed by a constraint induction process. This approach avoids the difficulty of learning context-sensitive grammars. In this paper, a specific method for learning AREs from positive examples is described, in which the RGI step is carried out by training a recurrent neural network for a prediction task [3] and extracting a DFA from the network dynamics [4]. The ARE learning method has been applied to the inference of a set of eight test CSLs, and good experimental results have been obtained.

1 Introduction

In order to extend the potential of application of the syntactic approach to pattern recognition, the efficient use of models capable of describing context-sensitive languages (CSLs) is needed, since usually, the involved patterns contain structural relationships that cannot be represented by regular or context-free languages. Moreover, learning such models from examples is an interesting challenge both for theoretical and practical purposes. Context-sensitive grammars (CSGs) [5] are not a good choice, since their parsing is computationally expensive and there is a lack of methods to infer them.

Indeed, work on CSL learning is extremely scarce in the literature of grammatical inference (GI). Twenty years ago, Chou and Fu [6] proposed a semi-automated heuristic procedure for inferring augmented transition networks (ATNs), which are powerful models capable of describing CSLs. However, no other work on ATN learning is known since then. On the other hand, some algorithms have been proposed to infer pattern languages from examples [7]. Pattern languages provide a limited mechanism to introduce some context influences [7], but they cannot describe even simple context-sensitive structures such as rectangles. Recently, Takada has shown that a hierarchy of language families that are properly contained in the family of CSLs (which includes even-linear grammars) can be learned using regular GI algorithms [8]. Nevertheless, the class of learnable CSLs seems to be rather restricted and does not cover most of the typical objects in pattern recognition tasks.

More recently, *Augmented Regular Expressions* (AREs) have been proposed by the authors as a formalism to describe and recognize a class of CSLs, that covers planar shapes with symmetries and other complex patterns [1, 2]. An ARE $\tilde{R}$ is formed by a regular expression R, in which the stars are replaced by natural-valued variables, called *star variables*, and these variables are related through a finite number of constraints (linear equations). Hence, regular expressions (REs) are reduced to AREs with no constraint among the star variables. A general approach to infer AREs from string examples has been reported elsewhere [2], that is based on a regular GI step followed by an inductive process which tries to discover the maximal number of linear constraints.

Therefore, a specific method for learning AREs can be obtained simply by selecting an RGI algorithm [9-11] for the former step. However, unless a teacher is available to classify the negative examples, it cannot be determined which negative examples should be rejected by the inferred RE (or DFA) and which ones should be accepted because they are due to constraint insatisfaction. This problem can be avoided by choosing an RGI method that only uses positive examples. Although several such methods exist [9], all of them are based on a pre-established heuristic criterion. As an alternative, recurrent neural networks (RNNs) have been shown to be able to learn some regular languages from just positive examples if they are trained to predict the next symbol in the positive strings [3]. Furthermore, clustering techniques may be used to extract from the trained RNN a DFA that is approximately emulated by the net [4].

In this paper, a specific method to infer AREs from positive examples is presented, in which the RGI step is carried out by training a second-order RNN for the next-symbol prediction task and extracting afterwards a DFA through hierarchical clustering [4]. This method has been applied to the inference of a set of eight test CSLs associated with ideal models of real patterns. The experimental results obtained show the feasibility of this approach to CSL learning.

2 Augmented Regular Expressions (AREs)

Let $\Sigma = \{a_1, ..., a_m\}$ be an *alphabet* and let λ denote the *empty string*. The *regular expressions (REs) over* Σ and the languages that they describe are defined recursively as follows: $\emptyset$ and λ are REs that describe the empty set and the set $\{\lambda\}$, respectively; for each $a_i \in \Sigma$ $(1 \leq i \leq m)$, a_i is a RE that describes the set $\{a_i\}$; if P and Q are REs describing the languages L_P and L_Q, respectively, then $(P + Q)$, (PQ), and (P^*) are REs that describe the languages $L_P \cup L_Q$, $L_P L_Q$ and L_P^*, respectively. By convention, the precedence of the operations in decreasing order is $*$ (star), (concatenation), $+$ (union). This precedence and the associativity of the concatenation and union operations allows to omit many parentheses in writing an RE. The language described by an RE R is denoted $L(R)$. Two REs P and Q are said to be *equivalent*, denoted by $P = Q$, if $L(P) = L(Q)$. REs and finite-state automata (FSA) are alternative representations of the class of regular languages, and there are algorithms to find an RE equivalent to a given FSA and viceversa [12].

Let R be an RE including ns star symbols ($ns \geq 0$). The set of *star variables* associated with R is an ordered set of natural-valued variables $V = \{v_1, ..., v_{ns}\}$, which are associated one-to-one with the star symbols that appear in R in a left-to-right scan. For $v_i, v_j \in V$, we say that v_i *contains* v_j iff the operand of the star associated with v_i in R includes the star corresponding to v_j; and we say v_i *directly-contains* v_j iff v_i *contains* v_j and there is no $v_k \in V$ such that v_i *contains* v_k and v_k *contains* v_j. The *star tree* $T = (N, E, r)$ associated with R is a general tree in which the root node r is a special symbol, the set of nodes is $N = V \cup \{r\}$, and the set of edges E is defined by the containment relationships of the star variables: (i) $\forall v_i \in V : (\neg \exists v_k \in V, v_k \text{ contains } v_i) \implies (r, v_i) \in E$; (ii) $\forall v_i, v_j \in V, i \neq j : v_i \text{ directly-contains } v_j \implies (v_i, v_j) \in E$. A star variable $v \in V$ can take as value any natural number, whose meaning is the number of consecutive times (cycles) the operand of the corresponding star (an RE) is instantiated while matching a given string. In such a case, we say that the star variable is *instantiated*. Given a string $s \in L(R)$, where R is the RE from which V has been defined, a data structure $SI_s(V) = \{SI_s(v_1), ...SI_s(v_{ns})\}$, called the set of *star instances* (of the star variables in V for s), can be built during the process of parsing s by R. Each member of the set $SI_s(V)$ is a list of lists containing the instances of a particular star variable:

$$\forall i \in [1..ns] : \quad SI_s(v_i) = (l_1^i \ ... \ l_{nlists(i)}^i) \quad \text{and} \quad nlists(i) \geq 0$$

$$\forall i \in [1..ns] \ \forall j \in [1..nlists(i)] : l_j^i = (e_{j1}^i \ ... \ e_{j(nelems(i,j))}^i) \quad \text{and} \quad nelems(i,j) \geq 1$$

The star instances stored in $SI_s(V)$ are organized according to the containment relationships described by the star tree T. To this end, each list l_j^i is associated with two pointers $father\_list(l_j^i)$ and $father\_elem(l_j^i)$ that identify the instance of the father star variable from which the instances of v_i in l_j^i are derived. All the star variables that are brothers in T will have the same structure of instances, provided that a special value, say -1, is stored when a star variable is not instantiated during a cycle of an instance of its father. Fig.1 shows an example of the set $SI_s(V)$ resulting from the parse of a string by an RE. Two efficient algorithms for *unambiguous*[1] RE parsing that construct the star instances structure have been reported [1].

Given a star tree T, a set of star instances $SI_s(V)$ for a string s, and two nodes $v_i, v_j \in V$, we say that v_i is a *degenerated ancestor* of v_j (for s) iff v_i is an ancestor of v_j in T and for each instance of v_i in $SI_s(v_i)$ all the values of the instances of v_j in $SI_s(v_j)$ that are derived from it are constant. By definition, the root r is a non-degenerated ancestor of any other node v_j. Let $v_i \in V \cup \{r\}$, $v_j \in V$; we say that v_i is the *housing ancestor* of v_j (for s) iff v_i is the *nearest non-degenerated*

---

[1] A RE R is *ambiguous* if there exists a string $s \in L(R)$ for which more than one parse of s by R can be made.

ancestor of v_j (for s). When a node is not housed by its father, then its redundant instances can be collapsed into the same list structure of its father, and this can be repeated until the housing ancestor is reached.

An *Augmented Regular Expression* (or ARE) is a four-tupla $(R, V, T, \mathcal{L})$, where R is a regular expression over an alphabet Σ, V is its associated set of *star variables*, T is its associated *star tree*, and $\mathcal{L}$ is a set of independent linear relations $\{l_1, ..., l_{nc}\}$, that partition the set V into two subsets V^{ind}, V^{dep} of independent and dependent star variables, respectively; this is

$$l_i \text{ is } v_i^{dep} = a_{i1}v_1^{ind} + .. + a_{ij}v_j^{ind} + .. + a_{i(ni)}v_{ni}^{ind} + a_{i0}, \text{ for } 1 \le i \le nc$$

where ni and nc are the number of independent and dependent star variables, respectively, $ns = nc + ni$, and the coefficients a_{ij} are always rational numbers.

$R = (a(b(ce^*c + df^*d)^*)^*)^*$ $R(V/*) = (a(b(ce^{v_1}c + df^{v_2}d)^{v_3})^{v_4})^{v_5}$
$V = \{v_1, v_2, v_3, v_4, v_5\}$ $T = (V \cup r, \{(r, v_5), (v_5, v_4), (v_4, v_3), (v_3, v_1), (v_3, v_2)\}, r)$

$s = abccdffdcecbddbdfdceecabceeec$

$SI_s(v_5) = ((2)^{\{-1,-1\}})$ $SI_s(v_1) = ((0\ -1\ 1)^{\{1,1\}}\ (-1)^{\{1,2\}}\ (-1\ 2)^{\{1,3\}}\ (3)^{\{2,1\}})$
$SI_s(v_4) = ((3\ 1)^{\{1,1\}})$ $SI_s(v_2) = ((-1\ 2\ -1)^{\{1,1\}}\ (0)^{\{1,2\}}\ (1\ -1)^{\{1,3\}}\ (-1)^{\{2,1\}})$
$SI_s(v_3) = ((3\ 1\ 2)^{\{1,1\}}\ (1)^{\{1,2\}})$

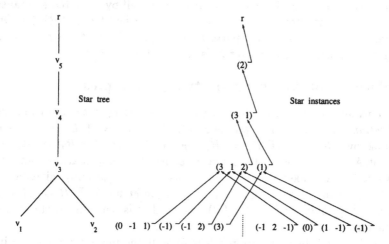

Fig. 1 *An example of star instances data structure.*

Now, let rewrite each constraint $l_i \in \mathcal{L}$ by removing all the terms of independent variables with coefficient zero in the r.h.s. of the equations, i.e. l_i is $v_i^{dep} = a_{i1}v_1' + .. + a_{il}v_{k_i}' + a_{i0}$, for $1 \le i \le nc$, such that $\forall j \in [1, k_i] : a_{ij} \ne 0$, and let $v_c \in V$ be the *deepest common ancestor* in T of the nodes $\{v_i^{dep}, v_1', ..., v_{k_i}'\}$. Then, we say that star instances $SI_s(V)$ *satisfy* the constraint $l_i \in \mathcal{L}$ iff

i) the *housing ancestors* (for s) of the nodes $\{v_i^{dep}, v_1', ..., v_{k_i}'\}$ are either v_c or an ancestor of v_c, or they satisfy a strict equality constraint, and

ii) the linear relation l_i is met by the corresponding instances of $\{v_i^{dep}, v_1', ..., v_{k_i}'\}$ that are derived for each instance of v_c.

The first condition implies structural similarity of instance lists and the second one requires the equation satisfaction. The star instances $SI_s(V)$ *satisfy* $\mathcal{L}$ iff $SI_s(V)$ satisfy each constraint $l_i \in \mathcal{L}$, for $1 \leq i \leq nc$. Finally, let $\tilde{R} = (R, V, \mathcal{T}, \mathcal{L})$ be an ARE over Σ, the language $L(\tilde{R})$ represented by $\tilde{R}$ is defined as $L(\tilde{R}) = \{\alpha \in \Sigma^* \mid \alpha \in L(R)$ and there exists a parse of α by R in which $SI_\alpha(V)$ *satisfy* $\mathcal{L}\}$. Hence, the recognition of a string s as belonging to $L(\tilde{R})$ can be clearly divided in two steps: parsing s by R, and if success, checking the satisfaction of constraints $\mathcal{L}$ by the star instances $SI_s(V)$ that result from the parse. If R is *unambiguous*, a unique parse and set of star instances $SI_s(V)$ is possible for each $s \in L(R)$, and therefore a single satisfaction problem must be analysed to test whether $s \in L(\tilde{R})$. An algorithm for constraint testing has been reported [1], that runs in $O(|\mathcal{L}| \cdot height(\mathcal{T}) \cdot |V| \cdot I(SI_s(V)))$, where $I(SI_s(V)) = \max_{i=1,|V|} \sum_{j=1}^{nlists(i)} nelems(i,j)$ is the maximal number of instances of a star variable yielded by parsing s.

AREs permit to describe a class of CSLs by defining a set of constraints that reduce the extension of the underlying regular language (see Fig.2). A very simple example is the language of rectangles described by the ARE $\tilde{R}_1 = (R_1, V_1, \mathcal{T}_1, \mathcal{L}_1)$, with $R_1(V_1/*) = aa^{v_1}bb^{v_2}aa^{v_3}bb^{v_4}$ and $\mathcal{L}_1 = \{v_3 = v_1, v_4 = v_2\}$. However, quite more complex languages with an arbitrary level of star embedment in the RE can be described as well by the ARE formalism. It has been proved that not all the CSLs can be described by an ARE [2]. On the other hand, AREs cover all the pattern languages [7], but the size of an ARE describing a pattern language over Σ is exponential in $|\Sigma|$ [2].

3 Inference of AREs from String Examples

Let us consider the problem of learning AREs. A strong statement concerns the *identification problem*: given a sample $S = (S^+, S^-)$ of a CSL L over Σ described by un unknown *target* ARE $\tilde{R}_T = (R_T, V_T, \mathcal{T}_T, \mathcal{L}_T)$, identify $\tilde{R}_T$, or at least an equivalent ARE $\tilde{R}_T'$, from S (and maybe some other information about $\tilde{R}_T$ or L, if available). A weaker statement concerns *data compatibility*: given a sample (S^+, S^-) of an unknown language L over Σ, *infer* an ARE $\tilde{R} = (R, V, \mathcal{T}, \mathcal{L})$ such that $S^+ \subseteq L(\tilde{R})$ and $S^- \cap L(\tilde{R}) = \emptyset$, and $\tilde{R}$ is determined through some *heuristic* bias.

A possible ARE learning approach is to split the inductive inference in two main stages: inferring the underlying RE R (where $L(R) \supseteq L$), and afterwards, inducing the constraints $\mathcal{L}$ included in the inferred ARE. A nice property of this approach is that if the RE R_T is identified in the first stage, then the target ARE $\tilde{R}_T$ can be identified in the second stage (in the limit) by inducing the maximal number of constraints satisfied by the positive examples.

Unfortunately, there is also a significant drawback. In order to infer the RE R correctly, we should be able to partition the negative sample S^- in the two subsets S_0^- and $(S^- - S_0^-)$, characterized by $S_0^- \cap L(R) = \emptyset$ and $(S^- - S_0^-) \subseteq L(R)$. Fig.2 displays the situation for a target ARE $\tilde{R}$ with k

constraints: starting with the language described by the underlying RE, each time an additional constraint of the ARE is imposed the extension of the represented language disminishes up to reach the target language. Thus, unless a teacher is available to partition the negative examples, or it is guaranteed that $S^- = S_0^-$, it is "dangerous" to supply S^- to the RGI method, since typically, an overfitting of the positive examples will occur. Consequently, a heuristic method based only on the positive examples will be generally preferred for the regular inference step.

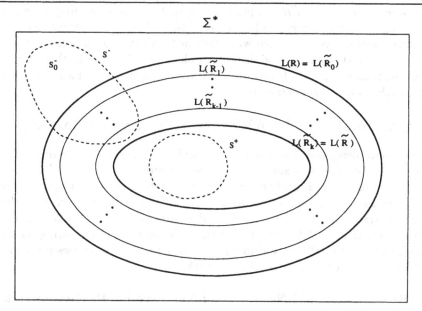

Fig. 2 *Representation of the languages involved in the ARE learning problem.*

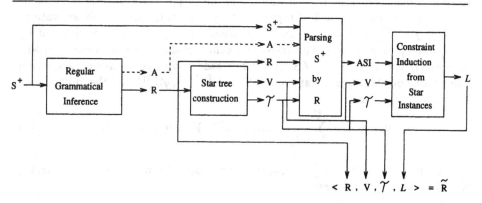

Fig. 3 *Block diagram of a general method to learn AREs from positive examples.*

The data flow of the process followed to infer an ARE from positive examples is depicted in Fig.3. The regular inference procedure must return an unambiguous RE R, and possibly, it may also yield a DFA A from which R has been obtained. Once the RE R is determined, the associated *star variables* V and *star tree* T are formed. Then, an "array of star instances" ASI is built containing the information recorded from parsing all the positive examples. The complexity of parsing a string s by an RE R is $O(|s| \cdot |R|)$, but if the equivalent DFA A is also available, a more efficient parsing algorithm can be applied [1]. Finally, the gathered star instances are analysed to induce the set of linear equations $\mathcal{L}$ of the inferred ARE $\tilde{R}$. If $\tilde{R}$ accepts a string in S^-, a new run may be started now giving some negative examples to a RGI procedure that searches consistent solutions. Several such runs, each with more negative examples, could be needed to obtain an ARE consistent with the sample $S = (S^+, S^-)$. In this case, the aforementioned overfitting behavior could arise, but data compatibility of the inferred ARE would be guaranteed.

4 A Method to Infer AREs from Positive Examples

In order to implement and test the ARE learning scheme, a specific method has to be chosen for the RGI step. As discussed before, a RGI method that uses only positive examples is preferred at first. The particular method that has been selected in the present work for the regular inference phase consists of three steps: i) to train a second-order RNN for the next-symbol prediction task, ii) to extract afterwards a DFA from the net through hierarchical clustering, and iii) to perform finally a DFA to RE mapping. Then the rest of processes shown in Fig.3 have been carried out to infer the ARE.

4.1 Recurrent Neural Network and Next-Symbol Prediction Task

We use a network architecture called Augmented Second-Order Recurrent Neural Network (or ASORN, for short). An ASORN has M inputs, a single-layer of N (second-order) recurrent hidden units, and an output layer of P non-recurrent units. The values at time t of inputs x_i ($1 \leq i \leq M$), hidden unit activations y_j ($1 \leq j \leq N$), and output unit activations o_l ($1 \leq l \leq P$) are denoted by x_i^t, y_j^t and o_l^t, respectively. The activation values of the recurrent units represent collectively the state of the ASORN. Each hidden unit computes its activation value based on the current state vector $S^t = [y_1^{t-1}, ..., y_N^{t-1}]^T$ and the input vector $I^t = [x_1^t, ..., x_M^t]^T$ as

$$y_k^t = g_1 \left(\sum_{i=1}^{M} \sum_{j=1}^{N} w_{kij} \, x_i^t \, y_j^{t-1} \right) \quad \text{for } 1 \leq k \leq N. \tag{1}$$

The output vector $O^t = [o_1^t, ..., o_P^t]^T$ is computed from the next-state vector S^{t+1} in a feed-forward way:

$$o_l^t = g_2 \left(w_{l0} + \sum_{j=1}^{N} w_{lj} y_j^t \right) \quad \text{for } 1 \leq l \leq P. \tag{2}$$

$\mathbf{W}_k = [w_{k11}, ..., w_{kMN}]^T$ and $\mathbf{W}_l = [w_{l0}, ..., w_{lN}]^T$ denote the vectors of weights of hidden and output units, respectively. Concerning the activation functions, an antisymmetric logarithm is used for g_1 and a sigmoid function is used for g_2.

For the next-symbol prediction task, both M and P equal the number of different symbols that can appear in the strings plus one (for a special end-of-string symbol). The positive examples are processed one symbol at each time step. Using a local encoding, the current symbol is introduced through the input signals, and the code of the next symbol is given as target for the output units. The network is trained using a gradient-descent learning algorithm to update the weights (e.g. back-propagation through time). The set of training examples is supplied to the net several times (epochs) up to reach a predetermined number of epochs, which must be large enough to let the network arrive at a minimum of the error function, where the total prediction error on the training set stabilizes.

4.2 DFA Extraction from a Trained Recurrent Network

After the training phase, the recurrent layer of the ASORN is supposed to have inferred approximately the state transition function of a DFA, while the output layer is supposed to have learned a function that, for each state, gives the probabilities of each symbol to be the next symbol in a valid string. To this end, it is assumed that the net has developed its own states in the form of clusters of the hidden unit activation vectors. Consequently, a clustering technique may be used to extract from the trained ASORN a DFA that is approximately emulated by the net. Initially, single-point clusters are associated with each state of the prefix tree of the sample. Then a hierarchical clustering, based on inter-cluster minimal distance, permits to guide a state merging process. Both processes are stopped when the inter-cluster minimal distance exceeds a certain threshold d. This threshold is fixed depending on the number of recurrent units N, according to the heuristic rule $d = 2\sqrt{N}/3$, that relates it to the diameter of the N-dimensional activation space.

4.3 DFA to RE Mapping

Given a DFA A, there can be many equivalent REs R satisfying $L(A) = L(R)$, and several algorithms are applicable to obtain such an RE [12]. By selecting a specific algorithm, a mapping $\psi : DFA \rightarrow REs$ can be established, i.e. a canonical RE R can be chosen for each DFA A, $R = \psi(A)$. The mapping ψ that we have selected is based on Arden's method [12], but, in order to facilitate the ARE induction, an inner modification of the algorithm and a final simplifying step have been included [2].

The resulting RE is always unambiguous (thus easing the RE parsing) and such that the star subexpressions due to loops are distinguished from those corresponding to the rest of circuits of the DFA. Since loops may represent indefinite length or duration of a basic primitive, this separation allows for a later induction of constraints relating the lengths or durations of the different parts of a pattern. Moreover, by increasing the number of stars in the RE, while preserving equivalence and unambiguity, the potential for inferring constraints that involve the instances of the star operations is also increased.

4.4 Inducing the ARE Constraints from Recorded Star Instances

Once an RE R has been inferred, the associated star variables V and star tree T are easily determined [1]. Then, the aim is to infer an ARE $\tilde{R} = (R, V, T, \mathcal{L})$ such that $\mathcal{L}$ contains the maximal number of linear constraints met by all the provided examples. In other words, $\tilde{R}$ should describe the *smallest language* L such that $L \supseteq S^+$ and L is accepted by an ARE with the given R as underlying RE. To this end, firstly, the positive strings in S^+ must be parsed by R giving rise to an array of sets of star instances $ASI_{S^+}(V)$.

A constraint induction algorithm has been reported [1], that returns a set $\mathcal{L}$ comprising all the linear constraints satisfied by the star instances throughout the examples. The algorithm follows the star tree T by levels and, for each star variable v_j, determines its *housing ancestor* (for S^+), say $h(v_j)$, forms a vector B with its *non-redundant* star instances in $ASI_{S^+}(V)$, and tries to establish a possible linear relation with respect to the housed descendents of $h(v_j)$ previously labeled as "independent". This is, a linear system $A \cdot X = B$ is built, where matrix A contains the instances of the independent housed descendents of $h(v_j)$. If the system has a solution then X contains the coefficients of a linear relation, and this relation is appended to $\mathcal{L}$; otherwise, v_j is put in the list of independent housed descendents of $h(v_j)$, and the associated vector B is stored for further constraint discovery. The algorithm time complexity is $O(|V|^3 \cdot I(ASI_{S^+}(V)))$, where $I(ASI_{S^+}(V))$ is the maximal number of instances of a star variable yielded by parsing the set of strings S^+.

5 Experimental Assessment

The ARE inference method described was applied to learn a set of eight test CSLs, associated with ideal models of real patterns, which are shown in Fig.4. Test languages L_1-L_4 are over the alphabet $\Sigma_1 = \{a, b, c, d, e, f, g, h\}$ and test languages L_5-L_8 are over the alphabet $\Sigma_2 = \Sigma_1 \cup \{i, j, k, l\}$. For each test language L_i ($1 \leq i \leq 8$), a global sample $SL_i = (SL_i^+, SL_i^-)$ containing 64 positive and 64 negative examples (without repetitions) was generated manually. The positive sample SL_i^+ was written by giving several values to each parameter (degree of freedom) of the language. The negative sample SL_i^- was divided in two groups: 48 strings (75%) corresponded to counterexamples for the target regular language $L(R_i)$ and they were generated from the positive examples by removing, inserting or substituting some subpatterns (near-misses); 16 strings (25%) corresponded to strings in $L(R_i)$ which did not satisfy at least one constraint in the target CSL L_i. Then, for each language, eight training samples S_{ij}^+ ($1 \leq j \leq 8$), each containing 16 positive examples, were defined such that the whole set SL_i^+ was used and each block of 8 strings was included in two consecutive samples S_{ij}^+ and $S_{i(j+1)}^+$. Every training sample S_{ij}^+ was structurally complete with respect to the minimal DFA describing $L(R_i)$.

For each test language L_i, an ASORN with 4 recurrent units, but different initial random weights, was trained from each sample S_{ij}^+ to learn the next-symbol prediction task. Every sample was processed 300 times (training epochs),

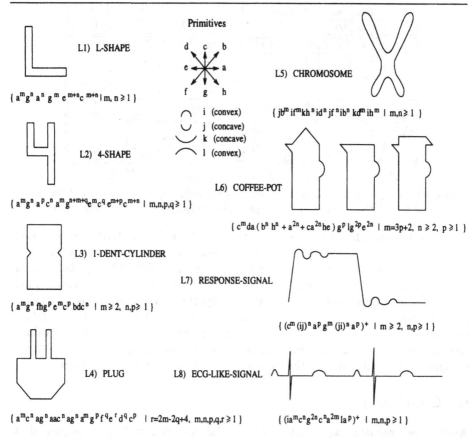

Primitives

L1) L-SHAPE

$\{\, a^m g^n\, a^n\, g^m\, e^{m+n} c^{\,m+n} \mid m, n \geqslant 1 \,\}$

i (convex)
j (concave)
k (concave)
l (convex)

L5) CHROMOSOME

$\{\, jb^m\, if^m kh^n id^n\, jf^{\,n} ib^n\, kd^m ih^m \mid m,n \geqslant 1 \,\}$

L2) 4-SHAPE

$\{\, a^m g^n\, a^p c^n\, a^m g^{n+m+q} e^m c^q\, e^{m+p} c^{\,m+n} \mid m,n,p,q \geqslant 1 \,\}$

L6) COFFEE-POT

$\{\, c^m da\, (\, b^n\, h^n + a^{2n} + ca^{2n} he\,)\, g^p\, lg^{2p} e^{2n} \mid m{=}3p{+}2,\ n \geqslant 2,\ p \geqslant 1 \,\}$

L3) 1-DENT-CYLINDER

$\{\, a^m g^n\, fhg^p\, e^m c^p\, bdc^n \mid m \geqslant 2,\ n,p \geqslant 1 \,\}$

L7) RESPONSE-SIGNAL

$\{\, (c^m (ij)^n\, a^p\, g^m\, (ji)^n\, a^p\,)^+ \mid m \geqslant 2,\ n,p \geqslant 1 \,\}$

L4) PLUG

L8) ECG-LIKE-SIGNAL

$\{\, a^m c^n\, ag^n\, aac^n\, ag^n\, a^m\, g^p\, f^q e^{\,r}\, d^q c^p \mid r{=}2m{-}2q{+}4,\ m,n,p,q,r \geqslant 1 \,\}$

$\{\, (ia^m c^n g^{2n} c^n a^{2m}\, la^p\,)^+ \mid m,n,p \geqslant 1 \,\}$

Fig. 4 *The eight test languages and the patterns described by them.*

using a learning rate of 0.005 and momentum of 0.5 in all the runs. A DFA A_{ij} was extracted from each trained ASORN and used to infer an equivalent RE R_{ij}. Finally, an ARE $\tilde{R}_{ij}$ was inferred using R_{ij} to parse the strings in S_{ij}^+ and the resulting star instances for constraint induction.

To assess the goodness of both the inferred ARE $\tilde{R}_{ij}$ and underlying RE R_{ij} (or DFA A_{ij}), an associated test sample was defined as $T_{ij} = (SL_i^+ - S_{ij}^+, SL_i^-)$ (i.e. the 48 positive examples not used for training and the whole 64 negative examples), and the correct classification rates on T_{ij} were computed. The results of the experiment are summarized in Table 1. Five features are displayed for each test language: the former three are averages over the eight learning samples of the correct positive, negative, and total classification rates, respectively; the fourth one refers to the arithmetic mean of the positive and negative classification rates [10]; and the fifth one (identification rate) is the percentage of times an ARE describing the target language was inferred. The last row of Table 1 displays the above features averaged over the 8 test languages.

	Pos.class		Neg.class		Tot.class		Av.class		Identif.	
	ARE	DFA	ARE	DFA	ARE	DFA	ARE	DFA	ARE	DFA
L_1	100.0	100.0	100.0	75.8	100.0	86.1	100.0	87.9	100.0	-
L_2	87.6	94.0	79.1	49.6	82.6	67.9	83.3	71.8	0.0	-
L_3	100.0	100.0	99.2	44.2	99.5	68.1	99.6	72.1	37.5	-
L_4	85.7	93.5	91.6	48.4	89.0	67.7	88.6	71.0	0.0	-
L_5	100.0	100.0	99.6	72.6	99.8	84.4	99.8	86.3	0.0	-
L_6	100.0	100.0	96.9	59.5	98.2	76.9	98.4	79.7	12.5	-
L_7	94.5	95.6	93.4	70.1	93.9	81.0	93.9	82.8	0.0	-
L_8	93.5	100.0	81.5	59.2	86.6	76.7	87.5	79.6	0.0	-
Mean	95.2	97.9	92.7	59.9	93.7	76.1	93.9	78.9	18.7	-

Table 1. *Performance features obtained by the ARE inference method (left) and just the (DFA) regular inference procedure (right) for the test languages.*

Table 1 shows the over-generalization carried out by the RGI step, which is indeed desirable to enable the discovery of context constraints afterwards, and the good classification results of the inferred AREs, with only L_2, L_4 and L_8 below 90% of correct classification rate. On the other hand, the results confirmed that ARE identification is hard. As it was expected, the inferred AREs notably outperformed the extracted DFA in the correct classification of the negative strings (by a rate difference that approaches to the percentage of "non-regular" negative examples), at the expense of a slight impairment in positive string recognition (which is due to the eventual induction of erroneous constraints).

6 Conclusions

Augmented regular expressions (AREs) [2] are compact descriptions that represent a non-trivial class of CSLs, including pattern languages, and permit to describe planar shapes with symmetries and other complex patterns. The recognition of a string as belonging to the language described by an ARE, which is based on parsing by the underlying RE and checking the constraints, is efficient (to the contrary of parsing by a CSG) [1]. A general approach to learn AREs from examples has been proposed that is based on splitting the process in two stages: inferring the underlying RE and inducing the maximal number of constraints afterwards. This learning strategy is not conceived as an identification method, but a heuristic method in which the inferred ARE strongly depends on the result of the RGI step. If negative examples are supplied, then the method cannot know which of them should belong to the regular language and which should not, unless an informant classified them in advance. Hence, an RGI algorithm using only positive examples seems more appropriate in this case. In addition, it must be biased to infer preferrably small-size descriptions (DFAs or REs) representing a high generalization with respect to the sample, both to ease the parsing of examples by the RE and to permit the discovery of the target constraints.

A specific method for inferring AREs has been described, in which the RGI procedure consists of three steps: training a recurrent neural network from the positive examples to learn the next-symbol prediction task, extracting a DFA from the net, and selecting an RE equivalent to the extracted DFA. This method has been implemented and applied to the inference of eight CSLs describing some planar shapes and signal patterns. The inferred AREs classified quite correctly samples of positive and negative strings not used during learning. However, although the test languages are rather simple, the exact identification of the CSL was rarely accomplished. It must be noticed that the cost of the DFA-to-RE transformation in the worst case is exponential in the number of states (e.g. for a fully-connected DFA). Although most of the DFAs that are typically induced from object contours or other physical patterns are sparsely connected and present a quite limited degree of circuit embedment, thus allowing the computation of the equivalent RE, it is clear that the worst-case behavior may defeat the learning method. A possible alternative is to use an RGI method that directly returns an RE (e.g. the $uv^k w$ algorithm [11]). We can say to conclude that the ARE learning strategy proposed is one of the most promising attempts by now to infer a large class of CSL acceptors from examples.

References

1. R. Alquézar and A. Sanfeliu, "Augmented regular expressions: a formalism to describe, recognize, and learn a class of context-sensitive languages," *Research Report LSI-95-17-R*, Universitat Politecnica de Catalunya, Spain (1995).
2. R. Alquézar and A. Sanfeliu, "Recognition and learning of a class of context-sensitive languages described by augmented regular expressions," *Pattern Recognition*, in press, (1996).
3. R. Alquézar and A. Sanfeliu, "Inference and recognition of regular grammars by training recurrent neural networks to learn the next-symbol prediction task," in *Advances in Pattern Recognition and Applications*, F.Casacuberta and A.Sanfeliu (eds.), World Scientific Pub., Singapore, 48-59, (1994).
4. R. Alquézar and A. Sanfeliu, "A hybrid connectionist-symbolic approach to regular grammatical inference based on neural learning and hierarchical clustering," in *Grammatical Inference and Applications*, R.C.Carrasco and J.Oncina (eds.), Springer-Verlag, Lecture Notes in Artificial Intelligence 862, 203-211, (1994).
5. A. Salomaa, *Formal Languages*, Academic Press, New York (1973).
6. S.M. Chou and K.S.Fu, "Inference for transition network grammars," *Proc. Int. Joint Conf. on Pattern Recognition, 3*, CA, 79-84 (1976).
7. D. Angluin, "Finding patterns common to a set of strings," *J. Comput. System Science* 21, 46-62 (1980).
8. Y. Takada, "A hierarchy of language families learnable by regular language learners," in *Grammatical Inference and Applications*, R.C.Carrasco and J.Oncina (eds.), Springer-Verlag, Lecture Notes in Artificial Intelligence 862, 16-24 (1994).
9. J. Gregor, "Data-driven inductive inference of finite-state automata," *Int. J. of Pattern Recognition and Artificial Intelligence* 8 (1), 305-322 (1994).
10. P. Dupont, "Regular grammatical inference from positive and negative samples by genetic search: the GIG method," in *Grammatical Inference and Applications*, R.C.Carrasco and J.Oncina (eds.), Springer-Verlag, LNAI 862, 236-245, (1994).
11. L. Miclet, "Inference of regular expressions," *Proc. of the 3rd Int. Conf. on Pattern Recognition*, 100-105, (1976).
12. Z. Kohavi, *Switching and Finite Automata Theory*, (2nd edition). Tata McGraw-Hill, New Delhi, India (1978).

Inducing Constraint Grammars

Christer Samuelsson[1], Pasi Tapanainen[2] and Atro Voutilainen[2]

[1] Universität des Saarlandes, FR 8.7, Computerlinguistik
Postfach 1150, D-66041 Saarbrücken, Germany
christer@coli.uni-sb.de
[2] Research Unit for Multilingual Language Technology
P.O. Box 4, FIN-00014 University of Helsinki, Finland
{tapanain,avoutila}@ling.helsinki.fi

Abstract. Constraint Grammar rules are induced from corpora. A simple scheme based on local information, i.e., on lexical biases and next-neighbour contexts, extended through the use of barriers, reached 87.3 % precision (1.12 tags/word) at 98.2 % recall. The results compare favourably with other methods that are used for similar tasks although they are by no means as good as the results achieved using the original hand-written rules developed over several years time.

1 Introduction

The present article describes experiments with inducing Constraint Grammars from annotated corpora. As described in Section 2, Constraint Grammar is a rule-based framework for morphological disambiguation and shallow syntactic parsing, where the rules are hand-coded by a linguistic expert. The present work does not aim at replacing the human grammar developer, but at supporting the grammar development task. It enables creating a first version of the grammar, which the grammarian can enhance in various ways, e.g. by discarding rules that are obviously incorrect, by adding additional constraints to rules that overgeneralise, and by adding linguistically motivated rules to cover phenomena that cannot readily be inferred from data. The only real advantage that the system has over the human is the ability to quantify what phenomena are common and what are not. Knowledge of this is essential for efficient grammar development, and the system can thus also find disambiguation rules that the human has overlooked.

The remainder of the article is organised as follows: The Constraint Grammar framework is presented in Section 2, while Section 3 describes the details of the various formats of the induced grammar rules. The learning procedure is explained in detail in Section 4, and the experimental results are reported and discussed in Section 5.

2 Constraint Grammar Framework

Constraint Grammar (CG), originally proposed by Karlsson [3], and fully documented in Karlsson et al. [4] and Tapanainen [6], is a reductionistic parsing framework based on the introduction and subsequent resolution of morphological and shallow syntactic ambiguities. The first mature CG parser, the English CG parser EngCG [11], consists of the following sequentially applied modules:

1. Tokenisation
2. Lookup of morphological tags
   (a) Lexical component
   (b) Rule-based guesser for unknown words
3. Resolution of morphological ambiguities
4. Lookup of syntactic function tags
5. Resolution of syntactic ambiguities

EngCG uses a morphological analyser, EngTWOL, with 90 000 lexical entries and a morphological description with about 180 ambiguity-forming morphological readings. Words not represented in EngTWOL are analysed with an accurate rule-based guesser. The following is an example of the output from EngTWOL:

```
"<campaign>"
    "campaign" <SV> <P/for> V SUBJUNCTIVE VFIN
    "campaign" <SV> <P/for> V IMP VFIN
    "campaign" <SV> <P/for> V INF
    "campaign" <SV> <P/for> V PRES -SG3 VFIN
    "campaign" N NOM SG
```

It contains the various readings of the word "campaign". This should be understood as follows: The word form is "campaign" as indicated by "<campaign>". There are five different readings. The word stem is "campaign" in all five of them as indicated by "campaign". The first four are verb readings, which is indicated by the V feature, while the last one is a noun reading bearing the N feature. The verb readings are in turn subjunctive ("They insisted that she campaign more effectively."), imperative ("Campaign more effectively!"), infinitive ("It is important to campaign more effectively."), and present indicative ("We campaign more effectively."). The first two readings, and the fourth one, are finite verb forms (VFIN). The first two features <SV> and <P/for> pertain to the possible syntactic subcategorization patterns of the verb readings: "They campaign." (intransitive) and "They campaign for it." (prepositional-phrase complement with "for" as the preposition).

The disambiguator uses a grammar of 1 200 constraint rules that refer to the global context and discard illegitimate morphological analyses in contexts specified by local or global contextual conditions. There are also some 250 heuristic rules for resolving remaining ambiguities.

EngCG is reported [11, 9, 7, 8] to assign a correct analysis to about 99.7 % of all words; on the other hand, each word retains on average 1.04–1.09 alternative analyses, i.e. some of the ambiguities remain unresolved. If also the heuristic constraints are used, about 50 % of the remaining ambiguities are resolved, but the error rate goes up to about 0.5 %.

3 Rule Typology

This section describes the different types of rules induced in the experiments.

3.1 Basic local-context rules

The basic format of the induced rules is:

REMOVE (V) (-1C (DET));

This should be read as: "Discard (REMOVE) any reading with the verb feature (V) if *all* readings (C) of the preceding word (-1) have the determiner feature (DET)." Omitting the C in -1C would mean "if *any* reading of the preceding word ..." The underlying idea of this particular rule is that readings bearing the V feature cannot intervene between a determiner and the head of the noun phrase. One might object that this would not hold for participles such as "given" in "the given example", but in the Constraint Grammar framework, these readings do not bear the V feature. The converse rule would be

REMOVE (DET) (1C (V));

and should be read as: "Discard any reading with the determiner feature if all readings of the *following* word have the verb feature".

These basic local-context rules can be induced by automatically inspecting an annotated corpus, and noting what features do not, or very seldom, occur on neighbouring words. In fact, the interesting quantities are the bigram feature counts and, as a comparison, the unigram feature counts, as explained in Section 4.1.

3.2 Combined local-context rules

Another well-motivated rule would be

REMOVE (V) (-1C (PREP));

and a number of other rules that discard verb readings if the preceding word carries some particular feature. These features can be collected into sets that can be referred to in the rules:

REMOVE (V) (-1C SET1);

Here SET1 is a set of features, and if all readings of the preceding word has some feature in this set, we can discard any reading of the current word that has a verb feature. In the example, SET1 would consist of DET and PREP, and other features as appropriate.

Note that this gives us more disambiguating power than the two original rules together; if the preceding word has one determiner reading and one prepositional reading, neither of the two original rules would be applicable, while the latter, combined local-context rule, would be. These rules can be automatically constructed from the previously discussed basic local-context rules.

3.3 Barrier rules

Barriers rules enable reference to tags whose precise position, relative to the ambiguous word in Position 0, is not known. In a barrier rule, some context conditions contain two parts each: (i) one part identifies some tag(s) somewhere to the left or right; (ii) the other (the barrier) states, what features are not allowed to occur in an intervening position. For instance, the following rule removes all readings with the tag V, if somewhere to the left there is an unambiguous determiner DET and there are no members of the set NPHEAD to the right of it, up to position -1.

REMOVE (V) (*-1C (DET) BARRIER NPHEAD);

The star * in (*-1C) means "one or more words", so *-1C (DET) means that for some word to the left, it is the case that all readings have the determiner feature DET. BARRIER is a reserved word of the CG description language and NPHEAD is a set of features that the grammarian has postulated, just like the set SET1 above. NPHEAD is here taken to be the set of features of the words that can function as heads of noun phrases, e.g., N for nouns, PRON for pronouns, NUM for numerals, etc. BARRIER means that there are no intervening words with any reading with any feature in the set following it. Thus, (*-1C (DET) BARRIER NPHEAD) means that somewhere to the left, we have a word that must bear the DET feature, and between this word and the current one, there are no words with remaining readings with any feature in the set NPHEAD, i.e., that can function as the head of the noun phrase. The intuition of this barrier rule is thus that if we have seen a verified determiner to the left, but no candidate NP head after that, we can safely remove all verb readings.

These rules can be induced from the basic local-context rules by noting what features actually occur between the features specified in those rules, e.g., by noting what features occur between determiners and verbs. These are collected and form the barrier sets, as described in Section 4.3.

3.4 Lexical rules

A third type of rule concerns rare readings of particular words, for example the verb reading of "table" as in "table the motion". The idea here is to see how many times a particular feature is proposed for a certain word in proportion to how many times it is actually in the correct reading. If this feature is not very often in the correct reading, it might be a good idea to remove any readings containing it. This would be effected by the rule

REMOVE (V) (0 ("<table>"));

The zero (0) refers to the current word and "<table>" refers to the word form "table". This rule will unconditionally remove the verb reading of the word form "table". It may seem a bit strange to first propose a particular reading for a word in the morphological analyser, and then write a rule that directly allows the disambiguator to discards it, but there is a very good reason for this: *The disambiguator is not allowed to remove the last remaining reading!* Thus, the system employs a Sherlock-Holmes strategy; if other rules have eliminated all other possible readings, then the remaining one, however unlikely, is the true one.

3.5   Rare-feature rules

Similarly, features that are very rarely the correct one, independent of what word form they are assigned to, can be removed in the same way. For example, the subjunctive reading of verbs is not often the correct one. The following rule discards these subjunctive readings:

REMOVE (SUBJUNCTIVE);

The last two rule types utilise the fact that it is possible to stratify the set of grammar rules, so that the disambiguation is first carried out with a first set of rules until no further readings can be eliminated, then with the first and a second set of rules, etc.

4   Learning Strategy

In this section, we describe how the various types of rules can be induced.

4.1   Local-context rules

First, unigram and bigram feature statistics are collected. Basic local-context rules such as

REMOVE (FEATURE) (-1C (CONTEXT));
REMOVE (FEATURE) (1C (CONTEXT));

remove any readings of the current word containing the feature FEATURE if all readings of the previous (or next) word contain the feature CONTEXT. These rules are induced if the probability of FEATURE drops drastically when conditioned on CONTEXT, i.e., if:

$$\frac{P(\text{FEATURE} \mid \text{CONTEXT})}{P(\text{FEATURE})} < \text{Threshold}$$

Note that this probability ratio is related to the mutual information statistics of FEATURE and CONTEXT, see [5], Section 2.2.2, and we will refer to this quantity as the score of the rule. Note also that due to the fact that each correct reading of any word can have a number of features, the probabilities do not necessarily sum to one over the features. P(FEATURE | CONTEXT) should therefore be interpreted as the probability of FEATURE showing up in the correct reading given CONTEXT.

Two modifications were made to this to avoid problems with sparse data. Firstly, only features and contexts with a reasonably high frequency count are allowed to participate in this phase. In the actual experiments, they were required to be at least 100. Secondly, instead of estimating P(FEATURE | CONTEXT) directly from the relative frequency of the feature in the context, a 97.5 % upper limit $\tilde{P}$ of this quantity is calculated. If there are no observations of the feature in the context, and if the frequency count of the context is N, this will be

$$\tilde{P} = 1 - \sqrt[N]{0.025} \tag{1}$$

Otherwise, with a non-zero relative frequency f, the usual (extended Moivre-Laplace) approximation using the normal distribution is employed (see, e.g., [5], Section 1.6):

$$\tilde{P} = f + 1.96 \cdot \sqrt{\frac{f \cdot (1 - f)}{N}} \tag{2}$$

Seeing that N was at least 100, this is an acceptable approximation.

Basic local-context rules with the same effect, and referring to the same neighbour (i.e., to the left or to the right), are collapsed into combined local-context rules with more disambiguating power as discussed in Section 3.2.

4.2 Rare-reading rules

Lexical rules are of the form

REMOVE (FEATURE) (0 (WORD));

and discard the feature FEATURE of the word form WORD. They are induced if

$$\frac{P(\text{FEATURE} \mid \text{WORD})}{\bar{P}_{FW}} < \text{Threshold}$$

where $\bar{P}_{FW}$ is the average probability over all features and words. Also here, an upper bound for P(FEATURE | WORD) is used instead of using this probability directly, and this bound is established exactly as in the previous case.

Similarly, rare-feature rules of the form

REMOVE (FEATURE);

unconditionally discard FEATURE regardless of which word bears it, and they are induced if

$$\frac{P(\text{FEATURE})}{\bar{P}_F} < \text{Threshold}$$

where $\bar{P}_F$ is the average probability over all features. Again, an upper bound is used instead of the probability itself.

4.3 Barrier rules

Barriers are established by collecting sets of candidate barrier features from the training data. One such set is constructed for each occurrence of two features that are ruled out as neighbours by any basic local-context rule. The candidate barrier set then simply consists of all features occurring between the two features. From the collection of candidate barrier sets, a minimal set of separating features is constructed for each feature pair using weighted abduction.

For example, if the only observed sequences of DET...V are

DET ADJ N PCP2 V (as in "The huge costs incurred are...")
DET NUM V (as in "The two will...")
DET N ADV V (as in "The shipments often arrive...")

we construct the candidate barrier sets

{ADJ,N,PCP2},{NUM} and {N,ADV}

Assuming that N is in the barrier set explains the first and third example, and assuming that NUM is in the barrier set explains the second one. It is easy to verify that no other barrier set of size two or less explains the observed sequences, and {N,NUM} is therefore chosen as the final set of barriers.

Here weighted abduction essentially means that we must choose (at least) one feature in each candidate barrier set. The cost of selecting a feature that has not previously been selected from any candidate barrier set is one unit, while the features that have already been selected from some candidate barrier set may be reused free of charge.

More formally, a Horn-clause program is constructed where each example will result in one clause for each candidate barrier feature. The conjunction of the examples is then proven at minimal cost. The examples above will result in the program

$$Ex_1 \leftarrow ADJ \quad (1) \qquad Ex_2 \leftarrow NUM \quad (4)$$
$$Ex_1 \leftarrow N \quad (2) \qquad Ex_3 \leftarrow N \quad (5)$$
$$Ex_1 \leftarrow PCP2 \quad (3) \qquad Ex_3 \leftarrow ADV \quad (6)$$

and the goal G to prove is Ex_1 & Ex_2 & Ex_3. Any RHS literal, i.e., any feature, may be assumed at the cost of one unit. We prove the goal G by employing an iterative deepening strategy, i.e., a proof of G is sought first at cost zero, then at cost one, then at cost two, etc. In the example, assuming N and NUM, at a total cost of two units, allows proving G through clauses (2), (4) and (5).

A couple of optimisations can be employed: Firstly, if the intersection of the candidate barrier sets is non-empty, any feature in the intersection can be chosen as a singleton barrier set. In practice, the intersection itself was used as a barrier. Secondly, each singleton candidate barrier set, such as {NUM} above, must be a subset of the final barrier set. This observation allows starting the abduction process from the union of all singleton sets, rather than from the empty set. Despite these optimizations, this turned out to be the most time-consuming phase of the induction process, due to the combinatorial nature of the abduction procedure.

This enables extending each basic local-context rule to long-distance dependencies, limited only by the corresponding induced barrier set. Note that this type of rules gives the learned grammar more expressive power than the rules induced in Brill's [1] learning framework. Also, the way the rules are applied is fundamentally different.

4.4 Redundancy and stratification

Some features always co-occur with others (within a reading), in which case there is a risk of inducing redundant rules. For example, the VFIN feature implies the presence of the V feature. Thus, there is no point in having a rule of the form

REMOVE (VFIN) (-1C (DET));

if there is already a rule of the form

REMOVE (V) (-1C (DET));

This is dealt with by keeping track of the observed feature co-occurrences and discarding candidate rules that are subsumed by other rules.

In the learning phase, the threshold is varied to stratify the rules. During disambiguation, several rule levels are employed. This means that the most reliable rules, i.e., those extracted using the lowest threshold, and that thus have the lowest scores, are applied first. When no further disambiguation is possible using these rules, the set of rules corresponding to the second lowest threshold is added, and disambiguation continues using these two sets of rules, etc. In the experiments reported in Section 5, ten rule levels were employed.

The threshold values and the subsumption test interact in a non-trivial way; low-score rules subsumed by high-score rules should not necessarily be eliminated. This is dealt with in a two-pass manner: In a first database-maintenance step, rules are only discarded if they are subsumed by another rule with a lower score. In a second step, when constructing each grammar level, redundancy within the upper and lower threshold values is eliminated.

Note that redundancy is more of a practical problem when inducing grammar rules, due to the limitations in available storage and processing time, than a theoretical problem during disambiguation: Exactly which rule is used to discard a particular reading is of no great interest. Also, the CG parser is sufficiently fast to cope with the slight overhead introduced by the redundancies.

5 Experiments

A grammar was induced from a hand-disambiguated text of approximately 55 000 words comprising various genres, and it was tested on a fresh hand-disambiguated corpus of some 10 000 words.

The training corpus as well as the benchmark corpus against which the system's output was evaluated was created by first applying the preprocessor and morphological analyser to the test text. This morphologically analysed ambiguous text was then independently disambiguated by two linguists whose task also was to detect any errors potentially produced by the previously applied components. They worked independently, consulting written documentation of the grammatical representation when necessary. Then these manually disambiguated versions were automatically compared. At this stage, about 99.3 % of all analyses were identical. When the differences were collectively examined, it was agreed that virtually all were due to clerical mistakes. One of these two corpus versions was modified to represent the consensus, and these "consensus corpora" were used, one for grammar induction and the other for testing the induced grammar. (For more details about a similar annotation experiment, see [10].)

A reasonable threshold value was established from the training corpus alone and used to extract the final learned grammar. It consisted of in total 625 rules distributed fairly evenly between the ten grammar levels. Of the learned rules, 444 were combined local-context rules, 164 were barrier rules, 10 were lexical rules and 7 were rare-feature rules.

The grammar was evaluated on a separate corpus of 9 795 words from the Brown corpus, manually annotated using the EngCG annotation scheme as described above. There were 7 888 spurious readings in addition to the 9 795 correct ones. The learned grammar removed 6 664 readings, including 175 correct ones, yielding a recall of 98.2 ± 0.3 % (with 95 % confidence degree) and a precision of 87.3 ± 0.7 %. This result is better than the results reported for Brill's [2] N-best tagger. He reports 98.4 % recall when the words have 1.19 tags on average (corresponding to 82.7 % precision) while the induced Constraint Grammar in the current experiments leaves less readings (1.12 per word) for the equivalent recall. However, the comparison to Brill's figures is only meant as an indication of the potential of our approach; more conclusive comparisons would require (i) accounting for the differences between the tag sets and (ii) the use of larger and more varied test corpora.

When these figures are compared with the reported EngCG performance using a hand-crafted grammar, it is obvious that although the proposed method is very promising, much still remains to be done. However, it should be remembered that this grammar was developed and debugged over several years. Thus, the rôle of the proposed method can be seen in three ways: (1) it is a bootstrapping technique for the development of a new grammar, (2) the remaining ambiguities of a linguistic (hand-written) grammar may be resolved by the empirical information (related work has been done in [7]), or (3) automatic induction may help the grammarian to discover new rules semi-automatically, so that the grammarian can remove the rules that are obviously incorrect and also fix and add sets and further contextual tests to the rules. In general, the exceptions to the rules are hard to detect and accommodate automatically, but using linguistic knowledge, the rules can be fixed relatively easily.

An advantage of the proposed approach is that the formalism itself does not restrict the scope of the rules to, say, bigrams. In the future, the result may be improved, for example, by adding linguistically sound predefined sets to guide the learning process towards better rules. Those sets may also be used to reduce the search space in the learning process, and that may make it possible to increase the number of the contextual tests in the rules to make them more accurate. Generally, the rôles of the different approaches can be characterized as follows: "linguistic knowledge is good for making generalisations, but the discovered rules can better distinguish between what is common and what is not."

References

1. Brill, E.: A Simple Rule-Based Part of Speech Tagger. Procs. the DARPA Speech and Natural Language Workshop (1992) 112–116. Morgan Kaufmann
2. Brill, E.: Some Advances in Transformation-Based Part-of-Speech Tagger. Procs. AAAI-94 (1994)
3. Karlsson, F.: Constraint grammar as a framework for parsing running text. Procs. CoLing-90 (1990) 3:168–173
4. Karlsson, F., Voutilainen, A., Heikkilä, J., Anttila, A. (eds.): Constraint Grammar. A Language-Independent System for Parsing Unrestricted Text. (1995) Mouton de Gruyter
5. Krenn, B., Samuelsson, C.: The Linguist's Guide to Statistics. (1994–1996) http://coli.uni-sb.de/~christer
6. Tapanainen, P.: The Constraint Grammar Parser CG-2. (1996) Department of General Linguistics, University of Helsinki
7. Tapanainen, P., Voutilainen, A.: Tagging accurately – don't guess if you know. Procs. ANLP-94 (1994) 47–52
8. Voutilainen, A.: A syntax-based part of speech analyser. Proc. EACL'95 (1995) 157–164
9. Voutilainen, A., Heikkilä, J.: An English constraint grammar (EngCG): a surface-syntactic parser of English. Fries, Tottie and Schneider (eds.), Creating and using English language corpora. (1994) Rodopi
10. Voutilainen, A., Järvinen, T.: Specifying a shallow grammatical representation for parsing purposes. Proc. EACL'95 (1995) 210–214
11. Voutilainen, A., Heikkilä, J., Anttila, A.: Constraint Grammar of English. A Performance-Oriented Introduction. (1992) Department of General Linguistics, University of Helsinki

Introducing Statistical Dependencies and Structural Constraints in Variable-Length Sequence Models

Sabine Deligne, François Yvon & Frédéric Bimbot

ENST - Dept. Signal & Dept. Informatique, CNRS-URA 820,
46 rue Barrault, 75634 Paris cedex 13, FRANCE, European Union.

1 Introduction

In the field of natural language processing, as in many other domains, the efficiency of pattern recognition algorithms is highly conditioned to a proper description of the underlying structure of the data. However, this hidden structure is usually not known, and it has to be learned from examples. The multigram model [1, 2] was originally designed to extract *variable-length* regularities within streams of symbols, by describing the data as the concatenation of *statistically independent sequences*. Such a description seems especially appealing in the case of natural language corpora, since natural language syntactic regularities are clearly of variable length: sentences are composed of a variable number of syntagms, which in turn are made of a variable number of words, which contain a variable number of morphemes, etc...

However, some previous experiments with this model [3] revealed the inadequacy of the independence assumption in the particular context of a grapheme-to-phoneme transcription task. In this paper, our goal is therefore twofold:

- to demonstrate theoretically the possibility to relax this important assumption of the original multigram model;
- to suggest, using a related model of dependent variable-length sequences, that relaxing this hypothesis is indeed effective.

This paper is organized as follows: in section 2 and 3, we briefly describe the original multigram model, and its multi-level generalization. We then present, in sections 4 and 5, two original stochastic extensions of the mono-dimensional model, in which the independence assumption is relaxed, and show theoretically that the estimation of these new models is indeed feasible. Section 6 introduces yet another approach for modeling dependencies between adjacent sequences, this time in a non-stochastic framework. Section 7 presents experiments suggesting the effectiveness of taking dependencies into account. We finally give in section 8 some indications regarding further extensions of these various models.

2 The Original Multigram Model

2.1 Formulation of the Model

Under the n-multigram approach, a string of symbols is assumed to result from the concatenation of non-overlapping sequences, each of which having a maximum length of n symbols. We note $\mathcal{D}_O = \{o_i\}_i$ the dictionary from which the emitted symbols are drawn, and $O = o_{(1)}o_{(2)}\cdots o_{(T_O)}$ any observable string of T_O symbols. Let L denote a possible segmentation of O into T_S sequences of symbols. We note S the resulting string of sequences: $S = (O, L) = s_{(1)}\cdots s_{(T_S)}$. The dictionary of distinct sequences, which can be formed by combining 1, 2,... up to n symbols from $\mathcal{D}_O$ is noted $\mathcal{D}_S = \{s_j\}_j$. Each possible segmentation L of O is assigned a likelihood value, and the overall likelihood of the string is computed as the sum of the likelihoods for each segmentation:

$$\mathcal{L}_{\mu gr}(O) = \sum_{L \in \{L\}} \mathcal{L}(O, L) \tag{1}$$

The decision-oriented version of the model parses O according to the most likely segmentation, thus yielding the approximation:

$$\mathcal{L}^*_{\mu gr}(O) = \max_{L \in \{L\}} \mathcal{L}(O, L) \tag{2}$$

The model is fully defined once the set of parameters Θ needed to compute $\mathcal{L}(O, L)$ for any particular segmentation L is known.

2.2 Computing the Likelihood under the Independence Assumption

If we now further assume that the multigram sequences are independent, the likelihood $\mathcal{L}(O, L)$ of any segmentation L of O can be expressed as:

$$\mathcal{L}(O, L) = \prod_{t=1}^{t=q} p\left(s(t)\right) \tag{3}$$

A n-multigram model is thus defined by the set of parameters Θ consisting of the probability of each sequence s_i in $\mathcal{D}_S$: $\Theta = \{p(s_i)\}_i$, with $\sum_{s_i \in \mathcal{D}_S} p(s_i) = 1$.

2.3 Maximum Likelihood Estimation of the Model Parameters

An estimation of the set of parameters Θ from a training corpus O can be obtained as a Maximum Likelihood (ML) estimation from incomplete data [4], where the observed data is the string of symbols O, and the unknown data is the underlying segmentation L. Thus, iterative ML estimates of Θ can be computed through an EM algorithm. Let $Q(k, k+1)$ be the following auxiliary function computed with the likelihoods of iterations k and $k+1$:

$$Q(k, k+1) = \sum_{L \in \{L\}} \mathcal{L}^{(k)}(O, L) \log \mathcal{L}^{(k+1)}(O, L) \tag{4}$$

It has been shown in [4] that if $Q(k, k+1) \geq Q(k, k)$, then $\mathcal{L}^{(k+1)}(O) \geq \mathcal{L}^{(k)}(O)$. The set of parameters $\Theta^{(k+1)}$ which maximizes $Q(k, k+1)$ at iteration $(k+1)$ also leads to an increase of the corpus likelihood. Therefore the reestimation formula of $p^{(k+1)}(s_i)$, i.e. the probability of sequence s_i at iteration $(k+1)$, can be derived directly by maximizing the auxiliary function $Q(k, k+1)$ over $\Theta^{(k+1)}$, under the constraint that all parameters sum up to one. Denoting by $c(s_i, L)$ the number of occurences of the sequence s_i in a segmentation L of the corpus, we rewrite the joint likelihood given in (3) so as to group together the probabilities of all identical sequences:

$$\mathcal{L}^{(k+1)}(O, L) = \prod_{i=1}^{i=m} (p^{(k+1)}(s_i))^{c(s_i, L)} \tag{5}$$

The auxiliary function $Q(k, k+1)$ can then be expressed as:

$$Q(k, k+1) = \sum_{i=1}^{m} \sum_{L \in \{L\}} \mathcal{L}^{(k)}(O, L) \, c(s_i, L) \, \log p^{(k+1)}(s_i) \tag{6}$$

which, as a function of $p^{(k+1)}(s_i)$, subject to the constraints $\sum_{i=1}^{m} p^{(k+1)}(s_i) = 1$ and $p^{(k+1)}(s_i) \geq 0$, is maximum for:

$$p^{(k+1)}(s_i) = \frac{\sum_{L \in \{L\}} c(s_i, L) \times \mathcal{L}^{(k)}(O, L)}{\sum_{L \in \{L\}} c(L) \times \mathcal{L}^{(k)}(O, L)} \tag{7}$$

where $c(L) = \sum_{i=1}^{i=m} c(s_i, L)$ is the total number of sequences in L. Equation (7) shows that the estimate for $p(s_i)$ is merely a weighted average of the number of occurences of sequence s_i within each segmentation. Since each iteration improves the model in the sense of increasing the likelihood $\mathcal{L}^{(k)}(O)$, it eventually converges to a critical point (possibly a local maximum).

The reestimation (7) can be implemented by means of a forward-backward algorithm [2]. The set of parameters Θ can be initialized with the relative frequencies of all co-occurences of symbols up to length n in the training corpus. Then Θ is iteratively reestimated until the training set likelihood does not increase significantly, or with a fixed number of iterations.

In practice, some pruning technique may be advantageously applied to the dictionary of sequences, in order to avoid over-learning. A straightforward way to proceed consists in simply discarding, at each iteration, the most unlikely sequences, i.e. those with probability value falling under a prespecified threshold.

3 The Joint Multigram Model

3.1 Formulation of the Model

The multigram model easily generalizes to the joint multigram model [3] to deal with the case of D observable streams of symbols, drawn from D distinct alphabets. The D strings are assumed to result from the parallel concatenation of D sequences, of possibly different lengths. As the model allows the D matched sequences to be of unequal length, it assumes a many-to-many alignment between the D strings.

In the following, we consider the case of two streams: $\begin{pmatrix} O = & o_{(1)}...o_{(T_O)} \\ \Omega = & \omega_{(1)}...\omega_{(T_\Omega)} \end{pmatrix}$, assumed to result from the concatenation of pairs of sequences $\begin{pmatrix} s_{(t)} \\ \sigma_{(t)} \end{pmatrix}$. A model restricting to n the length of a sequence $s_{(t)}$ in O, and to ν the length of a sequence $\sigma_{(t)}$ in Ω, will be refered to as a (n, ν)-joint multigram model. We note L_O (resp. L_Ω) a segmentation of O (resp. Ω) into sequences, and L the corresponding joint segmentation of O and Ω into paired sequences: $L = (L_O, L_\Omega)$. The likelihood of (O, Ω) is computed as the sum over all joint segmentations:

$$\mathcal{L}(O, \Omega) = \sum_{L \in \{L\}} \mathcal{L}(O, \Omega, L) \tag{8}$$

Assuming again that the subsequent pairs of sequences are independent, the likelihood of a joint segmentation is the product of each pair probability:

$$\mathcal{L}(O, \Omega, L) = \prod_t p\begin{pmatrix} s_{(t)} \\ \sigma_{(t)} \end{pmatrix} \tag{9}$$

3.2 Estimation of the Joint Multigram Model Parameters

The parameter estimation of a joint multigram model is based on the same principles as for the one-string multigram model. Let $\mathcal{D}_S = \{(s_i, \sigma_j)\}_{i,j}$ denotes a dictionary that contains all the pairs of sequences (s_i, σ_j), where s_i can be formed by combinations of 1, 2,... up to n symbols of the vocabulary of O, and σ_j can be formed by combinations of 1, 2,... up to ν symbols of the vocabulary of Ω. A joint multigram model is fully defined by the set Θ of each pair probability $p(s_i, \sigma_j)$. Replacing s_i by (s_i, σ_j), and O by (O, Ω) in (7), we can directly write the parameter reestimation formula at iteration $(k + 1)$:

$$p^{(k+1)}(s_i, \sigma_j) = \frac{\sum_{L \in \{L\}} c(s_i, \sigma_j, L) \times \mathcal{L}^{(k)}(O, \Omega, L)}{\sum_{L \in \{L\}} c(L) \times \mathcal{L}^{(k)}(O, \Omega, L)} \tag{10}$$

where $c(s_i, \sigma_j, L)$ is the number of occurences of the pair (s_i, σ_j) in L and $c(L)$ is the total number of matched sequences in L. The forward-backward algorithm implementing (10) is detailed in [3].

The training procedure jointly parses the two strings according to a maximum likelihood criterion. It produces a dictionary of pairs of sequences, which can be used for automatic transduction purposes, as explained below. As for the basic multigram model, additional pruning of this dictionary may advantageously be used in order to avoid over-learning. This can be done either a posteriori by discarding the most unfrequent pairs of sequences, or a priori, by taking into account only the pairs of sequences which are compatible with a known, possibly approximate, pre-alignment of the symbols between the two streams.

3.3 Application to a Grapheme-to-Phoneme Transduction Task

Since the joint multigram model assigns a probability to any pair of sequences, it can be used as a stochastic transducer. We study this application for a task of grapheme-to-phoneme transduction. Assume, for instance, that a joint multigram model is estimated on a training set where O and Ω are respectively a string of graphemes and a string of phonemes. The training process consists thus in mapping variable-length sequences of graphemes and variable-length sequences of phonemes. The resulting set of matched sequences, along with their probability of co-occurence, can be used to infer, through a sequence-by-sequence decoding process, the string of phonemes Ω corresponding to a test string of graphemes O, the pronunciation of which is unknown. This transduction task can be stated as a standard maximum a posteriori decoding problem, consisting in finding the most likely phonetic string $\widehat{\Omega}$ given the graphemic stream O:

$$\widehat{\Omega} = Argmax_\Omega \ \mathcal{L}(\Omega \mid O) = Argmax_\Omega \ \mathcal{L}(O, \Omega) \tag{11}$$

Assuming that $L^* = (L_O^*, L_\Omega^*)$, the most likely joint segmentation of the two strings, accounts for most of the likelihood, the inferred pronunciation results from the maximization of the approximated likelihood defined by (8):

$$\widehat{\Omega}^* = Argmax_\Omega \ \mathcal{L}(O, \Omega, L_O^*, L_\Omega^*) \tag{12}$$
$$= Argmax_\Omega \ \mathcal{L}(O, L_O^* \mid \Omega, L_\Omega^*) \, \mathcal{L}(\Omega, L_\Omega^*) \tag{13}$$

by application of Bayes rule. $\mathcal{L}(O, L_O^* \mid \Omega, L_\Omega^*)$ measures how well the graphemic sequences in the segmentation L_O^* match the inferred phonetic sequences in L_Ω^*. It is computed as $\prod p(s_{(t)} \mid \sigma_{(t)})$, where the conditional probabilities are deduced from the probabilities $p(s_i, \sigma_j)$ estimated during the training phase. The term $\mathcal{L}(\Omega, L_\Omega^*)$ measures the likelihood of the inferred pronunciation: it can be estimated as $\widetilde{\mathcal{L}}(\Omega, L_\Omega^*)$ using a language model. This decoding strategy is a way to impose syntagmatical constraints in string Ω (here phonotactical constraints). The maximization (13) thus rewrites as:

$$\widetilde{\Omega}^* = Argmax_\Omega \ \mathcal{L}(O, L_O^* \mid \Omega, L_\Omega^*) \ \widetilde{\mathcal{L}}(\Omega, L_\Omega^*) \tag{14}$$

In the experiments reported in Sect. 7, the phonotactical component $\widetilde{\mathcal{L}}(\Omega, L_\Omega^*)$ is computed by modeling the succession of the phonetic sequences with a bigram model. The conditional probabilities attached to those successions can be estimated on a parsed version of the phonetic training stream, during the last iteration of the estimation algorithm.

4 $\overline{n}$-Grams of n-Multigrams

4.1 Computation of the Observation Likelihood

If we relax the independence assumption between multigrams, we can model the correlations between sequences with a $\overline{n}$-gram model. Since each multigram sequence depends on the $(\bar{n} - 1)$ previous sequences, the likelihood value of a particular segmentation L is computed as:

$$\mathcal{L}(O, L) = \prod_t p(s_{(t)} \mid s_{(t-\bar{n}+1)} \ldots s_{(t-1)}) \tag{15}$$

As for the original model, the likelihood of O is computed as the sum over all possible segmentations (see (1)). A comparative example between an independent multigram model and a bi-gram of multigram model is given in Tab. 1.

$$\sum \begin{cases} p([a])\, p([b])\, p([c])\, p([d]) \\ p([a])\, p([b])\, p([cd]) \\ p([a])\, p([bc])\, p([d]) \\ p([a])\, p([bcd]) \\ p([ab])\, p([c])\, p([d]) \\ p([ab])\, p([cd]) \\ p([abc])\, p([d]) \end{cases} \qquad \sum \begin{cases} p([a] \mid \#)\, p([b] \mid [a])\, p([c] \mid [b])\, p([d] \mid [c]) \\ p([a] \mid \#)\, p([b] \mid [a])\, p([cd] \mid [b]) \\ p([a] \mid \#)\, p([bc] \mid [a])\, p([d] \mid [bc]) \\ p([a] \mid \#)\, p([bcd] \mid [a]) \\ p([ab] \mid \#)\, p([c] \mid [ab])\, p([d] \mid [c]) \\ p([ab] \mid \#)\, p([cd] \mid [ab]) \\ p([abc] \mid \#)\, p([d] \mid [abc]) \end{cases}$$

Table 1. The likelihood of $abcd$ for an independent 3-multigram model (left) and for a bi-gram of 3-multigram model (right). $\#$ refers to the empty sequence.

A $\bar{n}$-gram model of n-multigrams is fully defined by the set of parameters Θ consisting of the $\bar{n}$-gram conditional probabilities relative to any combination of $\bar{n}$ sequences from $\mathcal{D}_S$: $\Theta = \{p(s_{i_{\bar{n}}} \mid s_{i_1} \ldots s_{i_{\bar{n}-1}}) \mid s_{i_1} \ldots s_{i_{\bar{n}}} \in \mathcal{D}_S\}$, with $\sum_{s_{i_{\bar{n}}} \in \mathcal{D}_S} p(s_{i_{\bar{n}}} \mid s_{i_1} \ldots s_{i_{\bar{n}-1}}) = 1$.

4.2 Estimation of the model parameters

ML estimates of the parameters for the $\bar{n}$-gram model of multigrams can be derived exactly in the same way as in the case of independent multigrams, leading to the reestimation formula:

$$p^{(k+1)}(s_{i_{\bar{n}}} \mid s_{i_1} \ldots s_{i_{\bar{n}-1}}) = \frac{\sum_{L \in \{L\}} c(s_{i_1} \ldots s_{i_{\bar{n}-1}} s_{i_{\bar{n}}}, L) \times \mathcal{L}^{(k)}(O, L)}{\sum_{L \in \{L\}} c(s_{i_1} \ldots s_{i_{\bar{n}-1}}, L) \times \mathcal{L}^{(k)}(O, L)} \tag{16}$$

where $c(s_{i_1} \ldots s_{i_{\bar{n}}}, L)$ is the number of occurences of the combination of sequences $s_{i_1} \ldots s_{i_{\bar{n}}}$ in the segmentation L. It can be checked that, by taking $\bar{n}$ equal to 1, (16) reduces to (7), derived for the estimation of an independent multigram model. Equation (16) can be implemented by means of a forward-backward algorithm.

5 Embedded Multigrams

5.1 Computation of the Likelihood

In this section, the dependencies between the multigram sequences are modeled with a multigram model in a recursive way. A $\bar{n}$-multigram model is applied to any sequencement $S = s_{(1)} \ldots s_{(T_S)}$ resulting from a segmentation L of the observed string of symbols. Thus, the string S of multigram sequences is assumed to result from the concatenation of higher-level sequences, each of which is formed of either 1, 2,... or $\bar{n}$ sequences s_i from $\mathcal{D}_S$. We note $\bar{S} = \bar{s}_{(1)} \ldots \bar{s}_{(T_{\bar{S}})}$ any sequencement resulting from a possible segmentation $\bar{L}$ of S. Accordingly, $\mathcal{D}_{\bar{S}}$ denotes the set of sequences $\bar{s}_j$ formed of elements from $\mathcal{D}_S$. Further assuming a $\bar{\bar{n}}$-multigram structure to model the dependencies between the sequences within $\bar{S}$ would produce sequencements noted $\bar{\bar{S}}$, where each sequence $\bar{\bar{s}}_{(t)}$ would consist of either 1, 2, ... or $\bar{\bar{n}}$ elements from $\mathcal{D}_{\bar{S}}$, and so on...

This recursive process stops when all successively embedded multigrams are eventually grouped into a single highest-level sequence, spanning over the whole string of observation. Under this embedded multigram model, the observations are structured like in a tree (see an example on Fig. 1), the leaves of which consist of the symbols observed, and the non-terminal nodes of which have a maximum number of leaving branches equal to either n, $\bar{n}$, $\bar{\bar{n}}$... depending on the depth of the node in the tree. We assume in the rest of this section that the second-level sequences $\bar{s}_{(t)}$ are independent, so that the resulting model is a 2-level embedded multigram model. In this framework, the likelihood of a string O is computed as the sum of the likelihood values for each possible first-level and associated second-level segmentations L and $\bar{L}$:

$$\mathcal{L}(O) = \sum_{\{\bar{L}\}} \sum_{\{L\}} \mathcal{L}((O, L), \ \bar{L}) \tag{17}$$

where, in a 2-level scheme, the likelihood of any segmentation $\bar{L}$ of (O, L) is computed as:

$$\mathcal{L}((O, L), \ \bar{L}) = \prod_t p(\bar{s}(t)) \tag{18}$$

An example of a two-level embedded multigram model is given in Fig. 1.

The set of parameters Θ for a 2-level embedded multigram model is the set of probabilities of each sequence $\bar{s}_i$ in $\mathcal{D}_{\bar{S}}$: $\Theta = \{p(\bar{s}_i)\}_i$, with $\sum_{\bar{s}_i \in \mathcal{D}_{\bar{S}}} p(\bar{s}_i) = 1$.

5.2 Estimation of the model parameters

ML Estimates for the embedded multigram model can be derived using the same method as in the case of independent multigrams. By noting $c(\bar{s}_i, \bar{L} \mid L)$ the number of occurences of the sequence $\bar{s}_i$ in the second-level segmentation $\bar{L}$ performed on the sequencement (O, L), we have:

$$p^{(k+1)}(\bar{s}_i) = \frac{\sum_{L \in \{L\}} \sum_{\bar{L} \in \{\bar{L}\}} c(\bar{s}_i, \bar{L} \mid L) \times \mathcal{L}^{(k)}((O, L), \ \bar{L})}{\sum_{L \in \{L\}} \sum_{\bar{L} \in \{\bar{L}\}} c(\bar{L} \mid L) \times \mathcal{L}^{(k)}((O, L), \ \bar{L})} \tag{19}$$

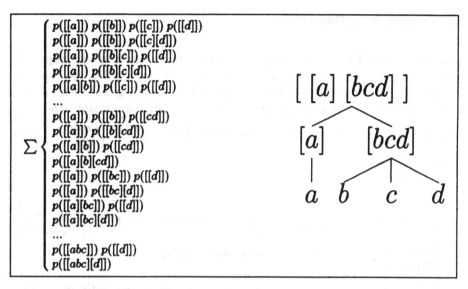

Fig. 1. The likelihood of *abcd* for a two-level embedded multigram model ($n = \bar{n} = 3$): all possible segmentations (left) and a tree-like representation of the particular segmentation $[\,[a]\,[bcd]\,]$ (right).

where $c(\overline{L} \mid L) = \sum_{\bar{s}_i \in \mathcal{D}_{\bar{s}}} c(\bar{s}_i, \overline{L} \mid L)$ is the total number of sequences in $\overline{L}$.

Equation (7) shows that the estimate for $p(\bar{s}_i)$ is merely a weighted average of the number of occurences of sequence $\bar{s}_i$ within each possible second-level segmentation $\overline{L}$. The reestimation formula (19) can be implemented by means of a forward-backward algorithm.

6 Non-Stochastic Models of Overlapping Sequences

In this section, we present an alternative transduction procedure relying upon the concatenation of sequences having a variable length. The main characteristic of this approach, in comparison to the stochastic model presented in the previous sections, is that it captures the dependency between successive sequences by imposing *overlapping constraints*.

We first present the constraints, and suggest how they could be used in a conjunction with a joint multigram model in the bi-dimensional case. We will then show that these constraints allows to define another kind of sequence modeling, where the notion of concatenation is extended to handle overlapping parts between adjacent pairs.

6.1 Overlapping Constraints

In the case of the joint multigram model, the pronunciation of a test graphemic string is obtained by selecting in a dictionary of matched pairs $\mathcal{D}_S$, the sequence maximizing the likelihood according to (12) or (14). Assuming that such a dictionary is available, the overlapping model adds the following constraints (the *overlapping constraints*) on any candidate sequence[1] $\begin{bmatrix} O(1) \cdots O(t_1) \\ \omega(1) \cdots \omega(t_1) \end{bmatrix} \begin{bmatrix} O(t_1+1) \cdots O(t_2) \\ \omega(t_1+1) \cdots \omega(t_2) \end{bmatrix}$

$\cdots \begin{bmatrix} O(t_n+1) \cdots O(T_O) \\ \omega(t_n+1) \cdots \omega(T_O) \end{bmatrix}$:

- $\exists\, t_1' \in [1; t_1],\ \exists\, t_2' \in [t_1 + 1; t_2], \ldots$ such that the pairs $\begin{bmatrix} O(t_1') \cdots O(t_2) \\ \omega(t_1') \cdots \omega(t_2) \end{bmatrix}$, $\begin{bmatrix} O(t_2') \cdots O(t_3) \\ \omega(t_2') \cdots \omega(t_3) \end{bmatrix}$, $\begin{bmatrix} O(t_3') \cdots O(t_4) \\ \omega(t_3') \cdots \omega(t_4) \end{bmatrix} \ldots$ can be found in $\mathcal{D}_S$,

- $\begin{bmatrix} O(1) \cdots O(t_1) \\ \omega(1) \cdots \omega(t_1) \end{bmatrix}$ (resp. $\begin{bmatrix} O(t_n+1) \cdots O(T_O) \\ \omega(t_n+1) \cdots \omega(T_O) \end{bmatrix}$) must be a prefix (respectively a suffix) of an existing lexical item.

Let us assume, for instance, that we wish to transcribe the word $O = abash$ by concatenating the 3 pairs $\begin{bmatrix} aba \\ əbæ \end{bmatrix}$, $\begin{bmatrix} s \\ ʃ \end{bmatrix}$ and $\begin{bmatrix} h \\ - \end{bmatrix}$, supposedly in $\mathcal{D}_S$. The concatenation of the first and the second pair will be allowed if and only if either the pair $\begin{bmatrix} bas \\ bæʃ \end{bmatrix}$, or the pair $\begin{bmatrix} as \\ æʃ \end{bmatrix}$ can also be found in $\mathcal{D}_S$, which warrants that the transition from the first to the second concatenated pair corresponds to an attested pronunciation. The expected advantage of such constraints is to reduce the set of all candidate pronunciations, by ruling out solutions including an unattested transition between two adjacent pairs.

The overlapping constraints appear as a way to introduce dependencies in a very crude way in a multigram model: whenever an overlap between two pairs is not found is the lexicon, the likelihood of any sequence where they would be adjacent is simply zeroed. Doing so would however be somewhat unsatisfying. Indeed, if we turn back to the example "abash", we feel intuitively that the transition between $\begin{bmatrix} aba \\ əbæ \end{bmatrix}$ and $\begin{bmatrix} s \\ ʃ \end{bmatrix}$ would be better warranted by the observation of $\begin{bmatrix} bas \\ bæʃ \end{bmatrix}$ than of $\begin{bmatrix} as \\ æʃ \end{bmatrix}$, on the ground that the former has a larger overlap with the first pair than the latter. It seems consequently appealing to use the observed overlap size as another clue of the transition likelihood, which is not possible if we use the constraints in a boolean fashion.

---

[1] We make here the additional assumption that the graphemic and phonemic strings have been aligned by inserting null symbols wherever needed. It shall be noted that this assumption is by no means necessary.

6.2 Overlapping Models

An alternative view of the overlapping constraints allows us to take this remark into account. In fact, the overlapping model is a model allowing the concatenation of **overlapping** pairs of sequences: the expression *O-concatenation* will refer to this extended notion of concatenation. Consider again the previous example of "abash": the transcription defined by the 3 **non-overlapping** pairs $\begin{bmatrix} aba \\ \partial b\ae \end{bmatrix}$, $\begin{bmatrix} s \\ \int \end{bmatrix}$ and $\begin{bmatrix} h \\ \cdot \end{bmatrix}$, with the additionnal constraint that the pairs $\begin{bmatrix} bas \\ b\ae\int \end{bmatrix}$ and $\begin{bmatrix} ash \\ \ae\int \end{bmatrix}$ can be found in $\mathcal{D}_S$, may also be stated as the O-concatenation of the **overlapping** pairs $\begin{bmatrix} aba \\ \partial b\ae \end{bmatrix}$, $\begin{bmatrix} bas \\ b\ae\int \end{bmatrix}$ and $\begin{bmatrix} ash \\ \ae\int \end{bmatrix}$.

This new formulation makes it possible to distinguish between identical segmentations produced with different overlaps, since they will correspond to distinct O-concatenations. The next stage is to rank these various O-concatenations: in this version of the model, this is performed according to a *ad-hoc* scoring function, which expresses formally that an O-concatenation which relies simultaneously upon "long" pairs and large overlaps should be preferred to a solution relying upon shorter pairs or smaller overlaps. Suppose the word O, of T_O graphemes, is viewed as an O-concatenation $S = s_{(1)}...s_{(T_S)}$ of T_S sequences. Denoting as $l(s_{(t)})$ the number of symbols in the sequence $s_{(t)}$, we define the scoring function C as:

$$C(S) = \frac{\sum_{s_{(t)}} l(s_{(t)})}{T_S \times T_O} \tag{20}$$

The form of $C(S)$ makes it possible to make a compromise between the size of the overlapping portions between successive sequences (the longer the overlap is, and the larger is the value at the numerator, since overlapping symbols are counted twice), and the number of sequences involved in the pronunciation (the greater the number of sequences is, and the larger is the value at the denominator). As a secondary criterion, the average frequency of the pairs involved in a given solution has been used to break possible ties.

7 The Advantage of Modeling Dependencies

In this section, we briefly review some results obtained in a grapheme-to-phoneme transduction task using the joint multigram model and the overlapping model. Our purpose here is not to present a complete evaluation of these models (see for instance [3] or [7]), but rather to provide the reader with a couple of results demonstrating the effectiveness of modeling dependencies in a variable sequence model.

Both models are evaluated on BDLEX, a database of about 22,500 French words [5]. Approximately 90% of the database is used for the training of the model, while the remaining 10% is used for the test. A transcription is judged to be correct when it exactly matches the pronunciation listed in the database at the phonemic level. The number of correct phonemes in a transcription is computed on the basis of the string-to-string edit distance with the target pronunciation. Table 2 reports only the best results obtained in our complete evaluation of each model, including an additionnal reference point obtained using a decision-tree learning technique, DEC [6]. The main outcome of this evaluation is that the

Model	% words	% phonemes
$(5, 5)$ Joint Multigram	64.5	92.3
$(3, 2)$ Joint Multigram	71.3	93.7
Overlapping Model	86.3	95.4
Decision Tree (DEC)	86.7	97.9

Table 2. Comparative evaluation of the joint multigram model and of the overlapping model on a grapheme-to-phoneme conversion task. For the $(3, 2)$ version of the joint multigram model, the decoding procedure additionally uses a bigram model of phonetic sequences (see (14)).

overlapping model significantly outperforms the non-overlapping model. A first obvious fact can readily account for this difference: the overlapping model uses a database where graphemic and phonemic entries have been aligned, whereas this kind of pre-processing is not used in the joint multigram model. But we believe that the superiority of the overlapping model also results from the fact that it efficiently constraints the transitions between the adjacent pairs of sequences. Conversely, the basic joint multigram model suffers from the assumption of independence between the successive pairs of sequences.

As far as the joint multigram model is concerned, this first evaluation is nevertheless encouraging, as it provides a completely unsupervised learning procedure for a task, which had so far been mainly treated in a supervised frameword (see [8] for a review). It also confirms the major weakness of the basic model used in these experiments, i.e. the assumption of independence between the successive joint sequences. As illustrated in the previous sections, this assumption is by no means required in the multigram approach. Thus, we expect the introduction of dependencies, *via* bigram models of joint sequences for instance, to improve these results.

As far as the overlapping model is specifically concerned, it is worth mentioning that the overlapping constraints may cause some input to remain unpronounced. In fact, this may be a desirable feature: for lack of better evidence, it is virtually impossible to transcribe accurately some very unusual forms, typically words borrowed from a foreign language.

8 Conclusions and Perspectives

The variable-length sequence modeling schemes offers a new framework for the description of many real-world data, such as those observed in the fields of natural language and speech processing, biological sequences modeling, and more generally discrete event systems.

The original (independent) multigram model can be generalized by introducing various kinds of statistical dependencies $\bar{n}$-grams of multigrams, embedded multigrams, etc...). An alternative way to account for contextual effects can be the use of structural constraints. For instance, the overlapping constraints appear to be efficient for grapheme-to-phoneme transcription.

This paper contributes in highlighting the links between both approaches. Their expression under a common formalism is a first step towards the integration of statistically- and structurally-based descriptions of symbolic streams. In particular, both models strongly relate to the goals of grammatical inference, for they describe the underlying structure of data in an unsupervised manner.

References

1. Frédéric Bimbot, Roberto Pieraccini, Esther Levin, and Bishnu Atal. Variable length sequence modeling: Multigrams. *IEEE Signal Processing Letters*, 2(6), 1995.
2. Sabine Deligne and Frédéric Bimbot. Language modelling by variable length sequences: theoretical formulation and evaluation of multigrams. In *Proceedings of the International Conference on Acoustics, Speech and Signal Processing (ICASSP)*, 1995.
3. Sabine Deligne, Frédéric Bimbot, and François Yvon. Phonetic transcription by variable length sequences: joint multigrams. In *Proceedings of the European Conference on Speech Communication and Technology (Eurospeech)*, Madrid, Sept. 1995.
4. A. P. Dempster, N. M. Laird, and D. B. Rubin. Maximum-likelihood from incomplete data via the EM algorithm. *Journal of the Royal Statistical Society*, 39(1):1–38, 1977.
5. Guy Pérennou, Monique de Calmès, Isabelle Ferrané, and Jean-Marie Pécatte. Le projet BDLEX de base de données lexicales du français écrit et parlé. Actes du séminaire lexique, Toulouse, Janv. 1992.
6. Kari Torkolla. An efficient way to learn English grapheme-to-phoneme rules automatically. In *Proceedings of the International Conference on Acoustics, Speech and Signal Processing (ICASSP)*, volume 2, Minneapolis, Apr. 1993.
7. François Yvon. Grapheme-to-phoneme conversion using multiple unbounded overlapping chunks. In *Proceeding of NeMLap'II*, Ankara, Turkey, 1996.
8. François Yvon. *Prononcer par analogie : motivations, formalisations et évaluations*. PhD thesis, École Nationale Supérieure des Télécommunications, Paris, 1996.

A Disagreement Count Scheme for Inference of Constrained Markov Networks

J. Gregor * and M.G. Thomason

Department of Computer Science, University of Tennessee, Knoxville, TN 37996 USA

Abstract. This paper describes a form of Markov chain, called a constrained Markov network, and its inference from finite-length sequences over a finite alphabet as a structural/statistical model of a class of strings for purposes of pattern analysis and recognition. In particular, we describe how the inference can be based on string alignments computed optimally by dynamic programming using an integer frequency-count disagreement cost function. We also discuss systematic reduction of network size by "pruning away" stages associated with low probability of observable symbols. Empirical results are reported for sequences representing band patterns in human chromosomes.

1 Introduction

For some patterns represented by finite length strings of symbols, a finite Markov chain is an effective model. Methods in the general area of creating or updating Markov chains by processing learning data include inference of stochastic finite-state automata and hidden Markov models; for example, see [1, 2, 3] for introductions. In this paper, we focus on a particular approach that creates a Markov network, a finite Markov chain with a unique initial state and no loops or cycles before a final, absorbing state [4]; similar pattern models are produced by the ECGIA algorithm [5, 6]. Sequence alignment computed optimally by dynamic programming is used to search for patterns which recur in samples but may be embedded in natural variations or random noise. By maintaining frequency counts of aligned symbols, a Markov network not only describes relative positions of symbols within learning data, but also imposes relative-frequency probabilities on symbol occurrences. Consequently, an appropriate cost function causes substrings that recur in approximately the same locations to align with one another and to emerge with relatively high probabilities, whereas nonrecurrent symbols tend to low probabilities. Overall effectiveness of these models in pattern recognition depends on the strings' having recurrent patterns suitable for approximation by first-order Markov chains and on the availability of learning data that is structurally and statistically typical of the classes. The remainder of the paper is devoted to the *constrained Markov network* [7] which is a simpler but more powerful model that resembles the "multivalued strings" defined in [8].

* Supported in part by a Professional Development Award from the University of Tennessee.

$$\begin{array}{c} 2 \\ 1 \\ 0 \end{array} \left[\begin{array}{cccccc} 23 & 2 & 0 & 12 & 8 & 1 \\ 7 & 21 & 2 & 15 & 8 & 28 \\ 0 & 7 & 28 & 3 & 14 & 1 \end{array} \right] \begin{array}{c} a \\ b \\ \epsilon \end{array}$$

$$\begin{array}{cccccc} 0 & 1 & 2 & 3 & 4 & 5 \end{array}$$

Fig. 1. An example of a CMN.

In particular, we introduce an integer based disagreement count cost function that in addition to being easy to compute also facilitates network-to-network alignment computations.

2 Constrained Markov Network (CMN)

The CMN topology is fixed to be a straightforward concatenation of stages. Each stage independently gives a choice of either an observable symbol α from the string alphabet Σ or the unobservable empty symbol ϵ; the latter is needed to align strings of different lengths and to align substrings in different strings optimally with one another. Within the ith stage, the jth symbol is assigned an integer frequency count f_{ij} ranging in value from 0 to F where F is the number of strings aligned to infer the network; also, $F = \sum_{j \in A} f_{ij}$ for all i where $A = \Sigma \cup \epsilon$. Figure 1 gives an example of a CMN in terms of a matrix (the bracketed part) whose rows and columns correspond to symbols and stages, respectively. We compute the relative-frequency probability of observing symbol j in stage i as f_{ij}/F. Thus, the probability of the unobservable empty symbol is $f_{i\epsilon}/F$, and the probability of an observable symbol is $1 - f_{i\epsilon}/F$. The CMN inference process involves updating the frequency counts and, as necessary, add new stages.

In conventional string-to-string and string-to-network alignments [9, 10], the edit operations match/substitute, insert, and delete are standard local operations on strings. Individual edits are assigned real-valued, additive costs. Optimal (minimum cost) edit sequences are conveniently computed by dynamic programming. CMN stages correspond directly to moves in the dynamic programming cost matrix during inference and are created by a single local operation *merge*. Alignment costs are based on symbol frequency counts. The number of stages in an inferred network and each stage's local frequency distribution are determined by optimal alignments during inference—an aspect of the method that adapts the costs to the specific learning data. The form of concatenated stages for CMNs makes it convenient and natural to describe all alignments as network-to-network computations—even when single strings are involved in which case $F = 1$. Although structurally identical, we will use $\mathcal{N}$ to refer to a CMN that truly is a network and S to refer to a CMN that merely represents a string.

Now consider the alignment of the two networks $\mathcal{N}_1$ and $\mathcal{N}_2$ which have been inferred from F_1 and F_2 samples and have N_1 and N_2 stages, respectively. We

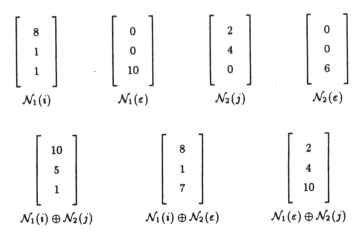

$$\begin{bmatrix} 8 \\ 1 \\ 1 \end{bmatrix} \qquad \begin{bmatrix} 0 \\ 0 \\ 10 \end{bmatrix} \qquad \begin{bmatrix} 2 \\ 4 \\ 0 \end{bmatrix} \qquad \begin{bmatrix} 0 \\ 0 \\ 6 \end{bmatrix}$$
$$\mathcal{N}_1(i) \qquad\qquad \mathcal{N}_1(\varepsilon) \qquad\qquad \mathcal{N}_2(j) \qquad\qquad \mathcal{N}_2(\varepsilon)$$

$$\begin{bmatrix} 10 \\ 5 \\ 1 \end{bmatrix} \qquad\qquad \begin{bmatrix} 8 \\ 1 \\ 7 \end{bmatrix} \qquad\qquad \begin{bmatrix} 2 \\ 4 \\ 10 \end{bmatrix}$$
$$\mathcal{N}_1(i) \oplus \mathcal{N}_2(j) \qquad \mathcal{N}_1(i) \oplus \mathcal{N}_2(\varepsilon) \qquad \mathcal{N}_1(\varepsilon) \oplus \mathcal{N}_2(j)$$

Fig. 2. Examples of CMN stage mergers.

define $\mathcal{N}_1(i) \oplus \mathcal{N}_2(j)$ to be the element-wise addition of the frequency counts of stage i from $\mathcal{N}_1$ and stage j from $\mathcal{N}_2$. This merge operation is equivalent to the match/substitute edit operation. Furthermore, we introduce the empty stage $\mathcal{N}_1(\varepsilon)$ (resp. $\mathcal{N}_2(\varepsilon)$) for which $f_{\varepsilon\alpha} = 0$ for all $\alpha \in \Sigma$ and $f_{\varepsilon\varepsilon} = F_1$ (resp. F_2). Such empty stages, which play a role in CMNs comparable to the empty symbol in ordinary strings, allow us to mimic the deletion and insertion edit operations by the merge operations $\mathcal{N}_1(i) \oplus \mathcal{N}_2(\varepsilon)$ and $\mathcal{N}_1(\varepsilon) \oplus \mathcal{N}_2(j)$. See Fig. 2 for examples of the CMN stage mergers. Finally, letting $\Delta(\ )$ denote the cost of a particular merge operation, the optimal alignment of $\mathcal{N}_1$ and $\mathcal{N}_2$ can be computed by standard dynamic programming using the recurrence relations:

$$d(0,0) = 0 \tag{1}$$

$$d(i,0) = d(i-1,0) + \Delta(\mathcal{N}_1(i) \oplus \mathcal{N}_2(\varepsilon)) \tag{2}$$

$$d(0,j) = d(0,j-1) + \Delta(\mathcal{N}_1(\varepsilon) \oplus \mathcal{N}_2(j)) \tag{3}$$

$$d(i,j) = \min \begin{cases} d(i-1,j) + \Delta(\mathcal{N}_1(i) \oplus \mathcal{N}_2(\varepsilon)) \\ d(i-1,j-1) + \Delta(\mathcal{N}_1(i) \oplus \mathcal{N}_2(j)) \\ d(i,j-1) + \Delta(\mathcal{N}_1(\varepsilon) \oplus \mathcal{N}_2(j)) \end{cases} \tag{4}$$

for $1 \le i \le N_1$ and $1 \le j \le N_2$. The computation fills in a $(N_1 + 1) \times (N_2 + 1)$ matrix. Each directed sequence of moves from the matrix origin at the upper left to its final entry at the lower right defines a candidate alignment of networks $\mathcal{N}_1$ and $\mathcal{N}_2$. The number of moves on these different alignments ranges from $\max(N_1, N_2)$ to $N_1 + N_2$. The CMN inferred by an alignment is the concatenation of stages created by the sequence of moves. There may be more than one optimal alignment. We break ties in practice by staying as close to the matrix "diagonal" as possible.

The above dynamic programming computation easily generalizes to simultaneous alignment of more than two CMNs via dynamic programming matrices with multiple axes; however, the matrix size grows as the product of the lengths of the networks, and the number of neighbors of each non-boundary position further grows exponentially with the number of axes d. The number of positions computed in a matrix with networks $\mathcal{N}_1, \mathcal{N}_2, \ldots, \mathcal{N}_d$ along d different axes is $\mathcal{O}(N_1 N_2 \ldots N_d)$. In terms of the number of neighbors checked to compute positions optimally, the complexity is $\mathcal{O}((2^d - 1)N_1 \ldots N_d)$. Sequential inference of a network for a class uses two axes by aligning the first two sample strings to produce the first network, then aligning each additional sample in turn with the existing CMN to produce an updated network until all F samples have been incorporated. All alignments in this paper are for two axes, so the computation complexity is $\mathcal{O}(3N_1 N_2)$.

3 Disagreement Count

There are many ways that costs can be assigned to the various merge operations. For string-to-network alignments, an option would be to aim for maximization of the alignment probability, i.e., the probability with which the updated network will generate the aligned string. This is achieved by [7]:

$$\Delta(\mathcal{N}(i) \oplus \mathcal{S}(j)) = -\log(f_{ij} + 1)/(F + 1) \qquad (5)$$

where $f_{ij} = f_{i\epsilon}$ if $j = \epsilon$ and $f_{ij} = 0$ if $i = \epsilon$. We take a different approach here and consider using an error measure in quadratic form to quantify the *disagreement* of frequencies within a stage. The resulting cost computation is straightforward integer summation and multiplication. Also, we note that the new cost function facilitates network-to-network alignments.

Let the disagreement count of the jth symbol in the ith stage of network $\mathcal{N}$ be defined as:

$$D_{ij}(\mathcal{N}) = f_{ij} \sum_{k \in A, k \neq j} f_{ik} \qquad (6)$$

$$= f_{ij}(F - f_{ij}). \qquad (7)$$

The value of $D_{ij}(\mathcal{N})$ ranges from a minimum of 0 if one symbol alone has non-zero frequency count, to a maximum of $F - 1$ if F different symbols have frequency count 1 each. By summing $D_{ij}(\mathcal{N})$ across all symbols in alphabet A we obtain the disagreement count of the ith stage itself:

$$D_i(\mathcal{N}) = \sum_{j \in A} D_{ij}(\mathcal{N}) \qquad (8)$$

$$= F^2 - \sum_{j \in A} f_{ij}^2. \qquad (9)$$

If we then sum $D_i(\mathcal{N})$ across all N stages, we obtain the disagreement count of network $\mathcal{N}$, namely:

$$D(\mathcal{N}) = \sum_{i=1}^{N} D_i(\mathcal{N}) \tag{10}$$

$$= NF^2 - \sum_{i=1}^{N} \sum_{j \in A} f_{ij}^2. \tag{11}$$

Suppose $\mathcal{N}$ is the network that results from aligning $\mathcal{N}_1$ and $\mathcal{N}_2$. Then we can specify minimization of $D(\mathcal{N})$ as the criterion for optimal network-to-network alignment. Thus, when we consider merging the mth stage of $\mathcal{N}_1$ with the nth stage of $\mathcal{N}_2$ we must compute:

$$\Delta(\mathcal{N}_1(m) \oplus \mathcal{N}_2(n)) = (F_1 + F_2)^2 - \sum_{j \in A} (f_{mj} + f_{nj})^2 \tag{12}$$

where $f_{mj} = F_1$ for $j = \varepsilon$ and 0 otherwise if $m = \varepsilon$ and, likewise, $f_{nj} = F_2$ for $j = \varepsilon$ and 0 otherwise if $n = \varepsilon$. For a string-to-network alignment we have that:

$$\Delta(\mathcal{N}(i) \oplus \mathcal{S}(j)) = D_i(\mathcal{N}) + 2(F - f_{ij}) \tag{13}$$

where $f_{ij} = f_{i\varepsilon}$ if $j = \varepsilon$, and $D_i(\mathcal{N}) = f_{ij} = 0$ if $i = \varepsilon$. This cost expression is particularly useful for sequential CMN inference during which $D_i(\mathcal{N})$ can be computed incrementally as the strings are aligned and incorporated one after the other.

An alternate interpretation of $D(\mathcal{N})$ gives additional insight into characteristics of optimal alignments. Specifically, if we sum $D_{ij}(\mathcal{N})$ across all stages before summing across all symbols and rearrange the various expressions, then we have that:

$$D(\mathcal{N}) = \sum_{j \in A} \sum_{i=1}^{N} D_{ij}(\mathcal{N}) \tag{14}$$

$$= Fn_\varepsilon + F \sum_{\alpha \in \Sigma} n_\alpha - \sum_{i=1}^{N} \sum_{j \in A} f_{ij}^2 \tag{15}$$

where $n_\varepsilon = \sum_{i=1}^{N} f_{i\varepsilon}$ and $n_\alpha = \sum_{i=1}^{N} f_{i\alpha}$. Equating (11) and (15) we find that:

$$n_\varepsilon = F(N - L) \tag{16}$$

where $L = (\sum_{\alpha \in \Sigma} n_\alpha)/F$ is the sample average length, a fixed value for a given sample set. Thus, in a network of N stages inferred from F samples, n_ε linearly tracks the number of stages in excess of the sample average length L. Because N must equal or exceed the length of the longest string in the learning data, we have $N \geq L$, and a necessary but not sufficient condition for $N = L$ is that all samples have the same length L. Given $F > 0$, then $N = L$ is a necessary and sufficient condition for $n_\varepsilon = 0$. But perhaps more importantly, substituting

$F(N-L)$ for n_ϵ, LF for $\sum_{\alpha \in \Sigma} n_\alpha$, and $F - \sum_{\alpha \in \Sigma} f_{i\alpha}$ for $f_{i\epsilon}$ in (15) we obtain an expression for $D(\mathcal{N})$ in terms of frequencies of observable symbols only, namely:

$$D(\mathcal{N}) = 2LF^2 - \sum_{i=1}^{N} \left[\sum_{\alpha \in \Sigma} f_{i\alpha}^2 + \left(\sum_{\alpha \in \Sigma} f_{i\alpha} \right)^2 \right] \tag{17}$$

Since $2LF^2$ is constant for a given sample set, $D(\mathcal{N})$ is minimized by maximizing the subtrahend. An optimal solution is thus a balance of two constraints: summing over moves in the dynamic programming matrix to maximize $\sum_{\alpha \in \Sigma} f_{i\alpha}^2$ emphasizes alignments in which individual observable symbols have larger frequency counts within stages, but without regard for how many stages the counts for different symbols are spread across; summing over moves to maximize $(\sum_{\alpha \in \Sigma} f_{i\alpha})^2$ seeks alignments that pack all observable symbols into the fewest number of stages. The first term represents the essential bias towards frequency reenforcements of individual observable symbols that signify recurrent patterns; the second term, which equals or exceeds the first in magnitude, simultaneously pushes n_ϵ towards lower values to bring N closer to L and produce a more compact network.

4 CMN Pruning

Consider the ith stage of network $\mathcal{N}$. The proportion of samples from which observable symbols were actually used to create that stage is $1 - f_{i\epsilon}/F$. If this proportion is relatively small, reasonable hypotheses are (1) that the stage is due to infrequent variants or noise rather than recurrent structure in the learning data, and (2) that removing the stage from $\mathcal{N}$ will produce a smaller, more compact network which may still retain crucial characteristics of recurrent structure.

Network pruning entails deleting from $\mathcal{N}$ every stage i with $1 - f_{i\epsilon}/F$ at or below a specific pruning level. The trend in the error rate in pattern classification is investigated by systematically increasing the pruning level and, at each level, pruning the CMNs for all classes and repeating the classification experiment with the same test data. Relatively minor fluctuations in error rate imply that structure distinguishing among classes is not being damaged by deletion of stages; a significantly escalating error rate implies that pruning has begun to remove significant structural information. A plot of expected number of observable symbols on paths versus pruning level also illustrates how a key ensemble characteristic of learning data, viz., L, is sacrificed as CMNs are made smaller by deletion of stages. An empirical study of pruning is given below.

5 Experimental Results

5.1 Data Material

In this section, we report network statistics and classification error rates for string representations of banded human chromosomes obtained from a database

Table 1. Learning and test data statistics.

Denver group	Chromosome types	Length characteristics Min	Max	Mean
A	1–3	59	106	78.9
B	4–5	56	74	64.0
C	6–12	44	72	52.2
D	13–15	36	46	40.5
E	16–18	30	38	34.4
F	19–20	26	32	28.6
G	21–22	21	38	24.5
Avrg	1–22	21	106	48.2

with approximately 7,000 samples that have been classified by cytogenetic experts. The centromere location, which is defined as the transition between the shorter p-arm and the longer q-arm, is coded into the data. Each digitized chromosome image is processed to obtain an idealized, one-dimensional density profile that emphasizes the band pattern along the chromosome. The idealized profile is mapped nonlinearly into a string composed of symbols from the alphabet {1,2,3,4,5,6}. Finally, this string is difference coded using the alphabet = for 0, A for +1, a for −1, ..., to represent signed differences of successive symbols in a left-to-right scan. See [11, 12] for more details on the raw data and the profile-to-string processing. Two balanced datasets, α and β, are formed for each of the 22 non-sex chromosome types by assigning every other of the 200 mid-length samples from the database to each of the datasets in turn. Table 1 lists length characteristics of the resulting 4400 samples by Denver group, a standard grouping in cytogenetics. Network statistics reported below are averages over the CMNs inferred from the α and β datasets. Likewise, the classification error rates reported below are the average results obtained by inferring using an α dataset and testing with a β dataset, and vice versa.

5.2 Network Inference

Each CMN is constructed by concatenating two sub-networks, namely, one inferred from the p-arm portion of the learning strings and one inferred from the q-arm portion; the learning strings are aligned and incorporated one at the time as described above. To compare the performance of the minimum disagreement count (DC) cost function (cf. (13)) we also carry out the inference using the maximum alignment probability (MP) cost function (cf. (5)). Network characteristics are listed in Table 2 as averages for Denver groups and for all types. We see that the disagreement count cost function produces shorter networks that have slightly more paths and higher path entropies than the maximum alignment

Table 2. CMN statistics and classification error rates.

Denver group	No. of Stages		No. of Paths[a]		Path Entropy[b]		Error Rate (%)	
	MP	DC	MP	DC	MP	DC	MP	DC
A	137	132	66	69	63	65	2.5	3.3
B	113	106	53	56	52	53	4.5	4.5
C	91	86	42	45	40	42	5.1	5.0
D	72	69	34	36	35	36	4.8	5.2
E	59	56	28	30	28	29	6.7	6.0
F	50	49	24	25	23	23	13.5	13.2
G	44	42	20	21	20	21	8.0	7.5
Avrg	84	80	40	42	39	40	5.9	5.9

[a] Order of magnitude. [b] $H = -\sum_{i=1}^{N} \sum_{j \in A} (f_{ij}/F) \log(f_{ij}/F)$.

probability cost function. Thus, the disagreement count cost function tends to focus on building more compact (shorter) networks whereas the maximum alignment probability cost function seems to aim for networks whose stages have their frequency mass concentrated in fewer symbols.

5.3 Classification

The disagreement count cost function is designed for inference and is not scaled appropriately for pattern classification involving comparisons across different networks. For classification purposes, we therefore use the maximum alignment probability cost function. The string is classified according to the network for which the largest value occurs[2]. There were no ties with this data. Table 2 lists the average classification error rates per Denver group and for all 22 chromosome types. The difference in the results obtained for the networks inferred using the disagreement count cost function and those inferred using the maximum alignment probability cost function is statistically insignificant. Thus, while the CMNs inferred using the disagreement count cost function perform no better than those obtained with the maximum alignment probability cost function they also perform no worse. Finally, we note that the CMN results in general compare well with the results obtained when applying other methods to the same database (cf. [7, 11, 12, 13]).

[2] The purpose of this experiment is direct comparison of the two types of CMNs as pattern models inferred from the same data; additional processing is therefore neither carried out before nor after alignments to improve the final classification results [13].

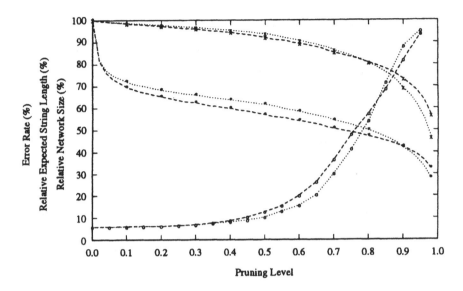

Fig. 3. Average CMN pruning results: relative network size (*), relative expected string length (x), and classification error rate (o) for the disagreement count (dotted) and maximum alignment probability (dashed) cost functions.

5.4 CMN Pruning

Average CMN pruning results are given in Fig. 3 for relative network size (number of stages), relative expected string length (expected number of observable symbols on paths), and classification error rate. Relative network size and expected string length is computed as the pruning level is changed by steps of 2 in frequency count; error rate is computed for steps of 5 in frequency count. Not all markers are shown. Relative size and expected string length for individual networks match these averages quite well at all pruning levels. The individual error rates for some networks are offset considerably from the average rate; but the trend for each network approximately parallels the average trend up to pruning level 0.6, beyond which there is increasing variance due to extensive damage to network structures.

Steep slopes in the graph of relative network size indicate that many stages are removed for a small increase in pruning level, i.e., that many stages exist with the same probability of an observable symbol. Likewise, a flatter slope shows that few stages exist at each pruning level. Figure 3 shows that about one-third of a typical CMN's stages produce an observable symbol with low probability (0.0–0.1) and another one-third with high probability (0.9–1.0). The remaining one-third of the stages are quite evenly distributed over a wide range of probabilities (0.1–0.9) with few stages for each value. This pattern appears consistently for all networks inferred for the chromosome data for both cost functions.

The expected string length of an unpruned network equals the sample average length of learning strings, L. The graph of relative expected string length shows that even extensive pruning causes little reduction in this network characteristic. For example, reducing average network size by 40% (pruning level 0.5) reduces the average expected string length only 5% (2.5 symbols).

Relatively minor change in average error rate as pruning level is increased implies that the network structure discriminating one class from another remains fairly intact; a more rapidly escalating error rate implies that essential structure is being lost. Up to pruning level 0.35, the error rate increases an average of 0.5% per change of 0.1 in pruning level; thereafter, the increase in error rate is more rapid and reaches an average of 25% per change of 0.1 in pruning level beyond level 0.65. We note that the maximum alignment probability inferred networks degenerate slightly faster than those inferred using disagreement count.

The long-run, joint probability of being in the ith stage at the observable symbol α is $\pi_{i\alpha} = f_{i\alpha}/(NF)$. Summing over all N stages gives the long-run, marginal probability of α among all observable and unobservable symbols in all paths, $\pi_\alpha = \sum_{i=1}^{N} \pi_{i\alpha} = n_\alpha/(NF)$. Further summing over all $\alpha \in \Sigma$ gives the long-run probability of an observable symbol at a random stage, $\pi_\Sigma = \sum_{\alpha \in \Sigma} \pi_\alpha = L/N$, and $\pi_\epsilon = 1 - L/N$. There is strong linear correlation between L and N across both types of networks. The correlation coefficient is 0.99. Linear regression yields an L-to-N ratio of approximately 0.60; hence, we have $\pi_\Sigma \cong 0.6$ and $\pi_\epsilon \cong 0.4$ for each unpruned chromosome network. The first levels of pruning yield networks for which the size decreases sharply but the expected string length remains very close to the original sample average L. This causes a distinct increase in the π_Σ value. For example, at pruning level 0.1 the average size of the disagreement count networks is 0.72 times the original, the average string length is $0.99L$, π_Σ has risen to 0.83, and π_ϵ has fallen to 0.17. Pruning level 0.5 gives networks with average size 0.62 times the original, average string length $0.94L$, $\pi_\Sigma = 0.91$, and $\pi_\epsilon = 0.09$. As pruning continues beyond 0.5, π_Σ approaches 1.0 but the escalating loss of observable symbols accelerates the damage to network structures and causes the rapidly increasing error rate. The results are similar for the maximum alignment probability networks.

6 Conclusion

We have presented a new integer disagreement count cost function for CMN inference. Network statistics and classification error rates are similar to those obtained for the maximum alignment probability cost function used previously. In addition to its computational simplicity, the disagreement count cost function has the advantage that it is directly applicable for network-to-network alignments.

References

1. L. Miclet, "Grammatical inference," in *Syntactic and Structural Pattern Recognition Theory and Applications* (H. Bunke and A. Sanfeliu, eds.), pp. 237–290, World Scientific, 1990.

2. J. Gregor, "Data-driven inductive inference of finite-state automata," *Int. J. Pattern Recogn. Artif. Intell.*, vol. 8, pp. 305–322, 1994.

3. M. G. Thomason and J. Gregor, "Inference of Markov chain models of sequences," *Current Topics in Pattern Recognition Research*, pp. 163–173, 1995.

4. M. G. Thomason and E. Granum, "Dynamic programming inference of Markov networks from finite sets of sample strings," *IEEE Trans. PAMI*, vol. 8, pp. 491–501, 1986.

5. H. Rulot and E. Vidal, "Modelling (sub)string-length based constraints through a grammatical inference method," in *Pattern Recognition Theory and Applications* (P. A. Devijver and J. Kittler, eds.), pp. 451–459, Springer-Verlag, 1987.

6. H. Rulot and E. Vidal, "An efficient algorithm for the inference of circuit-free automata," in *Syntactic and Structural Pattern Recognition* (G. Ferratè, T. Pavlidis, A. Sanfeliu, and H. Bunke, eds.), pp. 173–184, Springer-Verlag, 1988.

7. C. E. Guthrie, J. Gregor, and M. G. Thomason, "Constrained Markov networks for automated analysis of G-banded chromosomes," *Comput. Biol. Medicine*, vol. 23, pp. 105–114, 1993.

8. H. Bunke and D. Pasche, "Parsing multivalued strings and its application to image and waveform recognition," in *Structural Pattern Analysis* (R. Mohr, T. Pavlidis, and A. Sanfeliu, eds.), pp. 1–17, World Scientific, 1989.

9. R. A. Wagner and M. J. Fischer, "The string-to-string correction problem," *J. Assoc. Comput. Mach.*, vol. 21, pp. 168–173, 1974.

10. D. Sankoff and J. B. Kruskal, eds., *Time Warps, String Edits, and Macromolecules: The Theory and Practice of Sequence Comparisons.* Addison-Wesley, 1983.

11. E. Granum, M. G. Thomason, and J. Gregor, "On the use of automatically inferred Markov networks for chromosome analysis," in *Automation of Cytogenetics* (C. Lundsteen and J. Piper, eds.), pp. 233–251, Springer-Verlag, 1989.

12. E. Granum and M. G. Thomason, "Automatically inferred Markov network models for classification of chromosomal band pattern structures," *Cytometry*, vol. 11, pp. 26–39, 1990.

13. J. Gregor and M. G. Thomason, "Hybrid pattern recognition using Markov networks," *IEEE Trans. PAMI*, vol. 15, pp. 651–656, 1993.

Using Knowledge to Improve N-Gram Language Modelling Through the MGGI Methodology

Enrique Vidal and David Llorens
e-mail: evidal@dsic.upv.es

Departamento de Sistemas Informáticos y Computación
Universidad Politécnica de Valencia
SPAIN

Abstract. The structural limitations of N-Gram models used for Language Modelling are illustrated through several examples. In most cases of interest, these limitations can be easily overcome using (general) regular or finite-state models, without having to resort to more complex, recursive devices. The problem is how to obtain the required finite-state structures from reasonably small amounts of training (positive) sentences of the considered task. Here this problem is approached through a Grammatical Inference technique known as MGGI. This allows us to easily apply a priory knowledge about the type of syntactic constraints that are relevant to the considered task to significantly improve the performance of N-Grams, using similar or smaller amounts of training data. Speech Recognition experiments are presented with results supporting the interest of the proposed approach.

1 Introduction

A well known result in Grammatical Inference (GI) states that learning Regular Languages (RL) using only positive data is undecidable [10]. As a consequence, in order to learn RLs, additional information, not contained in the training (positive) examples themselves, is required. This information may take the form of *negative data* [11] [16] [13], *equivalence queries* [2] or *probabilistic information* [5] [19] [3]. Alternatively, this information can consist of the knowledge that the target languages of interest belong to a certain *subclass* of RLs that can be shown to be learnable from only positive data (*characterisable methods* [1]). Yet another alternative is to make more direct use of a-priori knowledge about the kind of syntactic constraints that are desired to be captured in the learned models. This generally leads to so called *heuristic methods*.

A step towards formalising this heuristic use of knowledge was introduced by Garcia et al. with the name "*Morphic Generator Grammatical Inference Methodology*" (MGGI) [8].

In this work we apply the MGGI approach to the problem of Language Modelling (LM). This problem has become central in the field of Automatic Speech Recognition (ASR). Current state-of-the-art ASR systems model the language of each ASR application through the use of *N-Grams*. However, it is argued that

---

* Work partially supported by the Spanish CICYT under grant TIC95–0984–C02–01

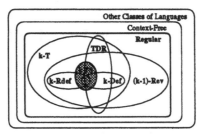

Fig. 1. Some families of Languages.

significant modelling improvements are required to overcome the most important limitations of current systems [12]. As we will see later on, languages described by N-Grams are equivalent to the so called stochastic *k-Testable Languages in the Strict Sense* (k-TS languages). This well known class of languages happens to be a very restricted subclass of (stochastic) Regular Languages that can only model *local or short-term* language constraints (Figure 1).

Even if we restrict ourselves to the class of Regular Languages (RL), many families or subclasses of languages exist that are significantly more powerful than k-TS/N-Grams, in the sense that they can help modelling more *global or long-term constraints*. Moreover, in many cases, adequate techniques do exist to learn the structures of the corresponding models from training sentences of the unknown target language [20]. However, learning structures that are significantly more complex than those underlying k-TSs may require large amounts of training data since all the relevant, perhaps long-term relations among the data that entail the corresponding syntactic restrictions have to be "shown" to the learning algorithm. Clearly, this may result prohibitive in many practical situations. The following example illustrates this fact along with the limited nature of k-TS/N-Gram models to capture certain syntactic constraints of interest.

Example 1 *The regular language $(a + d)b^+(c + e)$ (Figure 2 left), is 2-TS (2-Gram), 2-T and 1-Reversible. Conversely, a language such as $(ab^+c) + (db^+e)$ (Figure 2 right), which is also regular, 1-Reversible and 2-T, can by no means be adequately modelled by a k-TS model (k-Gram), for any possible k.* □

Fig. 2. Left: a model for the language $(a+d)b^+(c+e)$ which is 2-TS, 2-T and 1-Reversible. Right: a model for the language $(ab^+c)+(db^+e)$ which is also 2-T and 1-Reversible but can not be modelled by a k-TS model (k-Gram), for any possible k.

Real situations in LM in which syntactic restrictions of the kind just illustrated apply are rather common. For instance, in modelling the language for a telephone exchange, sentences like *"please, I wanted to talk to Mr. X"*, or *"may I speak with Mr. Y, please"* can be expected, but a sentence like *"please, I would like to talk to Mr. Z, please"*, would be very unlikely. Any attempt to (deterministically or probabilistically) model this language constraint would require a (finite-state) structure, similar to that schematically exemplified in **Figure 2** right, and no k-TS structure, for any k, can a approach this kind of restrictions properly. Nevertheless, it should be noted that learning other structures would demand at least twice the data required to learn a k-TS model which would miss the restrictions discussed.

As we will see in this paper, the MGGI approach readily allows the use of a-priori knowledge, not only to enforce the kind of syntactic constraints that are relevant for each application, but also to diminish the lack-of-data problem, yielding LMs that clearly outperform k-TS/N-Grams.

2 K-Testable Languages in the Strict Sense and N-Grams

This family of languages was introduced by Zalcstein in 1972 [21]. A *k-Testable Language in the Strict Sense* (k-TS) is often defined by means of a four-tuple $Z_k = (\Sigma, I, F, T)$ where Σ is the *alphabet*; I and F are, respectively, sets of *initial* and *final substrings* of length smaller than k; and T is a set of *forbidden substrings* of length k. A language associated with Z_k is defined by the following regular expression [21]:

$$L(Z_k) = I\Sigma^* \cap \Sigma^* F - \Sigma^* T \Sigma^* \tag{1}$$

In other words, $L(Z_k)$ consists of strings that begin with substrings in I, end with substrings in F and do not contain any substring in T. Instead of using the *forbidden* set T in the definition of Z_k the set of *permitted* substrings, $\Sigma^k - T$, can be more conveniently used in many cases.

Example 2 *(c.f. Figure 2 left)*
$Z_2 = (\{a, b, c, d, e\}, \{a, d\}, \{c, e\}, \{a, b, c, d, e\}^2 - \{ab, db, bb, bc, be\})$
$L(Z_2) = \{abc, abe, dbc, dbe, abbc, abbe, dbbc, dbbe, abbbc, abbbe, dbbbc, dbbbe, \ldots\}$ □

Particularly interesting is the $k = 2$ case (2-TS), traditionally known as *Local Languages*. On the other hand, a related family of languages is the class of *k-Testable* (k-T) languages (*not* in the strict sense) already mentioned in the previous section. A k-T language is defined as a finite boolean composition of k-TS languages [21]. This family of languages is significantly more general than the k-TS class (c.f. Fig. 1 and Example 2), but no *efficient* algorithm is known so far for learning this family from positive sentences only.

The inference of k-TS languages was considered in [9], where a simple algorithm called k-TSI was introduced. It starts building the sets Σ, I, F, T out of the training sentences and then builds a finite-state automaton from these sets. Alternatively, this automaton can also be directly built from the training sentences [20]. Properties of the k-TSI algorithm, studied in [9], include worst-case efficient computation and Identification in the Limit of the k-TS class.

The following example illustrates k-TS inference, along with the limited modelling capabilities of k-TS models.

Example 3

Let $R = \{abc, dbe, abbc, dbbe, abbbc, dbbbe\}$ be a sample drawn from the language of the automaton shown in Figure 2 right (Example 1). The automata produced by k-TSI for $k = 2$, $k = 3$ and $k = 4$ and the corresponding languages are shown in Figure 3. L_2 is the language of the automaton shown in Figure 2 left (Example 1 – see also Example 2). Both L_2 and L_3 are clear overgeneralisations, while L_4 is exactly the training sample. No language yields a satisfactory approximation to the target language in this case. □

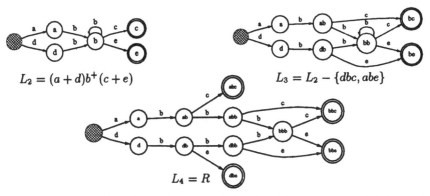

$$L_2 = (a + d)b^+(c + e) \qquad L_3 = L_2 - \{dbc, abe\}$$

$$L_4 = R$$

Fig. 3. Automata yield by k-TSI from $R = \{abc, dbe, abbc, dbbe, abbbc, dbbbe\}$ (see Figure 2 right), for $k = 2, k = 3$ and $k = 4$.

Since the models yield by k-TSI are deterministic and hence *unambiguous*, a max-likelihood estimation of the transition probabilities can be easily obtained from the frequency of use of each transition in the parsing of the training sentences. These frequencies can be trivially computed during execution of the k-TSI algorithm itself. The probabilities estimated in this way are quite directly related with N-Gram probabilities.

Let (q', w, q) be a transition of a model provided by k-TSI, where the name assigned to q' consists of a unique sequence of $k - 1$ words, $v_1 \dots v_{k-1}$, that lead to q'. This transition can then be written as $(v_1 \dots v_{k-1}, w, q)$ and its probability, $p((q', w, q))$, as $p((v_1 \dots v_{k-1}, w, q))$. Now, since the model is deterministic, the state q is uniquely specified by q' and w. Hence, $p((q', w, q))$ can be written as $p(w|q') = p(w|v_1 \dots v_{k-1})$; that is, the probability that the word w follows the sequence of previous words $v_1 \dots v_{k-1}$. In general, the following relation between k-TS models and N-grams can be formally established[2] [18]:

Fact 1 *Stochastic k-TS models are equivalent to N-Grams, with $N = k$.* □

---

[2] Two models are considered equivalent in this context if both assign the same probability to any string of *finite length*. Within the N-Gram paradigm, probabilities are assigned to *prefixes* of a unique infinite-length string assumedly generated by the model, and finite-length sentences are usually handled by using special symbols, not included in the vocabulary, to mark the beginnings and ends of the different sentences.

3 Morphism Theorem: Any Regular Language can be Represented using a 2-Gram

The capabilities of k-TS languages are strongly limited by the fact that they can only enforce local or short-term constraints. However, these languages (or, more specifically, the simplest case of $k = 2$; i.e., *Local Languages*) can be used as the basis for a technique that allows us to easily model any language from the whole class of Regular Languages. This is possible thanks to the following theorem [15]:

Theorem 1 (Morphism Theorem) *Let Σ be a finite alphabet and $L \subseteq \Sigma^*$ a regular language. There exist then a finite alphabet Σ', a letter-to-letter morphism[3] $h : \Sigma'^* \to \Sigma^*$, and a Local Language $l \subseteq \Sigma'$ such that $L = h(l)$.* □

The proof of this theorem is constructive (see [15] and [4], pag.18). If A is a DFA of L, Σ' is obtained by subindexing the symbols of Σ with the states of A they can be parsed through, and the Local Language l is built from the pairs of (subindexed) symbols associated with the possible pairs of consecutive transitions of A. The following example illustrates this construction:

Example 4

Let L be the language of the automaton shown in Figure 2 right, which is not k-TS for any value of k (Examples 1 and 3). It can be exactly represented by means of a morphism h and a 2-TS/2-Gram model $Z_2 = (\Sigma', I, F, T)$, where

$$\Sigma' = \{a_2, b_4, b_5, c_6, d_3, e_6\}, \qquad I = \{a_2, d_3\}, \qquad F = \{c_6, e_6\},$$
$$T = \Sigma'^2 - \{d_3b_5, b_5b_5, b_5e_6, a_2b_4, b_4b_4, b_4c_6\}$$

The corresponding 2-TS automaton is shown in Figure 4 left. The morphism h simply consists of removing the subindexes of the terminals. By applying this morphism and performing standard minimisation, an automaton identical to the original one (Figure 2) is obtained. □

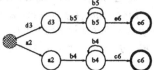

Fig. 4. Illustration of the construction used in the proof of the Morphism Theorem.

As a consequence of the morphism theorem and the equivalence of 2-TS and 2-Gram models, the popular 2-Grams can be considered as *"universal"* devices for the representation of *any regular Language Model*.

4 Learning General Regular Grammars: MGGI Approach

In the previous section we have seen how any *given* RL can be represented by a 2-TS/2-Gram model by simply relabelling the vocabulary. However, in many

---

[3] A letter-to-letter morphism between two alphabets Σ' and Σ is a function $h : \Sigma'^* \to \Sigma^*$ such that: $h(xy) = h(x)h(y) \; \forall x, y \in \Sigma'$; $h(\Sigma') = \Sigma$; and $h(\lambda) = \lambda$.

cases of interest, the target language unfortunately is not "given". Instead, it is an *unknown* language that we want to *"model"*; i.e., to *approach* using a model that belongs to a predefined class. As repeatedly mentioned throughout the previous sections, the currently most popular classes of models adopted for this *approximation* are N-Grams. In this section we will discuss how to obtain better (regular) models using the so called *Morphic Generator Grammatical Inference Methodology* (MGGI) [8].

While the construction used in the morphism theorem imposes the target language structure by labelling words according to the states they should be parsed through, in MGGI the lack of known target structure is compensated with a-priori knowledge about (perhaps long-term) *syntactic constraints* that are desired to be captured by the inferred model. As we will see later on, these constraints can often be quite naturally expressed also by means of appropriate word labelling schemes.

Let Σ and Σ' be two finite alphabets and $R \subset \Sigma^*$ a finite set of training sentences. The words of the sentences in R are renamed according to a suitable *"renaming function"*, g, obtaining a new set $R' = g(R) \subset \Sigma'^*$. From R' the corresponding 2-TS language, $l(g(R))$, is obtained and, then, another renaming process, h, is applied which, in this case, is a *letter-to-letter morphism*. The MGGI-inferred language is thus $L = h(l(g(R)))$. The goal is to restrict the overgeneralization of 2-TSs by means of appropriate definitions of the word-renaming functions g and h. While these functions are in principle independent of each-other, a natural choice is to make h the *inverse* of g. In this case, the following property holds [8]:

Theorem 2

Let $R \subset \Sigma^*$ be a finite set of sentences and $L = h(l(g(R)))$ the language obtained from R by MGGI. If $h(g(R)) = R$, then $R \subseteq L \subseteq l(R)$. □

Example 5

Let $R = \{abc, dbe, abbc, dbbe, abbbc, dbbbe\}$ be a training set of sentences drawn from a supposedly unknown language (c.f. Figure 2 and Examples 1, 3 and 4). By inspection of R one can guess that a key syntactic feature consists of correctly matching beginnings and ends of sentences. This suggests the use of a renaming function defined as:

$$g(R) = \{ab_{ac}c, db_{de}e, ab_{ac}b_{ac}c, db_{de}b_{de}e, ab_{ac}b_{ac}b_{ac}c, db_{de}b_{de}b_{de}e\} = R'$$

Using R' as a training set, the 2-TS algorithm yields an automaton isomorphic with that of Figure 4 left. According to the condition of Theorem 2 (i.e., $h(g(R)) = R$), the morphism h should simply consists in dropping the subindexes. After minimisation, this yields the automaton of Figure 2 right. □

5 MGGI and Language Modelling

Following the suggestions of the last section, we illustrate here how MGGI proves particularly adequate to improve the modelling accuracy of k-TS models, with the help of a-priori knowledge of the task under consideration.

The first example is drawn from the so-called *"Miniature Language Acquisition"* (MLA) task, originally introduced by Feldman et al. as a *"touch-stone"* for testing the capabilities of (language) learning systems [7]. The task consists of the description of simple two-dimensional visual scenes involving a few geometric objects with different shape, shade and size. In the simplest formulation of MLA [7], shapes may be *triangle, circle* and *square*, shades *dark* and *light* and sizes *large, medium* and *small*. These objects may be located in different relative positions: *above, below, touch*, etc. Only one positional relation can be expressed in each sentence and it may involve one or two geometric objects in a certain relative position with another object or pair of objects. Thus up to 4 geometric objects may be named in a sentence [7]. Although this implies a finite language, it is actually very large, with more than 10^7 different, equally likely sentences.

Example 6 *Consider the following training set from Feldman's MLA task:*

$R = \{$ a triangle and a small light circle are to the left of a small square,

a small light circle is to the right of a square and a triangle,

a circle and a triangle touch a medium square,

a small square touches a small light circle$\}$

The k-TS/k-Gram models obtained from these sentences for $2 \leq k \leq 6$ have 18, 29, 37, 41 *and* 43 *states and* 28, 36, 40, 42 *and* 42 *edges, respectively. The corresponding languages for $2 \leq k \leq 5$ are clear overgeneralisations, while for $k = 6$ no generalisation is obtained. All these languages contain the training set R. $L_5 - R$ consists of 6 sentences, from which 2 are correct generalisations and 4 are overgeneralization errors. $L_4 - R$ has 14 sentences, 4 correct and 10 errors. $L_3 - R$ is an infinite language; it has 788 sentences up to length 22 (the maximum correct in the MLA language), 39 of which are correct and 749 errors. $L_2 - R$, finally, is also infinite and contains more than $2 \cdot 10^6$ sentences up to length 22, the vast majority of which (more than 99.99%) are errors. Some examples of incorrectly generalised sentences are:*

L_2:

a triangle touch a triangle touch a circle

a medium square and a small square and a small light circle is to the right of a
.... circle and a square

L_2, L_3:

a triangle touch a medium square

a triangle and a triangle and a triangle and a triangle and a triangle

....

L_2, L_3, L_4:

a small light circle are to the left of a small square touches a small light circle

a small light circle is to the right of a square and a triangle touch a medium square

....

L_2, L_3, L_4, L_5:

a small square touches a small light circle are to the left of a small square

a small square touches a small light circle is to the right of a square and a triangle

....   □

One of the most prominent errors among these bad generalisations is improper *number agreement*; i.e., wrong use of *singular* and *plural* forms of the verbs. This is clearly caused by the merging of constructions corresponding to verb *subjects* which consist of single-objects with those that consists of a couple-of-objects.

Example 7

A better generalisation of the training set of Example 6 can be achieved through MGGI by labelling all the words of the training sentences that precede the verb so that the first (singular) and the second (plural) possible objects are distinguished:

$$g(R) = \{ \text{ } a_1 \text{ triangle}_1 \text{ and}_2 \text{ } a_2 \text{ small}_2 \text{ light}_2 \text{ circle}_2 \text{ are to the left of a small square,}$$
$$a_1 \text{ small}_1 \text{ light}_1 \text{ circle}_1 \text{ is to the right of a square and a triangle,}$$
$$a_1 \text{ circle}_1 \text{ and}_2 \text{ } a_2 \text{ triangle}_2 \text{ touch a medium square,}$$
$$a_1 \text{ small}_1 \text{ square}_1 \text{ touches a small light circle} \} = R'$$

By supplying R' to 2-TSI and applying the standard morphism h (dropping the subindexes), the automaton shown in Figure 5 is obtained. The language of this automaton is infinite. It contains 2185 sentences up to length 22, from which only 276 generalisations strictly comply the restrictions of the MLA task. Nevertheless, all the "errors" are sentences having more than two geometric objects on the right hand of the verb. Examples of these sentences are:

a circle is to the right of a medium square and a square and a triangle
a small square touches a medium square and a square and a small light circle

········· □

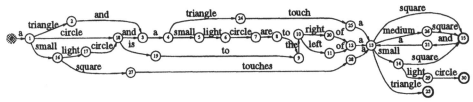

Fig. 5. Automaton obtained through MGGI from the (relabeled) training sentences of the MLA task (see Example 7).

It is worth noting that all these "bad" generalisations do involve *consistent number agreement* and can in fact be considered *correct* according to general English syntax. However, the pragmatics of the MLA task, as defined in [7], allows at most two geometric objects, not only as *subject*, but also as *object* or *complement* of a positional relation verb.

Example 8

All the restrictions on the numbers of objects involved in MLA sentences can be easily captured by applying a labelling similar to that of Example 7 also to the geometric objects that come after the verb. This labelling should thus allow to distinguish the syntactic roles of subject ("s") and object or complement ("o") within each sentence:

$g(R) =$

$\{$ a$_{s_1}$ triangle$_{s_1}$ and$_{s_2}$ a$_{s_2}$ small$_{s_2}$ light$_{s_2}$ circle$_{s_2}$ are to the left of a$_{o_1}$ small$_{o_1}$ square$_{o_1}$,

a$_{s_1}$ small$_{s_1}$ light$_{s_1}$ circle$_{s_1}$ is to the right of a$_{o_1}$ square$_{o_1}$ and$_{o_2}$ a$_{o_2}$ triangle$_{o_2}$,

a$_{s_1}$ circle$_{s_1}$ and$_{s_2}$ a$_{s_2}$ triangle$_{s_2}$ touch a$_{o_1}$ medium$_{o_1}$ square$_{o_1}$,

a$_{s_1}$ small$_{s_1}$ square$_{s_1}$ touches a$_{o_1}$ small$_{o_1}$ light$_{o_1}$ circle$_{o_1}$ $\}$ $= R'$

By supplying R' to 2-TSI and applying the standard morphism h (dropping the subindexes), the automaton shown in Figure 6 is obtained. Its language contains 94 generalised sentences, all of which are correct. Clearly, this appears to be the best possible generalisation of the given training data. □

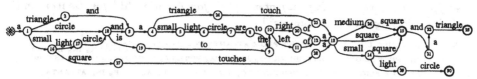

Fig. 6. Automaton obtained through MGGI from (relabeled) training sentences of the MLA task (see Example 8).

The last example is taken from the DARPA ATIS task [17]. ATIS stands for Air Travel Information System and the task was built around a subset of the OAG (Official Airline Guide) database. Sentences of this task consist of natural, spontaneous queries to this database. The ATIS task was designed for the development of speech understanding systems and is often used in experiments involving language modelling.

Example 9 *Consider the following training sentences from the ATIS task:*
$R =$

$\{$ I WOULD LIKE A TWA FLIGHT FROM ATLANTA TO SAN-FRANCISCO WITH A STOPOVER IN DENVER,

FIND THE CHEAPEST FLIGHT FROM DENVER TO ATLANTA WITH A STOPOVER IN PITTSBURGH,

I'D LIKE TO FIND A FLIGHT FROM PITTSBURGH TO DENVER WITH A STOP IN ATLANTA,

SHOW ME THE LATEST FLIGHT FROM DENVER TO PITTSBURGH WHICH SERVES DINNER $\}$

The k-TS/k-Gram models obtained from these sentences for $2 \leq k \leq 6$ have 27, 47, 52, 54 and 56 states and 46, 51, 53, 55 and 55 edges, respectively. The corresponding languages for $2 \leq k \leq 5$ are clear overgeneralisations, while for $k = 6$ no generalisation is obtained. All these languages contain the training set R. Both $L_5 - R$ and $L_4 - R$ consist of the same 5 sentences, from which 2 are overgeneralization errors. $L_3 - R$ has 36 sentences, 17 correct and 19 errors. $L_2 - R$, finally, is an infinite language that contains more than $3 \cdot 10^6$ sentences up to length 15, the majority of of which exhibit gross syntactic incorrectness and/or are semantically meaningless. Some examples of incorrect generalisations are:

L_2:

SHOW ME THE LATEST FLIGHT FROM DENVER WITH A STOPOVER IN DENVER

I'D LIKE A STOPOVER IN PITTSBURGH TO PITTSBURGH WHICH SERVES DINNER

. . . .

L_2, L_3:

I'D LIKE TO FIND A FLIGHT FROM DENVER TO ATLANTA WITH A STOP IN ATLANTA

FIND THE CHEAPEST FLIGHT FROM PITTSBURGH TO DENVER WITH A STOPOVER IN PITTSBURGH

. . . .

L_2, L_3, L_4, L_5:

SHOW ME THE LATEST FLIGHT FROM DENVER TO ATLANTA WITH A STOPOVER IN DENVER

FIND THE CHEAPEST FLIGHT FROM DENVER TO ATLANTA WITH A STOPOVER IN DENVER

. . . .

□

From these errors we can observe that most of the bad generalisations are directly or indirectly caused by improper merging of constructions involving different city names. While generalising these constructions can be beneficial in some situations, in this case it results in erroneously allowing *any* pair or triplet of city names within each sentence, including repetitions which are inconsistent with the pragmatics of the task.

Example 10

The required restrictions related with city names can be easily enforced by renaming all the words that refer to a (first) city in the sentence with a label specifying the corresponding city name ("a" for Atlanta, "d" for Denver and "p" for Pittsburgh, in our example[4]).

$g(R) = \{$I WOULD LIKE A TWA FLIGHT FROM ATLANTA TO$_a$ SAN-FRANCISCO$_a$ WITH$_a$ A$_a$ STOPOVER$_a$ IN$_a$ DENVER$_a$, FIND THE CHEAPEST FLIGHT FROM DENVER TO$_d$ ATLANTA$_d$ WITH$_d$ A$_d$ STOPOVER$_d$ IN$_d$ PITTSBURGH$_d$, I'D LIKE TO FIND A FLIGHT FROM PITTSBURGH TO$_p$ DENVER$_p$ WITH$_p$ A$_p$ STOP$_p$ IN$_p$ ATLANTA$_p$, SHOW ME THE LATEST FLIGHT FROM DENVER TO$_d$ PITTSBURGH$_d$ WHICH$_d$ SERVES$_d$ DINNER$_d$ $\} = R'$

By supplying R' to 2-TSI and applying the standard morphism h (dropping the subindexes), the automaton shown in Figure 7 is obtained. Its language contains 66 generalised sentences, all of which can be considered correct. □

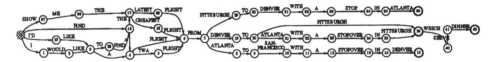

Fig. 7. Automaton obtained through MGGI from (relabeled) training sentences of the ATIS task (see Example 10).

All the examples of this section have dealt just with *structural* modelling issues. Nevertheless, it is important to note that, in a probabilistic framework, all the *bad generalisations* illustrated in these examples do entail *wasting probability mass* and hence reducing the probability of correct generalisations and increasing the perplexity. In general, the waste of probability mass tends to closely follow the rate of bad generalisation. For instance, in Example 6, with probabilities estimated as mentioned in Section 2, almost all the probability mass is wasted in the more than 99.99% incorrectly generated sentences.

6 Experiments

A series of experiments have been carried out in order to assess the ideas introduced in Sections 4 and 5 in a practical setting of Automatic Speech Recognition. The chosen task was a Spanish version of Feldman's MLA task introduced in Section 5 [7]. This version is slightly more complex than the English counterpart because of the more complex inflexion patterns of the Spanish language [6]. Examples of these sentences are:

---

[4] A more complete coverage of this type of restrictions would require both "from-city" and "to-city" labelling.

un círculo pequeño y claro esta muy por encima de un cuadrado y un triángulo oscuro,
un cuadrado toca a un círculo mediano y oscuro, ...

Three sets of 128, 1024 and 8192 text sentences of this task have been used for training different LMs. An independent set of 100 sentences (not included in any training set) of the same task has been reserved for testing. These sentences have been uttered by four different speakers, yielding 400 testing utterances in total.

All the LMs have been integrated with conventional lexical and acoustic-phonetic models. Lexical models are simple concatenation of phonemes, while acoustic-phonetic models consist of 26 context-independent, discrete-density Hidden Markov Models [14]. These models were trained with speech data (uttered by a different set of speakers) of an application different from that considered here.

Tree groups of (stochastic) LMs have been tested. The first group consists of k-TS/k-Grams for $k = 2$, $k = 3$ and $k = 4$. The second group encompasses two MGGI LMs, MGGI-0 and MGGI-1, obtained through renaming schemes similar to those suggested in Examples 7 and 8, respectively. The last group is just a manually built exact grammar for the Spanish MLA task with probabilities estimated from the same data used for the other types of automatically built LMs. Table I show the results of these experiments.

Table I

Word Error Rates(%) and Sizes of different LMs for the MLA task.

Tr. Set Size	Exact	2-TS	3-TS	4-TS	MGGI-0	MGGI-1
		Word Error Rate				
128	1.80	3.71	4.94	7.61	2.36	3.50
1024	1.80	3.71	3.62	3.12	2.11	1.80
8192	1.80	3.65	3.44	3.06	2.11	1.80
		Number of Edges				
128	78	77	184	384	132	156
1024	78	84	245	570	139	165
8192	78	84	248	606	139	165

7 Discussion and Conclusions

With all the training sets shown in Table I, both MGGI-0 and MGGI-1 LMs perform better than any k-TS/k-Gram model. For all the models, training can be considered complete with the set of 1024 sentences, since no significant improvement is obtained with the largest set of 8192 sentences. For these training set sizes, the MGGI-1 results are identical to those of the exact LM, which shows that the corresponding renaming scheme actually captured all the syntactic constraints relevant to this task. MGGI-0, on the other hand, performs closer to the exact model than to the best k-TS ($k = 4$). The increase in word error-rate of MGGI-0 with respect to the exact (and MGGI-1) model is 17%, while the corresponding degradations for the 4-TS, 3-TS and 2-TS models are 70%, 90% and 102%, respectively.

It is interesting to note in Table I that the good results of MGGI models are obtained with model sizes smaller than those of k-TS for $k > 2$. The number of arcs of each model essentially is the number of probabilities that have to be estimated. The exact model has the smallest amount and yields the best recognition results while, with nearly the same number of parameters, the 2-TS/2-Gram model yields the worst performance. Both MGGI models perform significantly better than k-TS, while having roughly twice as much parameters to train than the exact model and about one quarter than the best k-TS ($k = 4$).

These relations between performance and number of parameters to train clearly show that richer model structures are actually needed to effectively take advantage of the data available for improved probability estimation. The results also show how the MGGI approach facilitates the use of a-priory knowledge to help automatically capturing model structures that are significantly more appropriate than those of k-TS/k-Grams.

References

1. D. Angluin and C. H. Smith, "Inductive Inference: Theory and Methods", *Computing Surveys*, 15, no. 3, pp. 46-62, 1983.
2. D. Angluin, "Learning regular sets from queries and counter-examples", *Information and Computation*, 75, pp. 87-106, 1987.
3. D. Angluin, "Identifying Languages from Stochastic Examples", YALEU/DCS/RR-614. 1988.
4. J. Berstel, "Transduction and Context-Free Languages", B. G. Teubner Stuggrt, 1979.
5. R. C. Carrasco, J. Oncina, "Learning Stochastic Regular Grammars by Means of a State Merging Method", *Grammatical Inference and Applications, ICGI-94*, pp. 139-152, 1994.
6. A. Castellanos, I. Galiano, E. Vidal, "Application of OSTIA to Machine Translation Tasks", *Grammatical Inference and Applications, ICGI-94*, pp. 93-105, 1994.
7. J. A. Feldman, G. Lakoff, A. Stolcke and S. Hollbach Weber, "Miniature Language Acquisition: A touchstone for cognitive science International Computer Science Institute", TR-90-009. 1990.
8. P. Garcia, E. Vidal, F. Casacuberta, "Local Languages, The successor method, and a step towards a general methodology for the inference of regular grammars", *IEEE Trans. PAMI,*, vol. 9, no. 6, pp. 841-845, Nov. 1987.
9. P. Garcia, E. Vidal, "Inference of k-Testable Languages in the Strict Sense and Application to Syntactic Pattern Recognition", *IEEE Trans. PAMI.,*, vol. 12, no. 9, pp. 920-925, Sep. 1990.
10. M. Gold, "Language identification in the limit", *Inf. Control 10*, pp. 447-474, 1967.
11. M. Gold, "Complexity of automaton identification from given data", *Inf. Control 37*, pp. 302-320, 1978.
12. F. Jelinek, "Up from trigrams! The struggle for improved language Models", *EUROSPEECH 91*, pp. 1037-1039, 1991.
13. K. J. Lang, "Random DFAs can be Approximately Learned from Sparse Uniform Examples", COLT92.
14. D. Llorens, V. Jimenez, J, A. Sanchez, E. Vidal, H. Rulot, "ATROS, an Automatically Trainable Continuous-Speech Recognition System for Limited-Domain Tasks", Preprints of the VI Spanish Symp. of the AERFAI, Cordoba(Spain), 1995.
15. T. Yu. Medvedev, "On the Class of Events Representable in a Finite Automaton in Sequential Machines-Selected Papers", ed. E. F. Moor, Addison-Wesley, pp.227-315, 1964.
16. J. Oncina, P. Garcia, "Inferring Regular Languages in Polynomial Update Time", In "Pattern Recognition and Image Analysis", Perez, Sanfeliu, Vidal (eds.), 49-61, World Scientific, 1992.
17. P. J. Price, "Evaluation of Spoken Language Systems: the ATIS Domain," *Proc. of 3rd DARPA Workshop on Speech and Natural Language*, pp. 91-95, Hidden Valley (PA), June 1990.
18. E. Segarra, "Una Aproximacion Inductiva a la Comprension del Discurso Continuo", PhD diss. Univ. Politecnica de Valencia. 1993.
19. A. Stolcke, "Inducing Probabilistic Grammars by Bayesian Model Merging", *Grammatical Inference and Applications, ICGI-94*, Carrasco, Oncina (eds.), pp. 106-118, 1994.
20. E. Vidal, F. Casacuberta, P. Garcia, "Grammatical Inference and Automatic Inference Recognition", *Speech Recognition and Coding: New Advances and Trends*, J.Rubio and J.M.Lopez (eds.), Springer-Verlag, 1994.
21. Y. Zalcstein, "Locally Testable Languages", *JCSS*, 6, pp. 151-167, 1972.

Discrete Sequence Prediction with Commented Markov Models

Reinhard Blasig

International Computer Science Institute
Berkeley CA, USA
blasig@icsi.berkeley.edu

Abstract. This paper introduces the concept of *Commented Markov Models* (CMMs), an extension of the well known Markov Models, together with the relevant induction mechanisms. Given a discrete alphabet Σ and a source producing an input sequence $(s_1, s_2, \ldots, s_n)$ with $s_i \in \Sigma$, the task of sequence prediction is to guess the successive sequence element s_{n+1}. Here each element s_i may represent an object, a discrete event or any other discrete entity. Prediction with CMM is analogy-based. It is assumed that the final part of the input sequence describes the current state of the source. This final part is matched with earlier subsequences of the input, assuming that it will be continued the same way as was the 'most similar' subsequence. CMM learning involves the induction of objects, variables and object classes. While object and class creation are similar to the notions of *chunking* and *merging* in other grammatical inference approaches, the use of variables is a novel feature of CMM. It not only generalized the way subsequences can be matched, it also turns CMM from a pure sequence prediction algorithm into a computational model. I will show that CMM has sufficient expressiveness to represent any *primitive recursive function*. Thus it is not only capable of predicting e.g. the character 'u' to follow the sequence 'seq', but it can also extrapolate a sequence like '45 + 13 = ' by calculating the sum '58'.

1 Introduction

At the heart of sequence extrapolation lies an algorithm that – given a training sequence – searches for regularities in the sequence and creates a model to represent these regularities. Different kinds of models have been used for this purpose, the simplest of which is the so called n-gram. This approach only works for finite alphabets Σ and consists of an n-dimensional table T, comprising $|\Sigma|^n$ entries. The table entry $t_{x_{i_1}, \ldots, x_{i_n}}$, $x_{i_j} \in \Sigma$, simply stores, how often the character x_{i_n} has been following the sequence $(x_{i_1}, \ldots, x_{i_{n-1}})$ in a given sample. Extrapolating a sequence $(s_1, \ldots, s_{r-1})$ then amounts to calculating the empirical probabilities[1]

$$p(s_r = x_n | s_{r-n+1} = x_1, \ldots, s_{r-1} = x_{n-1}) = \frac{t_{x_1, \ldots, x_{n-1}, x_n}}{\sum_{x \in \Sigma} t_{x_1, \ldots, x_{n-1}, x}} \ . \quad (1)$$

---

[1] Let's assume that $r \geq n$.

Despite their simplicity, for some applications n-gram models exhibit a prediction performance that is hard to match by much more elaborate approaches. One disadvantage of the n-grams is the fact that the size of T grows exponentially with n. So if the domain is natural language text, with the corresponding number $|\Sigma|$ of different characters, the size of T becomes prohibitively large for n greater than 3 or 4. Also, since only a small portion of all possible 3- or 4-letter combinations actually appears in an ordinary text, most of the table entries will remain zero, rendering this kind of sequence model very inefficient.

To overcome these problems, suffix trees (see [9]) and prefix trees ([6],[11]) have been developed, which both base their predictions on variable length subsequences. To give an example, while the series of subsequences 'e', 'pe', 'ape', 'pape' provides increasing information on what the successive character may be in an English text, after the sequence 'q' there will most probably follow a 'u', no matter what the preceeding characters are. Usually, the depth of a suffix or prefix tree slowly increases during the learning process. While in the beginning the tree only represents short subsequences of the sample sequence, the stored subsequences grow longer, where the consideration of a longer 'history' can substantially improve prediction accuracy. Information theoretic measures are applied to weigh the improvement against the cost of storing longer subsequences. Tree-based sequence prediction algorithms for natural language text typically handle subsequences up to a length of 10 or 15 characters. This is usually sufficient, since in the natural language domain repetitive character sequences of much higher length are quite rare.

2 CMM induction

The three essential concepts describing sequence learning and representation as performed by CMM are **objects**, **variables** and **classes**. The following sections will introduce them one after the other. It will turn out that the concept of objects is closely related to the chunking operation found in some grammatical inference approaches. Also, the class concept is related to the merging operation. In contrast, CMM's variable concept is a novel feature in grammatical inference procedures[2], and it is the variables, that extends CMM from a sequence prediction algorithm to a model of computation.

2.1 Objects

CMM uses two main data structures: the **sequence graph**, which is a directed acyclic graph serving as internal representation of the input sequence, and a **dictionary** to store the descriptions of all objects known to CMM[3]. When presented

---

[2] Crutchfield [3] does mention the necessity of variable induction during ϵ-machine reconstruction, when models beyond the finite state level are used. However, no induction algorithm is provided.

[3] There are some similarities in functionality of the sequence graph and the dictionary to Copycat's workspace and slipnet, respectively (see [8]).

an input sequence, CMM reads the sequence from left to right, one character at a time, and scans it for objects stored in the dictionary.

Built-in objects. Before CMM starts learning (i.e. before processing the input) the dictionary already contains a number of *objects*. These comprise the upper and lower case letters, the digits and all the other characters that may appear in the input sequence. In addition to these primitive objects, CMM will learn new objects in the course of input processing. The new objects are sequences of smaller objects, of variables or of class descriptions. As a simple example, CMM may learn the object 'ABC' composed of the objects 'A', 'B' and 'C'.

Every object o has a label $label(o)$. For built-in objects, $label(o) = o$, thus $label('A') = 'A'$. Learned objects are labeled $O_1, O_2, \ldots$, so that the label of 'ABC' may be O_{14}. Learning a new object means storing the respective object description in the dictionary. An object description also states the length of an object. All built-in objects have length 1. The length of 'ABC' would be 3.

When processing the input sequence $(s_1, s_2, \ldots)$, CMM creates a *sequence cell* for every dictionary object that can be found in the input sequence. A sequence cell c carries the label of the object o it represents: $label(c) = label(o)$. Each cell has a *time stamp* $t(c)$, stating at which position in the input sequence the corresponding object starts. Thus, if a cell c represents the input character s_i, then $t(c) = i$. Also, each cell has a certain length $len(c)$, which is defined as the length of the object represented by c, and which can be determined by inspecting that object's dictionary entry. The cells are chained together and make up the sequence graph. Consider the example sequence

$$(s_1, s_2, \ldots) = \text{'H L C C L A F C C L \ldots'}.$$

Let's assume that CMM only knows the built-in objects and – just for demonstration purposes – one additional object O_1, that represents the character sequence 'C L'. The example sequence will then be transformed into the following sequence graph:

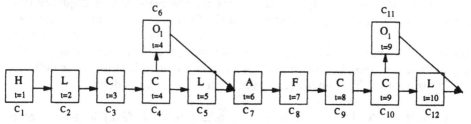

Fig. 1. Example sequence graph. The indices c_1 through c_{12} are just for reference purposes in the text below; they are of no significance for CMM. However, they do indicate the order, in which the cells have been created.

Note that the cells labeled O_1 carry the same time stamps as the 'C'-cells below them. The length of the O_1-cells is 2, which is the sum of the lengths of their composing objects. As the figure shows, the cells for the primitive objects (i.e. the input characters) build the 'backbone' of the sequence graphs. The cells for composed objects (as well as the cells for variables and classes, as we will later see) can be regarded as **comments** attached to the backbone graph. The task of the comments is to provide alterative paths and thus alternative inter-pretations of the input sequence. In the above figure, the subsequence 'C L' has been described as either a single composed object or a sequence of two simpler objects. The notion of *alternative interpretations* becomes more obvious in con-nection with variable comments and class comments. The name 'CMM' reflects the important role of these comments in representing alternative interpretations.

Sequence Prediction. CMM uses the sequence graph to model the input se-quence. As new characters of the input sequence are processed, CMM constantly looks for subsequences in the past, that are similar to the final part of the input sequence. The longer the final part and this *matching subsequence* are, the better a model is the subsequence for the final part, and the more likely is the final part (and thus the whole input sequence) continued the same way as was that matching subsequence. Let's make this more concrete. The input is $(s_1, s_2, \ldots)$, a sequence of discrete symbols, which is being transformed into a sequence graph as described in the previous section.

Definition 1: For two sequence cells c and d representing objects, the match-ing relation $=_m$ is defined as: $c =_m d$ iff $label(c) = label(d)$.

In later sections, $=_m$ will be extended to cells representing variables and classes.

Definition 2: The set $succ(c)$ of successors of a sequence cell c comprises the sequence cell d that c points to and all other sequence cells having the same time stamp as d.

Definition 3: A matching path $mp(c)$ for a given sequence cell c is a sequence $(d_1, d_2, \ldots, d_n)$ with d_n having a lower time stamp than c, such that there exists the sequence $(e_1, e_2, \ldots, e_n)$ with $succ(e_n) = succ(c)$ and $d_i =_m e_i$, $1 \le i \le n$. $MP(c)$ is the set of all matching paths for c.

In this definition, $(d_1, d_2, \ldots, d_n)$ represents the matching subsequence (see above) and $(e_1, e_2, \ldots, e_n)$ corresponds to the final part of the input sequence.

In the example of figure 1, the cell c_{11} has six matching paths: (c_2), (c_5), (c_4, c_5), (c_3, c_4, c_5), (c_6) and (c_3, c_6). For sequence prediction, the longest match-ing paths are especially interesting. This is how the length of a path is defined:

Definition 4: The length of a given path $(c_1, \ldots, c_n)$ is defined as
$$plen(c_1, \ldots, c_n) = \sum_{1 \le i \le n} len(c_i).$$

Definition 5: The set of *longest matching paths* $LMP(c)$ is defined as a subset of $MP(c)$:

$$LMP(c) = \{ (c_1, \ldots, c_n) \in MP(c) \mid \forall (d_1, \ldots, d_m) \in MP(c) :$$
$$t(d_m) > t(c_n) \Rightarrow plen(d_1, \ldots, d_m) < plen(c_1, \ldots, c_n)\} \qquad (2)$$

The longest matching paths are the 'best' models for the final part $(e_1, e_2, \ldots, e_n)$ of the input sequence, since they are the only paths that can provide a full explanation for this final part in terms of the sequence graph. Note that all paths in $LMP(c)$ cover the same input sequence $(s_j, \ldots, s_k)$. There may be several subsequences in the input sequence, that have maximum length and match the end of the input sequence. However, the time stamps are used in definition 5 to select those paths, which relate to the latest occurence of the matching subsequence in the input. To continue the above example, $LMP(c_{11}) = \{(c_3, c_4, c_5), (c_3, c_6)\}$.

Sequence prediction with CMM is based on the assumption, that the input sequence is continued in analogy to the the longest matching paths[4]. The continuation of a longest matching path $(c_1, \ldots, c_n)$ is given by $succ(c_n)$.

Note, that $succ(c_n)$ comprises the same set of sequence cells for all longest matching paths, although not all of these paths may share the same c_n. In the example, $succ(c_5) = succ(c_6) = \{c_7\}$. Thus, CMM expects the next character s_{11} to be an 'A'.[5]

It is interesting to compare the way how CMM and the prefix tree approach produce predictions. For both of them, the longest matching subsequence plays the central role. However, there are two main differences:

- CMM does not create a tree representation of the input sequence. As an advantage, this allows to take very long matching subsequences into account (dozens or hundreds of characters). In contrast, for prefix trees the maximum subsequence length is bounded by the tree depth, which is much smaller, as described in the introduction. The accessibility of long subsequences is essential, when long-range structures in the input sequence have to be detected. Another precondition for finding long-range structures is the capability to model a sequence in a more abstract way than by just matching identical character subsequences. I will show below, how the concepts of variables and classes are used to match character sequences, that are structurally similar, but not necessarily literally identical.
- When there are several longest matching subsequences being of the same length, the prefix tree prediction will contain all possible succeeding characters together with their estimated probability. In contrast, CMM only relies on the last (i.e. temporally closest) longest matching subsequence to provide a prediction. Both approaches are equally justified, the first one assuming a constant source producing the input sequence, and CMM assuming, that the source characteristics change with time[6].

---

[4] The term 'in analogy' here just means 'identically', since until now only objects are involved. However, as soon as variables and classes have been introduced, the term 'analogy' assumes its true, more general meaning.

[5] In the case that c_n and $succ(c_n)$ are both part of a larger object, it is assumed that this object represents the current state of the source and so the whole object will be predicted. The successor function as defined in section 3 provides an example.

[6] While Markov models are usually learned statistically, CMM's use of comments with their high representative power make an intelligent teacher necessary. He acts as a source with changing characteristics, providing simple learning tasks first and building on these to teach more complex tasks. This hierarchical way of learning fundamentally contradicts the Markov property of state-dependent (and time-independent) transition probabilities. CMM's predictions are not probability-based.

Learning new objects. CMM's object creation is based on the notion of *isolated paths*. Consider again the above example sequence. There is not much structure to it, except for the fact, that the subsequence 'C C L' appears twice. We could assume that the whole input sequence was just a string of random characters. However, the reoccurence of a three-letter subsequence would be very unlikely in this setting. Now, there are two possible conclusions depending on the continuation of the input sequence. If the upcoming sequence element s_{11} is an 'A', then 'C C L' is part of an even longer reappearing character subsequence. If s_{11} is any other character, the longest matching subsequence has been discontinued, isolating 'C C L' as a group of three successive characters, that appears at two places in the input sequence. It is these isolated groups that CMM turns into objects.

Definition 6: A longest matching path $(c_1, \ldots, c_n)$ becomes an isolated path, if the input sequence does not match the prediction $succ(c_n)$.

As already stated above, there may be several longest matching paths. Since they all lead to the same prediction, a failing prediction results in several isolated paths. CMM now has to select one of these paths to be transformed into an object. In the example, assuming $s_{11} \neq$ 'A', the task is to decide, whether the new object is created as ('CCL') or as ('C'O_1). CMM selects the cheapest of the isolated paths, applying a cost criterion, that accounts for the information necessary to describe the path given the sequence graph[7]. A path $(c_1, \ldots, c_m)$ can be described using the following code: given that the sequence graph contains N cells, $\log_2(N)$ bits are needed to describe the cell c_1. With $|succ(c_i)|$ denoting the number of immediate successors of c_i, there are $\log_2(|succ(c_i)|+1)$ bits necessary to describe cell c_{i+1}, where the 'additional successor' is used to code, if c_i is the last cell in the path or if the path continues. So altogether we have:

Definition 7: The cost of a path $(c_1, \ldots, c_m)$ is

$$C(c_1, \ldots, c_m) = \log_2(N) + \sum_{i=1 \ldots m-1} \log_2(|succ(c_i)|+1) \ . \tag{3}$$

Since $\log_2(N)$ is the same for all paths at a given time, this term can be neglected. The costs of the two above isolated paths are then:

$$C(c_3, c_4, c_5) = \log_2(2+1) + \log_2(1+1) = 2.585$$
$$C(c_3, c_6) \quad = \log_2(2+1) = 1.585$$

So CMM will create the object $O_2 = ($'C'$O_1)$.

2.2 Variables

From object creation it is only a small step to variable creation. As an example, consider the input sequence 's(100) = 101.'.

---

[7] This procedure is motivated by the *mtmtnum description length* principle. CMM constantly tries to model the input sequence and to explain new input characters, as they are processed. Searching for the longest and cheapest matching subsequence corresponds to explaining (or coding) the largest number of input characters with the least amount of information.

A human reader with some knowledge about binary numbers would probably realize, that the sequence is an example of calculating the successor of a binary number. Remember, that for CMM this is just a sequence of 13 characters, including the blanks and the period. The figure below shows the corresponding sequence graph created by CMM:

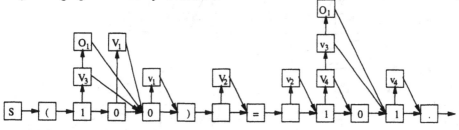

Fig. 2. Sequence graph with variable cells

As the commenting cells indicate, CMM has created the object O_1. Also, the variable cells labeled $V_1, \ldots, V_4$ and $v_1, \ldots, v_4$ have been created and attached to the sequence graph. Variable cells provide additional paths through the sequence graph and thus additional interpretations of the input sequence. Obviously, the two O_1-cells and the variable cells labeled V_3 and v_3 belong together. In fact, all of them have been created to account for the reappearing isolated group '10'. But while the object cells merely represent the hypothesis that the character group is an object on its own, the variable cells provide another interpretation of the reappearance: whatever character sequence occurs at the place of V_3, will reappear at the position marked by v_3. All the other V_i/v_i pairs in the sequence graph have been created after finding other isolated groups. However, no O_j-cells were built, because the groups only contain primitive objects (e.g. '0' corresponds to V_1/v_1) and the respective object cells are already in the graph.

Now one possible path[8] through the above graph reads 's($V_3$0) = $v_3$1.'. This already describes, how to calculate the successor of any even binary number.

An important consequence of variable induction is the fact that now matches between similar, but not necessarily identical sequences are possible. Let's assume that the above input sequence is continued by the characters 's(10110) = '. This sequence can be matched with 's(100) = ' by instantiating V_3 with '1011'. The longest matching path, which will consequently involve the V_3-cell, now has only one valid continuation: via the v_3-cell, yielding the prediction '1011', followed by '1' and '.'.

The following figure shows the sequence graph after processing the sequence 's(100) = 101;s(10110) = 10111.'. It shows the presence of a new object O_3, which has been built when with the final period the match of 's($V_2$0) = $v_2$1' with 's($V_5$0) = $v_5$1' became isolated. I mention this for two reasons. First of all it demonstrates that there is a special rule for matching variables:

---

[8] It has to be noted that a path with variable cells is *valid* only, if for every V_i in the path there is at least one corresponding v_i in the path and for each v_i there is also the corresponding V_i.

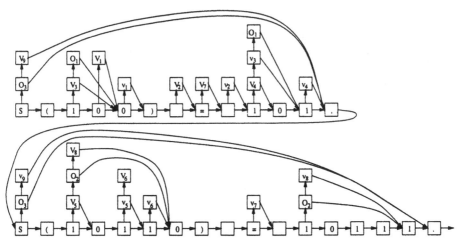

Fig. 3. Sequence graph with variable cells

Definition 8: Given the two paths $(c_1, \ldots, c_n)$ and $(d_1, \ldots, d_m)$, and given $label(c_i) = v_r$ and $label(d_i) = v_s$. Then $c_i =_m d_i$ iff $\exists j < i :\ label(c_j) = V_r$ and $label(d_j) = V_s$.

Secondly, O_2 is an object whose components are themselves composed objects. This means that CMM's object creation is hierarchical, building more and more complex objects out of simpler ones. As in the case of O_3, objects may incorporate variables, giving the objects the appearance of **rules**. Since objects and rules are handled in the same way by CMM, objects may represent rules about objects, rules about rules, ...

What about the path cost of variables? As before, the cost of a path is the path's description length (in bits) given the sequence graph. The cost of a V_j-cell is the same as that of an object cell, plus the cost for describing the content of the variable. So if $label(c_{i+1}) = V_j$, $C(c_{i+1}) = log_2(|succ(c_i)| + 1) + k * log_2(M)$, where k is the number of objects represented by the variable and M is the number of objects in CMM's dictionary. The cost of a v_j is 0, since v_j is only predicted when V_j is already in the path and then v_j is the only possible path continuation. Given this definition of the path cost of variables, and given the observation that $M \gg |succ(c_i)|$, it will always be cheaper to match identical objects directly than by using variables. For example, 'abbc' and 'addc' can be matched by the interpretation 'a$V_1 v_1$c'; two sequences 'abbc' can be matched either literally or again through 'a$V_1 v_1$c'. The first alternative will be cheaper and thus preferred, so that in the case of object creation the new object 'abbc' will be created.

2.3 Classes

The easiest way to introduce the mechanism of class induction is by considering it as a way of *approximate* matching. Take the following example:

digit(0);digit(1).

This sequence is made of two halves which are almost identical. To make a match possible, CMM uses an object labeled '%', which represents a *don't-care* symbol and matches any object or object sequence. CMM actually uses these cells if this makes the continuation of a longer match possible by 'bridging' a small unmatchable subsequence (see the figure).

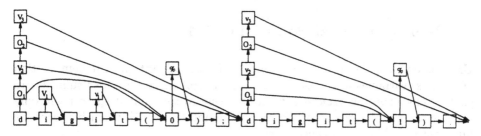

The introduction of the '%'-cells has several consequences. First of all, processing this sequence gives rise to an object $O_1 =$ 'digit(%)', where the don't-care is part of the object description. Secondly, since the don't-care in the newly built object has been matched with a '0' and a '1', CMM concludes that the two objects '0' and '1' are somehow **equivalent**. Their equivalence is given by the fact, that both objects have been found in the same **context**, which is defined by O_1. The use of the class concept is CMM's way to represent this equivalence. With the creation of O_1 or any other object containing a don't-care symbol, a class (C_1, say) is created collecting all objects that have been matched with this specific '%'. O_1 is said to be the class defining object for C_1. The class membership of '0' and '1' is represented in CMM by adding the class label C_1 to the respective object descriptions in the dictionary.

The class concept adds two important qualities to the concept of objects. Until now, objects were either made of sequences of simpler objects, in which case they just represented **abbreviations** to describe sequences. Or there were variables involved in the object description, which turns the object into a **rule**. Together with the class concept, objects can now be **class definitions** as well as **class members**. It is also interesting to note, that class induction and object induction are somehow dual mechanisms. CMM creates objects from matching subsequences, that have been found in different contexts. In contrast, classes are created, if non-matching subsequences appear in the same context. In the future, CMM will use *class cells* (i.e. sequence cells labeled with a C_i) to create comments within the sequence graph. A class cell either comments a don't-care cell or a V_j-cell and expresses CMM's hypothesis that the thus commented cell may only be matched with an object, that is a member of the respective class:

Definition 9: Given a class cell c, $label(c) = C_i$ and an object cell d, $label(d) = o$, then $c =_m d$ iff o is a member of class C_i according to the dictionary.

Until now, the creation of class cells is not fully implemented. For example, commenting a don't-care cell (which is related to a certain class C_j as described above,) with a class cell labeled C_i represents the hypothesis that the sets of class members of C_j and C_i are in a subset relationship. Hypotheses like this cannot be solely based on the matching mechanisms described in this paper, but they will also involve a probabilistic or information theoretic analysis of the membership entries in the dictionary. Some interesting work in this direction has already been done by other researchers (see [2], [8] and [10]), and I am currently investigating the extension of CMM in this respect.

3 Representational Power of CMM

CMM is not just an ordinary sequence prediction algorithm. The combination of objects, variables and classes results in a representative power sufficient to express any *primitive recursive function*[9]. Due to the limited space I will only provide a very informal proof. Following the notation of [5], primitive recursive functions over binary sequences are:

1. **The constant 0**: '0' is a CMM built-in object.
2. **The successor function** $succ(x) = x + 1$: The following three rules (or objects) are sufficient to determine the successor of any binary number:
   '[s($V_1$0)V_2][$v_1$1v_2]'
   '[s($V_3$1)V_4][s(v_3)0v_4]'
   '[s(1)V_5][10v_5]'
   The first rule is quite similar to the one examined in section 2.2. The variant shown here just uses the characters '[' and ']' to mark the beginning and the end of the two halves of each object, which can be perceived as the left-hand side and the right-hand side of a rewrite rule. There is no problem in teaching these three rules to CMM. Applied to e.g. '[s(1011)]' CMM prediction would produce the following sequence:
   '[s(1011)][s(101)0][s(10)00][1100]'.
3. **The projection function** $P_i(x_1, \ldots, x_n) = x_i$: In the framework of CMM the projection can be realized by applying the don't-care expression introduced in section 2.3. As an example, the following object would calculate $P_3(x_1, x_2, x_3, x_4)$:
   'P3(%,%,V_1,%') = v_1'.
4. **Function composition** $f(g_1(x_1, \ldots, x_n), \ldots, g_m(x_1, \ldots, x_n))$ with primitive recursive functions f and g_i: To evaluate composed functions, again '[' and ']' can be applied to mark an expression's beginning and end. Instead of learning functions as sequences like 'F($x_1, \ldots, x_n$) = y', the format
   '[V_αF($x_1, \ldots, x_n$)V_ω][$v_\alpha y v_\omega$]'
   with the auxiliary variables V_α and V_ω should be used: as an example, applying this to the above definition of the projection function would result in the object '[V_αP3(%,%,V_1,%')V_ω][$v_\alpha v_1 v_\omega$]', which can be used to evaluate a sequence like
   '[s(P3(111,10,100,0))]' by extrapolating it with '[s(100)][101]'.

---

[9] However, some simple constraints are necessary to guide the matching process, as described below.

5. **Primitive recursion** with primitive recursive functions f, g and h:

$$f(x_1,\ldots,x_n) = \begin{cases} g(x_1,\ldots,x_{n-1}) & \text{for } x_n = 0 \\ h(x_1,\ldots,x_n,f(x_1,\ldots,x_{n-1},x_n-1)) & \text{for } x_n \neq 0. \end{cases}$$

Primitive recursion can be handled similar to function composition, however two separate objects are necessary two account for $x_n = 0$ and $x_n \neq 0$:
'[F($V_1,\ldots,V_{n-1}$,0)][G($v_1,\ldots,v_{n-1}$)]' and
'[F($V_1,\ldots,V_{n-1},V_n$)] [H($v_1,\ldots,v_n$,F($v_1,\ldots,v_{n-1},v_n-1$))]'.

There is one important criterion for the matching process to make the above construction work: the matching has to preserve the **hierarchical structure** of composed functions. It must be made sure that e.g. '[P3(101,P2(0,10),11)]' is not matched with '[V_αP3(%,%,V_1,%)V_ω]' by instantiating V_1 with 'P2(0'. To achieve this, all variables and don't cares (except for the V_α and V_ω) must only be instantiated with sequences of zeros and ones, (i.e. $\{0,1\}^*$). Also, the V_α and V_ω must not be instantiated with sequences containing '[' or ']'. This can be accomplished by explicitly restricting the matching process accordingly. In a later version, CMM will utilize a more general class concept to achieve the same result. Note, that the restrictions imply *strict* function evaluation, i.e. the arguments of a function are evaluated, before the function itself is evaluated.

4   Computational Complexity

Given the high expressive power of CMM it comes as no surprise that learning with CMM is hard. In [1] Aho examines regular expressions augmented by variables. He proves that matching this kind of expressions with a character sequence is NP-complete. The setting is similar enough to CMM's matching process to conclude that NP-completeness also applies to CMM. However, Aho's proof is based on the fact, that the complexity of the considered matching process grows exponentially with the number of variables involved. CMM proceeds by limiting the number of variables per match. Although this will reduce the representative power of CMM, I believe that such a restriction (and maybe some additional ones) can make the matching process quite efficient without considerably impairing the practical usefulness of CMM. Some further theoretical investigation of this issue are certainly necessary.

Simulations on a SUN SPARC 20 indicate, that parsing an input sequence can be performed at a reasonable speed (several characters per second), as long as the sequence graph does not contain more than a few hundred cells. As the algorithm is implemented right now, CMM limits the size of the graph by pruning the oldest sequence cells first. Another interesting direction of research would lead to an assessment of the cells in order to delete the *least interesting* ones first. For example, if a sequence of primitive objects has been found to combine to a more complex object, the cells representing the primitives may be dispensible.

5 Conclusion and future work

The high expressive power of CMMs has been demonstrated. CMM can create objects, which, by applying variables and the class concept, may represent simple rules. Since CMM can hierachically build more complex objects out of simpler ones, it is also capable of representing rules about complex objects, rules about rules etc.. An important issue is of course the question of how these complex structures can be learned. It seems that statistical learning procedures as used to induce n-grams or prefix trees do not suffice. Instead, CMM needs an intelligent teacher who can divide a complex problem into simpler ones, teaches how to solve the simple problems first and then makes use of these solutions to deal with the complex one. Note, that the need for an intelligent teacher makes the assumption of time-varying source characteristics imperative.

There is a great variety of domains, where the phenomenon of reoccuring sequences plays an important role, like the chart analysis of stock values, the structure of music, natural language grammar or calculations in formal systems. As an important future task the viability of the CMM approach concerning some concrete applications in these domains remains to be shown.

As far as the induction of objects and variables is concerned, CMM is by now quite complete. Regarding the class concept, there is however still some work to be done. CMM *can* group objects into classes, but it is not yet able to merge classes, that may have different names, but identical or similar semantics. Another important direction of research is the improvement of CMM's efficiency. This can be accomplished by selectively pruning parts of the internal sequence representation and by applying restrictive heuristics to bound the complexity of the matching process.

References

1. Aho, A.V.: Algorithms for Finding Patterns in Strings. Handbook of Theoretical Computer Science, J. van Leeuwen, ed.. Elsevier Science Publishers B.V. (1990)
2. Brown, P.F., Della Pietra, V.J., DeSouza, P.V., Lai, J.C., Mercer, R.L.: Class-based n-gram models of natural language. Computational Linguistics **18** (1992) 467–479
3. Crutchfield, J.P.: The Calculi of Emergence: Computation, Dynamics and Induction. Physica D 75 (1994) 11–54
4. Hofstadter, D.R.: Fluid Concepts and Creative Analogies. Basic Books, NY (1995)
5. Hopcroft, J.E., Ullman, J.D.: Introduction to Automata Theory, Languages and Computation. Addison-Wesley, Reading, Mass. (1979)
6. Laird, P.: Discrete sequence prediction and its applications. Proceedings of the 9th National Conference on Artificial Intelligence, AAAI (1992)
7. Laird, P. and Saul, R.: Sequence Extrapolation. Proc. of the IJCAI (1993)
8. Michell, M.: Analogy-Making as Perception. Bradford Books, Cambr., MA (1993)
9. Ron, D., Singer, Y., Tishby, N.: The power of Amnesia. Advances in NIPS 6, Cowan, J., Tesauro, G., Alspector, J., eds. Morgan Kaufmann, San Mateo, (1994)
10. Stolcke, A.: Bayesian Learning of Probabilistic Language Models. University of California dissertation, Berkeley, CA (1994)
11. Williams, R.: Dynamic history predictive compression. Inf. Syst. **13(1)** (1988)

Learning k-Piecewise Testable Languages from Positive Data [*]

José Ruiz and Pedro García

Depto. de Sistemas Informáticos y Computación.
Universidad Politécnica de Valencia. Valencia (Spain).
email : jruiz@dsic.upv.es pgarcia@dsic.upv.es

Abstract. A k-piecewise testable language (k-PWT) is defined by the subwords (sequences of symbols which are not necessarely consecutive) no longer than k that are contained in its words. We propose an algorithm that identifies in the limit the class of k-PWT languages from positive data. The proposed algorithm has polynomial time complexity on the length of the received data. As the class of k-PTW languages is finite, the algorithm can be used for PAC- learning.

1 Introduction.

The central problem of grammatical inference is that of obtaining a representation of a formal language from examples. It is well known [8] that the problem of identifying a language from positive examples only has strong limitations. In fact, the simplest family of languages in Chomsky's hierarchy, the family of regular languages, is not identifiable from positive data in the limit. Inference from positive data seemed to be condemned to obtaining generalizations of the training sample by means of heuristics, without having the possibility of characterizing the obtained results [4], [9], [6]. However, there are nontrivial families of languages identifiable in the limit from positive presentation, and a characterization of those families has been proposed in [1], [16]. Afterwards, algorithms that identify in the limit certain interesting subclasses of regular languages have been proposed in [2], [15], [7] and [12]. Even a general framework to construct characterizable inference methods has been proposed in [10].

The family of *Piecewise Testable Languages (PWT)* has been previously studied by Simon [17, 11, 14]. It is a subclass of regular languages somewhat similar to the better known family of locally testable languages [5], [7]. The role played there by segments of a certain length is played here by subwords, also of certain length. By means of *subword* we understand, in this context, a sequence of non necessarily consecutive symbols taken from a word.

A language is said to be PWT if, for some integer k, if a word belongs to the language, any other word with exactly the same set of subwords of length k also belongs to the language. The family of PWT *languages* is a subclass of the class

---

[*] Work partially supported by the Spanish CICYT under grant TIC93-0633-CO2

of star-free languages neither comparable to the family of reversible languages [2] nor to the family of locally-testable languages.

For any positive integer k, the family of k-PWT languages is a finite class of languages and so, it is identifiable from positive data in the limit. For the same reason it is also PAC learnable.

We propose in this work an algorithm that identifies in the limit the family of k-PWT languages whose time complexity is polynomial in the sum of the lengths of the input words.

2 Definitions and notation.

Let Σ be a finite alphabet and Σ^* the free monoid generated by Σ with concatenation as the binary operation and λ as neutral element. The length of a word x will be denoted as $|x|$. Let $\Sigma^k = \{x \in \Sigma^* : |x| = k\}$ and $\Sigma^{\leq k} = \bigcup_{i=0}^{k} \Sigma^i$. The prefix $a_1 a_2 ... a_i$ of a word $x = a_1 a_2 ... a_n$ will be denoted as x_{1i}.

Given $x, y \in \Sigma^*$, we say that $x = a_1 a_2 ... a_n$, with $a_i \in \Sigma$, $i = 1, 2 ... n$ is a *subword* of y if $y = z_0 a_1 z_1 a_2 ... a_n z_n$ with $z_i \in \Sigma^*, i = 0, 1, 2 ... n$. We call this relationship *division* and denote it by $x \mid y$. This relationship is compatible with the concatenation, that is, $x \mid y \wedge x' \mid y' \Rightarrow xx' \mid yy'$.

Given a word $y \in \Sigma^*$, the set of subwords of y and their multiplicity (the number of ways each subword can be obtained from y) can be evaluated by using either Pascal's formula or Magnus transformation (see [11] for details). A problem with both methods is that they are exponential with the length of the considered word.

The inverse problem is to determine if for a given value of k and a set of words A there exists a word y such that A is the set of k-subwords of y. As far as we know, the problem has not been characterized yet (for example the set $\{ab, ba\}$ can not be the set of 2-subwords of any word y for it will also contain either the subword aa or bb).

Following [8], we say that an algorithm A identifies a class H of DFAs *in the limit* iff for any $M \in H$, on input of any presentation of $L(M)$, the infinite sequence of DFAs output by A converges to a DFA M' such that $L(M) = L(M')$.

A class of H of DFAs is *PAC-identifiable* by an algorithm A iff on input of any parameters ϵ, δ $(0 < \epsilon, \delta < 1)$, for any DFA $M \in H$ of size n, for any positive integer m and for any probability distribution D on strings of $\Sigma^{\leq m}$, if A obtains examples generated according to distribution D, A produces a DFA M' such that, with probability at least $1 - \delta$, the probability of the set $L(M) \oplus L(M')$ (where $\oplus$ means the symmetric difference) is at most ϵ. Any finite class of languages is potentially PAC-learnable, and any consistent algorithm for a potentially learnable class, PAC learns the class [3].

3 K-Piecewise Testable Languages.

For a word x, we define $S(x, k)$ and $NS(x, k)$ as follows:

$$S(x, k) = \begin{cases} \{x\} & if \ |x| < k \\ \{z \in \Sigma^k : z \mid x\} & if \ |x| \geq k \end{cases}$$

and

$$NS(x, k) = \Sigma^{\leq k} - S(x, k).$$

Let $\equiv_k$ be the equivalence relation defined in Σ^* as follows:

$$\forall x, y \in \Sigma^* \ (x \equiv_k y \Leftrightarrow S(x, k) = S(y, k)).$$

The above relationship is a congruence of finite index. We denote as $[x]_k$ the equivalence class of the word x, that is,

$$[x]_k = (\bigcap_{a_1 a_2 \dots a_k \in S(x,k)} \Sigma^* a_1 \Sigma^* a_2 \dots \Sigma^* a_k \Sigma^*) -$$

$$-(\bigcup_{a_1 a_2 \dots a_k \in NS(x,k)} \Sigma^* a_1 \Sigma^* a_2 \Sigma^* \dots \Sigma^* a_k \Sigma^*).$$

Properties [11]:

1. $\equiv_{k+1}$ is a refinement of $\equiv_k$.
2. Any equivalence class modulo $\equiv_k$ is either a singleton or has infinite words.
3. If $x = uv$ is such that $\exists \ a \in \Sigma$ with $S(ua, k) = S(u, k)$ then $\forall n > 0$, $ua^n v \in [x]_k$.

A language L is said to be *k-piecewise testable* iff it is the union of equivalence classes modulo $\equiv_k$. A language L is *piecewise testable* if there exists a value of k such that L is *k-piecewise testable*.

Following [17], a language $L \subseteq \Sigma^*$ is *piecewise testable* if and only if L belongs to the Boole Algebra generated by the languages of the form $\Sigma^* a_1 \Sigma^* a_2 \dots \Sigma^* a_k \Sigma^*$ with $k \geq 0$, $a_i \in \Sigma$, $i = 1, \dots, k$.

Given $x, y \in \Sigma^*$, we write that $x \leq_k y$ if and only if $S(x, j) \subseteq S(y, j)$, $\forall j \leq k$. This relationship is a partial order in Σ^*. It is easily seen that $x \mid y \Rightarrow x \leq_k y$, although the converse is not true (take, for example, $k = 2$, $x = abab$, $y = baba$).

The quotient set $(\Sigma^* / \equiv_k, \leq_k)$, being $\leq_k$ the above relationship extended to equivalent classes, is a finite lattice with an absolute maximum (the class of words x such that $S(x, k) = \Sigma^k$, which is always feasible) and an absolute minimum (the class of the empty word). With this order relation, the sequence $\{x_{1i}\}_{i=1}^n$ of the prefixes of a word $a_1 a_2 \dots a_n$ always form an ascending chain in the lattice.

Given a DFA $A = (Q, \Sigma, \delta, q_0, F)$, we say that $q \in Q$ is at *level i* iff $i = \min\{|x| : x \in \Sigma^*, \delta(q_0, x) = q\}$.

The following properties come out directly from the above definitions:

1. If L is a *k-piecewise testable* language, then L is *j-piecewise testable* language, $\forall j \geq k$.
2. If L is *k-piecewise testable* then L is *regular*.
3. If A is an automaton accepting a *k-piecewise testable* language L, there are no transitions in A from a state at level i to states at level j, $j < i$.

Input :	$k \in N$, *S set of words over* Σ^*
Output :	*DFA* $A = (Q, \Sigma, \delta, q_1, F)$, *consistent with the data:* $L(A) \subseteq L_k(S)$

Method :
$new = 1;$
$Q = \{q_1\};$
$\delta = \emptyset;$
$F = \emptyset;$
$\forall x = a_1 a_2 ... a_n \in S$ **do**
    $i = 1$
    $state = q_1;$
    While $(i \leq n \wedge \exists\, j : (state, a_i, q_j) \in \delta)$ **do**   **(1)**
        $state = q_j;$
        If $i = n$ **(2)**
        then $F = F \cup \{state\}$
        endif;
        $i = i + 1$
    EndWhile;
    While $(i \leq n)$ **do**   **(3)**
        If $(q_j, a_i, q_j) \in \delta$
        then $i = i + 1;$
        else
            $new = new + 1;$
            $j = new;$
            $Q = Q \cup \{q_j\};$
            $\delta = \delta \cup (state, a_i, q_j);$
            $st = S(a_1 a_2 ... a_i, k);$
            If $\exists\, a \in \Sigma : S(a_1 a_2 ... a_i a, k) = st$ **(4)**
            then $\delta = \delta \cup \{(q_j, a, q_j)\}$
            endif
            $state = q_j;$
            $i = i + 1;$
        Endif
    EndWhile
    $F = F \cup \{q_j\};$
  End $\forall$
  $A = (Q, \Sigma, \delta, q_1, F)$
EndMethod.

Fig. 1. Algorithm *k-PWTI*.

4. The class of k-piecewise testable languages is a finite class, bounded above by $\left|\mathcal{P}\left(\mathcal{P}\left(\Sigma^k\right)\right)\right| = 2^{2^{|\Sigma|^k}}$ (where $\mathcal{P}$ means the power set).

4 Smallest K-Piecewise Testable Language that contains a positive sample S. Learning Algorithm.

Given $k > 0$ we can associate to a positive sample $S = \{x_1, x_2, ...x_n\}$ a k-*piecewise testable* language $L_k(S)$ as follows:

$$x \in L_k(S) \Leftrightarrow \exists i, 1 \le i \le n : S(x, k) = S(x_i, k).$$

Properties :
It is easy to prove that :

1. $S \subseteq L_k(S)$.
2. $L_k(S)$ is the smallest k-piecewise testable language that contains S.
3. $S' \subseteq S$ implies that $L_k(S') \subseteq L_k(S)$.
4. $L_{k+1}(S) \subseteq L_k(S)$.
5. If $k > max_{x_i \in S}|x_i|$ then $L_k(S) = S$.

Based on the above definitions and properties, we propose a learning algorithm:*the k-Piecewise Testable Inference algorithm (k-PWTI)* that, with input of a positive sample S, outputs a DFA consistent with S that accepts a subset of the smallest k-PWT language that contains S. The algorithm is shown in Figure 1.

4.1 Example of run

Let $k = 2$ and $S = \{aba, aaba, aa\}$.

While, for better understanding, in figures 2, 3 and 4 each state of the shown automata is labelled with the set $S(a_1 a_2 ... a_i, k)$, in the algorithm we only need to maintain the set for the most recently created state.

The loop (1) is used when the algorithm has constructed part of the automaton, to try to analyze the longest prefix of new incoming word, so it is never used with the first word of the data. If intending to do so, the whole word is accepted, a new state is possibly added to the list of finals in (2).

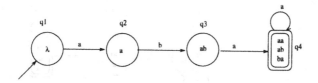

Fig. 2. Output automata when K-PWTI is executed on input aba.

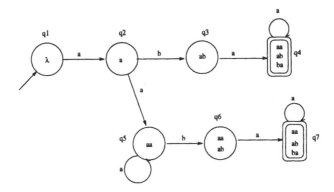

Fig. 3. Output automata when K-PWTI is executed on input $\{aba, aaba\}$.

So with the arrival of the first word "aba" the algorithm directly enters the loop (3) resulting the automaton shown in figure 2. Transitions of type (q, a, q) are created for all the prefixes of the word that meet the condition (4).

With the word "$aaba$", the algorithm executes (1) accepting the prefix "a". As the transition $\delta(q_2, a)$ does not exist, the algorithm enters the loop (2) creating the transition (q_2, a, q_5). The prefix "aa" meets condition (4) so (q_5, a, q_5) is added to the list of transitions. When it finishes evaluating the word, the resulting automaton is shown in figure 3. Observe that this automaton recognizes the language of all the words x such that $S(x, 2) = \{aa, ab, ba\}$.

At the arrival of the word "aa", which belongs to a different class modulo $\equiv_k$ as it meets condition (2), the algorithm establishes the already created q_5 as final state, outputting the algorithm shown in figure 4.

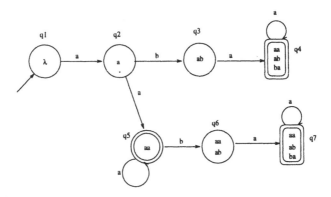

Fig. 4. Output automata when K-PWTI is executed on input $\{aba, aaba, aa\}$.

5 Convergence and time complexity

5.1 Convergence of the algorithm

Theorem 1. *The algorithm KWPTI identifies the class of k-Piecewise Testable languages in the limit.*

Proof. It is easily seen that the algorithm is consistent with the received data as for each set S outputs an automaton accepting the set $\{ua^n v, \forall uv \in S :$ $S(ua, k) = S(u, k), | u | \geq k, n \geq 0\} \subseteq L_k(S)$.

Convergence in the limit follows from the finiteness of the lattice established in section 3.

$\square$

A characteristic sample (a set of input words that make the algorithm to converge) for a class $[x]_k$ can be obtained as follows:

Let $l = \min \{| y | : y \in [x]_k\}$ (a way of calculating l is shown later). The set $\{z \in \Sigma^{l+k-1} : S(z, k) = S(x, k)\}$ is a characteristic sample for the class $[x]_k$ and algorithm k-*PWTLI* as with that sample we have every possible ascending chain in the lattice. The value $l + k - 1$ is necessary to obtain the loops at level $k + 1$ in the automaton (i.e.: transitions of the form $(S(a_1...a_k, k), a, S(a_1...a_k, k))$, $a \in \Sigma$).

The number l in the above definition can be iteratively evaluated from any word $y \in [x]_k$ as follows:

$y_1 = y$
Repeat
  If $\exists a \in \Sigma : y_i = uav$, $S(ua, k) = S(u, k)$ **then** $y_{i+1} = uv$
  else $y_{i+1} = y_i$
  endif
until $y_{i+1} = y_i$
$l = |y_i|$

Theorem 2. *The algorithm $k - PWTI$ is PAC-learnable for the class of k-Piecewise Testable languages*

Proof. It follows inmediately from the finiteness of the class and the consistency of the algorithm.

$\square$

5.2 Time complexity

Every state in the automaton can be represented by a set of subwords of length k. If m is the size of such a set, $m \leq |\Sigma|^k$. As every subword of length $k + 1$ contains $k + 1$ subwords of length k, the number of operations needed to create a new state (concatenating a symbol to the subwords of length k) is $m \cdot k$. As we have to test if every word of length k belongs to the new created state and this operation costs $k \cdot \lg m$, the total cost of creating a new state is $m \cdot k^2 \cdot \lg m$.

The operation described has to be done at most n times, being $n = \sum_{x \in S} |x|$, so the total cost is $(mk^2 \lg m)n \leq |\Sigma|^k k^2 \lg |\Sigma|^k n = k^3 |\Sigma|^k \lg |\Sigma| n$ in the worst case. Since $|\Sigma|$ and k can be considered as constants, the above algorithm is $O(n)$, where n is the sum of the lengths of the input data.

Acknowledgements

The authors gratefully acknowledge the thoughtful suggestions and corrections of anonymous referees.

References

1. Angluin, D. *Inductive inference of formal languages from positive data.* Information and Control, 45. pp. 117-135, 1980.
2. Angluin, D. Inference of reversible languages. Journal of the ACM 29 (3). pp. 741-765, 1982.
3. Anthony, M. and Biggs, N. *Computational Learning Theory. An Introduction.* Cambridge University Press, 1991.
4. Biermann A.W. and Feldman, J.A. *On the synthesis of finite state machines from samples of their behavior.* IEEE Trans. on Computers, Vol. C-21 pp. 592-597, 1972.
5. Brzozowski, J.A. and Simon, I. *Characterizations of Locally Testable Events.* Discrete Mathematics, 4. pp. 243-271. 1973.
6. Fu, K.S. *Syntactic Pattern Recognition and Applications.* Prentice Hall, 1982.
7. P.García and E. Vidal. *Inference of k-testable Languages in the Strict Sense and application to Syntactic Pattern Recognition.* IEEE Trans. Pattern Analysis and Machine Intelligence, Vol. PAMI-12 pp.920-925, 1990.
8. Gold, E.M. *Language identification in the limit.* Information and Control, 10. pp. 447-474, 1967.
9. González R.C. and Thomason, M.G. *Syntactic Pattern Recognition: An Introduction.* Addison Wesley, 1978.
10. Knuutila, T. *How to invent characterizable methods for regular languages.* Lecture Notes in Computer Science 744, Springer Verlag, pp. 209-222, 1993.
11. Lothaire, M. *Combinatorics on words.* Addison Wesley,1983.
12. Muggleton, S. *Inductive Acquisition of Expert Knowledge.* Addison-Wesley, 1990.
13. Natarajan, B. *Machine Learning: A theoretical aproach.* Morgan Kaufmann P. Inc.1991.
14. Pin, J.E. *Variétés de langages formels.* Masson, 1984.
15. Radhakrisnan, V. and Nagaraja, G. Inference of regular grammars via skeletons. IEEE Trans. System, Man, and Cybernetics, SCM-17. pp. 982-992, 1987.
16. Shyam Kapur and Gianfranco Bilardi *Language learning without overgeneralization.* Theoretical Computer Science 141, pp. 151-162, 1995.
17. Simon, I. *Piecewise testable events.* Lecture Notes in Computer Science, vol. 33, Springer Verlag, pp. 214-222, 1980.

Learning Code Regular and Code Linear Languages

J.D. Emerald, K.G. Subramanian and D.G. Thomas

Department of Mathematics, Madras Christian College
Tambaram, Madras - 600 059, India.

Abstract. In this paper, a subclass of regular languages, called code regular languages is defined. Algorithms for learning these languages are presented in the frame work of identification in the limit. Learning of analogous subclass of linear languages is also examined.

1. Introduction

Extensive research on the problem of learning of formal languages has been done in the literature. Learning subclasses of regular languages in the framework of identification in the limit from positive data, gained importance, in view of a result of Gold [4] that the class of languages containing all finite sets and one infinite set is not identifiable in the limit from positive data, as a consequence of which the class of regular languages is not identifiable in the limit from positive data.

Angluin [2] showed that the k-reversible languages which constitute a subclass of regular languages, are identifiable in the limit from positive data with the polynomial time of updating conjectures. Tanida and Yokomori [13] introduced another subclass of regular languages, called strictly regular languages (SRL), which is incomparable but not disjoint with k-reversible languages.

The notion of a strictly deterministic automaton (SDA) is introduced in [13], by extending the concept of usual deterministic automaton, with words labeling edges in the state transition graph of the automaton. But the SDA has certain restrictions, namely, i) a word in the finite set of labels, is the label of a unique edge ii) any two labels differ in their first letter and iii) there are no multiple edges. The learning algorithm to identify in the limit, a strictly regular language from positive examples, proposed in [13], involves an ingenious technique of decomposing an input string into different segments and thereby constructing the output automaton to be conjectured to accept the language. The identification algorithm runs in polynomial time for updating conjectures. Yokomori [14] relaxes the restriction of disallowing multiple edges in SDA and generalizes and strengthens the learning algorithm in [14], including forming characteristic samples for SRLs.

We introduce, in this paper the notion of a code deterministic automaton (CDA) in which the labels of the edges of the state transition graph of the automaton, constitutes a finite code set [3]. A finite set C of words over an alphabet Σ, forms a code, if every word over Σ has atmost one factorization over C. It is of interest to note that there is a linear time algorithm, due to Sardinas-Patterson [3] to check whether a finite set of words is a code or not. The SDA is a special case of CDA, since the labels of edges in a SDA also constitute a code. The identification algorithm in [13,14], does not straightaway apply for code regular languages (CRL) accepted by CDA. We propose an identification algorithm for a subclass of code regular languages. The languages in this subclass are accepted by CDA in which the labels of edges form a prefix as well as a suffix code set. In other words any word in the code set is neither a proper prefix nor a proper suffix of another word in the code set. The identification procedure involves techniques analogous to the identification algorithm for SDA proposed in [14], with a CDA being conjectured at each stage,the correct conjecture being arrived at when the characteristic sample is covered. On the other hand, the labels of the edges of a CDA are to be given as input for the identification algorithm in case the labels just form a code set without being a prefix or suffix code. In fact, the identification algorithm in this form does the same as Makinen's algorithm [6], since the input words can be parsed if the code set is given, yielding a regular left Szilard language to infer.

Application of the learning methods of SRL and CRL to picture recognition is shown. Digitized picture patterns and chain code pictures are encoded as strings which can be learnt when they constitute a SRL or a CRL. It is also of interest to note that certain splicing languages, introduced by Head [5] to represent the set of DNA molecules that may arise from an initial set of DNA molecules in the presence of specified enzyme activities, are SRL or CRL and thus the learning algorithms discussed here can be used for these splicing languages.

The problem of learning subclasses of linear languages has also been of interest. Grammatical inference algorithms for even linear grammars have been presented in [7,9,12]. Recently, Sempere and Garcia [10] have made an interesting study by providing a transformation to obtain a regular language from an even linear language. The associated automaton is then learnt by suitable learning methods available and the even linear grammar is recovered from the inverse transformation. Here we extend this notion by considering a linear language which is over a finite code set. The rules of a linear grammar are of the form A→uBv, or A→w, where u,v,w belong to a code set. A transformation σ, is then introduced to obtain a regular language $\sigma(L)$, from L. A code automaton can then be associated with $\sigma(L)$. When the code automaton is deterministic, it can be learnt by the learning algorithm described earlier, so that the corresponding linear grammar can be recovered from the extended inverse transformation σ^{-1}.

In section 2, we define code deterministic automata and in section 3, we describe an identification algorithm to learn a subclass of CRL in the limit from positive data. Section 4 deals with applications to pictures and DNA sequences. Section 5 deals with the problem of learning linear languages.

2. Code Deterministic Automata and Their Languages

We refer to [14] for the notion of polynomial time identification of a language in the limit from positive data.

We now recall the notion of an extended deterministic finite automaton (EDFA) and a strictly deterministic automaton (SDA) [13,14].

An extended deterministic finite automaton (EDFA) M over an alphabet Σ is a 5-tuple (Q,W,δ,q_0,F), where Q is a finite, nonempty set of states; W ($\subseteq \Sigma^+$) is a finite set of strings; $\delta : Q \times W \rightarrow Q$ is a state transition function partially defined; q_0 is the initial state in Q, and F($\subseteq Q$) is the set of final states.

The function δ is extended from $Q \times W$ to $Q \times W^*$ in the usual manner: for all $p \epsilon Q$, $x \epsilon W^*$, $u \epsilon W$, $\delta (p, \lambda) = p$, $\delta (p, xu) = \delta (\delta(p, x), u)$, where λ is the empty string.

The language accepted by M is $L(M) = \{w \epsilon \Sigma^* / \delta(q_0,w) \epsilon F\}$.

Let $M = (Q,W,\delta,q_0,F)$ be an EDFA. Then M is a strictly deterministic automaton (SDA) if and only if M satisfies the following:

1) for any $w \epsilon W$, there uniquely exists a pair (p,q) such that (p,w,q) $\epsilon \delta$.
2) for any w_1, $w_2 \epsilon W$, the first symbol of w_1 differs from that of w_2.

Yokomori [14] has shown that SRL are polynomial time identifiable in the limit from positive data. The identification algorithm [13,14] for SRL, has input a positive presentation of a strictly regular language (SRL) L, the output being a sequence of SDA. The algorithm has four subprocedures named "UPDATE", "REFINE", "PARSE" and "CONSTRUCT". The procedure UPDATE has a very elegant technique of decomposing the positive examples based on a 'strictly prefix-free' property and the other procedures describe the manner of constructing SDA by parsing the positive examples, creating a set of transitions of SDA and merging identical states. The existence of a characteristic sample for any SDA is shown in [14] and the construction of the characteristic sample is explicity exhibited.

We now introduce the notion of a code deterministic automaton.

Informally, the state transition graph of a code deterministic automaton has the following additional properties:

1) The finite set of labels of edges is a code set.

2) At a given node, the labels of two or more edges originating from the node differ in their first letter. On the otherhand, labels of two non-adjacent edges need not have this feature.

Definition (Code deterministic finite automaton)

Let $M = (Q, C, \delta, p_0, F)$ be an EDFA. M is a code deterministic finite automaton (CDA) if and only if M satisfies the following:

1) (Uniqueness of labels): for any $w \in C$, there exists a unique pair (p,q), $p,q \in Q$ such that $\delta(p,w) = q$.
2) (Code property): The set C forms a code over the alphabet Σ.
3) (Distinct first letter of labels of edges at a node): If $\delta(p,w_1) = q_1$ and $\delta(p,w_2) = q_2$ for any $w_1,w_2 \in C$, then the first symbol of w_1 differs from that of w_2.

A language L is called code regular, if $L = L(M)$ for some CDA M, where $L(M)$ denotes the language accepted by M.

Example:
Let $\Sigma = \{a,b,c\}$. Consider a CDA
$M = (\{q_0, q_1, q_f\}, \{ab, cab, cbb, cbaa\}, \delta, q_0, \{q_f\})$,
whose transition graph is given in Fig.1.

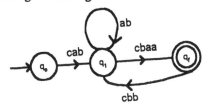

Fig.1

Proposition: The class of SRL $\subset$ the class of CRL.

Inclusion is clear. Proper inclusion is seen from the CDA in Fig.1 whose language is not a SRL.

3. Identification of CRL

Let L be a CRL over a code set $C = \{x_1,x_2,...,x_m\}$ which is both a prefix code (no word in C is a proper prefix of another word in C) and a suffix code (no word in C is a proper suffix of another word in C).

We present a learning algorithm IA for CDAs accepting the CRL over the code set C. The algorithm comprises of five subprocedures named "UPDATE", "REF-SUFFIX", "REFINE", "PARSE", and "CONSTRUCT". The last three subprocedures are as in [14] and are not explicitly given here.

We now give intuitive descriptions of the first two subprocedures.

The algorithm IA maintains a set $T = T_p \cup T_s$ of edge labels that, at any time, is sufficient to parse all example strings seen so far (where T_p and T_s consist of prefixes and suffixes of positive examples respectively). The goal of UPDATE is to update the sets T_p and T_s so that the new examples can be parsed, while maintaining the parsability of all previously seen examples. In general, the set T maintains a tentative set of edge labels of the CDA to be learned, and the elements of T always satisfy the code property. At any time, elements of T may be replaced, or they may be split into smaller pieces and new elements of T may be added. For performing this task, UPDATE refines the set T_p at each stage and immediately calls another subprocedure REF-SUFFIX to refine the set T_s. After updating T with a new example, the procedure REFINE takes as input each transition from the currently conjectured CDA, and breaks it up into the new smaller parse strings of the updated set T, introducing a chain of new states if necessary. Then, the procedure PARSE adds into the current automaton a new chain of states (using the updated set T of edge labels) that can exactly parse the new example. Finally, CONSTRUCT takes the refined automaton, along with new chain of states for the parse of the new example, and then converts it into a CDA.

Constructing characteristic sample for CRL is on lines similar to that of SRL in [14]. The characteristic sample for the CDA M in Fig.1 is formed as follows, using the notations as in [14].

For each $p \subset Q$, we choose u_p and v_p as follows:

$$u_{q_0} = \lambda, \qquad u_{q_1} = cab, \qquad u_{q_f} = cabcbaa$$

$$v_{q_0} = cabcbaa, \quad v_{q_1} = cbaa, \quad v_{q_f} = \lambda$$

Then, construct
$$X_{q_0} = \{cabcbaa\}, \; X_{q_1} = \{abcbaa, cbaa\}, \; X_{q_f} = \{\lambda, cbbcbaa\}$$

Finally,
$$S_M = \{cabcbaa, cababcbaa, cabcbaa, cabcbaacbbcbaa,$$
cabababcbaa, cabcbaacbbabcbaa$\}$.

In the procedure, the following notations are used.

- Common-prefix (x,y) denotes the string which is the longest common prefix of x and y.
- Remove prefix (x,α) denotes the string ß such that $x = \alpha$ß.
- min(A) denotes the set of all elements of minimum length in the finite set A.
- first (x) denotes the first letter of the string x.

Procedure UPDATE (T_p, T_s, x)
begin
   if $T_p = \phi$ then $T_p = \{x\}$
   else
      begin
      if first (y) = first (x) for some $y \epsilon T_p$ then
         begin
            α = common-prefix (y,x)
            ß = remove-prefix (y,α)
            γ = remove-prefix (x,α)
            $T_p = (T_p \setminus \{y\}) \cup \{\alpha\}$
            if $ß \neq \lambda$ then $T_s = T_s \cup \{ß\}$
            if $\gamma \neq \lambda$ then $T_s = T_s \cup \{\gamma\}$
         end
      else
         $T_p = T_p \cup \{x\};$
      call REF-SUFFIX (T_s)
      end
end

Procedure REF-SUFFIX (T_s)
begin
   flag = true;
   while (flag) do
   begin
      flag = false
      $T_f = \phi$
      while $(T_s \neq \phi)$ do
      begin
         $T_m = \min (T_s)$
         $T_s = T_s \setminus T_m$
         do for each $\delta \epsilon T_m$
            do for each $y \epsilon T_s$
               if $y = \delta^n y'$ or $y = y' \delta^n$ $(n \geq 1)$ or $y = \delta^n y' \delta^m$
                  then begin
                      $T_s = T_s \setminus \{y\}$
                      $T_f = T_f \cup \{y'\}$
                      flag=true
                  end
            end do
         end do
         $T_f = T_f \cup T_m$
      end
      $T_s = T_f$
   end
end.

From the manner of updating T, it is clear that update gives a correct set of labels C, which is not necessarily unique to L.

Identification algorithm IA

Input: A positive presentation of the code regular language L.
Output: A sequence of CDAs for code regular languages.

Procedure

Initialize $i = 0$;
Initialize the sets T, T_p, T_s to ϕ;
Let $M_0 = (\{p_0\}, \phi, \phi, p_0, \phi)$ be the initial CDA;
repeat (forever)
begin
   let $i = i+1$;
   let $M_{i-1} = (Q_{i-1}, W_{i-1}, \delta_{i-1}, p_0, F_{i-1})$ be the (i-1)st conjectured CDA;
   read the next positive example w_i ;
   if $w_i \epsilon L(M_{i-1})$ then output $M_i(=M_{i-1})$ as the i-th conjecture;
   else
      begin
         call UPDATE (T_p, T_s, w_i);
         let $T_i = T_p \cup T_s$;
         for all $t \in \delta_{i-1}$, make REFINE(T_i, M_{i-1}, t);
         for w_i, make PARSE(T_i, M_{i-1}, w_i);
         let Δ_i be the unions of each
            REFINE(T_i, M_{i-1}, t) $(t \in \delta_{i-1})$ and
            PARSE(T_i, M_{i-1}, w_i);
         let $M_i = $ CONSTRUCT (Δ_i);
         output M_i as the i-th conjecture;
      end
end.

Remark

1) If the code set $C = \{x_1, x_2, ..., x_m\}$ is not a prefix code or a suffix code, then the code set is also given as an input in the above algorithm. The factorization of a positive example presented over the code C can be done using a pattern matching machine [1] in linear time. Hence the CDA is constructed using the REFINE, PARSE and CONSTRUCT procedures directly, as $T = \{x_1, x_2, ..., x_m\}$.

2) If the code set C is a uniform code of length k, it is enough to input k instead of the elements of the finite set C. The algorithm will then factorize the word w_i as $w_i = u_1 u_2 ... u_n$ where length of u_i is k for $i=1,2,...,n$ and obtain $T_i = \{u_1, u_2, ..., u_n\}$. The CDA is then constructed using the REFINE, PARSE and CONSTRUCT procedures.

4. Application to Learning of Pictures and DNA Sequences

The learning methods described earlier could be applied to the problems of learning of picture languages and DNA sequences.

Syntactic methods of generation of digitized pictures has been widely investigated. One of the basic references in this direction is [11]. A digitized picture as in Fig.2 where the body of a's represents the token L in a background of b's, can be encoded into a string of the form $(ab^4)^6 a^5$. The picture describing token L of fixed width in fig.2 can thus be represented by elements of the language $\{(ab^4)^n a^5/n \geq 1\}$. This language is accepted by a code deterministic automaton and the learning algorithm discussed earlier is applicable here. The language is learnt and is then interpreted to give rise to the pictures. b stands for blank and is not shown in fig.2.

```
a
a
a
a
a
a
a a a a a
```
Fig.2 : Token L of a's

Likewise, patterns described by chain codes [8] can also be learnt using the learning algorithm described earlier. The picture "staircases" in Fig.3 can be encoded as a string $(ru)^2 rdr(dr)^3$, where r,u,d respectively, stand for moving one unit line to the right, up, down from the current point. (The encoding depends on the starting point and ending point). The pictures as in Fig.3 are thus represented by elements of the language $\{(ru)^n rdr(dr)^m/n, m \geq 1\}$, which is also accepted by a code deterministic automaton. Again, the learning technique described earlier is applicable here, with the chain-coded language being learnt and interpreted to give chain code pictures.

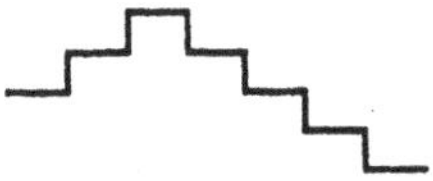

Fig. 3 : Staircases

Head [5] introduced splicing languages as mathematical models to formalize the effect of restriction enzymes and a ligase that allow DNA molecules to be cleaved and reassoicated to produce further molecules. Languages obtained by persistent splicing systems are regular [5]. For example the language $\{aba(ba)^n/n \geq 1\}$ is a persistent splicing language. A biochemical interpretation of this language, is that its elements consist of all molecules that can be potentially arised from the action of enzyme ClaI with an appropriate ligase on copies of the molecule

[A/T][T/A][C/G][G/C][A/T][T/A][C/G][G/C][A/T][T/A]
which is encoded by the string ababa on taking
a = [A/T][T/A] and b = [C/G][G/C]

The language $\{aba(ba)^n / n \geq 1\}$ is indeed a SRL and thus the learning algorithm for SRL is applicable.

5. Learning of Linear Languages

Learning of subclasses of linear languages such as even linear languages has been proposed in [7,9,12]. Recently, Sempere and Garcia [10] have provided a nice characterization of even linear languages and have shown its application to the learning of these languages.

We consider here linear languages over a finite code set generated by a linear grammar called code linear grammar (CLG) $G = (N,\Sigma,C,P,S)$ where N, Σ are respectively the nonterminals and terminals; C is a finite code set over Σ; $S\epsilon N$ is the start symbol and P consists of rules of the forms $A \rightarrow uBv$, $A \rightarrow w$ where $u,v,w\epsilon C$. A CLG is deterministic, if i) whenever $A \rightarrow uBv$, $A \rightarrow uCv$ are in P, then $B=C$ and ii) each $x\epsilon C$ occurs in the rightside of atmost one rule in P.

We extend here the notion of a transformation introduced in [10]. We define the transformation σ, called extended joined extreme as follows: If $x = uyv$ is a word over a code set C, where $u,v\epsilon C$ then $\sigma(x) = uv\sigma(y)$ and $\sigma(x) = x$, if $x\epsilon C$. The inverse transformation σ^{-1} is defined by $\sigma^{-1}(x) = x$, if $x\epsilon C$ and $\sigma^{-1}(uvx) = u\sigma^{-1}(x)v$, where $u,v\epsilon C$ and x is a word over C.

It can be seen that, if L is a linear language over a finite code set C generated by a code linear grammar then $\sigma(L)$ is regular. In fact, given a linear language L generated by a deterministic code linear grammar $G = (N,\Sigma,C,P,S)$, a code deterministic automaton A to accept $\sigma(L)$ is formed as follows: $A = (Q,C,\delta,q_0,F)$ where $Q = N\cup\{q_f\}$, $q_f\notin N$, $q_0 = S$, $F = \{q_f\}$, and δ is defined by the following steps:

     i) $B \epsilon \delta(A,uv)$, if $A \rightarrow uBv \epsilon P$, $u,v\epsilon C$
and   ii) $\delta(A,w) = \{q_f\}$, if $A \rightarrow w \epsilon P$, $w\epsilon C$

Conversely, if CDA A of the type constructed above is given, then a deterministic code linear grammar can be formed to generate $\sigma^{-1}(L(A))$, where $L(A)$ is the language accepted by the CDA A.

A deterministic code linear grammar and an associated CDA are shown in Fig.4 and Fig.5.

G: S → ru S dr
     S → r
with code set C = {ru, dr, r}

Fig.4: A Deterministic Code Linear Grammar

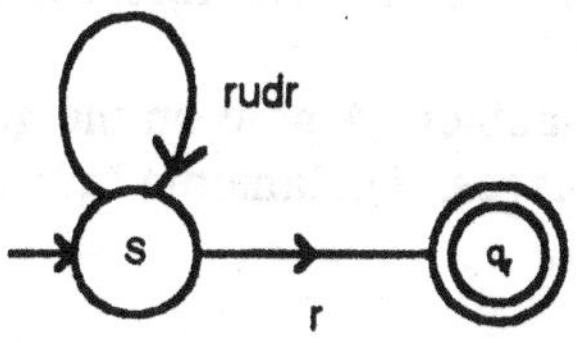

Fig. 5: Associated CDA

Learning algorithms developed earlier can be applied to learn $\sigma(L) = L(A)$, where A is a CDA and the deterministic code linear grammar to generate the given linear language L can then be obtained.

Applications of the learning algorithms to learn pictures represented by the deterministic code linear languages can be done as in the earlier section. For instance, the chain code picture corresponding to the word $(ru)^3 r (dr)^3$ in the grammar considered above, is shown in Fig.6.

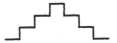

Fig.6 : Staircases of equal size

Acknowledgement: The authors thank the referees for their very useful and elaborate comments, which enabled a thorough revision of the paper. The authors are grateful to the Department of Atomic Energy and the National Board for Higher Mathematics for financial support for this work done under Project No.48/4/94-G/2207.

References

1. A.V.Aho and M.J.Corasick, Efficient string matching: an aid to bibliographic search, Communications of the ACM 18(6), 338-340, 1975.

2. D.Angluin, Inference of reversible languages, Journal of the ACM, 29(3), 741-765, 1982.

3. J.Berstel and D.Perrin, Theory of Codes, Academic Press, New York/London, 1985.

4. E.M. Gold, Language identification in the limit, Information and Control, 10, 447-474, 1967.

5. T.Head, Formal language theory and DNA:An analysis of the generative capacity of specific recombinant behaviours, Bulletin of Mathematical Biology, 49, 737-759, 1987.

6. E. Makinen, The grammatical inference problem for the Szilard languages of linear grammars, Information Processing Letters, 36, 203-206, 1990.

7. E. Makinen, A note on the grammatical inference problem for even linear languages, Fundamenta Informaticae, 25(2), 175-181, 1996.

8. H.A.Maurer, G.Rozenberg and E.Welzl, Using string languages to describe picture languages, Information and Control, 54, 155-185, 1992.

9. V.Radhakrishnan and G.Nagaraja, Inference of even linear grammars and its application to picture description languages, Pattern Recognition, 21(1), 55-62, 1988.

10. J.M.Sempere and P.Garcia, A characterisation of even linear languages and its application to the learning problem, Lecture Notes in Artificial Intelligence 914, 38-44, Springer Verlag.

11. G.Siromoney, R.Siromoney and K.Krithivasan, Abstract families of matrices and picture languages, Comp. Graphics and Image Proc., 1, 234-307, 1972.

12. Y.Takada, Grammatical inference of even linear languages based on control sets, Information Processing Letters, 28(4), 193-199, 1988.

13. N.Tanida and T.Yokomori, Polynomial time identification of strictly regular languages in the limit, IEICE Transactions on Information and Systems, E75-D, 125-132, 1992.

14. T.Yokomori, On polynomial-time learnability in the limit of strictly deterministic automata, Machine Learning, 19, 153-179, 1995.

Incremental Regular Inference

Pierre Dupont

Carnegie Mellon University
Pittsburgh, PA 15213, USA
E-mail : pdupont@cs.cmu.edu

Abstract

In this paper, we extend the characterization of the search space of regular inference [DMV94] to sequential presentations of learning data. We propose the RPNI2 algorithm, an incremental extension of the RPNI algorithm. We study the convergence and complexities of both algorithms from a theoretical and practical point of view. These results are assessed on the Feldman task.

1 Introduction

Regular inference is the problem of learning a regular language from a positive sample, that is, a finite set of strings supposed to be drawn from a target language. Whenever a negative sample, that is, a finite set of strings not belonging to the target language, is also available, the problem may be solved by the RPNI algorithm[1] proposed by Oncina and García [OG92] and, independently, by Lang [Lan92].

The RPNI algorithm has been shown to identify in the limit any regular language with polynomial complexity as a function of the positive and negative sample sizes. However, this algorithm requires the positive and negative information to be presented as a whole, that is, it uses a *presentation from given data.* If new learning data become available, the inference process must be restarted from scratch. The objective of the present work is to overcome this limitation by extending the RPNI algorithm to deal with *sequential presentation.* In this case, the learning data are presented one at a time in a random order, each example being labeled either as positive or negative.

In section 2, we recall the theoretical framework of regular inference by specifying its *search space* and its *border set*, that is, the limit of possible generalizations of a positive sample under the control of a negative sample [DMV94]. We also discuss identification in the limit for the two data presentations.

Section 3 is devoted to the description of the RPNI algorithm. We formally define the notion of a characteristic sample that guarantees the correct identification of an unknown language. Two related theorems are presented which characterize the solution produced by this algorithm.

---

[1] RPNI stands for Regular Positive and Negative Inference.

We pursue the characterization of the search space proposed in [DMV94] for a sequential data presentation. Some interesting properties of an incrementally constructed search space are proved in section 4.

In section 5 we propose the RPNI2 algorithm[2], the incremental extension of the RPNI algorithm. Here, we observe that the asymptotic complexities of both algorithms are equal while a practical complexity reduction may be expected with RPNI2. This expectation is confirmed by experimental results detailed in section 6.

2 Theoretical Framework[DMV94]

The reader familiar with the classical definitions of automata theory and regular inference may omit section 2.1. We introduce these notions here for the sake of completeness.

2.1 Definitions and Notations

Let Σ denote a finite alphabet, let u, v, w denote elements of Σ^*, i.e. strings over Σ, and let λ denote the empty string. Let $|u|$ denote the length of the string u. We say that u is a *prefix* of v if there exists w such that $uw = v$. We say that u is a *suffix* of v if there exists w such that $wu = v$. A language L is any subset of Σ^*. Let $Pr(L) = \{u|\exists v, uv \in L\}$ denote the set of prefixes of L. Let $L/u = \{v|uv \in L\}$ denote the *right-quotient* of L by u. This is also called the *set of tails* of u in L. We have $L/u \neq \phi$ if and only if $u \in Pr(L)$.

A *finite automaton* is a 5-tuple $(Q, \Sigma, \delta, q_0, F)$ where Q is a finite set of *states*, Σ is an *alphabet*, δ is a *transition function*, i.e. a mapping from $Q \mathrm{x} \Sigma$ to 2^Q, q_0 is the *initial state* and F is a subset of Q identifying the *final* or *accepting states*. If for any q in Q and any a in Σ, $\delta(q, a)$ has at most one member (exactly one member) the automaton A is said to be *deterministic* (respectively, *complete)*. Henceforth we shall denote using DFA (NFA) a deterministic (respectively, a non-deterministic) finite automaton.

If $A = (Q, \Sigma, \delta, q_0, F)$ is an automaton, the automaton A/π *derived from A with respect to the partition* π of Q, also called the *quotient automaton* $A/\pi = (Q', \Sigma, \delta', B(q_0, \pi), F')$, is defined as follows:

$Q' = Q/\pi = \{B(q, \pi)|q \in Q\}$, $F' = \{B \in Q'|B \cap F \neq \phi\}$,

$\delta' : Q' \mathrm{x} \Sigma \to 2^{Q'} : \forall B, B' \in Q', \forall a \in \Sigma, B' \in \delta'(B, a) \Leftrightarrow \exists q, q' \in Q, q \in B, q' \in B'$ and $q' \in \delta(q, a)$.

The states of Q belonging to the same block B of the partition π are said to be *merged* together.

Let I_+ (respectively, I_-) denote some *positive sample* (respectively, *negative sample)* of an unknown language[3] L. Let $A(L)$ denote the *canonical acceptor* of L, i.e. the *minimal DFA* accepting L. We say that an automaton is *compatible* with a positive sample (with a negative sample) if it accepts (respectively, rejects) any string from the sample. Let $PTA(I_+)$ denote the *prefix tree acceptor* built

---

[2] **RPNI2** stands for *Regular Positive and Negative Incremental Inference*.
[3] By default, "language" refers here to a *regular* language.

from a positive sample I_+ and let $MCA(I_+)$ denote the *maximal canonical acceptor* of I_+.

Let $P(A)$ denote the set of partitions of the state set of an automaton A. Let $r(\pi_i)$, or simply r_i, denote the number of blocks of the partition π_i. Let $\pi_1 = \{B_{11}, \ldots, B_{1r_1}\}$ and π_2 be two partitions of $P(A)$. We say that π_2 *directly derives from* π_1 if the partition π_2 is constructed from π_1 as follows: $\pi_2 = \{B_{1j} \cup B_{1k}\} \cup (\pi_1 \setminus \{B_{1j}, B_{1k}\})$, for some j, k between 1 and r_1, $j \neq k$. Consequently, $r_2 = r_1 - 1$.

This derivation operation defines a partial order relation on $P(A)$, which we shall denote $\preceq$. In particular, we have $\pi_1 \preceq \pi_2$. Let $\ll$ denote its transitive closure. In other words, $\pi_i \ll \pi_j$ if and only if π_i is finer than π_j. By extension, we say that A/π_i is *finer than* A/π_j and that A/π_j *derives from* A/π_i. The set of automata partially ordered by the relation $\preceq$ is a lattice, which we shall denote $Lat(A)$. In particular, we shall consider $Lat(PTA(I_+))$, the lattice of automata derived from the $PTA(I_+)$.

By construction of a quotient automaton, we have the language inclusion property which may be stated as follows [FB75]: $A/\pi_i \ll A/\pi_j$ if $L(A/\pi_i) \subseteq L(A/\pi_j)$. In other words, the derivation operation gives rise to a *language generalization* in a lattice of automata.

We say that I_+ is *structurally complete* with respect to an automaton A accepting a language L if there exists an acceptance of the strings of I_+ by A such that every transition of A is exercised and every element of the final state set of A is used as accepting state.

The search space of possible solutions to the regular inference problem is defined by the following theorem [Ang82, DMV94].

Theorem 2.1 *Let I_+ be a positive sample of any regular language L and let $A(L)$ be the canonical automaton accepting L. If I_+ is structurally complete with respect to $A(L)$ then $A(L)$ belongs to $Lat(PTA(I_+))$.*

In other words, if we assume the structural completeness of the positive sample with respect to an unknown canonical automaton, this automaton may be found by searching the lattice $Lat(PTA(I_+))$.

The *border set* $BS_{PTA}(I_+, I_-)$ is the set of automata which are at a *maximal depth* in the lattice [DMV94], that is, the set of automata which are compatible with I_+ and I_-, and from which there are no compatible automata that can be derived. The border set of $Lat(PTA(I_+))$ is the set of automata which correspond to the limit of generalization, by merging states of the $PTA(I_+)$, under the control of the negative sample. The *minimal DFA consistency problem*, i.e. finding the smallest DFA compatible with I_+ and I_-, can then be viewed as the discovery of the smallest DFA in $BS_{PTA}(I_+, I_-)$.

The minimal DFA consistency problem has been shown to be NP-hard [Ang78, Gol78] in the general case. However, as detailed in section 3, this problem may be solved by the RPNI algorithm if the sample is supposed to be *characteristic*. Note that the RPNI algorithm also offers a good generalization of the learning data even if the sample is not characteristic. This last point will be illustrated experimentally in section 6.

2.2 Language Identification in the Limit and Characteristic Samples

The language identification in the limit paradigm was introduced by Gold [Gol67]. For a sequential presentation of data, the identification in the limit is guaranteed if an inference method is guaranteed to converge to a correct representation of the language to be identified. Gold also proposed a related identification paradigm for fixed learning data [Gol78] called *identification from given data*. In this case, the learning set D is made of a pair of samples respectively positive and negative, that is, $D = (I_+, I_-)$. We restate Gold's definition to introduce the notion of *characteristic sample* $D^c = (I_+^c, I_-^c)$.

Definition 2.1 An inference method M *identifies* a language L *from given data* if there exists a sample $D^c = (I_+^c, I_-^c)$ such that for any data set $D = (I_+, I_-)$, with $I_+ \supseteq I_+^c$ and $I_- \supseteq I_-^c$, the hypothesis $H(D)$ proposed by the method M is correct, that is $L(H(D)) = L$. The sample D^c is called *characteristic* for the language L and the inference method M.

This definition gives a general characterization of an inference method. It does not prescribe, for a given method M and a language L, how to specify D^c. Since the canonical automaton $A(L)$ of a regular language is unique, the specification of a characteristic sample is usually based on this automaton. However, an inference method which would identify a regular language represented by an NFA might require another specification.

The following theorem, proved for instance in [Dup96], states the equivalence of the two related identification paradigms.

Theorem 2.2 *An inference method M identifies a language L from given data if and only if it identifies the language L from a sequential presentation.*

3 The RPNI Algorithm

3.1 Characteristic Sample Specification

Given a regular language L, represented by its canonical automaton $A(L)$, we shall detail the conditions that the learning data must satisfy to be characteristic for the language L and the RPNI algorithm. To this end, Oncina and García define the *short prefixes* and *kernel* of a language [OG92]. Henceforth, we will denote the standard order[4] on the strings of an alphabet Σ by the symbol "$<$".

3.1.1 The Set of Short Prefixes and the Kernel

Definition 3.1 The set of *short prefixes* $Sp(L)$ of a language L is defined as

$$Sp(L) = \{x \in \Pr(L) \mid \nexists u \in \Sigma^* \text{ with } L/u = L/x \text{ and } u < x\}$$

---

[4] According to the standard order the first strings on the alphabet $\Sigma = \{a, b\}$ are $\lambda, a, b, aa, ab, ba, bb, aaa, \ldots$

We know that in the canonical automaton $A(L)$ of the language L, there are as many states as the number of tails L/x of strings x belonging to the prefixes of L. The set of short prefixes is the set of the first strings in standard order, each of which leads to a particular state of the canonical automaton. Consequently, there are as many short prefixes as states in $A(L)$.

For example, the set of short prefixes of the language accepted by the automaton presented in figure 1 is $Sp(L) = \{\lambda, b\}$. Note that λ and b are the two first strings in standard order leading respectively to state 0 and state 1.

Figure 1: A canonical automaton.

Definition 3.2 The *kernel* $N(L)$ of the language L is defined as

$$N(L) = \{\lambda\} \cup \{xa \mid x \in Sp(L), a \in \Sigma, xa \in \mathrm{Pr}(L)\}$$

The kernel is made of the string λ and of the prefixes of the language corresponding to the short prefixes extended by one letter. By construction $Sp(L) \subseteq N(L)$. The kernel elements represent the transitions of the canonical automaton $A(L)$ since they are obtained by adding one letter to the short prefixes which represent the states of $A(L)$. Moreover, all elements of the kernel that also belong to the language represent the accepting states of $A(L)$. The kernel of the language of our example is $N(L) = \{\lambda, a, b, ba, bb\}$. The strings λ, a and bb belong to L ; they lead to an accepting state in the automaton presented in figure 1.

Note that if $|Q|$ denotes the number of states of the canonical automaton $A(L)$, the kernel has at most $1 + |Q| \cdot |\Sigma|$ elements.

Definition 3.3 A sample $D^c = (I_+^c, I_-^c)$ is *characteristic* for the language L and the algorithm RPNI if it satisfies the following conditions

1. $\forall x \in N(L)$, *if* $x \in L$ *then* $x \in I_+^c$ *else* $\exists u \in \Sigma^*$ *such that* $xu \in I_+^c$.

2. $\forall x \in Sp(L), \forall y \in N(L)$ *if* $L/x \neq L/y$ *then* $\exists u \in \Sigma^*$ *such that* $(xu \in I_+^c$ *and* $yu \in I_-^c)$ *or* $(xu \in I_-^c$ *and* $yu \in I_+^c)$.

Condition 1 guarantees that each element of the kernel belongs to I_+^c if it also belongs to the language or, otherwise, is prefix of a string of I_+^c. One can easily check that this condition implies the structural completeness of the sample I_+^c with respect to $A(L)$. In this case, theorem 2.1 assures that the automaton $A(L)$ belongs to the lattice $Lat(PTA(I_+^c))$. When an element x of the short prefixes and an element y of the kernel do not have the same set of tails $(L/x \neq L/y)$, they necessarily correspond to distinct states in the canonical automaton. In this case, condition 2 guarantees that a suffix u would distinguish them. In other words, the merging of a state corresponding to a short prefix x in the $PTA(I_+^c)$ with another state corresponding to an element y of the kernel is made incompatible by the existence of xu in I_+^c and yu in I_-^c or the converse.

There may exist several distinct characteristic samples for a given language L as several suffixes u may satisfy condition 1 or 2. Since the set of short prefixes contains $|Q|$ elements and the kernel has $\mathcal{O}(|Q| \cdot |\Sigma|)$ elements, the size of a characteristic sample is given by

$$|I_+^c| = \mathcal{O}(|Q|^2 \cdot |\Sigma|) \text{ and } |I_-^c| = \mathcal{O}(|Q|^2 \cdot |\Sigma|).$$

For a fixed alphabet Σ, this size only depends on the number of states of the canonical automaton to be identified.

One can verify that $D^c = (I_+^c, I_-^c)$, with $I_+^c = \{\lambda, a, bb, bba, baab, baaaba\}$ and $I_-^c = \{b, ab, aba\}$, forms a characteristic sample for the language accepted by the canonical automaton of figure 1.

3.2 Outline of the RPNI Algorithm

Algorithm RPNI

input I_+, I_-
output A DFA compatible with I_+, I_-

begin

// N is the number of states of $PTA(I_+)$

$\pi \leftarrow \{\{0\}, \{1\}, \dots, \{N-1\}\}$ // One block for each prefix in the order $<$
$A \leftarrow PTA(I_+)$

for $i = 1$ to $|\pi| - 1$ // Loop on the blocks of partition π
  for $j = 0$ to $i - 1$ // Loop on the blocks of lower rank
    $\pi' \leftarrow \pi \backslash \{B_j, B_i\} U \{B_i U B_j\}$ // Merging of block B_i and block B_j
    $A/\pi' \leftarrow$ *derive* (A, π')
    $\pi'' \leftarrow$ *determ_merge* (A/π')
    if *compatible* $(A/\pi'', I_-)$ then   // Deterministic parsing of I_-
      $A \leftarrow A/\pi''$
      $\pi \leftarrow \pi''$
      break   // Break j loop
    end if
  end for   // End j loop
end for   // End i loop
return A
end RPNI

The RPNI algorithm performs an ordered search in the lattice $Lat(PTA(I_+))$. By construction of the $PTA(I_+)$, each of its states corresponds to a unique prefix. The prefixes may be sorted according to the standard order. This order also applies on the prefix tree states. A partition in the state set of the $PTA(I_+)$ is made of an ordered block set, each block receiving the rank of its state of minimal rank. The RPNI algorithm proceeds in $N - 1$ steps where $N = \mathcal{O}(\|I_+\|)$ is the number of states[5] of $PTA(I_+)$. The partition $\pi(i)$ at step i is obtained by

---

[5] $\|I_+\|$ denotes the sum of the lengths of the strings belonging to I_+.

merging the two first blocks, according to the standard order, of the partition $\pi(i-1)$ at step $i-1$ such that $PTA(I_+)/\pi(i)$ is a compatible automaton.

The function *derive* (A, π') returns the quotient automaton A with respect to partition π'. The automaton A/π' may be non-deterministic. The function *determ_merge* (A/π') returns the partition π'' obtained by recursively merging all blocks of π', which creates a non-determinism. If A/π' is deterministic, the partition π'' is equal to partition π'. This is the "determinization by merging" operation. The function *compatible* $(A/\pi'', I_-)$ returns TRUE if the quotient automaton is compatible with the negative sample, FALSE otherwise.

Given that $PTA(I_+)$ has $\mathcal{O}(\|I_+\|)$ states, the time complexity of *determ_merge* is $\mathcal{O}(\|I_+\|)$. Moreover, since the quotient automaton A/π'' is necessarily deterministic, the compatibility checking with I_- has a $\mathcal{O}(\|I_-\|)$ complexity. Since the inside loop (on index j) is performed $\mathcal{O}(\|I_+\|^2)$ times, the global complexity of the RPNI algorithm is $\mathcal{O}((\|I_+\| + \|I_-\|) \cdot \|I_+\|^2)$.

3.3 Identification in the Limit

Theorem 3.1 *The RPNI algorithm identifies in the limit the class of regular languages.*

Two distinct proofs of this theorem may be found in [OG92] and in [Dup96].

Theorem 3.2 *When the learning data contains a characteristic sample for the language L, the canonical automaton $A(L)$ is the DFA having the least number of states and belonging to $BS_{PTA}(I_+, I_-)$. Consequently, $A(L)$ is the solution to the minimal DFA consistency problem.*

A proof of this theorem may be found in [Dup96].

This theorem characterizes the search space independently of the inference algorithm. As a result the definition of a characteristic sample becomes more general. In short, theorem 3.2 guarantees the existence of a notable element of the border set while theorem 3.1 guarantees that this element may be found by applying the RPNI algorithm.

The polynomial complexity of the RPNI algorithm and theorem 3.2 do not contradict the NP-hardness of the minimal DFA consistency problem. This is because in order to guarantee the identification, the RPNI algorithm must be provided with learning data that contain a characteristic sample.

4 Incremental Search Space

In this section, we study the structure of the search space for a sequential presentation of the learning data.

4.1 Induction Hypothesis

We suppose that the current solution $A(k)$ at step k is a DFA compatible with the first k data received. More precisely, the current positive sample $I_+(p)$ is defined by the first p examples, which may be stored as a prefix tree $PTA(I_+(p))$, and the current negative sample $I_-(q)$ is defined by the first q negative examples, with $k = p + q$. The solution $A(k)$ is supposed to belong to the border set $BS_{PTA}(I_+(p), I_-(q))$.

We can initialize this induction by applying the RPNI algorithm on the first example. If the first example is positive, the solution will be the universal automaton, otherwise the solution will be the empty automaton.

4.2 Incremental Lattice Construction

Property 4.1 defines the relation between successive lattices when a new positive example is received[6].

Property 4.1 $Lat(PTA(I_+(p))) \not\subseteq Lat(PTA(I_+(p+1)))$.

Proof : Both lattices could be completely distinct, i.e. $Lat(PTA(I_+(p))) \cap Lat(PTA(I_+(p+1))) = \phi$. When the $(p+1)^{th}$ example introduces a new symbol, the universal automaton on the new alphabet is not in $Lat(PTA(I_+(p)))$. Since the universal automaton may be derived from any automaton belonging to $Lat(PTA(I_+(p+1)))$, none of them belong to $Lat(PTA(I_+(p)))$. When, on the contrary, the $(p+1)^{th}$ example does not introduce a new symbol, the universal automaton belongs to both lattices, but $Lat(PTA(I_+(p))) \not\subseteq Lat(PTA(I_+(p+1)))$ because $PTA(I_+(p)) \notin Lat(PTA(I_+(p+1)))$. Indeed, $I_+(p+1)$ is not included in the language accepted by $PTA(I_+(p))$. Since the language accepted by any automaton in $Lat(PTA(I_+(p+1)))$ includes $I_+(p+1)$, $PTA(I_+(p))$ does not belong to this lattice. $\square$

4.2.1 New Example Acceptance

Given a solution $A(k)$, the membership of a new example x to $L(A(k))$ may be checked and $A(k)$ may be extended by *the shortest suffix* of x. This operation consists in finding the longest prefix u of x accepted by the automaton $A(k)$. This acceptance defines a state q such that $q \in \delta^*(q_0, u)$. Since $A(k)$ is deterministic, the state q is unique. From state q, the automaton $A(k)$ is extended by the suffix v to accept $x = uv$.

Let $A^x(k)$ denote the automaton obtained by the shortest suffix extension of x from the automaton $A(k)$. By construction, $A^x(k)$ is deterministic. If x is already accepted by $A(k)$, the shortest suffix v is the empty string and hence $A^x(k) = A(k)$.

Figure 2: Shortest suffix extension.

Suppose that the current solution $A(k)$ is the automaton presented in figure 2 (left). Assume also that the new example is $bbbaab$. The longest accepted prefix is bbb, which leads to state 1. The resulting automaton, presented at figure 2 (right), is obtained by extension using the suffix aab from state 1.

The shortest suffix extension may cause an incompatibility with the current negative sample even if $A(k)$ is compatible. In our example, $L(A(k)) = (bb)^*$. The extension guarantees the acceptance of the string $bbbaab$ but also of any

---

[6]If a positive example has already been presented, the prefix tree acceptor remains unchanged, as does the associated lattice.

string of the form $b(bb)^*aab$. If, for instance, the string $baab$ belongs to the current negative sample, the extended solution is incompatible. The solution to this problem is presented in section 5.1.

The property 4.2 states that the shortest suffix extension guarantees that, if the current solution at step k belongs to the lattice built from the first p examples, then the extended automaton necessarily belongs to the lattice built by adding the new example.

Property 4.2 $A(k) \in Lat(PTA(I_+(p))) \Rightarrow A^x(k) \in Lat(PTA(I_+(p+1)))$, with x being the $(p+1)^{th}$ example.

Proof : By hypothesis, $A(k)$ is a quotient automaton of $PTA(I_+(p))$. Thus $I_+(p)$ is structurally complete with respect to $A(k)$. Let v be the shortest suffix corresponding to the extension of $A(k)$ to get $A^x(k)$. Let w be the shortest suffix corresponding to the extension of $PTA(I_+(p))$ to get $PTA(I_+(p+1))$. By construction, v is suffix of w and, consequently, $I_+(p+1)$ is structurally complete with respect to $A^x(k)$. In other words, $A^x(k) \in Lat(MCA(I_+(p+1)))$. Finally, since $A^x(k)$ is deterministic, it belongs to $Lat(PTA(I_+(p+1)))$. □

Property 4.3 states that if the automaton $A(k)$, which, by induction hypothesis, belongs to the border set of the lattice obtained at step k, accepts the new example, then it also belongs to the border set of the new lattice.

Property 4.3 $A(k) \in BS_{PTA}(I_+(p), I_-(q))$ and $A(k) = A^x(k) \Rightarrow A^x(k) \in BS_{PTA}(I_+(p+1), I_-(q))$, with x being the $(p+1)^{th}$ example.

Proof : We have $A(k) = A^x(k)$ if and only if the string x belongs to the language accepted by $A(k)$. By induction hypothesis, $A(k)$ belongs to $BS_{PTA}(I_+(p), I_-(q))$, i.e. it is at a maximal depth in $Lat(PTA(I_+(p)))$. Since the negative sample has not been modified, $A(k)$ is also at a maximal depth in the new lattice $Lat(PTA(I_+(p+1)))$. □

4.2.2 Dealing with a new Negative Example

The reception of a new negative example does not modify the search space since, by theorem 2.1, the solution is to be found in the lattice built from the prefix tree acceptor of the positive sample. On the other hand, the border set is generally modified at the reception of a new negative example. In other words, the current solution $A(k)$ belonging to $BS_{PTA}(I_+(p), I_-(q))$ may not belong to $BS_{PTA}(I_+(p), I_-(q+1))$. The property 4.4 states that if an automaton $A(k)$, which, by induction hypothesis, belongs to the border set at step k, does not accept the new negative example then it also belongs to the border set of the same lattice after treating the additional negative example.

Property 4.4 $A(k) \in BS_{PTA}(I_+(p), I_-(q))$ and $x \notin L(A(k)) \Rightarrow A(k) \in BS_{PTA}(I_+(p), I_-(q+1))$, with x being the $(q+1)^{th}$.

Proof : Since the string x does not belong to the language accepted by $A(k)$ it does not modify the compatibility of $A(k)$ with respect to the negative sample. Since the automaton $A(k)$ is at a maximal depth after the first q negative examples, it remains at a maximal depth after receiving the new negative example. Consequently, $A(k)$ belongs to $BS_{PTA}(I_+(p), I_-(q+1))$.□

5 The RPNI2 Algorithm

5.1 The Guarantee of Compatibility with I_-

The properties proved in section 4 characterize the search space and its border set when new learning data are received. As we have seen, there are two possible cases of incompatibility with the negative sample. The first case results from the shortest suffix extension. This operation extends the current solution to obtain an element of the new search space. This element may be incompatible with the negative sample as illustrated in section 4. The second case results from the adding of a new negative example that is not rejected by the current solution.

These two incompatibility cases may be dealt in the same way. Let A be a DFA belonging to $Lat(PTA(I_+))$ with $L(A) \cap I_- \neq \phi$, and let π be the partition such that $A = PTA(I_+)/\pi$. This partition may be stored from one step to the next and easily adapted when the shortest suffix extension is performed.

Let us consider the prefix tree and a deterministic quotient automaton A presented in figure 3. The data already received are $I_+ = \{\lambda, a, bb, bba, baab, baaaba\}$ and $I_- = \{abbb\}$.

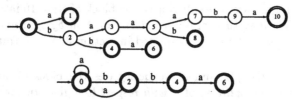

Figure 3: A prefix tree and a deterministic quotient automaton.

One can easily check that the partition π such that $A = PTA(I_+)/\pi$ is given by $\pi = \{\{0, 1, 3, 5, 7, 10\}, \{2, 8, 9\}, \{4\}, \{6\}\}$.

Let us assume that the next negative example is b. The automaton A accepts the string b and thus becomes incompatible with $I_- = \{b, abbb\}$. The incompatibility is due to at least one state merging that allows for accepting b. Consequently, we look for the partition π' finer than π such that $PTA(I_+)/\pi'$ is compatible with I_-.

We know that the negative examples aim at distinguishing between kernel elements and short prefixes that do not share the same set of tails. More precisely, let a negative example w be in a characteristic sample. There must exist a prefix $u \in Pr(L)$ and a string v such that $w = uv$ and $uv \in I_-^c$. Knowing the negative example w and the prefix tree acceptor, one can determine the strings u and v. In our case, the negative example b leads to state 2 in $PTA(I_+)$. We have $u = b$ and $v = \lambda$. Since the negative example is accepted by the quotient automaton, there exists a state q_v of which v is a suffix and which belongs to the block of u. In our example, state q_v has λ as a suffix and corresponds to state 8 in $PTA(I_+)$. This state belongs in partition π to the block of state 2. The definition of state q_v will be called the *acceptance prefix definition*. It also determines the *rank* of state q_v. We say that the block of state q_v is *split* or that state q_v is taken out of its block to create the new block $\{q_v\}$.

5.1.1 Conforming with the Standard Order

We look for a partition π' finer than partition π such that the quotient automaton $PTA(I_+)/\pi'$ is compatible. We know by the proof of convergence of the RPNI algorithm that it is essential to respect the standard order of merging [Dup96]. Therefore if, by the splitting operation, we negate the merging of state q_v with any other state, the merging of any state of higher rank has to be negated as well. In our example, q_v corresponds to state 8, meaning that state 8, 9 and 10 have to be taken out of their respective blocks. We perform these splittings in reverse order, starting with state 10.

Figure 4: Splitting of a DFA.

5.1.2 Determinization by Splitting

While the original automaton was deterministic, the splitting may create non-determinism. In our case, the splitting of the block of state 10 introduces a non-determinism. We may then apply a *determinization by splitting*, the converse of the determinization by merging quoted in section 3. It is formally defined as follows.

> If $A = PTA(I_+)/\pi$ and if Bq designates the block of state q in partition π, the *splitting* of π *with respect to* q gives rise to the new partition
> $$\pi' = (\pi \setminus Bq) \cup \{Bq \setminus q\} \cup \{q\}$$
> **If** in $PTA(I_+)$ state q has a predecessor q_p on letter a, i.e. $q \in \delta_{PTA}(q_p, a)$, **and if** $\exists Bq_p, B' \in \pi'$ with $B' \neq \{q\}$ and $\delta(Bq_p, a) \supseteq \{\{q\}, B'\}$ in $PTA(I_+)/\pi'$ **then** apply the splitting of π' with respect to q_p.

In other words, the splitting with respect to q introduces a non-determinism on letter a since there exists a state q_p belonging to block Bq_p, predecessor of q, from which there exists another transition on letter a in the quotient automaton $PTA(I_+)/\pi'$. In this case, a splitting of π' with respect to q_p is performed.

Determinization by splitting is a recursive operation. In order to respect the standard order, each time a splitting of a partition π with respect to a state q is performed, the states belonging to the tails of q in $PTA(I_+)$ must also be taken out of their respective blocks.

Property 5.1 *[Dup96] Determinization by splitting necessarily stops at a deterministic automaton.*

The determinization by splitting applied in the previous example yields a compatible DFA presented in figure 5.

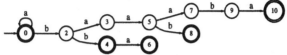

Figure 5: Compatible DFA obtained by recursive splitting.

5.2 Outline of the RPNI2 Algorithm

Each time a new positive example x is received, the prefix tree is extended by the function $extend\ (PTA(I_+(p)), x)$. The function $compatible\ (A, I)$ returns TRUE if the automaton A is compatible with the sample I, otherwise it returns FALSE. When I is a positive sample, the compatibility means the acceptance of all strings in I. Conversely, when I is a negative sample, compatibility means the rejection of all strings in I. If the previous solution remains compatible after adding the new example, this solution is returned. When an incompatibility with a new positive example x is found, the previous solution is extended by the shortest suffix of x. This operation is implemented by the function $suffix\_extension\ (A/\pi, x)$. At this stage, the current automaton A belongs to the search space defined by all the data received. However, it may be incompatible with the current negative sample I_-. The function $acceptance\_prefix\ (A, I_-)$ returns the minimal rank of the state with respect to which partition π must be split. The function $determ\_split\ (A/\pi, j)$ performs the splitting of automaton A/π with respect to state j and seeks, by recursive splitting, to find a compatible DFA. Finally, the RPNI algorithm is applied starting with the automaton obtained after splitting. Since, in the worst case, the automaton obtained after splitting is the prefix tree, the RPNI algorithm is applied without making use of the previously constructed solution. However, in practice, the RPNI algorithm will generally be applied starting with a smaller automaton than the prefix tree. That is, the search will be performed on a sub-lattice of $Lat(PTA(I_+))$.

Algorithm RPNI2
```
input PTA(I₊(p))              // Prefix Tree Acceptor of the first p positive examples
      I₋(q)                    // Negative sample made of the first q negative examples
      A/π                      // The current solution
      x                        // The new example
output A DFA compatible with (I₊(p), I₋(q)) and x
begin
if x is a positive example then
   PTA(I₊(p + 1)) ←extend (PTA(I₊(p)), x)        // Prefix tree extension
   if compatible (A/π,{x}) then                   // Acceptance checking
      return A/π
   else
      A/π' ← suffix_extension (A/π, x)            // Shortest suffix extension
      A ← A/π'
      π ← π'
   end if
end if
```

```
if x is a negative example then
  if compatible (A/π,{x}) then                    // Rejection checking
    return A/π
  else
    A ← A/π'
    π ← π'
  end if
end if


i ← acceptance_prefix (A, I_)                     // Minimal rank of states to be split
// N is the number of states of the PTA
for j = N to i                                    // State splitting in reverse order <
  A/π' ← determ_split (A/π, j)
  π ← π'
end for
A ← A/π


// RPNI algorithm applied from automaton A
for i = 1 to |π| − 1                              // Loop on the blocks of partition π
  for j = 0 to i − 1                              // Loop on the blocks of lower rank
    π' ← π\{Bj, Bi}U{BiUBj}                       // Merging block Bi and block Bj
    A/π' ← derive (A, π')
    π'' ← determ_merge (A/π')
    if compatible (A/π'',I_) then                 // Deterministic parsing of I_
      A ← A/π''
      π ← π''
      break                                       // Break j loop
    end if
  end for                                         // End j loop
end for                                           // End i loop
return A
end RPNI2
```

5.3 Identification in the Limit and Complexity

Theorem 5.1 *The RPNI2 algorithm identifies in the limit the class of regular languages.*

Theorem 5.1, proved in [Dup96], guarantees the identification of the correct automaton when the data, received one by one, include a characteristic sample. The identification in the limit may also be obtained with the RPNI algorithm. This requires the storage of all the data received sequentially and the application of the RPNI algorithm as if the data were given as a whole. However, the RPNI algorithm cannot make use of the solution constructed from the previous data set. In this regard, the RPNI2 algorithm offers a possible complexity reduction. We showed that the asymptotic space and time complexities of both algorithms are the same [Dup96]. The advantage of the RPNI2 algorithm lies, then, in a practical complexity reduction which arises because the core of the algorithm, the double loop, is generally applied on a smaller search space. This point is experimentally confirmed in section 6.

6 Experimental Results

6.1 Learning Task and Experimental Protocol

The Feldman task [FLSW90] was proposed for language acquisition studies. It is not meant to study the whole cognitive process of learning a language but it offers a clear framework which may be easily extended. This task has served as a benchmark for research in different domains such as cognitive science [FLSW90], estimation of probabilistic attribute grammars [Sto94] and transducer learning [CGV94].

In its original formulation, the Feldman task consists in building an automatic system capable of classifying as true or false statements about object positions on a screen. Typically, we might have the following statements:

"A circle is to the right of a triangle",
"A triangle and a circle are above a square".

We consider here an extension of the original task including actions on the objects:

"Delete the triangle on the right of the square",
"Add a medium size square above a light circle and a small dark triangle".

Positive learning samples are randomly generated from the canonical automaton of the Feldman task[7]. Neither the structural completeness nor the inclusion of a possible characteristic sample are guaranteed. Negative samples are obtained by randomly corrupting independently generated positive samples according to a Markov process. Each string is corrupted by allowing insertion, substitution and deletion of symbols. The corrupted data are checked to eliminate those strings that are positive. In general 95 % of the corrupted strings generated in this fashion were negative examples of the Feldman language.

We generate 10 independent pairs of positive and negative samples. The size $|I_+|$ of each positive sample is fixed at 2,500 examples. Each example having on the average about 10 symbols, the total number of symbols $||I_+||$ is about 25,000 from an alphabet of 29 symbols. The size of the prefix tree built on a full positive sample is about 10,000 states and 10,000 transitions. The total number of symbols in each negative sample $||I_-||$ is about 20,000 while the size $|I_-|$ of a negative sample is typically 2,250. Following the same procedure, we generate a new pair of positive and negative samples each containing 500 strings. This pair of samples form the test set on which we compute the correct classification rate of positive and negative test strings with respect to the target automaton.

For each pair of positive and negative samples, the data are presented sequentially by picking at random either the next positive or the next negative example. At each step of this sequential presentation the inference algorithm proposes a solution. The RPNI2 algorithm uses the preceeding solution to build the new one. The incremental use of the RPNI algorithm consists in returning the previous solution if it is compatible with the new data, and otherwise in inferring from the prefix tree built on the positive examples already received.

---

[7] This canonical DFA contains 57 states and 149 transitions.

6.2 RPNI and RPNI2 Comparative Results

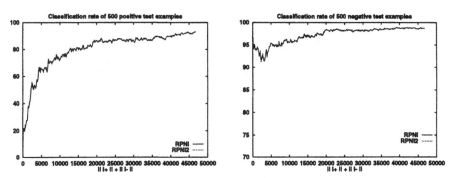

Figure 6: RPNI and RPNI2 : classification rates on the test data.

Figure 6 presents the classification rates of positive and negative test examples as a function of $||I_+|| + ||I_-||$, the number of training symbols received. These curves are averaged over the 10 independent pairs of training samples. On these tests, both algorithms have nearly identitical classification rates as illustrated by their remarkable similarity in figure 6. Let us remark that the identification in the limit only guarantees that both curves reach 100 % correct classification at the same time.

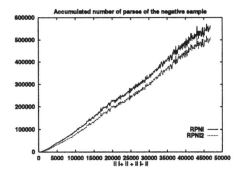

Figure 7: RPNI and RPNI2 : practical complexities.

Figure 7 presents the accumulated number of parses of the negative sample I_- performed during the entire incremental learning process. At each step we measure the number of calls to the compatibility checking function, as it dominates the practical cost of both algorithms.

At the end of the sequential presentation, the RPNI algorithm has performed 10.2 % more calls than the RPNI2 algorithm. The observed gain may depend on the order of presentation which is in this case purely random. An interesting property is that the gain increases monotonically with the size of the learning samples.

7 Conclusion

In this work, we propose a new characterization of the incremental search space of regular inference. The exhibited properties resulted in the design of the RPNI2 algorithm, the incremental extension of the RPNI algorithm. We study the characterization of these algorithms, together with their theoretical and practical complexities. Both algorithms experimentally converge at the same rate. RPNI2 allows for monotonically decreasing the practical complexity as a function of the learning data size.

While the RPNI2 algorithm has been designed in such a way that the identification in the limit may be proved, examples previously received could be forgotten, for instance, by memorizing only the last n examples. It would then offer a natural tradeoff between the space complexity and the convergence rate, the exact identification not being guaranteed.

References

[Ang78]   D. Angluin. On the complexity of minimum inference of regular sets. *Information and Control*, pages 337–350, 1978.

[Ang82]   D. Angluin. Inference of reversible languages. *Journal of the Association for Computing Machinery*, 29(3):741–765, 1982.

[CGV94]   A. Castellanos, I. Galiano, and E. Vidal. Application of OSTIA to machine translation tasks. In *Grammatical Inference and Applications, ICGI'94*, number 862 in Lecture Notes in Artificial Intelligence, pages 93–105. Springer Verlag, 1994.

[DMV94]   P. Dupont, L. Miclet, and E. Vidal. What is the search space of the regular inference ? In *Grammatical Inference and Applications, ICGI'94*, number 862 in Lecture Notes in Artificial Intelligence, pages 25–37. Springer Verlag, 1994.

[Dup96]   P. Dupont. *Utilisation et Apprentissage de Modèles de Langage pour la Reconnaissance de la Parole Continue*. Thèse de Doctorat, Ecole Nationale Supérieure des Télécommunications, Paris, France, 1996.

[FB75]   K.S. Fu and T.L. Booth. Grammatical inference: Introduction and survey, part 1. *IEEE Transactions on Systems, Man and Cybernetics*, 5:85–111, 1975.

[FLSW90] J.A. Feldman, G. Lakoff, A. Stolcke, and S.H. Weber. Miniature language acquisition: A touchstone for cognitive science. Technical Report TR-90-009, International Computer Science Institute, Berkeley, California, 1990.

[Gol67]   E.M. Gold. Language identification in the limit. *Information and Control*, 10(5):447–474, 1967.

[Gol78]   E.M. Gold. Complexity of automaton identification from given data. *Information and Control*, 37:302–320, 1978.

[Lan92]   K.J. Lang. Random DFA's can be approximately learned from sparse uniform examples. In *5th ACM workshop on Computational Learning Theory*, pages 45–52, 1992.

[OG92]   J. Oncina and P. García. Inferring regular languages in polynomial update time. In N. Pérez de la Blanca, A. Sanfeliu, and E.Vidal, editors, *Pattern Recognition and Image Analysis*, volume 1 of *Series in Machine Perception and Artificial Intelligence*, pages 49–61. World Scientific, 1992.

[Sto94]   A. Stolcke. *Bayesian Learning of Probabilistic Language Models*. Ph. D. dissertation, University of California, 1994.

An Incremental Interactive Algorithm for Regular Grammar Inference*

Rajesh Parekh & Vasant Honavar

Artificial Intelligence Research Group
Department of Computer Science
Iowa State University, Ames, IA 50011. U.S.A.
{parekh|honavar}@cs.iastate.edu

Abstract. We present provably correct interactive algorithms for learning *regular grammars* from positive examples and membership queries. A *structurally complete* set of strings from a language L(G) corresponding to a target regular grammar G implicitly specifies a lattice of finite state automata (FSA) which contains a FSA M_G corresponding to G. The lattice is compactly represented as a version-space and M_G is identified by searching the version-space using membership queries. We explore the problem of regular grammar inference in a setting where positive examples are provided intermittently. We provide an incremental version of the algorithm along with a set of sufficient conditions for its convergence.

1 Introduction

Regular Grammar Inference [3, 5, 9, 12] is an important machine learning problem with applications in pattern recognition and language acquisition. It is defined as the process of learning an unknown regular grammar (G) given a finite set of positive examples S^+, possibly a finite, non-empty set of negative examples S^-, and possibly a knowledgeable teacher who can answer queries posed by the learner. We present an algorithm for *regular grammar inference* in an *active learning* framework wherein the learner's task is to infer the unknown grammar using the teacher supplied positive examples and answers to *membership* queries.

A *Regular Grammar* is a finite set of rewrite (production) rules of the form $A \longrightarrow aB$ or $A \longrightarrow b$ where A and B are called *non-terminals* and a and b are called *terminals*. These rules are applied recursively to generate *strings* (containing terminal symbols only). The *language* L(G) is the set of all strings generated by the grammar G. *Finite State Automata* (FSA) are recognizers for regular grammars. A *deterministic* FSA (DFSA), A, is a quintuple $A = (Q, \delta, \Sigma, q_0, F)$ where, Q is a finite set of states, Σ is the finite set of input symbols called the alphabet, $F \subseteq Q$ is the set of accepting states, $q_0 \in Q$ is the start state, and δ is the transition function $Q \times \Sigma \longrightarrow Q$ that gives the next state of the automaton

* Vasant Honavar is grateful to National Science Foundation (grant NSF IRI-9409580) and the John Deere Foundation for supporting his research. The authors would like to thank Professor Giora Slutzki for several helpful discussions related to this work.

upon reading a particular symbol. Fig. 1 shows the state transition diagram for a sample FSA. A *non-deterministic* FSA without ϵ-transitions (NFSA) is defined exactly like the DFSA except that the transition function $\delta: Q \times \Sigma \longrightarrow 2^Q$ where 2^Q is the power set of Q. Intuitively, there might be multiple transitions out of a state on any letter of the alphabet. DFSA and NFSA are equivalent in expressive power. Two FSA M_1 and M_2 are equivalent iff $L(M_1) = L(M_2)$. A *subautomaton* (A_s) of a FSA A is a FSA and is defined by $A_s = (Q_s, \delta_s, \Sigma, q_0, F_s)$ where $Q_s \subseteq Q$, $F_s \subseteq F$, and $\delta_s \subseteq \delta$ in the sense that $\forall p, q \in Q_s$ and $a \in \Sigma$, if $\delta_s(p, a) = q$ then $\delta(p, a) = q$. Clearly, $L(A_s) \subseteq L(A)$. For a detailed treatment of this subject see [10].

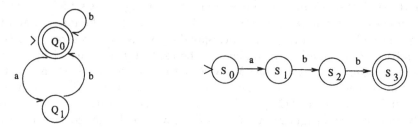

Fig. 1. Finite State Automaton   **Fig. 2.** MCA - M_{S^+}

This paper is organized as follows: Sect. 2 describes a non-incremental version of the grammar inference algorithm and proves its correctness. Sect. 3 explains the incremental version of the algorithm. Finally, Sect. 4 provides a summary, discussion of related work, and directions for future research.

2   Inference given a Structurally Complete S^+

Initially, we present a non-incremental algorithm for inference of a FSA (not necessarily deterministic) that is equivalent to a FSA corresponding to the target regular grammar (G). A knowledgeable teacher provides a set S^+ of positive examples (i.e., $S^+ \subseteq L(G)$) which is restricted to be a *structurally complete* set in order to facilitate theoretical analysis. A structurally complete set of strings covers each production rule of G at least once. Equivalently, if M_G is a FSA corresponding to the grammar G, then each transition of M_G must be covered by at least one string in S^+ and for each accepting state of M_G there must be at least one string in S^+ which terminates in that accepting state. In what follows, we use the terms target grammar and target FSA interchangeably.

The teacher provides a structurally complete set S^+ which implicitly defines a lattice (or version space) Ω of candidate FSA or the initial hypothesis space that is guaranteed to contain a FSA (M_G) corresponding to the target grammar (G) [14, 15, 4]. At all times, the learner maintains two sets of lattice elements — $\mathcal{S}$ and $\mathcal{G}$ — which correspond respectively to the most specific and most general FSA consistent with the data (sample strings, queries) processed so far. Thus, $\Theta = [\mathcal{S}, \mathcal{G}]$ provides a compact representation of Ω. The learner generates strings and queries the teacher about their membership in G. The teacher's response to a query results in pruning of the hypothesis space while ensuring that M_G is not eliminated in the process. The interaction between the learner and the teacher proceeds until a single FSA (or a set of equivalent FSA) equivalent to M_G remains in Ω.

2.1 Lattice of Grammars Specified by S^+

Given S^+, a FSA called the *maximal canonical automaton* (MCA), M_{S^+}, that accepts every string in S^+ and no other is constructed. This MCA provides a path from the start state to an accepting state for each string in the set S^+. For example, suppose the grammar G of the FSA M_G in Fig. 1 is to be inferred and the teacher provides $S^+ = \{abb\}$. The corresponding MCA M_{S^+} is shown in Fig. 2. The lattice Ω of candidate grammars can be explicitly constructed by systematically merging the states of the MCA M_{S^+} to form partitions. Each partition yields an element of Ω. The language corresponding to the FSA defined by a partition is a superset of $L(M_{S^+})$. Thus, successive state mergings yield progressively more general languages as explained below. The lattice constructed from the MCA (Fig. 2) is depicted in Fig. 3. A MCA with m states yields an initial hypothesis space that contains: $E_m = \displaystyle\sum_{j=0}^{m-1} \binom{m-1}{j} E_j$ grammars where $E_0 = 1$.
Therefore, explicit representation of Ω is generally impractical. The proposed algorithm represents Ω implicitly using $\Theta = [\mathcal{S}, \mathcal{G}]$.

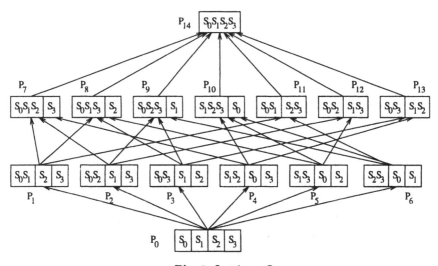

Fig. 3. Lattice - Ω

Each element of the lattice (i.e., a partition of the set of states of M_{S^+}) represents a FSA M. The states of M correspond to the blocks of the partition. For the FSA M, the start state is the block which contains the start state of

M_{S^+}, the accepting states are the blocks which contain one or more accepting states of M_{S^+}, the alphabet is the same as that of M_{S^+}, and the transition function for M, δ_M, is defined on the basis of the transitions within M_{S^+}. If several states of M_{S^+} are merged together in a block c in a partition, then the transitions into (out of) each of those states become transitions into (out of) the state represented by c in M. Transitions between two states that get merged in block c form self loops on the state resulting from the merger. The FSA M_2 corresponding to the partition P_2 (of Fig. 3) is shown in Fig. 4.

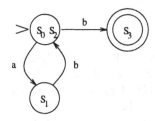

Fig. 4. FSA corresponding to the partition P_2

The lattice Ω of grammars (or equivalently FSA, or partitions) is ordered by the *grammar cover* relation. This property is exploited during the search for M_G. If each block of a partition P_i at one level of the lattice is contained in some block of a partition P_j in the level above, we say that P_j *covers* P_i ($P_i \preceq P_j$). Let M_i and M_j be the FSA and L_i and L_j be the regular languages that correspond to the partitions P_i and P_j respectively. Clearly, if $P_i \preceq P_j$, $L_i \subseteq L_j$. This is indicated in Fig. 3 by an arrow from P_i to P_j. If there is an arrow from P_i to P_j, we say that P_i is an immediate *lower-bound* of P_j and analogously, P_j is an immediate *upper-bound* of P_i. Grammar cover is a transitive property. Thus, if $P_i \preceq P_j$ and $P_j \preceq P_k$ then $P_i \preceq P_k$ and we say that P_i is *more specific than or equal to* (MSE) P_k (which is conversely *more general than or equal to* (MGE) P_i). The MSE (MGE) test can be performed efficiently by just examining the partitions under consideration.

2.2 Query-Aided Bi-Directional Search of the Lattice

Ω is implicitly represented by $\Theta = [\mathcal{S}, \mathcal{G}]$ where $\mathcal{S}$ is the set of maximally *specific* elements and $\mathcal{G}$ is the set of maximally *general* elements of Ω that are consistent with all the data gathered by the learner at any time. Initially, $\mathcal{S} = \{P_0\}$, the partition corresponding to the MCA M_{S^+} and $\mathcal{G} = \{P_{E_m-1}\}$, the partition corresponding to the most general element of Ω i.e., the one with all states of the MCA merged together in a single block. Note that E_m is the total number of partitions in the lattice Ω. The learner constructs FSA $M_i = \{S, \delta_s, \Sigma, s_0, A\}$ and $M_j = \{T, \delta_t, \Sigma, t_0, B\}$ corresponding to partitions $P_i \in \mathcal{S}$ and $P_j \in \mathcal{G}$ respectively. M_i and M_j are compared for equivalence. If they are not equivalent then there exists a string y such that $\delta_s(s_0, y) \in A$ but $\delta_t(t_0, y) \notin B$ or vice-versa (in which case the roles of M_i and M_j are simply reversed). The shortest such string y

belonging to the language of the difference machine $M_i - M_j = \{W, \delta_w, \Sigma, w_0, C\}$ where, $W = S \times T$, $w_0 = (s_0, t_0)$, $\delta_w((s,t), \sigma) = (\delta_s(s, \sigma), \delta_t(t, \sigma))$ for all $\sigma \in \Sigma$ and $C = \{(s,t) \mid s \in A \text{ and } t \in T - B\}$ [7] forms the query "$y \in L(G)$"? that is posed to the teacher. Based on the teacher's response Θ is pruned and elements of S and $\mathcal{G}$ become progressively *more general* and *more specific* respectively. Since the lattice Ω defines a partial order and the MSE (MGE) test can be performed efficiently on the elements of the lattice, the *version-space* algorithm [13] can be adapted for candidate elimination.

Algorithm:

1. Set $S = \{P_0\}$ and $\mathcal{G} = \{P_{E_m - 1}\}$.
2. While there exists an element $P_i \in S$ and $P_j \in \mathcal{G}$ such that the corresponding FSA $M_i \not\equiv M_j$ pick the shortest string $y \in L(M_i - M_j)$ or $L(M_j - M_i)$ and pose the query $y \in L(G)$? Based on the teacher's response modify Θ as described below (see candidate elimination).
3. Return the FSA corresponding to the partition to which the search of the lattice (Ω) converges.

Candidate Elimination:

1. If y is a positive example
   (a) Remove any $P_k \in \mathcal{G}$ such that the FSA M_k rejects y.
   (b) Minimally generalize any $P_l \in S$ if M_l does not accept y. Retain only those partitions in S that are MSE some partition in $\mathcal{G}$.
   (c) Remove any element from S that is MGE some other element in S.
2. If y is a negative example
   (a) Remove any $P_k \in S$ such that the FSA M_k accepts y.
   (b) Minimally specialize any $P_l \in \mathcal{G}$ if M_l accepts y. Retain only those partitions in $\mathcal{G}$ that are MGE some partition in S.
   (c) Remove any element from $\mathcal{G}$ that is MSE some other element in $\mathcal{G}$.

Minimally generalizing a $P_l \in S$ when M_l does not accept a positive example y involves replacing P_l by its immediate upper bounds. Any of these upper bounds not accepting y are minimally generalized and so on till all the generalizations thus obtained accept y. *Minimal specialization* is defined analogously for elements of $\mathcal{G}$. The choice of elements of S and $\mathcal{G}$ to be compared at each step is arbitrary. Alternatively, this may be guided by a suitable heuristic. The following example illustrates the working of the algorithm given $S^+ = \{abb\}$ which defines the lattice shown in Fig. 3. The algorithm terminates with a solution M_9 which is the target FSA. Note that at step 3, if M_3 is compared with M_{13} (instead of M_9) convergence would need an additional query.

Example

Step	Θ	$M_i \equiv M_j$?	Query y	Modified Θ
1	$S = \{P_0\}$; $\mathcal{G} = \{P_{14}\}$	$M_0 \not\equiv M_{14}$	$\lambda \in L(G)$	$S = \{P_3\}$; $\mathcal{G} = \{P_{14}\}$
2	$S = \{P_3\}$; $\mathcal{G} = \{P_{14}\}$	$M_3 \not\equiv M_{14}$	$a \notin L(G)$	$S = \{P_3\}$; $\mathcal{G} = \{P_9, P_{13}\}$
3	$S = \{P_3\}$; $\mathcal{G} = \{P_9, P_{13}\}$	$M_3 \not\equiv M_9$	$b \in L(G)$	$S = \{P_9\}$; $\mathcal{G} = \{P_9\}$

2.3 Proof of Correctness

The correctness of the algorithm follows from the following theorems.

Theorem 1[1]: A FSA M_G corresponding to the target grammar G lies in the lattice Ω defined by a structurally complete set of strings for M_G.

Theorem 2: Let P_{M_G} be the partition corresponding to the target FSA M_G. The following invariance condition holds at all times during the execution of the algorithm: $\exists\, P_z \in \mathcal{G}$ and $\exists\, P_y \in \mathcal{S}$ such that $P_y \preceq P_{M_G} \preceq P_z$.

Proof: By induction.
Base Case: Initially, $\mathcal{S} = \{P_0\}$ and $\mathcal{G} = \{P_{E_m-1}\}$. Therefore, the hypothesis space $\Theta = [\mathcal{S}, \mathcal{G}]$ implicitly includes the entire lattice Ω. Theorem 1 guarantees that P_{M_G} lies within Ω, and hence in the hypothesis space Θ. Clearly, the invariance condition holds if we set P_y to P_0 and P_z to P_{E_m-1}.
Induction Hypothesis: Assume that the invariance condition holds at some time during the execution of the algorithm (just before processing a query).
Induction Proof: We prove that the invariance condition continues to hold after processing the query. If the query string y is a positive example:

1. Any $P_k \in \mathcal{G}$ such that the FSA M_k rejects y is removed. Clearly, no such P_k could be P_z or else M_G would also reject y.
2. A partition $P_l \in \mathcal{S}$ is minimally generalized if M_l does not accept y. Consider that the partition P_l generalized is P_y. Since $P_y \preceq P_{M_G}$ there is a sequence of one or more generalizations leading from P_y to P_{M_G} such that at least one of these generalizations accepts the positive string y. This generalization (which could be P_{M_G}) becomes the new P_y. Only those partitions in $\mathcal{S}$ that are MSE some partition in $\mathcal{G}$ are retained. Since the new $P_y \preceq P_{M_G} \preceq P_z$ it is clear that the new P_y will not be eliminated from $\mathcal{S}$.
3. Finally, any partition in $\mathcal{S}$ that is MGE some other partition in $\mathcal{S}$ is removed. If the designated P_y is eliminated the partition in $\mathcal{S}$ to which it is MGE takes over as the new P_y.

At the end of each step above we see that the invariance is preserved. A symmetric argument can be presented for the case when y is a negative example.

3 An Incremental Algorithm for Grammar Inference

Often in practical inductive learning scenarios the entire training data is not available to the learner at the start. This motivates the need for incremental learning algorithms that enable the learner to develop suitable hypotheses based on the available data and, when presented with additional training data, update the hypotheses appropriately without having to reprocess the previous data.

---

[1] The proof of theorem 1 is originally due to Pao and Carr [14] and has been reworked in [15]. It was also independently proven by Miclet (see [4]).

Suppose a set S_0^+ of positive examples that is not necessarily structurally complete is provided at the start. We ask whether it is possible, using S_0^+, to infer a hypothesis that has a well-defined relationship with the target and whether it is possible to incrementally update the hypothesis as and when additional positive examples are provided until eventually the hypothesis converges to the target when a structurally complete set has been processed. The answer to this question is affirmative provided certain conditions are satisfied: First, the teacher must provide positive examples in non-decreasing order by length (see [16] for an explanation). Second, the teacher must provide an upper bound N on the number of states of the target automaton M_G (or by some other means indicate when the learner has processed a structurally complete set of samples). Third, only *safe queries* (see below) must be used for candidate elimination.

The algorithm works as follows: Let S^+ be a structurally complete set of examples with respect to the target FSA M_G. Based on a set S_0^+ of positive examples provided by the teacher, the learner constructs the lattice Ω_0 represented by $\Theta_0 = [S_0, G_0]$ and proceeds to prune Ω_0 using the teacher's responses to safe queries. When the teacher provides an additional example the lattice is incrementally updated to Ω_1 (see Sect. 3.1) corresponding to $S_1^+ = S_0^+ \cup \{s\}$. This interleaving of *lattice expansion* and *safe candidate elimination* is repeated until at some step n, S_n^+ is structurally complete with respect to M_G. At this point, all queries are treated as safe and the algorithm converges to the target.

At any time, the teacher can only be expected to answer queries with respect to the target (M_G). At step k in the inference process, S_k^+ is structurally complete with respect to a subautomaton M_{G_k} of M_G (where $L(M_{G_k}) \subseteq L(M_G)$). An example that is not accepted by M_G will not be accepted by M_{G_k}. However, a positive example not accepted by M_{G_k} might be accepted by M_G. This makes it unsafe to perform candidate elimination using positive query strings of length greater than that of the longest positive example in S_k^+. Such query strings are unsafe and are simply ignored by the learner. All other query strings are safe for candidate elimination. At some $k = n$, when S_k^+ is structurally complete with respect to M_G any query can be safely used for candidate elimination.

Given an upper bound N on the number of states in M_G, it can be shown that there exists a structurally complete set S^+ with respect to M_G such that no string in S^+ has length greater than $2N - 1$ [16]. Thus, if the teacher provides examples in increasing order by length, the learner can infer that a structurally complete set of examples has been processed when an example of length greater than $2N - 1$ is provided. (Note that this does not require the teacher to provide every positive example of length up to $2N - 1$).

3.1 Incremental Lattice Update

Given the current representation of the lattice $\Theta_k = [S_k, G_k]$ and a new positive example s the lattice update operation $\oplus$ defines the new lattice $\Theta_{k+1} = \Theta_k \oplus s$ represented by $[S_{k+1}, G_{k+1}]$. If s is accepted by the FSA corresponding to every partition in S_k then $\Theta_{k+1} = \Theta_k$; otherwise S_k and G_k are modified as follows.

Assume that M_s (with n states) is the MCA (with the corresponding partition P_s) that accepts only the string s. For each partition $P_y \in \mathcal{S}_k$, a new partition $P_y' \in \mathcal{S}_{k+1}$, is constructed by fusing the blocks corresponding to the start states of M_y and M_s together into a single block and appending the other blocks of P_y and P_s as distinct blocks of P_y'. Thus, $L(M_y') = L(M_y) \cup L(M_s)$. If P_y contains m blocks and P_s contains n blocks then P_y' contains $m + n - 1$ blocks. For each partition of $P_z \in \mathcal{G}_k$ a set of partitions $\{P_z'\} \in \mathcal{G}_{k+1}$ (where the number of blocks in each P_z' is exactly the same as the number of blocks in P_z) is constructed by fusing the blocks containing the start states of M_z and M_s together and then distributing the remaining $n - 1$ blocks of P_s with the m blocks of P_z in $\mathcal{D}_m^{n-1}$ ways[2].

Algorithm:

1. The teacher provides a bound, N, on the number of states in the target FSA and a set of positive examples S_0^+. Using S_0^+ construct $M_{S_0^+}$ and Ω_0 represented by $\Theta_0 = [S_0, \mathcal{G}_0]$. If the longest string in S_0^+ is of length at most $2N - 1$ then set $k = 0$ and go to step 2; otherwise S_0^+ is structurally complete with respect to M_G. Use the non-incremental version of the algorithm to infer the target grammar.

2. While there exists an element $P_i \in \mathcal{S}_k$ and $P_j \in \mathcal{G}_k$ such that the corresponding FSA $M_i \not\equiv M_j$, pick the shortest string $y \in L(M_i - M_j)$ or $L(M_j - M_i)$ and pose the query $y \in L(G)$? If the query is safe then modify Θ_k according to the candidate elimination algorithm. Ignore the query otherwise. If further safe eliminations in Θ_k are not possible then await additional positive examples.

3. When the teacher provides a string s of length $|s|$ do one of the following
   (a) If $|s| \leq 2N - 1$ then update Θ_k, set $k = k + 1$ and go to step 2.
   (b) If $|s| > 2N - 1$ then since structural completeness is achieved, resume the search for the target FSA in Θ_k treating all queries to be safe. Return the solution to which the candidate elimination procedure converges.

For a description of the correctness of the incremental version see [16].

Example

We use the incremental algorithm to infer the FSA in Fig. 1. Consider that the teacher provides a bound on the number of states $N = 2$ (from which the learner infers that positive samples of length 4 or greater will not be necessary to form a structurally complete set of examples) and the example b. Thus, $S_0^+ = \{b\}$. The lattice Ω_0 is shown in Fig. 5. The result of the first query is shown below.

---

[2] $\mathcal{D}_B^E = \sum_{i=0}^{E} \binom{E}{i} \mathcal{D}_{B-1}^{E-i}$ is the number of ways of distributing E distinct elements among B distinct boxes. $\mathcal{D}_B^0 = 1$ and $\mathcal{D}_1^E = 1$.

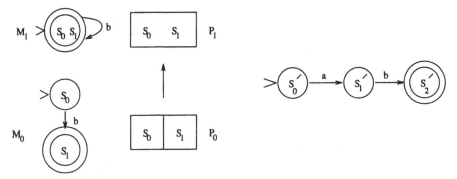

Fig. 5. Lattice Ω_0 **Fig. 6.** MCA for $s = ab$

	Θ	$M_i \equiv M_j$?	Query y	Modified Θ
1	$\mathcal{S}_0 = \{P_0\}; \mathcal{G}_0 = \{P_1\}$	$M_0 \not\equiv M_1$	$\lambda \in L(G)$ (SAFE)	$\mathcal{S}_0 = \{P_1\}; \mathcal{G}_0 = \{P_1\}$

The learner then waits for more positive examples. Consider that ab is provided. The MCA for $s = ab$ is shown in Fig. 6. $S_1^+ = \{b, ab\}$. ab is not accepted by the FSA corresponding to the partition $P_1 \in \mathcal{S}_0$. The lattice update operation (shown in Fig. 7) results in the lattice Ω_1 (Fig. 8) that is implicitly represented by $\Theta_1 = [\mathcal{S}_1, \mathcal{G}_1]$.

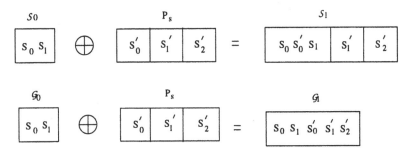

Fig. 7. Lattice Update Operation $\oplus$

The processing of the next two queries is summarized below.

	Θ	$M_i \equiv M_j$?	Query y	Modified Θ
2	$\mathcal{S}_1 = \{P_0\}; \mathcal{G}_1 = \{P_4\}$	$M_0 \not\equiv M_4$	$a \notin L(G)$ (SAFE)	$\mathcal{S}_1 = \{P_0\}; \mathcal{G}_1 = \{P_2\}$
3	$\mathcal{S}_1 = \{P_0\}; \mathcal{G}_1 = \{P_2\}$	$M_0 \not\equiv M_2$	$abb \in L(G)$ (UNSAFE)	$\mathcal{S}_1 = \{P_0\}; \mathcal{G}_1 = \{P_2\}$

At this point no safe query can be posed so the learner is forced to wait for more examples. Note that S_1^+ is structurally complete with respect to the target FSA in Fig. 1. The teacher can now provide $abab$ which is not necessary for structural completeness (since its length is greater than $2N - 1 = 3$). The learner infers that S_1^+ is structurally complete with respect to M_G and the lattice is not updated. After processing a safe query the algorithm converges to the target.

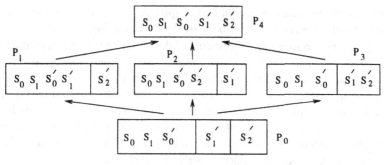

$$\boxed{S_0\ S_1\ S'_0\ S'_1\ S'_2}\ P_4$$

P_1 $P_2\uparrow$ P_3

$$\boxed{S_0\ S_1\ S'_0\ S'_1\ \big|\ S'_2}\qquad \boxed{S_0\ S_1\ S'_0\ S'_2\ \big|\ S'_1}\qquad \boxed{S_0\ S_1\ S'_0\ \big|\ S'_1\ S'_2}$$

$$\boxed{S_0\ S_1\ S'_0\ \big|\ S'_1\ \big|\ S'_2}\ P_0$$

Fig. 8. Lattice Ω_1

	Θ	$M_i \equiv M_j$?	Query y	Modified Θ
4	$S_1 = \{P_0\}; \mathcal{G}_1 = \{P_2\}$	$M_0 \not\equiv M_2$	$abb \in L(G)$ (SAFE)	$S_1 = \{P_2\}; \mathcal{G}_1 = \{P_2\}$

If the teacher had given examples like bb or bab when no more candidates from Ω_1 could be eliminated the lattice would not have been updated as M_0 accepts both those examples. If however, the teacher had provided an example like abb (instead of $abab$) that is potentially necessary for structural completeness the lattice would have had to be updated.

4 Summary and Discussion

Grammar inference is an important machine learning problem with several practical applications in speech recognition, computational biology, language acquisition, syntactic pattern classification, and cryptography. We have presented provably correct non-incremental and incremental versions of an algorithm for regular grammar inference. We have adopted the idea of mapping the structurally complete set of examples to an ordered lattice from the grammar inference algorithm proposed by Pao and Carr [14]. Their algorithm is not incremental and requires explicit enumeration of the entire lattice. The hypothesis space Ω defined by the set S^+ is too large to be represented explicitly or to be searched exhaustively. Our algorithm uses a compact representation of the hypothesis space in terms of S and $\mathcal{G}$. The operations on the version space sets take time polynomial in the size of the S and $\mathcal{G}$ sets. The efficiency of our algorithm thus relies on the fact that the size of these sets at any time is not unreasonably large. The proposed algorithm uses an efficient bidirectional search strategy inspired by Mitchell's [13] version space algorithm which enables elimination of large parts of the hypothesis space based on a single query and also to make unambiguous inferences even when the algorithm has not converged. Given a current representation of the lattice in the incremental version if an example is accepted by all FSA in S_k then clearly, the example is positive. When the structurally complete sample set has been acquired, an example that is not accepted by all FSA in $\mathcal{G}_k$ can be classified as negative. The idea of incremental lattice update was inspired by Hirsh's work on *Incremental Version-Space Merging* [8]. The set $\mathcal{G}$ in our algorithm, which represents the set of most general FSA of the lattice that do not accept any negative strings identified by the queries during the inference process is analogous to the *border set* described by Dupont *et al* [4].

Angluin [1] has proposed an algorithm (*ID*) to infer the target grammar from a *live complete set* of examples (which can be constructed from a structurally complete set) using a polynomial number of membership queries. A trivial upper bound on the number of queries needed in our procedure is exponential in the number of states of M_{S+}. We do not yet have an expected case analysis for the number of queries. Our approach offers an alternative to the *ID* procedure when a structurally complete set of samples is available. A direct extension of the *ID* procedure to the incremental version has not been studied.

Porat and Feldman [17] have proposed an algorithm that uses a complete ordered sample and membership queries and is guaranteed to converge in the limit. They maintain a single working hypothesis that gets modified after the presentation of each sample. Their algorithm uses a sub-routine that generates all strings in the ordered sample to check the consistency of the modified hypothesis. Since the complete ordered sample up to a particular length m is exponential in m, a trivial time complexity bound on their procedure is exponential. One potential advantage we see in maintaining a space of hypotheses (as is the case in our method) is the ability to make unambiguous inferences even when the algorithm has not converged to the target.

VanLehn and Ball [19] have proposed a version-space approach to learning context-free grammars from a set of positive and negative examples that returns a set of grammars consistent with the given sample set. Their algorithm is also based on a lattice of partitions and involves lattice updating to accommodate more evidence in the form of examples. The learner is required to store all the examples seen earlier for future reference and the version-space is represented by a triple $[S^+, S^-, \mathcal{G}]$ where S^+ and S^- represent sets of positive and negative examples respectively and $\mathcal{G}$ is the set of generalizations. By restricting our approach to inference of regular grammars our version-space is finite and compactly represented by $[\mathcal{S}, \mathcal{G}]$. Our algorithm does not store the previous examples and is guaranteed to converge to the desired target instead of a set of candidate solutions as is the case for VanLehn and Ball's method.

Angluin [2] has proposed a polynomial time algorithm (L^*), which allows the learner to infer the target grammar by posing both membership and equivalence queries. The L^* procedure can be adapted to the *PAC* learning framework to learn from membership queries and examples alone. Rivest and Schapire [18] have suggested a *diversity* based mechanism dealing with *homing sequences*. Giles *et al* [6] use recurrent neural networks to learn FSA from positive and negative samples. Lankhorst [11] has presented a genetic algorithms based approach for learning context free grammars.

The experimental estimation of expected case time and space complexity of the proposed algorithm, generation of informative queries so as to speed up learning, sampling strategies for obtaining a structurally complete set with a high probability using a relatively small number of random samples, and extension of the proposed approach to regular *tree* and *attributed* grammars are under investigation.

References

1. Angluin, D. A Note on the Number of Queries Needed to Identify Regular Languages. *Information and control*, 51. '81. pp 76-87.
2. Angluin, D. Learning Regular Sets from Queries and Counterexamples. *Information and Computation*, 75. '87. pp 87-106.
3. Biermann, A., and Feldman, J. A Survey of Results in Grammatical Inference. In Watanabe S. (ed), *Frontiers of Pattern Recognition*. Academic Press. '72. pp. 31-54.
4. Dupont, P., Miclet, L., and Vidal, E. What is the Search Space of the Regular Inference?. In *Proceedings of the ICGI-94*, Alicante, Spain, Sept. '94. pp. 25-37.
5. Fu, K. Syntactic Pattern Recognition and Applications. *Prentice-Hall, N.J.* '82.
6. Giles, C., Chen, D., Miller, H., Sun, G., and Lee, Y. Second-order Recurrent Neural Networks for Grammatical Inference. In *Proceedings of the International Joint Conference on Neural Networks 91*, vol. 2, pp. 273-281, July '91.
7. Harrison, M. Introduction to Switching and Automata Theory. *McGraw-Hill*, '65.
8. Hirsh, H. Incremental Version-Space Merging: A General Framework for Concept Learning. *Kluwer Academic Publishers*, '90.
9. Honavar, V. Toward Learning Systems That Integrate Different Strategies and Representations. In: Artificial Intelligence and Neural Networks: Steps toward Principled Integration. Honavar, V. & Uhr, L. (eds) *New York: Academic Press*, '94.
10. Hopcroft, J., and Ullman, J. Introduction to Automata Theory, Languages, and Computation. *Addison-Wesley*, '79.
11. Lankhorst, M. A Genetic Algorithm for Induction of Nondeterministic Pushdown Automata. *University of Groningen, Computer Science Report CS-R 9502*, The Netherlands. '95.
12. Miclet, L. and Quinqueton J. Learning from Examples in Sequences and Grammatical Inference. In Ferrate, G., *et al* (eds) Syntactic and Structural Pattern Recognition. *NATO ASI Series* Vol. F45, '86. pp. 153-171.
13. Mitchell, T. Generalization as search. *Artificial Intelligence*, 18. '82. pp 203-226.
14. Pao, T., and Carr, J. A solution of the Syntactic Induction-Inference Problem for Regular Languages. *Computer Languages*, Vol. 3, '78, pp. 53-64.
15. Parekh R., and Honavar, V. An Efficient Interactive Algorithm for Regular Language Learning. *Computer Science TR95-02*, Iowa State University, '95. (Preliminary version appeared in *Proceedings of the 5th UNB AI Symposium*, Fredericton, Canada, '93).
16. Parekh, R., and Honavar, V. An Incremental Interactive Algorithm for Regular Grammar Inference. *Computer Science TR96-03*, Iowa State University, '96.
17. Porat S., and Feldman J. Learning Automata from Ordered Examples. *Machine Learning*, 7, pp 109-138. '91.
18. Schapire, R., The Design and Analysis of Efficient Learning Algorithms. *MIT Press*, '92.
19. VanLehn, K. and Ball, W. A Version Space Approach to Learning Context-Free Grammars. *Machine Learning 2*, '87. pp 39-74.

Inductive Logic Programming for Discrete Event Systems

David Lorenzo

Computer Science Dept.,
University of A Coruña, Spain
david@dc.fi.udc.es

Abstract. Inductive modelling of dynamic systems attempts to create a model for a system based on observed data. In this work we make possible that methods of *Inductive Logic Programming* (ILP) can be applied to induce the discrete-event specification of a system from its behaviour. The self-activation capacity of DEVS increases the complexity of this work by introducing time-dependent conditions in the transition functions. Besides, we will show how a new set of "state variables" can be derived from the time-dependent data when the initial set is not sufficiently relevant.

1 Introduction

The DEVS formalism is a mathematical, computer language and application independent system formalism introduced by Zeigler [9, 7] for the simulation and modelling of dynamic systems. Some ad-hoc works exist that attempt to create a model for a system based on observed data. However, the temporal characteristics of dynamic systems have made not feasible the application of classical rule induction methods. In this work we make possible that methods of *Inductive Logic Programming* (ILP) can be applied to induce the discrete-event specification of a system from its behaviour.

The aim of the inductor will be to obtain a set of rules that help to explain the current state of a system from the sequence of states that the system has gone through so far. Discrete-event specified systems are able to change its state without an external event by scheduling their next activation time point. Furthermore, the function that schedules these activation points can be different for each state.

This self-activation capacity of DEVS increases the complexity of this work by introducing time-dependent conditions in the transition functions. This involves also a great complexity in the training data compared to non-temporal applications of rule induction, because the history of each variable is provided to the inductor and thus, it involves a very large search space of possible hypotheses.

ILP has arosen as an appropiate method for the acquisition of rules from temporal data, whereas attribute-based learning has not, given that in the latter, the learned descriptions are limited to non-relational descriptions of objects. To this end, temporal data must be translated into a predicate logic representation that ILP methods can manage.

Besides, sometimes the temporal data describing the behaviour of a system do not include sufficiently relevant state variables for the inductor to obtain a set of predictive rules. Hence, we will show how a new set of "state variables" can be derived from the temporal data that enhance the description of each training instance, thus helping the inductor obtain a set of accurate rules.

This paper is organized as follows. Firstly, section 2 contains a brief description of DEVS as well as a set of steps that must be done to make feasible the application of rule induction methods. In section 3, the problem will be formulated in terms of Inductive Logic Programming and finally in section 4, we will show how new state variables can be derived from the initial data.

2 Induction of DEVS structures

2.1 Discrete Event Systems

The DEVS formalism is a mathematical, computer language and application independent system formalism introduced by Zeigler [9, 7] for discrete event simulation and modelling.

A discrete event system (DEVS) is a structure:

$$DEVS = (X, Y, S, \delta_{int}, \delta_{ext}, \lambda, t_a)$$

where X is the set of external events, Y is the set of outputs, S is the set of sequential states, $\delta_{ext} : Q * X \rightarrow S$ is the external transition function, $\delta_{int} : S \rightarrow S$ is the internal transition function, $\lambda : S \rightarrow Y$ is the output function, $t_a : S \rightarrow \mathcal{R}_o^+ \cup \{\infty\}$ is the time advance function and $Q = \{(s, e) | s \in S, 0 \leq e \leq t_a(s)\}$ is the set of states with e representing the elapsed time since the last event.

Discrete Event Systems have a continuous time base $\mathcal{R}$ but inputs and state transitions occur at discrete time instances. Two events -internal and external events- are responsible for the state changes. The external transition function δ_{ext} is executed whenever an input arrives and the times of execution of the internal transition function δ_{int} are scheduled by the time advance function $t_a(s)$.

Input values can arrive at arbitrary time instances. If at time t the system has been in state s for a time $e \leq t_a(s)$ and there arrives an external input, then the system has to execute its external transition function and the system will transit from s to $s'' = \delta_{ext}(s, e, x)$ where it will remain either to the next external event or $ta(s'')$ time units. If there is no external event, the system will stay in state s until it has been in s exactly $t_a(s)$ time units, then an internal event is generated that will transit from s to $s' = \delta_{int}(s)$. The output value is determined based on the state s by the output function $\lambda(s)$.

A system consisting of a single **CPU** that executes one job at a time and an input queue where the jobs wait to enter CPU will be used as an example along this paper. There exist many other similar applications of this type, for instance, a supermarket with a limited number of cashiers, a bank (cashiers), a pub (waiters, glasses, ...) [4], a shipyard (repair stations and vessels) [8] and so on. In the present example, multiple CPU scheduling policies can be considered, e.g. FIFO, Round Robin, Prioritized queue, and so on.

For instance, as to FIFO discipline, jobs enter CPU according to their arrival time, and they stay there until their required execution time is completed (the system undertakes an internal transition). Jobs wait to enter CPU on a *queue*, so that a new job is inserted at the end of the queue whereas the job at the head of the queue will enter CPU when the job currently in CPU leaves the system.

2.2 Formulating the problem

The trajectory of a discrete-event system is controlled by the four functions mentioned above that govern the behaviour of the system. Thus, the problem lies in obtaining this set of functions. To this end, the inductor will be presented with a sequence of states of the system to be modelled together with a set of state variables describing them. In figure 1 we show the sequence of states corresponding to a trajectory of an example simulation experiment (CPU scheduling example).

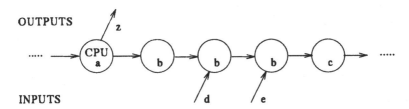

Fig. 1. CPU scheduling

In this example, the data that will be given as input to the inductor will consist, for each state, of the job entering the system (**e-event**), the job leaving the system (**lambda**), a predicate establishing if an internal transition was scheduled at that state (**i-event**) and the job being executed in CPU at each state.

On the other hand, let us suppose an observer records the arrival and departure of jobs from the system (figure 2). The arrival of jobs corresponds to input events, and the departure of jobs corresponds to output events. The number of jobs in the system is increased (decreased) by one whenever a job enters it (departs from it). Instead of specifying the number of jobs in the system, the observer may keep an ordered record of the jobs entering the system, while removing from the list any job departing from it.

This ordered record is included in each example thus describing the waiting jobs (if any) at each state. Besides, each job will be described through its *name*, its required *CPU time* (**tcpu**) and its position on that internal list. And finally, we will use the variable e to register the elapsed time from each state to the next one.

Once formulated the problem, the formalism of DEVS and ILP must be made compatible in order to translate input data into a form usable by the

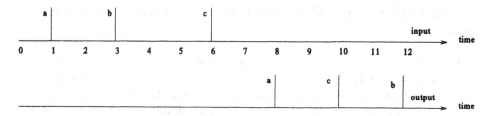

Fig. 2. An input/output trajectory

inductor [6]. We have chosen to arrange an independent classification problem for each function, where the legal set of values of each function identify the classes, whereas the system's states become the *domain's objects*. Thus, the induced rules will determine the current value of a function at each state, i.e., the output of a function f at the state represented by the example E is f_1 (a class), if the values of the attributes included in E match those in the right-hand side of the rule.

In section 2.1, we showed that the time points at which the system changes its state are identified by the arrival of external events and by the *time advance function* t_a. To induce the *time advance* function we must search for the condition fulfilled by the set of states at which an internal transition occurred, i.e., justify the existence of a new state at that time point when no external event arrives. Hence, its expression must include a time-dependent condition (elapsed time from a previous state).

Besides, we must determine an expression for each state variable, included in the initial data (those defining the structure of the system, e.g., **cpu**) and the function $\lambda(s)$, that determines the output element (if any) from the Y set that will depart from the system at the state s.

The goal we have followed, i.e., obtaining the model from the behaviour, has not been, to our knowledge, posed before. This is the reason why we need for instance more complete examples including the internal structure of the intended model, in order to build the model of the system. Nevertheless, the additional information we need is usually known by the designer of the system -in a cpu system, it is important to know which is the job in cpu-. The learning system will discover and model the behaviour: the scheduling policy.

In a related work [8], the system to be modelled is considered as a black box and the predictions are based only on the observed sequence of inputs and outpus to and from the system. From these data, the algorithm try to predict the particular *output segment* that corresponds to each *input segment* (the input trajectory is partitioned into a set of segments). The hypothesis formulated is retracted or confirmed with the arrival of new data. The objective is trying to know as much as possible about the system's structure.

3 Inductive Logic Programming from time-dependent data

Inductive logic programming (ILP) has arosen as a powerful means for the acquisition of rules from time-dependent data. Our work is inspired by the work of Feng and Muggleton [3] who apply an ILP algorithm (Golem) to the diagnosis of power-supply failures in the Skynet satellite, which usually require the history diagnosis of related components.

Unlike other non-temporal applications of rule induction methods, the training instances presented to the inductor consist of the temporal sequence of states that a single object has gone through rather than descriptions of a single state of multiple objects. Thus, *time instances* become the objects of the domain, and so, each training instance describes the state of a system at a time point.

On the other hand, in ILP each domain's descriptor is represented as a predicate p(arg, ...) that assert some properties about the domain's objects. The first argument of each predicate is now the time point at which an example was generated whereas the meaning of the remaining arguments depends on each particular predicate. Thus, a positive example class(15, c_1) states that at time instance 15 an example of the class "c_1" was generated.

Background knowledge records the status of the remaining descriptors (e.g., sensors in the satellite) at each time point, e.g. sensor1(15,+), and at the same time it allows us to represent knowledge in the form of logic programs, as the succession of time instants, represented by means of the predicate succ defined intensionally as:

$$\text{succ}(X,Y) \text{ :- } Y \text{ is } X\text{-1}.$$

which is applied multiple times to refer to values of previous states, by chaining a sequence of states. Thus, the rules can include references to facts occurred 1, 2, ... states ago.

class(A,a):- sensor7(A,+), succ(A,C), sensor12(C,-), ...

This is the usual specification as used by Feng and Muggleton in their work, where states are equidistant, i.e., states are generated by sampling a system at regular intervals. With respect to DEVS, a more complex specification must be considered. The domain's objects are the states (situations) of a system (i.e., the time points at which an external event enters the system or at which an internal transition was scheduled). Thus, states are not equidistant and consequently we need to include a variable (e) in the description of each state that measures the elapsed time between each pair of adjacent states. Background knowledge records the status of the remaining variables, e.g., i-event(s1), e-event(s2,j) and so on.

Initially, as in [3], states were represented as integer numbers, however the ILP algorithm sometimes did wrong substitutions, given that, e.g., temporal differences and states are represented by the same data type, thus obtaining non-sense clauses. We reserved the numeric type for expressing temporal differences whereas for states we used a character type, e.g. s1,s2,s3,..., using types with disjoint domains to implement different sorts of objects, e.g., jobs, that are represented by letters, e.g. a,b,c,.... However, the predicate **succ** needs now to be expressed extensionally, i.e., succ(s1,s2), succ(s2,s3),....

The predicate **succ** allows to include in a clause references to the state before the current one, the state before this one and so on (succ(A,B),succ(B,C),...). However, in this case, it is not useful to know how many states ago occurred an event, i.e., the behaviour depends not on the distance between states. Thus, we have to refer to states by the properties that hold in an state, and not only through a sequence of states, e.g.:

- the (last/first) state at which an (internal/external) transition occurred.
- the (last/first) state at which any element left the system.
- the (last/first) state at which any other event ocurred (e.g. a particular external event, a particular value of a state variable, and so on).

This can be expressed by means of a set of predicates like, e.g., last-cpu(s-,s',j), asserting at the state s that the last state at which the job j was in CPU is s' or input(j,s), asserting that s is the state at which the external event j entered the system, and so on. These predicates let us establish a connection between a set of states based on a more complex criterion than that of being adjacent, e.g.

```
class(S,a):- p(S), last_deltai(S,S'), q(S'), ...
```

As in many other examples of *multiple predicate learning*, additional problems may arise given that the predicates can be mutually dependent. Hence, it is necessary avoid mutual recursion between them, which would cause that no ground facts could be derived from their definition in simulation experiment. Mostly, the recursion is avoided by removing one of the predicates involved.

Many algorithms could be used to deal with this problem. However, given the efficiency and the possibility of using intensional background knowledge, we have used **Progol** [5]. Progol uses a set of examples $E = E^+ \cup E^-$ and background knowledge B and induces a set of clauses that help to explain the positive examples and none of the negative ones. Progol does "Mode-directed Inverse Resolution", i.e., uses a set of mode declarations to delimit the language used during the learning process. The predicate definitions in the input file (file.pl) for the CPU scheduling problem can be seen in figure 3 [1].

The **modeh** predicate establishes which predicate will be generalized, i.e., the predicate at the head of the induced clauses, whereas **modeb** establishes the predicates that will appear in the body of the clauses. The first argument of **modeb** specifies an upper bound number of successful calls to the predicate (*recall*). The type of the arguments of each predicate is preceded by a character (+,-, #), that is used in susbstituting constants for variables.

---

[1] The internal record is represented as a list, by means of the predicates **first**, **last**, **next** and **empty** for each state, according to the order of arrival of jobs.

```
% Predicate definitions
:-modeh(1,class(+state,...))?       /* Each class to be induced      */
:-modeb(1,i-event(+state))?         /* Internal transition           */
:-modeb(1,e-event(+state,-job))?    /* A new job entered the system  */
:-modeb(1,lambda(+state,-job))?     /* A job leaves the system       */
:-modeb(1,e(+state,-time))?         /* t elapsed since the prev. state */
:-modeb(1,tcpu(+job,-time))?        /* The CPU time needed by a job   */
:-modeb(1,next(+state,+job,-job))?  /* The next job in the input queue */
:-modeb(1,first(+state,-job))?      /* The oldest job in the queue    */
:-modeb(1,last(+state,-job))?       /* The newest job in the queue    */
:-modeb(1,empty(+state))?           /* The input queue is empty       */
:-modeb(1,cpu(+state,-job))?        /* The job currently in CPU       */
:-modeb(1,succ(+state,-state))?     /* The previous state             */
:-modeb(1,idle(+state))?            /* The system is idle             */
:-modeb(1,slice(+time))?            /* Time slice of the processor    */
```

Fig. 3. Input file used by Progol for the CPU scheduling problem

Progol admits the use of the negation operator not, but it must be explicitly declared for each predicate in the mode language. Besides, Progol has a set of parameters that can be modified to control the complexity of the language, setting an upper bound on the *nodes* to be explored by Progol when searching for a consistent clause, on the *number of literals* in the body of a consistent clause, on the *depth* of the theorem prover, on *layers of new variables*, e.g., $succ(A,B), succ(B,C), \ldots$, and on the *number of negatives* that can be covered by an acceptable clause.

4   Feature construction

Once the problem has been formulated so that ILP methods can manage it, we have a temporal sequence of states that the system has gone through, and a set of attributes describing them, from which Progol can be applied to try to obtain a set of rules. If the set of initial descriptors is complete, Progol can success. On the contrary, Progol will not be able to generalize or it will obtain poor generalizations, i.e., low compression rates.

In the second case, the temporal sequence of states provided as input, do not include enough *state variables* as to obtain accurate predictions. It is possible, however, that certain combinations or functions of the original variables are highly relevant to the problem. This process in induction is called *Feature Construction* and is essential for difficult domains, i.e., those that involve hard concepts or have their structure "hidden" by poor representations. When it is based on an analysis of data, it is said to be data-driven [1, 2].

FC generates new features by combining the original features with a set of operators. The most appropiate set of operators is always difficult to determine.

The set of operators shown below do not pretend to be complete but is a minimal set that has been found of interest in the experiments carried out. The new variables generated are intimately connected to the temporal nature of data and translate the dynamic behaviour of the system into a set of state variables.

- Time-elapsed-since(s,e) returns the elapsed time since the last ocurrence of the event e or from the last [input/output/internal transition].
- Number-of(s,e) returns the number of occurrences of the event e or kind of events [input/output/variable/internal transition].
- Previous(s,E) returns the previous value of a state variable E (different from its current value).
- Duration(s,e) returns the elapsed time from an state s' from which an event e has been occurring uninterruptedly.
- [First,Last]([input,output]) returns the first or last [input/output] to or from the system respectively.
- max, min, +, -, $\sum$ are applied to numerical events.

Some operators can be applied over a different set of states, e.g., the complete sequence of states (since the initial state) or all the states since any particular preceding state, e.g., first(output) since last input.

- since (first/last) transition (internal or external)
- since (first/last) output
- since initial state
- since the last ocurrence of a particular event (e.g., since last cpu(a)).

The feature constructor applies three strategies for enhancing the mode language of Progol (see below). In the first case, all candidate features are identified and the set of applicable operators are selected. Thus, a new set of features are constructed for each state. The second one, does not introduce new features but allows to reference relevant old states directly, i.e., without using succ. The last one, allows Progol to explore a larger search space.

- Apply an operator.
- Include references to relevant old states in a clause (e.g. last-cpu(s,s',a)).
- Modify settings of Progol (number of literals, number of layers of new variables, and so on)

From the possible set of new features, the constructor must select the most relevant for each domain. However, the only completely reliable way to test for relevant variables, whose relevance depends on their interrelations with other variables is trying to produce rules using them. Hence, the data enhanced with the new attributes are used to generate rules which are then evaluated by a *rule quality* function, e.g., their accuracy on a *testing set*. Thus, attribute construction and rule generation are repeated until a termination condition is satisfied, i.e., a complete set of rules is obtained or no improvement is achieved in the rules in a number of iterations (due to an insufficient language).

To illustrate the process, we will use the CPU scheduling problem [7] because it is significantly more complex than the other systems considered. Initially Progol was provided with the initial set of features (FIFO) together with the succ predicate. From these data Progol generated a complete set of rules only for the cpu and **lambda** predicates, however, it obtained a very low compression for the **i-event** predicate. Hence, new predicates were included in the description of each state (figure 4).

```
% state 20
e(s20,4).
e-event(s20,h).
cpu(s20,f).
% Ordered list of waiting jobs
first(s20,f). tail(s20,h). next(s20,f,g). next(s20,g,h).
% Derived features
te_first_cpu(s20,f,4).
last_ievent(s20,s19).
previous_cpu(s20,f).
    ....
```

Fig. 4. Description of state 20 in the language of Progol

To show the utility of the new features, we will comment on the clauses induced by Progol[2]. Progol initially induced a partially good solution for the **i-event** predicate. This solution is valid only for those cases where an only job exists or where no input arrives since a job enters CPU till it leaves the system.

```
i-event(S):-succ(S,S1),cpu(S1,J),tcpu(J,T),e(S,T).
```

The problem is that any input causes e to reset its value to zero. Thus it is necessary to know the time elapsed since the the job first entered CPU not since the previous state. When this time equals the required execution time of the job executing in CPU, the system undertakes an internal transition and that job leaves the system. As to the cpu predicate, the first job in the input queue, i.e., the one that has been waiting more time than any other job, is always the one executing in CPU.

```
i-event(S):-succ(S,S1),cpu(S1,J),te_first_cpu(S,J,T),tcpu(J,T).
lambda(S,J):-succ(S,S1),i_event(S),cpu(S1,J).
cpu(S,J) :- first(S,J).
```

As to *round robin*, and unlike the FIFO discipline, jobs enter and leave CPU several times. Progol induced initially an incomplete solution covering those cases where a job leaves CPU when the time slice is elapsed and -as with FIFO- there have not been an input since the last internal transition, i.e., e is equivalent to the time elapsed since the last internal transition.

---

[2] The variables returned by Progol have been renamed for clarity (S=state, J=job, T=time).

```
i_event(S):-e(S,T),slice(T).
```

However, it was unable to compress the remaining cases, i.e., when a job in CPU is interrupted by an external event and when a job needs to be in CPU for a time shorter than the time slice. In the first case, we need to know how much time has been a job in CPU uninterruptedly (duration-cpu(s,j,t)). When this time equals the time slice of the processor (slice(t)) the system undertakes an internal transition and that job must leave CPU. As to the second case, when the total execution time consumed by the job currently in CPU (sum-duration-cpu(s,p)) equals its required execution time, the system undertakes an internal transition and that job leaves the system.

```
i-event(S):-duration_cpu(S,J,T),slice(T).
i-event(S):-sum_duration_cpu(S,J,T),tcpu(J,T).
lambda(S,J):-i-event(S),tcpu(J,T),sum_duration_cpu(S,J,T).
```

The clauses headed by cpu(S,J) describe the discipline followed by the jobs waiting to enter CPU. Jobs enter and leave CPU several times and both new jobs and the jobs that must leave CPU (when the time slice is elapsed) are positioned at the end of the queue. Thus, the order of the waiting jobs in the ordered list included in the examples, does not correspond to the order of jobs entering CPU. The most simple cases were easy to induce by Progol, i.e., when there is an only job in the system and when an external event arrives the system, because it does not change the job in CPU.

```
cpu(S,J):-first(S,J),tail(S,J).
cpu(S,J):-e-event(S,J),succ(S,S1),cpu(S1,J).
```

However, Progol was initially unable to explain the remaining cases, i.e., when there are more than one job and an internal transition is scheduled. In this case, if a job j has never been in CPU (e in figure 5), it is necessary to know if at the state at which j entered the system (input(S,j)), j was the first input since the last internal transition (i.e., there was an internal transition at the previous state). If so, j will follow the job that was previously in CPU (a in figure 5). If not so, j will follow the job that entered before it (d in figure 5).

```
cpu(S,J):-i-event(S),input(J,S1),previous_cpu(S1,J1),succ(S1,S2),
          i-event(S2),succ(S,S3),cpu(S3,J1).
cpu(S,J):-i-event(S),input(J,S1),succ(S1,S2),e-event(S2,J1),
          succ(S,S3),cpu(S3,J1).
```

On the other hand, if a job j has already been in CPU (b in figure 5), it is necessary to know if there was any input during the last time (last-cpu(S,j,S')). If so, the next time, j will follow the job that entered the system at that state (e in figure 5). If not so, j will follow the job that was in CPU before it (previous-cpu(S,j)) (a in figure 5).

```
cpu(S,J):-i-event(S),last_cpu(S,J,S1),e-event(S1,J1),succ(S,S2),
          cpu(S2,J1).
cpu(S,J):-i-event(S),last_cpu(S,J,S1),i-event(S1),previous_cpu(S1,J1),
          succ(S,S2),cpu(S2,J1).
```

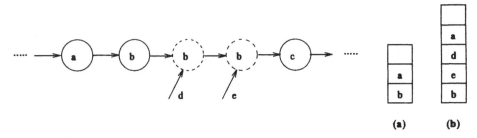

Fig. 5. Queue of jobs waiting to enter CPU

5 Conclusions

The temporal characteristics of dynamic systems have made not feasible the application of classical rule induction methods for inductive modelling. In this work we make possible that methods of *Inductive Logic Programming* (ILP) can be applied to induce the discrete event specification of a system from its exhibited behaviour. To this end, temporal data must be translated into a predicate logic representation that ILP methods can manage.

The inductor is provided with a temporal sequence of states that the system has gone through, and a set of attributes describing them, from which it must obtain the rules governing the behaviour of the system. The self-activation capacity of DEVS introduces time-dependent conditions in the transition functions. This involves a great complexity in the learning process compared to non-temporal applications of rule induction.

But sometimes the set of initial state variables is not complete and thus the inductor is not able to obtain a good generalization. We have shown how a set of new *state variables* can be derived from the temporal data that enhance the description of each state. The new features have proven to be useful in all the domains considered.

Acknowledgements This research was supported in part by the Government of Galicia (Spain), grant XUGA10503B/94. We would also like to thank Stephen Muggleton for allowing the public use of Progol.

References

1. E. Bloedorn and R.S. Michalski. Data driven constructive induction in AQ17-PRE: A method and experiments. *Proceedings of the Third International Conference on Tools for AI, San Jose, CA*, pages 9–14, 1991.
2. E. Bloedorn, R.S. Michalski, and J. Wnek. Multistrategy constructive induction: AQ17-MCI. *Proceedings of the 2nd International Workshop on Multistrategy Learning, Harpers Ferry, VW*, pages 188–203, 1993.
3. C. Feng. *Inducing Temporal Fault Diagnostic Rules from a Qualitative Model*, chapter 24. Academic Press Limited, 1992.

4. D. Mladenic, I. Bratko, R.J. Paul, and M. Grobelnik. Knowledge adquisition for discrete event systems using machine learning. *ECAI 94. 11th European Conference on Artificial Intelligence*, 1994.

5. S. Muggleton. Inverse entailment and progol. *New Generation Computing Journal*, (13):245–286, 1995.

6. R. P. Otero, D. Lorenzo, and P. Cabalar. Automatic induction of DEVS structures. *Lecture Notes in Computer Science*, (1030):305–315, 1996.

7. F. Pichler and H. Schwärtzel (Eds.). *CAST, Methods in Modelling*. Springer Verlag, 1992.

8. Hessam S. Sarjoughian. *Inductive Modeling of Discrete-event Systems: A TMS-based Non-monotonic Reasoning Approach*. PhD thesis, University of Arizona, 1995.

9. B. P. Zeigler. *Multifaceted Modelling and Discrete Event Simulation*. London: Academic Press, 1984.

Stochastic Simple Recurrent Neural Networks

Mostefa Golea1 and Masahiro Matsuoka2 and Yasubumi Sakakibara3

[1] Neurocomputing Research Center
Queensland University of Technology
of Technology
Brisbane, Australia
email: golea@fit.qut.edu.au
[2] Institute for Social Information Science
Fujitsu Laboratories Ltd.
140, Miyamoto, Numazu, Shizuoka 410-03, Japan
e-mail: (mage,yasu)@iias.flab.fujitsu.co.jp
[3] Department of Information Sciences
Tokyo Denki University
Hatoyama, Hiki-gun, Saitama 350-03, Japan
email: yasu@j.dendai.ac.jp

Abstract. Simple recurrent neural networks (SRNs) have been advocated as an alternative to traditional probabilistic models for grammatical inference and language modeling. However, unlike hidden Markov Models and stochastic grammars, SRNs are not formulated explicitly as probability models, in that they do not provide their predictions in the form of a probability distribution over the alphabet. In this paper, we introduce a *stochastic* variant of the SRN. This new variant makes explicit the functional description of how the SRN solution reflects the target structure generating the training sequence. We explore the links between the stochastic version of SRNs and traditional grammatical inference models. We show that the stochastic single-layer SRN can be seen as a generalized hidden Markov model or a probabilistic automaton. The two-layer stochastic SRN can be interpreted as a probabilistic machine whose state-transitions are triggered by inputs producing outputs, that is, a probabilistic finite-state sequential transducer. It can also be thought of as a hidden Markov model with two alphabets, each with its own distinct output distribution. We provide efficient procedures based on the forward-backward approach, used in the context of hidden Markov models, to evaluate the various probabilities occurring in the model. We derive a gradient-based algorithm for finding the parameters of the network that maximize the likelihood of the training sequences. Finally, we show that if the target structure generating the training sequences is unifilar, then the trained stochastic SRN behaves deterministically.

1 Introduction

Grammatical Inference entails inferring a model for an unknown language from a finite set of sample strings in the language [8, 10]. Ideally, a grammatical inference model should provide the ability to assign each string a probability of occurrence, and to predict which symbols are most likely to follow a given sub-string. Because predictions are usually ranked by their likelihood, an inference model that gives its prediction in the form of a probability distribution over the alphabet is desirable. Hence, traditionally, the grammatical inference prob-lem has been approached using Hidden Markov Models (HMMs), Probabilistic Automata, and Stochastic Grammars.

Recently, Simple Recurrent Networks (SRNs) have been advocated as an al-ternative to traditional probabilistic models for grammatical inference and lan-guage modeling [4, 6, 9, 13]. A SRN is basically a two-layer feedforward network with an extra layer of *context units*. The latter holds a *copy* of the hidden unit activations at the previous time slice. At each time step, the values of the context units are fed into the hidden units, along with the input values. The output of the hidden units and output units is then evaluated in the usual manner. Be-cause at each time step the activations of the hidden units are copied back to the context layer, the context unit values depend on all the previous inputs to the networks, and hence constitute a compressed record of the past history of the sequence. Empirical studies have shown that SRNs has the potential to develop internal representations that are useful encodings of the *temporal* properties of a sequence of inputs [4, 13].

Training SRNs is usually formulated as a prediction task: the network is presented with the current element of the string as input and it is trained to produce the next element of the string as output [4, 13]. SRNs can also be trained to translate a sequence of input strings to the corresponding sequence of output strings [7]. The basic algorithm for SRNs is a modification of the well known backpropagation algorithm, the optimization criterion being the square error between the targets and the network predictions.

The above formulation of learning in SRNs suffers from two problems. First, unlike HMMs and stochastic grammars, SRNs are not formulated explicitly as probabilistic models, in that they do not provide their predictions in the form of a probability distribution over the alphabet. Rather, symbols associated with output units that have activation larger than a pre-set threshold are accepted as valid continuation of the string [13]. Second, a functional description of how the SRN solution reflects the target structure is not an explicit part of the SRN model. Instead, a post-learning phase is required to *extract* an interpretation, e.g. in form of a stochastic grammar, from the SRN solution [6, 13, 14].

This paper proposes a new, probabilistic formulation of learning in SRNs. Within the new formulation, interpreting the learning results of SRN and ex-tracting equivalent stochastic grammars is straightforward. We introduce the concept of *stochastic* SRNs. Loosely speaking, in a stochastic SRN each unit takes on values at random according to a probability that depends on the states of the other nodes. The probability model governing the behavior of the stochas-tic SRN is introduced via the Statistical Physics concept of *energy*. This concept has been applied previously to different neural networks, e.g. Hopfield networks, Boltzman machine, and the combination machine (see [5] and references therein).

We investigate both single-layer and two-layer stochastic SRNs. We show that the stochastic single-layer SRN can be thought of as a generalized HMM [11] with a *distributed* state-representation. We show that if the target structure generating the strings is unifilar [12], then the (trained) stochastic single-layer SRN behaves deterministically. For the stochastic two-layer SRN, if the probability model is looked at generatively, it can be interpreted as (stochastically) synthesizing an *input-dependent* sequence of states in the hidden-layer, and then turning this sequence of hidden states into a sequence of observations in the output layer. Thus, the stochastic SRN model can be viewed as a generalized HMM whose state-transitions are triggered by inputs producing outputs, that is, a probabilistic finite-state sequential transducer.

The learning problem is formulated as that of choosing the parameters of the stochastic SRN that maximize the likelihood of the probability model, given the training sample. We derive an efficient gradient-based learning algorithm using dynamic programming for maximizing the likelihood of the model (the algorithm can be seen as an extension of back-propagation).

Our work is motivated by, and make use of techniques from, the recent work of Freund and Haussler [5] on learning time-independent probability distributions. The probability model of Section 3 can be seen as an extension of their work on the combination machine [5] to single-layer SRNs.

Due to the limited space, the learning algorithm for stochastic SRNs and the experimental results will appear in the full paper.

2 The Network

The simple recurrent network architecture is shown in Figure 1a. We consider a network with d input units, m hidden units, and c outputs. The random variables represented by the input, hidden, context, and output units take values in $\{0,1\}$. The context units simply hold a *copy* of the states of the hidden units from the previous time step.

We denote by $\mathbf{x}^{(t)} = (x_1^{(t)}, \ldots, x_d^{(t)}) \in \{0,1\}^d$ the state of the d input units at time t, by $\mathbf{h}^{(t)} = (h_1^{(t)}, \ldots, h_m^{(t)}) \in \{0,1\}^m$ the state of the m hidden units at time t, by $\mathbf{h}^{(t-1)} \in \{0,1\}^m$ the state of the context units at time t, and by $\mathbf{y}^{(t)} = (y_1^{(t)}, \ldots, y_c^{(t)}) \in \{0,1\}^c$, the state of the c output units at time t

Let $\mathbf{w}_j = (w_{j1}, \ldots, w_{jd}) \in \mathcal{R}^d$ represent the connection weights between the input units and the jth hidden unit, and $\theta_j \in \mathcal{R}$ represent the bias of the jth hidden unit. Let $\mathbf{u}_j = (u_{j1}, \ldots, u_{jm}) \in \mathcal{R}^m$ represent the connection weights between the context units and the jth hidden unit. Finally, let $\mathbf{v}_l = (v_{l1}, \ldots, v_{lm}) \in \mathcal{R}^c$ be the weight vector connecting the hidden units to the lth output unit and $\beta_l \in \mathcal{R}$ be the bias of the lth output unit. The set of parameters that defines both the SRN network and the resulting distribution model is denoted by (Φ, Ψ) where $\Phi = \{(\mathbf{w}_1, \mathbf{u}_1, \theta_1), \ldots, (\mathbf{w}_m, \mathbf{u}_m, \theta_m)\}$ denotes the parameters of the hidden layer and $\Psi = \{(\mathbf{v}_1, \beta_1), \ldots, (\mathbf{v}_c, \beta_c)\}$ denotes the parameters of the output layer. For a given model (Φ, Ψ), the *state* of the network at time t is defined by $(\mathbf{x}^{(t)}, \mathbf{h}^{(t)}, \mathbf{y}^{(t)})$.

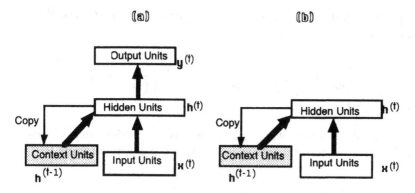

Fig. 1. a) Simple recurrent neural network. b) Single-Layer Simple Recurrent Network.

3 Grammatical Inference: Stochastic Single-Layer SRNs

Suppose a grammatical model is to be inferred from a set of strings. Then the information about the underlying grammar process generating the strings is encoded solely in the *order* in which symbols appear in the strings. Thus, predicting the next possible symbol(s) following a substring is what guides the grammatical inference process. In the case of SRNs, this translates into predicting the next possible input(s) to the network given the past inputs. Usually an output layer is used to represent the predictions of the network. But here, we formulate the prediction/inference problem solely in terms of a stochastic single-layer SRN consisting of the input, hidden, and context layers (Figure 1b). We will show later how to extend the analysis to include the output units.

3.1 The Probability Model

We define the energy of a state configuration $(\mathbf{x}^{(t)}, \mathbf{h}^{(t)})$ of the stochastic single-layer SRN at time t, given the parameters of the model Φ and the state of context units $\mathbf{h}^{(t-1)}$, by

$$E(\mathbf{x}^{(t)}, \mathbf{h}^{(t)} \mid \mathbf{h}^{(t-1)}, \Phi) = -\sum_{j=1}^{m}(\mathbf{w}_j \cdot \mathbf{x}^{(t)} + \mathbf{u}_j \cdot \mathbf{h}^{(t-1)} + \theta_j)h_j^{(t)} \qquad (1)$$

where $\mathbf{w}_j \cdot \mathbf{x}^{(t)} = \sum_{i=1}^{d} w_{ji}x_i^{(t)}$ and $\mathbf{u}_j \cdot \mathbf{h}^{(t-1)} = \sum_{k=1}^{m} u_{jk}h_k^{(t-1)}$. This energy function is an adaptation of the one introduced by Freund and Haussler for the combination model [5]. As we will see later, this particular definition has the advantage of assigning a meaningful interpretation to the random variables $\mathbf{h}^{(t)}$ in terms of the output of their corresponding units.

The probability of a state $(\mathbf{x}^{(t)}, \mathbf{h}^{(t)})$ at time t is defined to be

$$P(\mathbf{x}^{(t)}, \mathbf{h}^{(t)} \mid \mathbf{h}^{(t-1)}, \Phi) = \frac{1}{Z_t}e^{-E_t(\mathbf{x}^{(t)}, \mathbf{h}^{(t)} \mid \Phi, \mathbf{h}^{(t-1)})} \qquad (2)$$

where Z_t is the appropriate normalization factor. Defining $\mathbf{w}(\mathbf{h}^{(t)}) = \sum_{j=1}^{m} h_j^{(t)} \mathbf{w}_j$, we get

$$Z_t = \sum_{\mathbf{h}^{(t)} \in \{0,1\}^m} \left[\exp\left(\sum_{j=1}^{m} h_j^{(t)}(\mathbf{u}_j \cdot \mathbf{h}^{(t-1)} + \theta_j) \right) \prod_{i=1}^{d}(1 + e^{\mathbf{w}(\mathbf{h}^{(t)})_i}) \right] \quad (3)$$

The probability distribution over possible states of the hidden units at time t, again given the parameters of the model Φ and the state of context units $\mathbf{h}^{(t-1)}$, is given by

$$P(\mathbf{h}^{(t)}|\mathbf{h}^{(t-1)}, \Phi) = \sum_{\mathbf{x}^{(t)} \in \{0,1\}^n} P(\mathbf{x}^{(t)}, \mathbf{h}^{(t)} \mid \mathbf{h}^{(t-1)}, \Phi)$$

$$= \frac{\exp\left(\sum_{j=1}^{m} h_j^{(t)}(\mathbf{u}_j \mathbf{h}^{(t-1)} + \theta_j) \right) \prod_{i=1}^{d}(1 + e^{\mathbf{w}(\mathbf{h}^{(t)})_i})}{\sum_{\mathbf{h}^{(t)} \in \{0,1\}^m} \exp\left(\sum_{j=1}^{m} h_j^{(t)}(\mathbf{u}_j \mathbf{h}^{(t-1)} + \theta_j) \right) \prod_{i=1}^{d}(1 + e^{\mathbf{w}(\mathbf{h}^{(t)})_i})} \quad (4)$$

The distribution over possible states of the input units at time t is given by

$$P(\mathbf{x}^{(t)} \mid \mathbf{h}^{(t-1)}, \Phi) = \sum_{\mathbf{h}^{(t)} \in \{0,1\}^m} P(\mathbf{x}^{(t)}, \mathbf{h}^{(t)} \mid \mathbf{h}^{(t-1)}, \Phi)$$

$$= \sum_{\mathbf{h}^{(t)} \in \{0,1\}^m} \Pr(\mathbf{h}^{(t)} \mid \mathbf{h}^{(t-1)}, \Phi) P(\mathbf{x}^{(t)} \mid \mathbf{h}^{(t)}, \mathbf{h}^{(t-1)}, \Phi)$$

$$= \sum_{\mathbf{h}^{(t)} \in \{0,1\}^m} \Pr(\mathbf{h}^{(t)} \mid \mathbf{h}^{(t-1)}, \Phi) \prod_{i=1}^{d} \frac{e^{\mathbf{w}(\mathbf{h}^{(t)})_i x_i^{(t)}}}{1 + e^{\mathbf{w}(\mathbf{h}^{(t)})_i}} \quad (5)$$

where the last equality follows from the fact that

$$P(\mathbf{x}^{(t)} \mid \mathbf{h}^{(t)}, \mathbf{h}^{(t-1)}, \Phi) \equiv P(\mathbf{x}^{(t)} \mid \mathbf{h}^{(t)}, \Phi) = \prod_{i=1}^{d} \frac{e^{\mathbf{w}(\mathbf{h}^{(t)})_i x_i^{(t)}}}{1 + e^{\mathbf{w}(\mathbf{h}^{(t)})_i}} \quad (6)$$

Further, it is straightforward to show that

$$P(\mathbf{h}^{(t)} \mid \mathbf{h}^{(t-1)}, \mathbf{x}^{(t)}, \Phi) = \prod_{j=1}^{m} \frac{e^{(\mathbf{w}_j \cdot \mathbf{x}^{(t)} + \mathbf{u}_j \cdot \mathbf{h}^{(t-1)} + \theta_j) h_j^{(t)}}}{1 + e^{(\mathbf{w}_j \cdot \mathbf{x}^{(t)} + \mathbf{u}_j \cdot \mathbf{h}^{(t-1)} + \theta_j)}} \quad (7)$$

$$P(h_j^{(t)} = 1 \mid \mathbf{h}^{(t-1)}, \mathbf{x}^{(t)}, \Phi) = \text{logistic}(\mathbf{w}_j \cdot \mathbf{x}^{(t)} + \mathbf{u}_j \cdot \mathbf{h}^{(t-1)} + \theta_j) \quad (8)$$

where $\text{logistic}(a) = 1/(1 + e^{-a})$.

3.2 Interpretation

In SRNs, the output of a hidden unit is usually defined as the logistic function
of the total input to the unit

$$O_j^{(t)} = \text{logistic}(\mathbf{w}_j \cdot \mathbf{x}^{(t)} + \mathbf{u}_j \cdot \mathbf{h}^{(t-1)} + \theta_j) \qquad t = 1, 2, \ldots, \qquad j = 1, \ldots, m$$

In light of Equation 8, $O_j^{(t)}$ can be interpreted as the *expected value* of the hidden
variable $h_j^{(t)}$, given the input $\mathbf{x}^{(t)}$.

The stochastic single-layer SRN model has an intuitive interpretation in
terms of HMMs. Equation 4 can be interpreted as the transition probability
from state $\mathbf{h}^{(t-1)} \in \{0, 1\}^m$ to state $\mathbf{h}^{(t)} \in \{0, 1\}^m$. Similarly, Equation 6 is
the output probability distribution at state $\mathbf{h}^{(t)}$. This output distribution is a
Bernouli product distribution [5]. Therefore, the model defined by the stochastic
single-layer SRN is a generalized HMM with a distributed state-representation,
where the inputs to the network play the role of the observations in the traditional HMM.

The stochastic single-layer SRN model can also be interpreted in terms of
probabilistic automata [12]. Equation 2 is the probability of a transition from
state $\mathbf{h}^{(t-1)}$ to state $\mathbf{h}^{(t)}$ with the output of the symbol $\mathbf{x}^{(t)}$.

Yet another interpretation of stochastic single-layer SRNs is the following. If
we restrict the feedback to each hidden unit to be *only* from the unit itself, i.e.

$$\mathbf{u}_j = (0, 0, \ldots, 0, u_{jj}, 0, \ldots, 0) \qquad j = 1, \ldots, m$$

then this corresponds to having a hidden representation that is a *cross product* of
several independent and time varying hidden causes: Each hidden unit represents
a 2-state HMM, and the stochastic single-layer SRN represents a cross product
of these m 2-state HMMs.

3.3 Recovering the Traditional Discrete HMM

An interesting special case of the stochastic single-layer SRN model is when
the input vectors are restricted to have one bit on and the rest zero, i.e a local
representation for the symbols [13]. Then, there are exactly d possible inputs
(symbols) of the form

$$\mathbf{x}(l) = (0, 0, \ldots, 0, 1_l, 0, \ldots, 0) \qquad l = 1, \ldots, d$$

If we restrict the admissible hidden vectors $\mathbf{h}$ likewise, i.e. one bit on and the
rest zero, then there are exactly m possible state vectors of the form

$$\mathbf{h}(s) = (0, 0, \ldots, 0, 1_s, 0, \ldots, 0) \qquad s = 1, \ldots, m$$

Starting from Equation 1 and summing only over the d possible inputs and the
m possible hidden unit vectors, one can show that the resulting stochastic single-
layer SRN model is exactly equivalent to a (traditional) discrete HMM with m
states and d symbols [11]. The transition probability from state k to j is given
by $\frac{e^{u_{jk}}}{\sum_{j=1}^m e^{u_{jk}}}$, and the probability of outputing the ith symbol while in state j
is given by $\frac{e^{w_{ji}}}{\sum_{i=1}^d e^{w_{ji}}}$, where we have assumed w.l.o.g. that $\theta_j = 0$.

3.4 Stochastic vs. Deterministic SRN

Consider the case where the target structure generating the strings is such that, given a state S in the structure and a symbol σ, there is at most one outgoing edge from S labeled by σ. This is referred to in the case of HMMs as the *unifilar* property [12]. Note that deterministic SRNs can not represent target structures that are not unifilar.

When learning such target structures, and assuming learning is successful, the trained stochastic single-layer SRN behaves deterministically, in that given the state of the context units $\mathbf{h}^{(t-1)}$ and the current input $\mathbf{x}^{(t)}$, there is only one hidden state, that we denote by $\mathbf{h}_0^{(t)}$, such that

$$
P(\mathbf{h}^{(t)} \mid \mathbf{h}^{(t-1)}, \mathbf{x}^{(t)}, \Phi) = \begin{cases} \text{arbitrary close to 1} & \text{if } \mathbf{h}^{(t)} = \mathbf{h}_0^{(t)} \\ \text{arbitrary close to 0} & \text{otherwise} \end{cases}
$$

for $t = 1, 2, \ldots$. Recalling that a hidden unit output $O_j^{(t)}$ is the expected value of hidden variable $\mathbf{h}^{(t)}$ given the input $\mathbf{x}^{(t)}$, one can immediately see that $O^{(t)} = \mathbf{h}_0^{(t)}$. In this case, letting the context units stand for the hidden unit previous state is equivalent to feeding back the hidden unit outputs, as usually done in SRNs. In other words, given a sequence of inputs, the stochastic single-layer SRN behaves deterministically.

3.5 Efficient Forward-Backward Evaluation of the Likelihood

Given a string of observations $\mathbf{x}^{(1)}, \mathbf{x}^{(2)}, \ldots, \mathbf{x}^{(t)}$ and a model Φ, the first basic problem is to calculate the likelihood of the string, i.e., the probability that the observed sequence is produced by the stochastic SRN model. Here we present an efficient method for the evaluation of the likelihood. The method is a variant of the well-known Baum-Welch (forward-backward) algorithm for HMMs [11].

The probability of a sequence $\mathbf{x}^{(1)}, \mathbf{x}^{(2)}, \ldots, \mathbf{x}^{(t)}$, given a model Φ, can be written as $\Pr(\mathbf{x}^{(1)}, \ldots, \mathbf{x}^{(t)} \mid \Phi) = \sum_{\mathbf{h}^{(t)} \in \{0,1\}^m} \Pr(\mathbf{x}^{(1)}, \ldots, \mathbf{x}^{(t)}, \mathbf{h}^{(t)} \mid \Phi)$.. Assuming an initial state probability distribution $\Pr(\mathbf{h}^{(0)} \mid \Phi)$ for $\mathbf{h}^{(0)} \in \{0,1\}^m$, the forward probability $\Pr(\mathbf{x}^{(1)}, \ldots, \mathbf{x}^{(t)}, \mathbf{h}^{(t)} \mid \Phi)$ is calculated inductively:

1. Base step: $\Pr(\mathbf{x}^{(1)}, \mathbf{h}^{(1)} \mid \Phi) = \sum_{\mathbf{h}^{(0)} \in \{0,1\}^m} \Pr(\mathbf{x}^{(1)}, \mathbf{h}^{(1)} \mid \mathbf{h}^{(0)}, \Phi) \cdot \Pr(\mathbf{h}^{(0)} \mid \Phi)$
2. Induction step: $\Pr(\mathbf{x}^{(1)}, \ldots, \mathbf{x}^{(t)}, \mathbf{h}^{(t)} \mid \Phi) = \sum_{\mathbf{h}^{(t-1)} \in \{0,1\}^m} \Pr(\mathbf{x}^{(t)}, \mathbf{h}^{(t)} \mid \Phi, \mathbf{h}^{(t-1)}) \cdot \Pr(\mathbf{x}^{(1)}, \ldots, \mathbf{x}^{(t-1)}, \mathbf{h}^{(t-1)} \mid \Phi)$

The backward probability $\Pr(\mathbf{x}^{(t+1)}, \ldots, \mathbf{x}^{(N)} \mid \mathbf{x}^{(t)}, \mathbf{h}^{(t)}, \Phi)$, which is used in the learning algorithm, can be calculated in a similar way.

3.6 Learning the Parameters of the Model from Training Sequences

Given a string [4] of inputs $S = \mathbf{x}^{(1)}, \ldots, \mathbf{x}^{(N)}$, learning is formulated as the problem of choosing the set Φ of parameters of the stochastic single-layer SRN that minimize the negative log-likelihood $\text{NLL} = -\log \Pr(\mathbf{x}^{(1)}, \ldots, \mathbf{x}^{(N)} \mid \Phi)$ of the sequence S. For gradient-based minimization procedures, we need the derivatives of the likelihood with respect to the parameters Φ:

$$\frac{\partial - \log \Pr(\mathbf{x}^{(1)}, \ldots, \mathbf{x}^{(N)} \mid \Phi)}{\partial \Phi_i}$$

$$= \sum_{\mathbf{h}^{(0)}, \ldots, \mathbf{h}^{(N)}} \Pr(\mathbf{h}^{(0)}, \ldots, \mathbf{h}^{(N)} \mid \mathbf{x}^{(1)}, \ldots, \mathbf{x}^{(N)}, \Phi) \frac{\partial - \log \Pr(\mathbf{x}^{(1)}, \ldots, \mathbf{x}^{(N)}, \mathbf{h}^{(0)}, \ldots, \mathbf{h}^{(N)} \mid \Phi)}{\partial \Phi_i}$$

$$= \sum_{t=1}^{N} \sum_{\mathbf{h}^{(t-1)}, \mathbf{h}^{(t)} \in \{0,1\}^m} \Pr(\mathbf{h}^{(t-1)}, \mathbf{h}^{(t)} \mid \mathbf{x}^{(1)}, \ldots, \mathbf{x}^{(N)}, \Phi) \frac{\partial - \log \Pr(\mathbf{x}^{(t)}, \mathbf{h}^{(t)} \mid \mathbf{x}^{(t-1)}, \mathbf{h}^{(t-1)}, \Phi)}{\partial \Phi_i}.$$

The first term in the above formula is calculated efficiently using the forward-backward technique of Section 3.5:

$$\Pr(\mathbf{h}^{(t-1)}, \mathbf{h}^{(t)} \mid \mathbf{x}^{(1)}, \ldots, \mathbf{x}^{(N)}, \Phi)$$
$$= \frac{\Pr(\mathbf{x}^{(1)}, \ldots, \mathbf{x}^{(t-1)}, \mathbf{h}^{(t-1)} \mid \Phi) \cdot \Pr(\mathbf{x}^{(t)}, \mathbf{h}^{(t)} \mid \mathbf{h}^{(t-1)}, \Phi) \cdot \Pr(\mathbf{x}^{(t+1)}, \ldots, \mathbf{x}^{(N)} \mid \mathbf{x}^{(t)}, \mathbf{h}^{(t)}, \Phi)}{\Pr(\mathbf{x}^{(1)}, \ldots, \mathbf{x}^{(N)} \mid \Phi)}.$$

Evaluating the gradient in the second term results in the following formulas. For the weight vector $\mathbf{w}_j$ connecting the jth hidden unit to the input units, we get

$$\frac{\partial - \log \Pr(\mathbf{x}^{(t)}, \mathbf{h}^{(t)} \mid \mathbf{h}^{(t-1)}, \Phi)}{\partial w_{ji}} =$$

$$-h_j^{(t)} x_i^{(t)} + \sum_{\mathbf{h}^{(t)'} \in \{0,1\}^m} \Pr(\mathbf{h}^{(t)'} \mid \mathbf{h}^{(t-1)}, \Phi) h_j^{(t)'} \text{logistic}(w(\mathbf{h}^{(t)'})_i)$$

where $\Pr(\mathbf{h}^{(t)} \mid \mathbf{h}^{(t-1)}, \Phi)$ is given by Equation 4. The derivatives with respect to the weight vectors $\mathbf{u}_j$ and the bias parameters θ_j $(j = 1, \ldots, m)$ can be obtained in a similar way. For updating the initial state probabilities $(t = 0)$, we get

$$P(\mathbf{h}^{(0)} \mid \Phi) = \sum_{\mathbf{h}^{(1)} \in \{0,1\}^m} \Pr(\mathbf{h}^{(0)}, \mathbf{h}^{(1)} \mid \mathbf{x}^{(1)}, \ldots, \mathbf{x}^{(N)}, \Phi)$$

The time complexity of estimating the derivatives and the likelihood is $O(2^m)$. As suggested in [5], we can reduce the complexity by limiting the number of hidden units that can be on at the same time, say to at most k hidden units. This approach has also been suggested for the Boltzman machines. With

---

[4] The same holds for multiple strings, assuming we restart the context units at the beginning of each string.

such restriction, the number of hidden states reduces from 2^m to $O(m^k)$, which is polynomial in m. [5]

4 Mapping Input sequences to Output Sequences: The Stochastic SRN

As mentioned in the introduction, SRNs can be trained to translate a strings of inputs into the corresponding strings of outputs. For example, SRNs has been applied for acoustic-to-phonetic mapping, a typical problem in speech recognition [7]. In this section, we extend the stochastic formulation of the previous sections to include the output nodes (Figure 1).

Given a pair of strings $\mathbf{x}^{(1)}, \mathbf{x}^{(2)}, \ldots, \mathbf{x}^{(t)}, \ldots$ and $\mathbf{y}^{(1)}, \mathbf{y}^{(2)}, \ldots, \mathbf{y}^{(t)}, \ldots$, we are interested in predicting $\mathbf{y}^{(t)}$ based on $\mathbf{x}^{(1)}, \mathbf{x}^{(1)}, \ldots, \mathbf{x}^{(t)}$. [6] We will formulate the stochastic SRN model such it provides predictions in the form of a probability distribution over the output alphabet.

We find it useful to think of the stochastic SRN as the aggregation of two conceptually distinct components: a hidden layer implementing an input-dependent state-transition probability function

$$(\mathbf{h}^{(t-1)}, \mathbf{x}^{(t)}) \longrightarrow \mathbf{h}(t)$$

and an output layer implementing a state-dependent output probability function for predictions

$$\mathbf{h}^{(t)} \longrightarrow \mathbf{y}^{(t)}$$

We have already seen how the deal with the first component. For the second component, we define the energy of an output state $\mathbf{y}^{(t)}$, given the state of the hidden units $\mathbf{h}^{(t)}$ and the parameters of the output layer Ψ, by

$$E(\mathbf{y}^{(t)} | \Psi, \mathbf{h}^{(t)}) = -\sum_{l=1}^{c} (\mathbf{v}_l \cdot \mathbf{h}^{(t)} + \beta_l) y_l^{(t)} \tag{9}$$

The probability distribution over possible outputs $\mathbf{y}^{(t)}$, again given the state of the hidden units $\mathbf{h}^{(t)}$ and Ψ, is

$$P(\mathbf{y}^{(t)} | \Psi, \mathbf{h}^{(t)}) = \frac{1}{Z'_t} e^{-E(\mathbf{y}^{(t)} | \Psi, \mathbf{h}^{(t)})} \tag{10}$$

where $Z'_t = \sum_{\mathbf{y}^{(t)} \in \{0,1\}^c} e^{-E(\mathbf{y}^{(t)} | \Psi, \mathbf{h}^{(t)})}$ is the normalization factor. A straightforward calculation yields

$$P(\mathbf{y}^{(t)} | \Psi, \mathbf{h}^{(t)}) = \prod_{l=1}^{c} \frac{e^{(\mathbf{v}_l \cdot \mathbf{h}^{(t)} + \beta_l) y_l^{(t)}}}{1 + e^{(\mathbf{v}_l \cdot \mathbf{h}^{(t)} + \beta_l)}} \tag{11}$$

---

[5] Note that the time complexity $O(2^m)$ does not mean that our procedure is inefficient. This complexity is *necessary* because the stochastic SRN with m hidden units is equivalent to a HMM with 2^m states. Hence the time complexity of $O(2^m)$ is reasonable from the viewpoint of a HMM or a finite automaton.

[6] For Grammatical inference, $\mathbf{y}^{(t)} = \mathbf{x}^{(t+1)}$.

Thus, given the state of the hidden units $\mathbf{h}^{(t)}$, $\mathbf{y}^{(t)}$ is distributed according to a Bernouli product distribution, where

$$P(y_l^{(t)}|\Psi,\mathbf{h}^{(t)}) = \frac{e^{(\mathbf{v}_l\cdot\mathbf{h}^{(t)}+\beta_l)y_l^{(t)}}}{1+e^{(\mathbf{v}_l\cdot\mathbf{h}^{(t)}+\beta_l)}}$$

$$P(y_l^{(t)} = 1|\Psi,\mathbf{h}^{(t)}) = \text{logistic}\left(\mathbf{v}_l\cdot\mathbf{h}^{(t)}+\beta_l\right)$$

for $l = 1,\ldots,c$. Hence, the output of an output unit, as usually defined in SRNs

$$f_l^{(t)} = \text{logistic}\left(\mathbf{v}_l\cdot\mathbf{h}^{(t)}+\beta_l\right)$$

is the *expected value* of the random variable $y_l^{(t)}$, given the state of the hidden units.

Two quantities are of interest. First, the conditional probability of a given output $\mathbf{y}^{(t)}$, given the current input and the state of the context units,

$$P(\mathbf{y}^{(t)}\mid\mathbf{x}^{(t)},\mathbf{h}^{(t-1)},\Psi,\Phi) = \sum_{\mathbf{h}^{(t)}\in\{0,1\}^m} P(\mathbf{h}^{(t)}\mid\mathbf{x}^{(t)},\mathbf{h}^{(t-1)},\Phi)\times P(\mathbf{y}^{(t)}\mid\mathbf{h}^{(t)},\Psi)$$

$$= \sum_{\mathbf{h}^{(t)}} P(\mathbf{h}^{(t)}\mid\mathbf{x}^{(t)},\mathbf{h}^{(t-1)},\Phi)\times P(\mathbf{y}^{(t)}\mid\mathbf{h}^{(t)},\Psi)$$

$$= \sum_{\mathbf{h}^{(t)}} \prod_{j=1}^m \frac{e^{(\mathbf{w}_j\cdot\mathbf{x}^{(t)}+\mathbf{u}_j\cdot\mathbf{h}^{(t-1)}+\theta_j)h_j^{(t)}}}{1+e^{(\mathbf{w}_j\cdot\mathbf{x}^{(t)}+\mathbf{u}_j\cdot\mathbf{h}^{(t-1)}+\theta_j)}} \prod_{l=1}^c \frac{e^{(\mathbf{v}_l\cdot\mathbf{h}^{(t)}+\beta_l)y_l^{(t)}}}{1+e^{(\mathbf{v}_l\cdot\mathbf{h}^{(t)}+\beta_l)}}$$

$$(12)$$

where the last equality follows from Equations 7 and 11. The second quantity of interest is the *join* distribution over the inputs and the outputs, given the state of the context units,

$$P(\mathbf{y}^{(t)},\mathbf{x}^{(t)}\mid\mathbf{h}^{(t-1)},\Psi,\Phi) = \sum_{\mathbf{h}^{(t)}} P(\mathbf{h}^{(t)}\mid\mathbf{h}^{(t-1)},\Phi)\times P(\mathbf{x}^{(t)}\mid\mathbf{h}^{(t)})\times P(\mathbf{y}^{(t)}\mid\mathbf{h}^{(t)},\Psi)$$

$$(13)$$

The stochastic SRN probability model may be interpreted in two different ways. First, in light of Equation 12, the model can be seen as *probabilistic machine* whose state-transitions are triggered by inputs producing outputs, i.e. a probabilistic finite-state sequential transducer

Alternatively, starting at the hidden units and looking outward to the input and output layers, Equation 13 can be interpreted as a (hidden) Markov Chain whose state-transitions are given by Equation 4. Two output distributions are associated with each state in the chain: one distribution for the symbols represented by network inputs (Equation 6) and one for the symbols represented by network outputs (Equation 11). That is, the model represents two sequences *coupled* through a hidden Markov chain. Learning can then be thought of as finding the parameters of the model that best explain *both* output sequences.

If the target structure generating the pair of sequences is known to be unifilar (Section 3.4), then we can show that the trained stochastic SRNs behave deterministically. In this case, the stochastic model is used for the purpose of training the network, but we can use the ordinary deterministic SRN set-up [4] for information processing after training is completed. The advantage of starting with a stochastic set-up is the possible speed-up in the learning phase [7] and, most importantly, the straightforward interpretation of the learning results.

4.1 Learning The Parameters of the Stochastic SRN

Given a pair of input-output strings $\mathbf{x}^{(1)}, \ldots, \mathbf{x}^{(N)}$ and $\mathbf{y}^{(1)}, \ldots, \mathbf{y}^{(N)}$, the first problem is to estimate the likelihood of the pair of string, given the parameters of the model (Φ, Ψ)

$$
\begin{aligned}
\text{LL} &= \log \Pr(\mathbf{x}^{(1)}, \ldots, \mathbf{x}^{(N)}, \mathbf{y}^{(1)}, \ldots, \mathbf{y}^{(N)} \mid \Phi, \Psi) \\
&= \log \Pr(\mathbf{x}^{(1)}, \ldots, \mathbf{x}^{(N)} \mid \Phi) + \log \Pr(\mathbf{y}^{(1)}, \ldots, \mathbf{y}^{(N)} \mid \mathbf{x}^{(1)}, \ldots, \mathbf{x}^{(N)}, \Phi, \Psi)
\end{aligned}
$$

The first term in the above equation represents the log-likelihood of the input sequence, and the second term represents the log-likelihood of the output sequence conditioned on the input sequence. Both terms can be evaluated efficiently using the forward-backward procedure of Section 3.5.

Learning is formulated as that of finding the parameters (Φ, Ψ) of the network that minimize the negative log-likelihood of the model, given a training set of pairs of strings. We derived a gradient-based approach for solving the learning problem. The learning algorithm makes use of dynamic programming and can be seen as an extension of backpropagation. Due to the limited space, the details of algorithm and the experimental results will appear in the full paper.

5 Conclusion and Related Work

There has been a great interest lately in relating neural networks and HMMs. For example, the capacity of connectionist models to capture the implicit statistical regularities in the input data has been used to estimate *a posteriori probabilities* required by HMMs [3]. A modular architecture that implement an input/output HMM is introduced in [2].

The present work is quite distinct from the previous ones, in that we are not proposing a modular architecture to represent the constituent structures of HMMs. Our networks are stochastic in their own nature, so their behavior is described by probability distributions and stochastic dynamics. The links between the stochastic version of SRNs and HMMs are a by-pass of the probabilistic formulation. Our main purpose is to provide an explicit description of how the SRN solution reflects the target structure.

---

[7] Many researchers have pointed out that even if a network is deterministic, it is sometimes effective to train it as it it were stochastic. The stochastic set-up has also been used for training (deterministic) networks with *threshold* activation functions [1].

Finally, the present analysis can be easily extended to handle real-valued inputs and/or outputs, and to other networks that are based on the SRN architecture [6, 15].

Acknowledgements

We would like to thank Peter Bartlett and Yoav Freund for very useful suggestions and comments on an earlier draft of the paper.

References

1. P. Bartlett (1992). Using Random Weights to Train Multilayer Networks of Hard-Limiting Units. IEEE Trans. Neural Networks, Vol. 3, p. 202.
2. Y. Bengio and P. Frasconi (1995). An Input Output HMM Architecture. In G. Tesauro et al (Eds), Advances in Information Processing Systems (NIPS) 7. MIT Press.
3. H. Boulard and C. Wellekens (1990). Links Between HMMs and Multilayer Perceptrons. IEEE Trans. pattern An. Mach. Intell., Vol. 12, p. 1167.
4. J.L. Elman (1991). Distributed Representations, Simple Recurrent Networks, and Grammatical structure. *Machine Learning*, Vol. 7, p. 195.
5. Y. Freund and D. Haussler (1994). Unsupervised Learning of Distribution over Binary Vectors using Two-layer networks. *UCSC-CRL-94-25*. Also, *Neural Information Processing Systems*, Vol. 4, p. 912.
6. C.L. Giles and C.W. Omlin. Extraction, insertion, and refinement of symbolic rules in dynamically-driven recurrent neural networks. Connection Science, Vol. 5, p. 307, 1993.
7. M. Hanes, S. Ahalt, and A. Krishnamurthy. (1994). Acoustic-to-Phonetic Mapping Using Recurrent Neural Networks. IEEE Trans. on Neural Networks, Vol. 5, p. 659.
8. King-Sun Fu and Taylor L. Booth. Grammatical inference: Introduction and survey - part I and II. IEEE Transactions on Pattern Analysis and Machine Intelligence, PAMI-8(3), May 1986.
9. S.C. Kremer (1995). On the Computational Power of Elman-Style Recurrent Networks. IEEE Trans. on Neural Networks, Vol. 6, p. 1000.
10. S.M. Lucas. New directions in grammatical inference. In IEE Colloquim on Grammatical Inference : Theory, Applications and Alternatives, pages 1/1–7, April 1993.
11. L.R. Rabiner (1989). A Tutorial on Hidden Markov Models and Selected Applications in Speech Recognition. *Proceedings of the IEEE*, Vol. 77, p. 257.
12. D. Ron (1995). Automata Learning and its Applications. Ph.D. Thesis, Hebrew University.
13. D. Servan-Schreiber, A. Cleeremans, and J.L. MacClelland (1991). Graded State Machines: The Representation of Temporal Contingencies in Simple Recurrent Networks. *Machine Learning*, Vol. 7, p. 161.
14. P. Tino, B. Horne, and L. Giles (1995). Finite State Machines and Recurrent Neural Networks - Automata and Dynamical Systems Approaches", Technical Report-UMCP-CSD:CS-TR-3396, University of Maryland, College Park.
15. P. Tino and J. Sajda (1995). Learning and Extracting Initial Mealy Automata with Modular Neural Models. Neural Computation, Vol. 7, p.822.

Inferring Stochastic Regular Grammars
with Recurrent Neural Networks

Rafael C. Carrasco, Mikel L. Forcada, Laureano Santamaría

Departamento de Lenguajes y Sistemas Informáticos
Universidad de Alicante
E-03071 Alicante, Spain.
E-mail: {carrasco, mlf, laureano}@dlsi.ua.es.

Abstract. Recent work has shown that the extraction of symbolic rules improves the generalization performance of recurrent neural networks trained with complete (positive and negative) samples of regular languages. This paper explores the possibility of inferring the rules of the language when the network is trained instead with stochastic, positive-only data. For this purpose, a recurrent network with two layers is used. If instead of using the network itself, an automaton is extracted from the network after training and the transition probabilities of the extracted automaton are estimated from the sample, the relative entropy with respect to the true distribution is reduced.

1 Introduction

A number of papers [1, 2, 3, 4] have explored the ability of second-order recurrent neural networks to infer simple regular grammars from complete (positive and negative) training samples. The generalization performance of a finite state automaton extracted from the trained network is better than that of the network itself [1, 2, 5]. In most cases, they find that once the network has learned to classify all the words in the training set, the states of the hidden neurons visit only small regions (clusters) of the available configuration space during recognition. These clusters can be identified as the states of the inferred deterministic finite automaton (DFA) and the transitions occurring among these clusters when symbols are read determine the transition function of the DFA. Although automaton extraction remains a controversial issue [6], it has recently been has shown [7] that a recurrent neural network can robustly model a DFA if its state space is partitioned into a number of disjoint sets equal to the number of states in the minimum equivalent automaton. An automaton extraction algorithm can be found in [5]. The extraction is based on partitioning the configuration hypercube $[0.0, 1.0]^N$ in smaller hypercubes, such that at most one of the clusters falls into each defined region. An improved algorithm which does not restrict clusters to point-like form is described in [8].

However, complete samples, which include both examples and counterexamples, are scarce and, in most cases, only a source of random (or noisy) examples is available. In such situations, inferring the underlying grammar will clearly improve the estimation of the probabilities, above all, for those strings which do not appear in the sample. In this paper, the possibility of extracting symbolic rules from a recurrent network trained with stochastic samples is explored. The architecture of the network is described in next section, and it can be viewed as an Elman net [9] with a second-order next-state function, as used in [8]. The related work of [10] uses an Elman architecture to predict the probability of the next symbol, but it does not address the question of what symbolic representation is learned by the net. An alternate, algorithmic approach to the inference of stochastic regular languages can be found in [11].

2 Network architecture

Assume that the input alphabet has L symbols. Then, the second-order recurrent neural network consists of N hidden neurons and L input plus $L + 1$ output neurons, whose states are labeled S_k, I_k and O_k respectively (see Fig. 1).

The network reads one character per cycle (with $t = 0$ for the first cycle) and the input vector is $I_k = \delta_{kl}$ when a_l (the l-th symbol in the alphabet) is read[1]. Its output $O_k^{[t+1]}$ represents the probability that the string is followed with symbol a_k for $k = 1, ... L$ and $O_{L+1}^{[t+1]}$ represents the probability that the string ends there. The dynamics is given by the equations:

$$O_k^{[t]} = g(\sum_{j=1}^{N} V_{kj}\ S_j^{[t]})$$ (1)

$$S_i^{[t]} = g(\sum_{j=1}^{N}\sum_{k=1}^{L} W_{ijk}\ S_j^{[t-1]}\ I_k^{[t-1]})$$ (2)

where $g(x) = 1/(1 + \exp(-x))$.

The network is trained with a version of the Real Time Recurrent Learning (RTRL) algorithm [12]. The contribution of every string w in the sample to the energy (error function) is given by

$$E_w = \sum_{t=0}^{|w|} E_w^{[t]}$$ (3)

where

$$E_w^{[t]} = \frac{1}{2}\sum_{k=1}^{L+1}\left(O_k^{[t]} - I_k^{[t]}\right)^2,$$ (4)

$I_k^{[|w|]} = \delta_{k,L+1}$, and $I_{L+1}^{[t]} = 0$ for $t < |w|$. It is not difficult to prove that this energy has a minimum when $O_k^{[t]}$ is the conditional probability of getting symbol a_k after reading the first t symbols in w. Because a probability one (or zero) is difficult to learn, a contractive mapping $f(x) = \epsilon + (1 - 2\epsilon)x$, with ϵ a small

---

[1] The Kronecker's delta δ_{kl} is 1 if $k = l$ and zero otherwise.

output

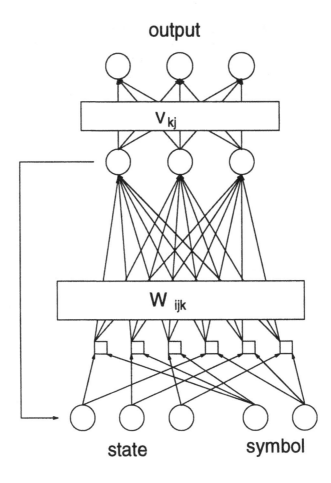

Fig. 1. Second-order recurrent neural network with $N = 3$ and $L = 2$

positive number, is applied to inputs (outputs are correspondingly expanded). This mapping does not affect the essentials of the formalism presented here.

Usually, the weights are set to random values and then learned, but the initial states of the hidden neurons $S_i^{[0]}$ cannot change during training. As remarked in [13], there is no reason to force the initial states to remain fixed, and the behavior of the network improves if they are also learned. This is even more important here, because the predicted probability $O_k^{[t]}$ depends on the states $S_i^{[t]}$, while in a mere classification task it suffices that the accepting states are in the acceptance region and the rest in the non-acceptance region. In order to keep $S_i^{[t]}$ within the range $[0.0, 1.0]$ during gradient descent, one rather defines the net inputs $\sigma_i^{[t]}$ such that $S_i^{[t]} = g(\sigma_i^{[t]})$ and take $\sigma_i^{[0]}$ as the parameters to be optimized.

Therefore, all parameters V_{kj}, W_{ijk} and $\sigma_i^{[0]}$ are initialized to small random values before training, but then learned together. Every parameter P is updated according to gradient descent:

$$\Delta P = -\alpha \frac{\partial E}{\partial P} + \eta \Delta' P \tag{5}$$

with a learning rate α and a momentum term η. The value $\Delta' P$ represents the variation of parameter P at previous iteration.

The contribution of every symbol in w to the energy derivative is:

$$\frac{\partial E_w^{[t]}}{\partial P} = \sum_{b=1}^{L+1} (O_b^{[t]} - I_b^{[t]}) O_b^{[t]} (1 - O_b^{[t]}) \sum_{a=1}^{N} \left(\frac{\partial V_{ba}}{\partial P} S_a^{[t]} + V_{ba} S_a^{[t]} (1 - S_a^{[t]}) \frac{\partial \sigma_a^{[t]}}{\partial P} \right) \tag{6}$$

where the derivative of the sigmoid function $g'(x) = g(x)(1 - g(x))$, was used.

The derivatives with respect to V_{kj} may be evaluated in a single step:

$$\frac{\partial E_w^{[t]}}{\partial V_{kj}} = (O_k^{[t]} - I_k^{[t]}) O_k^{[t]} (1 - O_k^{[t]}) S_j^{[t]} \tag{7}$$

However, the derivatives with respect to $\sigma_i^{[0]}$ and W_{ijk} are computed in a recurrent way, using the following equations:

$$\frac{\partial \sigma_m^{[0]}}{\partial W_{ijk}} = 0 \tag{8}$$

$$\frac{\partial \sigma_i^{[0]}}{\partial \sigma_j^{[0]}} = \delta_{ij} \tag{9}$$

$$\frac{\partial \sigma_i^{[t]}}{\partial \sigma_j^{[0]}} = \sum_{a=1}^{N} S_a^{[t-1]} (1 - S_a^{[t-1]}) \sum_{b=1}^{L} W_{iab} \frac{\partial \sigma_a^{[t-1]}}{\partial \sigma_j^{[0]}} I_b^{[t-1]} \tag{10}$$

$$\frac{\partial \sigma_m^{[t]}}{\partial W_{ijk}} = \delta_{im} S_j^{[t-1]} I_k^{[t-1]} + \sum_{a=1}^{N} S_a^{[t-1]} (1 - S_a^{[t-1]}) \sum_{b=1}^{L} W_{mab} \frac{\partial \sigma_a^{[t-1]}}{\partial W_{ijk}} I_b^{[t-1]} \tag{11}$$

3   Results and discussion

The behavior of the network has been checked using the following stochastic deterministic regular grammar:

$$
\begin{aligned}
S &\to 0S \ (0.2) \\
S &\to 1A \ (0.8) \\
A &\to 0B \ (0.7) \\
A &\to 1S \ (0.3) \\
B &\to 0A \ (0.4) \\
B &\to 1B \ (0.1)
\end{aligned}
\tag{12}
$$

where the numbers in parenthesis indicate the probability of the rules. The end-of-string probability for a given variable is the difference between 1 and the sum of the probabilities of all rules with that variable on the left. Two input neurons ($L = 2$) and three output neurons (corresponding to 0, 1 and end-of-string respectively) were used, while the number of hidden neurons in the network was set to $N = 4$. The network was trained with 800 random[2] examples generated by grammar (12) and all of them were used at every iteration of the learning algorithm. The learning rate was $\alpha = 0.004$ and the momentum term $\eta = 0.2$. The training process for a given sample involved 1000 iterations. Figure 2

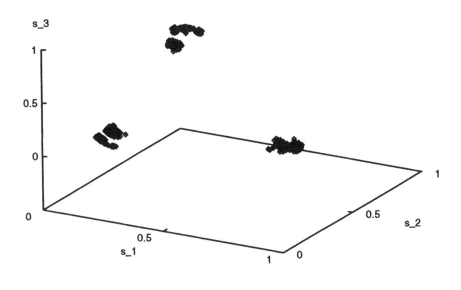

Fig. 2. Configuration space after training with 800 examples.

shows a typical section of the configuration space $[0.0, 1.0]^N$ for a trained net. Every point represents a vector $S^{[t]}$, generated for all words of length up to 10. As seen in the figure, only some regions are visited and three clusters appear corresponding to the three variables in the grammar. Clusters were observed in all the experiments.

[2] The sample contained an average of 200 different strings.

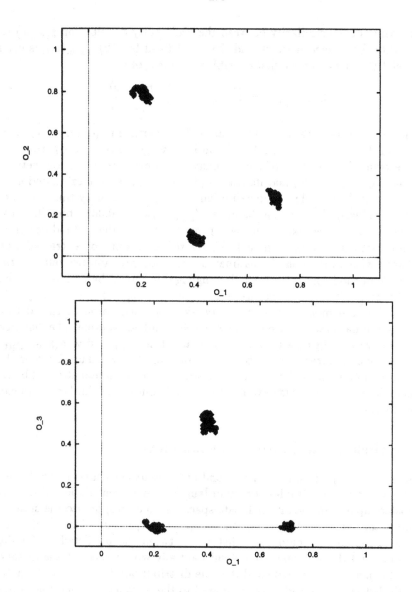

Fig. 3. Output probabilities after training.

In Fig. 3, the projection to the output space (O_1, O_2, O_3) is plotted. The clusters map into the regions around $(0.2, 0.8, 0.0)$, $(0.7, 0.3, 0.0)$ and $(0.4, 0.1, 0.5)$, in agreement with the true probabilities. Note that, even if not required by the model, the sum of all three components is approximately 1. Note also that due to the contractive mapping (we take $\epsilon = 0.1$) one gets some values slightly below zero which should be treated as rounding errors. As observed in the picture, the trained network is able to predict the probability of the next symbol with good accuracy.

A measure of the similarity between the probability distribution $p_{net}(w)$ estimated with the trained network and the one defined by (12), $p_{grm}(w)$, is given by the relative entropy or Kullback–Leibler distance [14]:

$$d(p_{grm}, p_{net}) = \sum_w p_{grm}(w) \log_2 \frac{p_{grm}(w)}{p_{net}(w)} \tag{13}$$

which gave an average value of 0.05 bits in 10 experiments (obtained by summing for all strings w in canonical order until convergence is reached). However, when the transition diagram of the automaton was extracted from the network (using the algorithm in [5]) and its transition probabilities were estimated using the statistics of the sample, the distribution $p_{ext}(w)$ generated by this stochastic automaton reduced the average distance $d(p_{grm}, p_{ext})$ to 0.0015 bits (this distance may be computed exactly using a generalization of the method described in [14] for stationary Markov chains). Therefore, the automaton extracted from the network with experimentally estimated transition probabilities outperforms the network in modeling the stochastic language. It should be emphasized that generalization performance is not assessed here by using a test set, but by comparing the inferred model (either the network or an automaton extracted from it) to the grammar that was used to generate the synthetic sample. The distances obtained above may be shown to be very small when compared to $d(p_{sam}, p_{grm})$ (with p_{sam} the actual frequencies observed in the sample), which is 1.2 bits in this case[3]; this gives another indication of the degree of generalization attained by the inference process. The results obtained for other grammars of similar complexity are comparable.

4   Conclusions and future developments

The generalization performance of a second-order recurrent neural network when trained with stochastic samples of regular languages has been studied. It is found that clusters appear in the internal state space which correspond to the states in the finite automaton used to generate the sample. If the probabilities are estimated with the extracted automaton, the distance between the predicted probability distribution and the true one reduces substantially with respect to the distance between the network's estimate and the true distribution; it also has to be noted that both distances are negligible compared to the distance between the sample and the true distribution. This last fact shows by itself the generalization ability of the inference method. The results suggest that second-order recurrent neural networks may become suitable candidates for modeling stochastic processes when grammatical algorithms are not yet developed.

We are currently studying the application of the more rigorous automaton extraction algorithm of [8] to our networks, as well as the effect of having a finite sample that gives an incorrect estimation for under-represented strings on the quality of the internal representation inferred by the network.

---

[3] The distance $d(p_{grm}, p_{sam})$ is infinity due to the fact that the sample is finite.

Acknowledgments: We wish to thank the Dirección General de Investigación Científica y Técnica of the Government of Spain for support through projects TIC93-0633-C02 and TIC95-0984-C02-01. We also thank Ramón Ñeco for suggestions regarding the manuscript.

References

1. Giles, C.L., Miller, C.B, Chen, D., Chen, H.H., Sun, G.Z., Lee, Y.C.: "Learning and Extracting Finite State Automata with Second-Order Recurrent Neural Networks" *Neural Computation* **4** (1992) 393–405.
2. Giles, C.L., Miller, C.B, Chen, D., Sun, G.Z., Chen, H.H., Lee, Y.C.: "Extracting and Learning an Unknown Grammar with Recurrent Neural Networks", in *Advances in Neural Information Processing Systems 4* (J. Moody et al., eds.), Morgan-Kaufmann, San Mateo, CA, 1992, p. 317–324.
3. Watrous, R.L., Kuhn, G.M.: "Induction of Finite-State Automata Using Second-Order Recurrent Networks" *Advances in Neural Information Processing Systems 4* (J. Moody et al., Eds), Morgan-Kaufmann, San Mateo, CA, 1992, p. 306–316.
4. Watrous, R.L., Kuhn, G.M.: "Induction of Finite-State Languages Using Second-Order Recurrent Networks" *Neural Computation* **4** (1992) 406–414.
5. Omlin, C.W., Giles, C.L.: "Extraction of Rules from Discrete-Time Recurrent Neural Networks" *Neural networks* **9**:1 (1996) 41–52.
6. Kolen, J.F.: "Fool's Gold: Extracting Finite-State Automata from Recurrent Network Dynamics" in *Advances in Neural Information Processing Systems 6* (C.L. Giles, S.J. Hanson, J.D. Cowan Eds.), Morgan-Kaufmann, San Mateo, CA, 1994, 501–508.
7. Casey, M.: "The Dynamics of Discrete-Time Computation with Application to Recurrent Neural Networks and Finite State Machine Extraction" *Neural Computation* (1996), to appear.
8. Blair, A.D., Pollack, J.B.: "Precise Analysis of Dynamical Recognizers". Tech. Rep. CS-95-181, Comput. Sci. Dept., Brandeis Univ. (1996).
9. Elman, J.: "Finding Structure in Time" *Cognitive Science* **14** (1990) 179–211.
10. Castaño, M.A., Casacuberta, F., E. Vidal, E: "Simulation of Stochastic Regular Grammars through Simple Recurrent Networks", in *New Trends in Neural Computation* (J. Mira, J. Cabestany and A. Prieto, Eds.). Lecture Notes in Computer Science **686**, Springer-Verlag, Berlin, 1993, p. 210–215.
11. Carrasco, R.C., Oncina, J.: "Learning Stochastic Regular Grammars by Means of a State Merging Method" in *Grammatical Inference and Applications* (R.C. Carrasco and J. Oncina, Eds.), Lecture Notes in Artificial Intelligence **862**, Springer-Verlag, Berlin, 1994, p. 139–152.
12. Williams, R.J., Zipser, D.: "A learning algorithm for continually running fully recurrent neural networks" *Neural Computation* **1** (1989) 270–280.
13. Forcada, M.L., Carrasco, R.C.: "Learning the Initial State of a Second-Order Recurrent Neural Network during Regular-Language Inference" *Neural Computation* **7** (1995) 923–930.
14. Cover, T.M. and Thomas, J.A.: *Elements of Information Theory*, John Wiley and Sons, New York, 1991.

Maximum Mutual Information and Conditional Maximum Likelihood Estimations of Stochastic Regular Syntax-Directed Translation Schemes *

F. Casacuberta
fcn@iti.upv.es

Departamento de Sistemas Informáticos y Computación
Universidad Politécnica de Valencia
SPAIN

Abstract. Formal translations have become of great interest for modeling some Pattern Recognition problems, but they require a stochastic extension in order to deal with noisy and distorted patterns. A Maximum Likelihood estimation has been recently developed for learning the statistical parameters of Stochastic Regular Syntax-Directed Translation Schemes. The goal of this paper is the study of estimation criteria in order to take into account the problem of sparse training data. In particular, these are the Maximum Mutual Information criterion and the Conditional Maximum Likelihood criterion. Some experimental results are reported to compare the three criteria.

1 Introduction

A translation is a process that maps strings from a given language (input language) to strings from another language (output language). Initially, translations were proposed in Syntactic Pattern Recognition as a framework for a fine presentation of error-correction models [10]. However, this formalism has recently become of great interest as a model in some practical Pattern Recognition problems in which the classification paradigm is not adequate [15], since the number of classes could be large or even infinite. In this case, the most general paradigm of Interpretation seems to be a better framework for problems of this type which can be tackled through formal translations. For example, many tasks in Automatic Speech Recognition can be viewed as simple translations from acoustic sequences to sublexical or lexical sequences (Acoustic-Phonetic Decoding) or from acoustic or lexical sequences to sequences of commands to a data-base management system or to a robot (Semantic Decoding). Other more complex applications of formal transducers are Language Translations (i.e. English to Spanish). Another interest in formal machines for translation comes from the fact that these machines can be learned automatically from examples [13]. In general, however, the application of formal machines to Syntactic Pattern Recognition

---

* Work partially supported by the Spanish CICYT under grant TIC95-0884-C04-01

needs a stochastic extension due to the noisy and distorted patterns under consideration which make the process of interpretation ambiguous [8]. Maximum Likelihood algorithms for automatically learning the statistical parameters of Stochastic Regular Syntax-Directed Translation Schemes from examples have recently been proposed [5]. Under this criterion, for each input string, the learning process only affects the correct output string. Under the Maximum Mutual Information criterion [3] [4], for each pair of strings, the learning process also affects all the output strings which are possible translations of an input string of the training pair as well as all the possible input strings whose translation is the output string of the training pair. Similarly, in the Conditional Maximum Likelihood [12] approach for each pair of strings, the learning process affects all possible output strings which are possible translations of the same input string of the training pair. These criteria can be particulary useful when the training data is sparse. Some experimental results are also reported in order to study the influence of the size of the training data over the percentage of the correctly translated sentences.

2 Stochastic Regular Syntax-Directed Translation Schema

A *Stochastic Regular Syntax-Directed Translation Schema* (SRT) is defined to be a system $T = (N, \Sigma, \Delta, R, S, P)$, where N is a finite set of non-terminal symbols, Σ and Δ are finite sets of input and output terminal symbols, respectively, and $S \in N$ is the starting symbol, R is a set of rules of the form $A \rightarrow aB, zB$ or $A \rightarrow a, z$ for $A, B \in N$ $a \in \Sigma$, $z \in \Delta^*$ and $P : R \rightarrow]0, 1]$ is an assignment of probabilities to the rules such that the sum of the probabilities of all rules for rewriting A is equal to one (proper SRT [10]).

A *translation form* for a *translation* $(x, y) \in \Sigma^* \times \Delta^*$ is a finite length sequence of rules $tf = (r_1, r_2, ..., r_n)$ such that: $tf : (S, S) \overset{*}{\Rightarrow} (x, y)$, where $(S, S) \overset{r_1}{\Rightarrow} (x_1 A_1, y_1 B_1) \overset{r_2}{\Rightarrow} (x_1 x_2 A_2, y_1 y_2 B_2) \overset{r_3}{\Rightarrow} ... \overset{r_n}{\Rightarrow} (x, y)$ and the corresponding probability is

$$Pr(tf|\Phi(P)) = P(r_1)P(r_2)...P(r_n) \tag{1}$$

where $\Phi(P)$ defines the set of statistical parameters related to P.

For a translation form *tf* from *(S,S)* to *(x,y)*, *output(tf)* and *input(tf)* will denote y and x, respectively.

A SRT is *ambiguous*, if for some $(x, y) \in \Sigma^* \times \Delta^*$, there is more than one translation form *tf* such that $tf : (S, S) \overset{*}{\Rightarrow} (x, y)$. In this case, the probability of the translation *(x,y)* is

$$Pr(x, y|\Phi(P)) = \sum_{\forall tf / input(tf) = x \land output(tf) = y} Pr(tf|\Phi(P)) . \tag{2}$$

Alternatively, a Viterbi score for *(x,y)* can be defined as

$$\hat{P}r(x, y|\Phi(P)) = max_{\forall tf/input(tf)=x \wedge output(tf)=y} Pr(tf|\Phi(P)) \ . \tag{3}$$

Given an input string $x \in \Sigma^\star$, the *stochastic translation* (or the *Maximum A Posteriori probability translation* -MAP-) of x by a SRT T is $y \in \Delta^\star$ such that

$$y^* = argmax_{y \in \Delta^*} Pr(y|x, \Phi(P)) \ . \tag{4}$$

According to Bayes' rule, the above expression can be rewritten as:

$$y^* = argmax_{y \in \Delta^*} Pr(x, y|\Phi(P)) \tag{5}$$

since the $Pr(x|\Phi(P))$ does not depend on the index of maximization $\bar{y}$.

As an approximation to (5), the *approximate strochastic translation* is

$$y^{**} = argmax_{y \in \Delta^*} \hat{P}r(x, y|\Phi(P)) \ . \tag{6}$$

The computation of (5) is a **NP**-Hard problem [7]. The only algorithmic solution is the use of some type of **A*** algorithm (i.e. the Stack-Decoding [1]). However, there is a polynomial algorithm for computing (6) that corresponds to the computation of the optimal translation form for a given x, independently of the output y. This computation can be formally presented as:

$$y^{**} = output(argmax_{\forall tf/input(tf)=x} Pr(tf|\Phi(P))) \ . \tag{7}$$

Then, to obtain the maximum of (7), the following algorithm can be used for $x \in \Sigma^\star$:

$$\begin{aligned} t(\lambda, S) &= 1 \\ t(x_1, ..., x_i, A) &= max_{\forall A' \in N \wedge z \in \Delta^*} t(x_1, ..., x_{i-1}, A')P(A' \rightarrow x_i A, zA) \end{aligned} \tag{8}$$

where λ is the empty string.

Finally, from (8)

$$max_{\forall tf/input(tf)=x} Pr(tf|\Phi(P)) = t(x, F) \tag{9}$$

where F is a new non-terminal which is not in N that takes into account rules of the form $A \rightarrow a, z$ which becomes $A \rightarrow aF, zF$, for $a \in S$ and $z \in \Delta^\star$.

The iterative algorithm is $O(|x| \cdot |R|)$. The obtainment of a translation from the optimal translation is straightforward: let $(S \rightarrow x_1 A_1, z_1 A_1)$, $(A_1 \rightarrow x_2 A_2, z_2 A_2)$,..., $(A_{|x|-1} \rightarrow x_{|x|} F, z_{|x|} F)$ be the optimal translation form obtained from (8), the approximate stochastic translation of x is $z_1 z_2 ... z_{|x|}$.

A Maximum Likelihood Estimation (MLE) of the statistical parameter $\Phi(P)$ of SRT was proposed in [5]. The learning algorithm was obtained through the use of rule transformations in a general paradigm of Expectation-Maximization algorithms to maximize [2] [11]:

$$R_{MLE}(\Phi(P)) = \prod_{(x,y) \in TT} Pr(x, y|\Phi(P)) \ . \tag{10}$$

where TT is a *training sample*[2].

---

[2] A *sample* is any finite collection of translations with repetitions allowed (a multiset drawn from $\Sigma^\star \times \Delta^\star$).

3 Maximum Mutual Information Estimation of Stochastic Regular Syntax-Directed Translation Schema

Given $(x, y) \in \Sigma^* \times \Delta^*$, the Mutual Information (MI) between the input string and the output string is

$$I_{\Phi(P)}(x, y) = \log \frac{Pr(x, y|\Phi(P))}{Pr(x|\Phi(P))Pr(y|\Phi(P))} \quad . \tag{11}$$

The Maximum MI Estimation (MMIE) [3] attempts to find a parameter set $\hat{\Phi}(P)$ that maximizes $I_{\Phi(P)}(x, y)$.

The expansions of the terms in the denominator of (11) are

$$Pr(x|\Phi(P)) = \sum_y Pr(x, y|\Phi(P)) \quad Pr(y|\Phi(P)) = \sum_x Pr(x, y|\Phi(P)) \tag{12}$$

In MLE the goal is to increase $Pr(x, y|\Phi(P))$ for a training pair (x, y). However, in MMIE, taking into account (12), the goal is to increase $Pr(x, y|\Phi(P))$ for a training pair (x, y), as well as to decrease $Pr(x, y'|\Phi(P))$ for every output string $y' \neq y$ and to decrease $Pr(x', y|\Phi(P))$ for every input string $x' \neq x$.

When for each output string y there is only one input string x, the MMI criterion is not adequate since the probability $Pr(x, y|\Phi(P)) = Pr(y|\Phi(P))$, and then the maximization of (11) becomes a minimization of $Pr(x|\Phi(P))$.

For a training sample TT, the estimation criterion can be formulated as:

$$R_{MMIE}(\Phi(P)) = \prod_{(x,y) \in TT} \frac{Pr(x, y|\Phi(P))}{Pr(x|\Phi(P))Pr(y|\Phi(P))} \quad . \tag{13}$$

The reestimation formulae can be obtained using gradient descent methods or through an extension of the Growth Transformations proposed by Gopalakrishnan et. al. which enable us to use an iterative Expectation-Maximization-like algorithm for maximizing (13) [11]. Let Q_{TT}^{MMIE} be a transformation from the space of the parameter set $\Phi(P)$ to itself. Then: $\forall (A \to aB, zB) \in R$

$$Q_{TT}^{MMIE}(P(A \to aB, zB)) = \frac{P(A \to aB, zB) \left(\frac{\delta \log R_{MMIE}(\Phi(P))}{\delta P(A \to aB, zB)} + C \right)}{\sum_{a', z', B'} P(A \to a'B', z'B') \left(\frac{\delta \log R_{MMIE}(\Phi(P))}{\delta P(A \to a'B', z'B')} + C \right)} \tag{14}$$

where

$$P(A \to aB, zB) \frac{\delta \log R_{MMIE}(\Phi(P))}{\delta P(A \to aB, zB)} =$$

$$\sum_{(x,y) \in TT} \left(\frac{1}{Pr(x, y|\Phi(P))} P(A \to aB, zB) \frac{\delta Pr(x, y|\Phi(P))}{\delta P(A \to aB, zB)} - \frac{1}{Pr(x|\Phi(P))} P(A \to aB, zB) \frac{\delta Pr(x|\Phi(P))}{\delta P(A \to aB, zB)} - \right.$$

$$\frac{1}{Pr(y|\Phi(P))}P(A \to aB, zB)\frac{\delta Pr(y|\Phi(P))}{\delta P(A \to aB, zB)}\Big)$$

$$(15)$$

and C is an admissible constant [11].

The first term in the sum is proportional to the expected number of times that the rule is used in the training set in the Maximum Likelihood reestimation approach and can be computed as in [5]. The second term is proportional to the expected number of times that the rule of the *input grammar* of T is used for parsing the set of inputs of the training translations. This input grammar is $G_i = (N, \Sigma, R_i, S, P_i)$, where if $(A \to aB, zB) \in R$, then $(A \to aB) \in R_i$ and $P_i(A \to aB) = P(A \to aB, zB)$. The formulae obtained for a MLE with Stochastic Grammars can be used to compute this term [6]. Similarly, the third term is proportional to the the expected number of times that the rule of the *output grammar* of T is used for parsing the set of outputs of the training translations. This grammar is $G_o = (N, \Delta, R_o, S, P_o)$, where if $(A \to aB, zB) \in R$, then $(A \to zB) \in R_o$ and $P_o(A \to zB) = P(A \to aB, zB)$. As for the second term, a simple modification of formulae in [6] can be used to compute the third term.

4 Conditional Maximum Likelihood Estimation of Stochastic Regular Syntax-Directed Translation Schema

The Conditional ML Estimation (CMLE) is based on the search of a parameter set $\hat{\Phi}(P)$ that translates the input of the training translations with minimum error [4]:

$$\forall (x, y) \in TT, Pr(y|x, \hat{\Phi}(P)) \geq Pr(y'|x, \hat{\Phi}(P)) \quad \forall y' \in \Delta^\star . \quad (16)$$

A possible way to achieve this is to maximize *Conditional Likelihood* [12] $Pr(y|x, \Phi(P))$ over $\Phi(P)$, that is:

$$argmax_{\Phi(P)}Pr(y|x, \Phi(P)) = argmax_{\Phi(P)}\frac{Pr(x, y|\Phi(P))}{Pr(x|\Phi(P))} . \quad (17)$$

The CMLE and MAP translation maximize the same function, but the maximization is done over different arguments and using different data [12]. On the other hand, in CMLE the goal is to increase $Pr(x, y|\Phi(P))$ for a training pair (x, y), as well as to decrease $Pr(x, y'|\Phi(P))$ for every output string $y' \neq y$.

From the definition of the MI in (11), the CMLE can be related to MMIE through

$$argmax_{\Phi(P)}Pr(y|x, \Phi(P)) = argmax_{\Phi(P)}\big(I_{\Phi(P)}(x, y) + \log Pr(y|\Phi(P))\big) . \quad (18)$$

In the case that $Pr(y|\Phi)$ does not depend on Φ, the MMIE is the same criterion as CMLE [12]. In the other case, for a training sample TT, this estimation criterion can be formulated as:

$$R_{CMLE}(\Phi(P)) = \prod_{(x,y)\in TT} \frac{Pr(x,y|\Phi(P))}{Pr(x|\Phi(P))} \ . \tag{19}$$

As in the previous section, let Q_{TT}^{CMLE} be a transformation from the space $\Phi(P)$ of the parameter set to itself [11]. Then:

$$Q_{TT}^{CMLE}(P(A \to aB, zB)) = \frac{P(A \to aB, zB)\left(\frac{\delta \log R_{CMLE}(\Phi(P))}{\delta P(A \to aB, zB)} + C\right)}{\sum_{a',z',B'} P(A \to a'B', z'B')\left(\frac{\delta \log R_{CMLE}(\Phi(P))}{\delta P(A \to a'B', z'B')} + C\right)} \tag{20}$$

where

$$P(A \to aB, zB)\frac{\delta \log R_{CMLE}(\Phi(P))}{\delta P(A \to aB, zB)} =$$

$$\sum_{(x,y)\in TT}\left(\frac{1}{Pr(x,y|\Phi(P))}P(A \to aB, zB)\frac{\delta Pr(x,y|\Phi(P))}{\delta P(A \to aB, zB)} - \frac{1}{Pr(x|\Phi(P))}P(A \to aB, zB)\frac{\delta Pr(x|\Phi(P))}{\delta P(A \to aB, zB)}\right)$$

$$\tag{21}$$

and C is an admissible constant [11].

As for MMIE, the first term in the sum is proportional to the expected number of times that the rule is used in the training set in the MLE approach and can be computed as in [5]. The second term is proportional to the expected number of times that the rule of the input grammar of T is used for parsing the set of inputs of the training translations.

5   Experiments

Some experiments were carried out to compare the methods presented here using the MLE proposed in [5]. The selected task was the translation of binary input strings to the corresponding transcription in strings of Spanish orthographic decimal numbers. For example, an input string can be "111" and a possible transcription is "TRES-UNO" ("three-one" in Spanish). This translation is ambiguous because the previous input string could be translated into "UNO-UNO-UNO" ("one-one-one") or into "UNO-TRES" ("one-three") or into "SIETE" ("seven"). The SRT used for generating translation pairs was the one shown in Figure 1.

Three series of training/test data were generated from the SRT of Figure 1. The probability distribution of this SRT was quasi uniform. Each one of the series consisted of training sets of 10, 20, 30, 40, 50, 100, 150, 200 translation pairs (each set is included in the previous one) and an independent test set of 10,000 translation pairs. The training process was performed using the MLE algorithm in [5] and the MMIE and CMLE algorithms proposed in the previous sections.

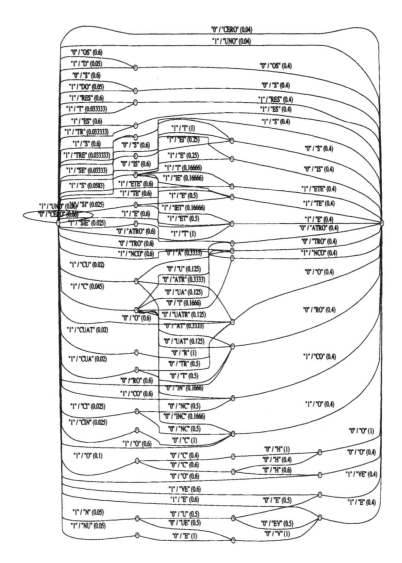

Fig. 1. A Stochastic Regular Syntax-Directed Scheme for generating translation pairs of strings of binary inputs and strings of Spanish orthographic decimal numbers. The number of non-terminal symbols is 40 and the number of rules is 100.

When the reestimation of the probability of a rule was under some specified threshold, the probability of this rule was set to the value of this threshold. The algorithms iterate until the corresponding values of the objective function do not significantly change. For testing, the input of each translation pair of the test data is supplied to the algorithm (8), (9) and (10) and the output of this algorithm is compared to the output of the translation pair. The results are the relative number of times that this comparison is performed successfully (in

Table 1. Experimental results: the size of the training set is presented in the first column ; the number of correctly translated sentences using a MLE approach is presented in the second column (in %) together with the numer of iterations of the training algorithm in parenthesis (iter); the number of correctly translated sentences using a MMIE approach is presented in the third column (in %) when only 5 iterations were run; the number of correctly translated sentences using a CMLE approach is presented in the fourth column (in %) together with the number of iterations of the training algorithm in parenthesis.

Training Set Size	MLE (iterations)	MMIE (iterations)	CMLE (iterations)
10	49,8 (2)	71,3 (5)	66,9 (388)
20	64,2 (2)	71,3 (5)	68,5 (644)
30	68,9 (3)	71,3 (5)	68,7 (446)
40	70,5 (4)	71,3 (5)	70,2 (1389)
50	69,4 (3)	71,2 (5)	70,4 (1604)
100	69,0 (2)	71,3 (5)	68,7 (2475)
150	70,6 (3)	71,3 (5)	71,3 (2469)
200	71,7 (7)	71,3 (5)	71,8 (2200)

Table 2. Perplexity of the test set: the size of the training set is presented in the first column; the perplexity obtained with the test set is presented in columns 2 through 4 for each estimation criterion.

Training Set Size	MLE	MMIE	CMLE
10	1,96	1,12	1,40
20	1,41	1,12	1,34
30	1,21	1,12	1,26
40	1,19	1,12	1,25
50	1,19	1,12	1,21
100	1,13	1,12	1,14
150	1,13	1,12	1,13
200	1,12	1,12	1,11

%). The proposed SRT verifies that, for each output string y, there is only one input string x, therefore the MMIE does not seem adequate and the experiments showed very different results for the three series of training/test data. However, another experiment was performed in which only five iterations were done using the MMIE. This number of iterations was set small heuristically in order not to obtain an excesive decrease of $Pr(x|\Phi(P))$.

The results of the experiments are shown in Table 1 and Table 2. In the first table, The first column corresponds to the size of the training pairs used. The second column corresponds to the results when the MLE was used, and the number of iterations required is in parenthesis. The third column corresponds to the results when the MMIE approach was used and only 5 iterations were allowed. The last column corresponds to the results with the CMLE approach, and the number of iterations required is in parenthesis. All the results are the mean of the corresponding results for each series of training/test data. From this table, it can be observed that the MMIE and CMLE outperform the MLE results until the number of training pairs is 30. After this, only the results with the MMIE approach are better than the MLE results until the number of training pairs is 150. After this, the results are the same. Note that with CMLE the number of iterations required is considerably higher than with the other approaches. In the second table, the perplexity of the test set is presented for new series of training/test data and for each estimation criterion.

6 Concluding Remarks

Stochastic Formal Translation is a powerful framework for dealing with many current problems in Syntactic Pattern Recognition, with the Stochastic Regular Syntax-Directed Schemes being particular cases of such formalisms. Two learning criteria, the Maximum Mutual Information and the Conditional Maximum Likelihood, are proposed in this paper for learning the statistical parameters of such models from training translations. The time complexity of the application of the corresponding formulae are linear with the product of the length of the input and output string of training translations. These two criteria correspond to different ones in the case of Stochastic Regular Syntax-Directed Schemes as opposed to when these criteria are used in the conventional acoustic training of subword models.

One of the main characteristics of these criteria is the influence of the training translations on the rest of the alternative translations (negative training samples) and therefore a more effective use of the training translations is performed. This could be the reason that the experimental results with MMIE and CMLE were better than the ones obtained with MLE when the number of training pairs was small.

Acknowledgements

The author wish to thank the two anonymous reviewers for their criticisms and suggestions, and Dr. North for providing the *"dot"* software [9] used to draw the grammar of Figure 1.

References

1. L.R.Bahl, F.Jelinek, R.L. Mercer: *A Maximum Likelihood Approach to Continuous Speech Recognition.* IEEE Transactions on Pattern Analysis and Machine Intelligence. Vol. 5 (2). pp. 179-196. 1983.

2. L.E.Baum: *An Inequality and Associated Maximization Technique in Statistical Estimation for Probabilistic Functions of Markov Processes.* Inequalities. Vol. 3, pp. 1-8. 1972.

3. P.F. Brown: *The Acoustic-Modeling Problem in Automatic Speech Recognition.* Ph.D. dissertation. Dept. Comput. Sci. Carnegi-Mellon Univ. Pittsburgh, PA. 1987.

4. R.Cardin, Y.Normandin,R.DeMori: *High Performance Connected Digit Recogntion using Maximum Mutual Information Estimation.* IEEE Trans. on Speech and Audio processing. Vol. 2 (2). pp 300-311. 1994.

5. F.Casacuberta : *Probabilistic Estimation of Stochastic Regular Syntax-Directed Translation Schemes* Proc. of the VI Spanish Symposium on Pattern Recognition and Image Analysis. pp. 201-207. 1995

6. F.Casacuberta. *Growth Transformations for Probabilistic Functions of Stochastic Grammars.* International Journal on Pattern Recognition and Artificial Intelligence. Vol. 10. No. 3. 1996.

7. F.Casacuberta, C.de la Higuera *Some Difficult Problems in Pattern Recognition.* To be published. 1996.

8. K.S.Fu: *Syntactic Pattern Recognition and Applications.* Ed. Prentice-Hall. 1982.

9. R. Gansner, E. Koutsofios, S.C. North, K.P. Vo: *A Technique for Drawing Directed Graphs..* IEEE Trans. Software Engineering. March, 1993.

10. R.C.Gonzalez, M.G.Thomason :*Syntactic Pattern Recognition: an Introduction.* Ed. Addison-Wesley. 1978.

11. P.S Goplakrishnan, D.Kanevsky, A.Nadas, D.Nahamoo: *An Inequality for rational Functions with Applications to some Statistical Estimation Problems.* IEEE Trans. Information Theory. Vol. IT-37 (1). pp 107-113. 1991.

12. A.Nadas,D.Hahamoo,M.Picherny: *On a Model-Robust Training Method for Speech Recognition.* Trans. on Acoustic, speech and Signal Processing. Vol. 36 (9), pp 1432-1435. 1988

13. J. Oncina, P. Garcia and E. Vidal: *Learning Subsequential Transducers for Pattern Recognition Interpretation Tasks.* IEEE Transactions on Pattern Analysis and Machine Intelligence, May 1993.

14. L.R. Rabiner. *A Tutorial on Hidden Markov Models and Selected Applications in Speech Recognition.* Proceedings of the IEEE, 77, pp. 257-286, 1989.

15. E.Vidal, F.Casacuberta, P.Garía: *Grammatical Inference and Speech Recognition* in *New Advances and Trends in Speech Recognition and Coding.* NATO ASI Series. pp. 174-191. Springer-Verlag. 1995.

Grammatical Inference Using Tabu Search

Jean-Yves Giordano

Genset
1, rue Robert & Sonia Delaunay
75011 PARIS
e-mail: giordano@genset.fr

Abstract. Grammatical inference is the problem of learning a language from examples and counter-examples of words in this language. The common formulations of this problem make the fundamental hypothesis of the existence of a formal language underlying the data, to be discovered. Here we follow another approach, based on the following remarks. First of all, the initial hypothesis of a formal language to be identified does not hold for real data. Secondly, the algorithmic complexity of language identification is huge, even in the case of the simplest class of languages. Our approach aims at removing these two limitations. It allows the grammars produced to discriminate the sample words imperfectly, while it introduces the use of classic optimization techniques. Here we apply Tabu Search to the inference of regular grammars.

1 Introduction

The problem of grammatical inference is commonly stated as follows (e.g. [Gol67] or [Ang88]): given a language L on X^*, and two sets of strings $I^+ \subseteq L$ and $I^- \subseteq X^* - L$, find a description for L (i.e. a grammar, an automaton or an expression). For the most part, this formalization led to the development of methods that deal with the inference of regular grammars, i.e. the simplest in the Chomsky hierarchy. In conformity with the basic hypothesis of a language to be learnt, these methods aim at producing a grammar or an automaton that describes the strings in I^+ and I^-, that is a grammar or an automaton that accepts every string in I^+ and rejects every string in I^-. In practice, the grammatical inference algorithms have to be adapted in order to fit the nature of the data available in pattern recognition. A first way to palliate the inadequation between the descriptions produced and the data consists in extending the notion of recognized language, by allowing the insertion or deletion of characters in the strings of the language (error-correcting techniques). This technique makes the algorithms more efficient when applied to real data, for one thing because it allows to deal with noise. Another approach is to associate probabilities with the production rules. Several models are based on this idea: inference of stochastic grammars, fuzzy automata and to a certain extent of Markov models. The problem is better stated this way, but it is more complex too, as not only do the rules of the grammar have to be determined but also their associated probability.

However, the basic formulation corresponds to an ideal situation, for one knows that real patterns are not regular or context-free. This remark led us to consider that the point of grammatical inference is less to identify a supposedly existing language than to find a grammar that best discriminates the examples and counter-examples. Given two finite sets of strings I^+ and I^-, the problem comes to optimize the quality of the discrimination the grammar induces on I^+ and I^-.

The descriptions produced are formal grammars as in the classic formulation, but this approach allows more flexibility in the description of the data (e.g. it takes account of atypic examples or badly classified data), and can be combined with the existing mechanisms (particularly the error-correcting techniques).

The methods corresponding to this approach differ from the classic ones. It is *a priori* possible to apply the standard optimization techniques, as well as using the algebraic properties of the class under consideration to build specific methods. Here we study the inference of the simplest class of grammars (regular grammars) using Tabu Search. The tests are run on a typical set of difficult problems, the goal being the production of a grammar that exactly discriminates the examples and counter-examples.

2 Identifying vs. Discriminating

The presentation method for our approach corresponds to the standard situation in inductive learning when two finite sets (positive and negative instances) are given to the system, from which a concept is to be produced.

2.1 Discriminating Finite Samples

The identification of a language from examples and counter-examples can be assimilated to the production of a language that exactly discriminates these sets of strings. Here we relax the identification constraint, allowing the algorithm to produce a solution that imperfectly discriminates the samples:

Given two finite sets of strings I^+ and I^-, and a set E of grammars, find the grammar of E that induces the best discrimination on I^+ and I^-.

The set E of grammars has to be determined in accordance with the aims of the programmer. In the next section we suggest as a general setting that E be restricted to the set of grammars with a bounded number of non terminals, which allows the grammars to realize an inductive leap, and restricts the search to a finite space.

The descriptions produced are formal grammars as in the classic formulations, but this approach allows more flexibility in the description of the data:

- The case of atypic examples is treated correctly. While such an example has an effect on the solution produced by classic methods (since it must be accepted by this solution), an imperfect discrimination treats them explicitly as particular cases, which are excluded from the description. The same remark holds for atypic counter-examples.
- This approach allows dealing with noisy or badly classified data. In practice this case is similar to the previous one.
- Real data often corresponds to complex languages. While identifying such a language is difficult, approximating the language underlying the data with a formal language is a less demanding task. It allows the production of grammars which may not be exact solutions but constitute a better or worse description of the target language, according to the quality of the method. Within this framework, the identification of a language determined in advance can be seen as a limit case, to be used as a validation procedure.

2.2 Necessity of an Inductive leap

Learning a concept from instances means producing a description that discriminates these instances. Now, the set of examples itself constitute such a description (rote learning). In some way, the description must generalize the set of examples, i.e. cover more instances than those presented to the system.

Concerning grammatical inference, a factor that clearly acts on the capacity of a grammar to generalize a set of examples is the number of non terminals of this grammar. At the extremes, a one non terminal grammar generalizes too much in most cases, while a grammar with enough non terminals will learn the examples by rote.

In order to realize an inductive leap we propose to restrain the set of concepts to the set of grammars with a bounded number of non terminals. In practice, the number of non terminals is arbitrary. It allows the programmer to make a compromise between the size of the search space and the performance of the system, in that it limitates the complexity of the grammars produced (this approach could be extended by repeatedly running the search with a growing number of non terminals). Some factors that can intervene in the choice of the number of non terminals are for example the size of the samples, the quality of the discrimination or the complexity of the description required.

Besides, the notion of number of non terminals corresponds to the intuitive notion of structural complexity of a language, and could be related to the MDL principle (*Minimum Description Length*) developed by Rissanen ([Ris89]).

3 Application of Tabu Search to the Inference of Regular Grammars

In the following sections, we apply a classic optimization technique to the inference of regular grammars. The tests are conducted in the case where a grammar exists that discriminates the examples and counter-examples.

3.1 Tabu Search

Tabu Search is a recent optimization technique proposed by F. Glover ([Glo89], [Glo90]). It has been applied to a number of combinatorial problems (traveling salesman problem, graph coloring, graph partitioning, scheduling problems...). One of its advantages is the simplicity and genericity of its basic principle, which by itself often suffices to the development of efficient algorithms. According to the specificities of the application, several auxiliary mechanisms can be implemented. We shall present the mechanisms we chose to implement.

Other techniques could be applied to this problem, such as simulated annealing. The reason we chose Tabu Search is its simplicity and that few parameters have to be tuned in order to get good results.

Background and Notations Let's consider an optimization problem presented in the following form:

$$\text{Maximize } c(x) : x \in X$$

The condition $x \in X$ is assumed to constrain x to discrete values, and c is a function from X in R.

Many optimization methods can be characterized by reference to sequences of *moves* that lead from an hypothesis (an $x \in X$) to another. A move consists of a mapping defined on a subset $X(s)$ of X:

$$s : X(s) \rightarrow X$$

$X(s)$ is the set of elements of X to which s can apply. Conversely, for an element x of X, we note $S(x)$ the set of moves that can apply to x :

$$S(x) = \{s \mid x \in X(s)\}$$

In general, the set of hypotheses is clearly defined (e.g. the set of hamiltonian circuits for a traveling salesman problem). The notion of move corresponds to the neighborhood of an hypothesis. It may vary for a given problem, but in all cases it should maintain part of the hypothesis to which it applies (for a TSP problem it can be the permutation of the ends of two edges). The principle of the optimization methods based on the use of moves is to explore the space in search of a solution. Therefore it is preferable that the search space should be connected, i.e. that for any two hypothesis there exists a sequence of moves leading from one to the other.

Algorithm Tabu Search (TS) can be viewed as an elaboration of the common heuristic known as *hill-climbing*. The principle of this heuristic is to progress from a starting point to a local optimum:

Procedure Hill-climbing

1. Select an initial $x \in X$.
2. While there exists an $s \in S(x)$ such that $c(s(x)) > c(x)$ Do
    a. Select such an s
    b. $x := s(x)$
3. Return x.

Several efficient methods are based on this simple procedure (the simplex method for example), which was used in grammatical inference as early as 1976 ([CRA76], [Tom82]). Its main limitation is that the local optimum obtained at its stopping point may not be a global optimum. The idea of TS is to continue the search, without falling back into a local optimum from which it previously emerged. For this purpose the algorithm maintains a set $T \subset S$ containing a set of tabu moves that may lead back to a solution visited in the past. The algorithm is:

Tabu Search

1. Select an initial $x \in X$.
   Let $x^* := x$ be the best solution reached so far,
   $T := \emptyset$ the Tabu list,
   $k := 0$ the iteration counter and k_{max} the maximum number of iterations.
2. While $S(x) - T \neq \emptyset$ and $k \neq k_{max}$ Do
   a. Select an $s_k \in S(x) - T$ such that $c(s_k(x)) = \max_{s \in S(x) - T} c(s(x))$
   b. $x := s_k(x)$
   c. If $c(x) > c(x^*)$ then $x^* := x$
   d. Update T
   e. $k := k + 1$
3. Return x^*.

The choice of the set T depends on the characteristics of the problem. In general, T is a short term memory containing the reverses of the moves made in the t most recent iterations. This choice is based on the assumption that the likelihood of cycling is inversely related to the distance of the current hypothesis to that previous solution.

It is worth noting that at each step a "best" move is chosen. Indeed, there is no reason to delay the approach to a local optimum since such an optimum does not present a barrier. On the contrary, this allows one to quickly obtain a good solution, and intensify the search in regions where solutions are good.

3.2 Application to Grammatical Inference

In this section we present an application of TS to the inference of regular grammars. First we define the search space, and then the moves that are used. Next the auxiliary mechanisms we implemented are described. In the last section some experiments are conducted on a typical set of languages to be learnt.

Implementation It is preferable that the search space should be finite. Besides, the learning phase must realize an inductive leap, i.e. the examples have to be generalized. As we indicated in section 2.2, these two requirements can be fulfilled by restraining the search to grammars with a fixed number of non terminals.

Bounding the number of non terminals ensures that the inferred grammars realize an inductive leap, if the number of non terminals allowed is small enough. Moreover, if n is the maximal number of non terminals of the grammars, and t is the number of terminals, the number of possible production rules is $tn(n + 1)$ (the rules are under the form $A \rightarrow aB$ and $A \rightarrow a$, where A and B are non terminal symbols and a is a terminal symbol). Thus the number of grammars in the search space is $2^{tn(n+1)}$. For $t = 2$ and $n = 5$, the size of the search space is $2^{60} \approx 10^{18}$, which is reasonable in comparison with the optimization problems to which this type of method has been applied (e.g. the number of hamiltonian circuits for a TSP of 30 towns is around 10^{32}).

We quantify the quality of a discrimination by the correct classification rate the grammar produces on the samples. In order to compensate for the different sizes of the positive and negative samples, the classification rate is taken as the mean of the correct classification rates on the two samples.

The moves are operated by deleting or adding a rule. These operations maintain part of the information present at each step, and realize the connectedness of the search space. Furthermore, they are simple to implement, and the computational cost of an iteration remains low (if n is the number of non terminals and t the number of terminals, only $tn(n + 1)$ grammars have to be examined to determine the next hypothesis). Then our TS algorithm for inferring regular grammars is (d represents the correct classification rate):

Tabu Grammatical Inference

1. Let R be the set of rules of the grammars in the search space,
   G an initial grammar,
   $G^* := G$ the best solution reached so far,
   $T := \emptyset$ the Tabu list of the rules in R that cannot occur in the next transition,
   $k := 0$ the iterations counter and k_{max} the maximum number of iterations.
2. While $k \neq k_{max}$ Do
   a. Select a rule r in $R - T$, such that the deletion of r from G or the addition of r to G realizes the maximum of d on I
   b. Accordingly, delete r from G or add r to G
   c. If $d(G) > d(G^*)$, let $G^* := G$
   d. Update T
   e. $k := k + 1$
3. Return G^*.

T is a queue containing the t last rules that were added or deleted. T is updated in the following way:

Procedure Update(T, r)

1. If $card(T) \leq n$, delete its last element from T.
2. Add r as the first element of T.

Smallest grammars are preferred, in conformity with the principle of Occam's Razor. In the context of inference, Occam's Razor is taken to mean that among competing hypotheses, the simplest is preferable. This general approach has been taken in a number of practical and theoretical settings ([Sol64], [Gol78], [AS83], [LV89]). In the context of grammatical inference, this suggests that we choose grammars with the fewest number of rules. Accordingly, for an equal value of d, deleting a rule is preferred to adding a rule at step 2.a of the algorithm. For the same reason, at step 2.c, if $d(G) = d(G^*)$ and G has less rules than G^* then G is chosen as the best solution found so far.

Auxiliary Mechanisms The performance of the algorithm is increased by applying some of the auxiliary techniques described by Glover. First, we found that the main reason why the optimum is not always reached is the exploration of local optima that constitute strong attractors. Once visited, such optima can be left behind only by an especially strong effort. This problem is not specific to our application, and some mechanisms are proposed in [Glo89] to quickly withdraw from such regions. We chose to delete from the grammars involved the rule that keeps the search in the same region, i.e. the rule that has been present in the grammars for the largest number of iterations. More precisely, if the discrimination achieved has been the same for a number of iterations, the oldest rule is removed from the grammar (this allows to diversify the search, too). Experiments showed that the best results were obtained by fixing the allowed number of iterations to 6.

The second improvement concerns the Tabu list and best solutions obtained so far. The idea is that when such an solution is reached, there is no reason for forbidding the t last moves. Hence, the Tabu list is reinitialized to the empty set such a solution is reached.

Experimental Assessment We carried out an implementation of the algorithm given in the last sections, with the size of T being equal to 7. Other values were tried: we found that too small a list doesn't keep the process from cycling, while a too large list often precludes interesting moves. The number of iterations for each run was fixed to 300.

We considered the case where the sample strings can actually be discriminated by a grammar in the search space. Though this limit case does not illustrate the advantages of our approach (i.e. deal with badly classified data, approximate more complex data with a simple language), this test is significant with regard to the capacity of the algorithm to produce a good discrimination on real data.

The benchmark is composed of fourteen languages used in [Tom82] and [Dup94] :

L_1 : a^*
L_2 : $(ab)^*$
L_3 : any string without an odd number of consecutive a's after an odd number of consecutive b's
L_4 : any string on $\{a, b\}$ without more than two consecutive a's
L_5 : any string with an even number of a's and an even number of b's
L_6 : any string such that the number of a's differs from the number of b's by 0 modulo 3
L_7 : $a^*b^*a^*b^*$
L_8 : a^*b
L_9 : $(a^* + c^*)b$
L_{10} : $(aa)^*(bbb)^*$
L_{11} : any string with an even number of a's and an odd number of b's
L_{12} : $a(aa)^*b$
L_{13} : any string on $\{a, b\}$ with an even number of a's
L_{14} : $(aa)^*ba^*$
L_{15} : $bc^*b + ac^*a$

This test set is considered as "typical" of the regular languages, even though the sizes of the corresponding grammars are small. In particular, the inference of languages L_2, L_3, L_4, L_5 and L_{10} is known as a difficult problem. Indeed, there is no simple expression for them, and the languages met in practical situations are much more simple.

The samples used for each language are random samples used in [Dup94]. The average size of $I^+ \cup I^-$ is about 40. The maximal number of non terminals is fixed to 5. For each language we performed 10 independent runs on each of the 10 samples. In the table below the results are averaged over the 100 runs. The second column corresponds to the number of non terminals of the grammar associated with each language. The average value of $d(I)$ the solution reaches is in the third column. The next two columns indicate the number of iterations needed to find the solution, and the CPU time consumed at this point (in C on a Sparc5 station). The quality of the grammar produced (in the sense that it describes the language underlying the samples) is evaluated by the quality of the discrimination it induces on $\bar{I} = \Sigma^l - I$, where Σ^l is the set of strings in X^* up to a given length l, and $I = I^+ \cup I^-$. The value of $d(\bar{I})$ for $l = 9$ is given in the sixth column. The last column indicates the value of $d(\bar{I})$ obtained with the solution grammar having the fewest number of rules over the 10 runs.

The results are excellent concerning the ability of the system to discriminate the sample strings. Yet, the discrimination induced on $\bar{I}$ is of lesser quality, i.e. the grammar found is less representative of the target language than it is of the samples. Yet, the results are comparable to those obtained with other algorithms concerned with the identification of a language ([OG92], [Dup94]).

	Nt	$d(I)$	k	t(s)	$d(\bar{I})$	best
L_1	1	100.0	49	1	100.0	100.0
L_2	2	100.0	57	1	100.0	100.0
L_3	4	99.8	130	35	84.3	89.6
L_4	3	100.0	120	13	86.6	92.9
L_5	4	98.3	141	9	72.6	84.5
L_6	3	99.9	128	6	80.8	91.5
L_7	4	99.9	144	22	82.2	87.6
L_8	1	100.0	38	1	100.0	100.0
L_9	3	100.0	73	6	99.2	99.2
L_{10}	5	99.0	137	17	92.8	96.5
L_{11}	4	99.1	142	9	75.8	86.3
L_{12}	2	100.0	57	2	100.0	100.0
L_{13}	2	100.0	94	3	89.9	95.5
L_{14}	3	100.0	81	3	90.9	95.2
L_{15}	3	100.0	90	8	97.4	100.0
Mean	-	99.7	99	9	90.2	94.6

4 Conclusion

The approach we chose here is adapted to the nature of the data available in real world problems, and relates to a class of methods specially concerned with combinatorial problems. We have presented a first application of such a method to the inference of regular grammars.

The use of optimization techniques in the field of grammatical inference is recent (except for Hill-Climbing). Few works are concerned with these techniques, and most of them deal with genetic algorithms (e.g. [Dup94] or [Wya94]). The experimental results obtained make this kind of methods attractive. However, the authors aim at identifying a language from the data, and the use of genetic algorithms is justified by their convergence properties. Still, optimization methods do not aim at producing an optimal solution, which is considered to be too costful, but a reasonably good solution.

We consider to develop this work in three directions:

It is possible to have the system produce several "solutions", i.e. grammars that imperfectly discriminate the strings of the samples. Concerning the classification of real data, these solutions can be seen as decision rules, to be integrated into a more general, multi-criteria decision system. More precisely, decision trees could be built, each node of which would correspond to an imperfectly discriminating grammar.

We mentioned in this paper the existing link between the MDL principle and the size of the grammars in the search space. If this factor is clearly linked to Kolmogorov complexity, we feel that a more precise analysis of the connection between the size of the grammars and the statistic notion of stochastic complexity introduced by Rissanen should be useful for a number of practical applications, in particular those that aim at the development of a symbolic classification system.

Most of the works in grammatical inference deal with regular languages, which can only describe simple syntactic structures. Inferring context-free grammars is difficult within the existing formalisms. Still, these grammars allow accounting for more complex structures, such as self-embedding structures that are essential in a number of potential domains of application. We think the approach proposed is an interesting alternative for learning context-free grammars, since it does not hold on the specific properties of the class under consideration.

References

[Ang88] D. Angluin. Queries and concept learning. *Machine Learning*, 2:319–342, 1988.

[AS83]   D. Angluin and C.H. Smith. Inductive inference: Theory and methods. *Computing Surveys*, 15(3):237–269, 1983.

[CRA76] C.M. Cook, A. Rosenfeld, and A.R. Aronson. Grammatical inference by hill-climbing. *Information Sciences*, 10:59–80, 1976.

[Dup94] P. Dupont. Regular grammatical inference from positive and negative samples by genetic search : the gig method. In *Proceedings of the Second International Colloquim on Grammatical Inference*, pages 236–245. Springer-Verlag, 1994.

[Glo89] F. Glover. Tabu search - part i. *ORSA Journal on Computing*, 1(3):190–206, 1989.

[Glo90] F. Glover. Tabu search - part ii. *ORSA Journal on Computing*, 2(1):4–32, 1990.

[Gol67] E.M. Gold. Identification in the limit. *Information and control*, 10:447–474, 1967.

[Gol78] E. M. Gold. Complexity of automaton identification from given data. *Information and Control*, 37:302–320, 1978.

[LV89]   M. Li and P. Vitanyi. Inductive reasoning and kolmogorov complexity. In *Proceedings of the 4th Annual IEEE Conference on Structure in Complexity Theory*. IEEE Computer Society Press, June 1989.

[OG92]   J. Oncina and P. Garcia. Inferring regular languages in polynomial updated time. In *Proceedings of the IVth Spanish Symposium on Pattern Recognition and Image Analysis*, 1992.

[Ris89] J. Rissanen. *Stochastic Complexity in Statistical Inquiry*, volume 15 of *Series in Computer Science*. World Scientific, 1989.

[Sol64] R. J. Solomonoff. A formal theory of inductive inference. *Information and Control*, 7:1–22,224–254, 1964.

[Tom82] M. Tomita. Dynamic construction of finite-automata from examples using hill-climbing. In *Proceedings of the 4th Annual Cognitive Science Conference*, pages 105–108, 1982.

[Wya94] P. Wyard. Representational issues for context-free grammars induction using genetic algorithms. In *Proceedings of the Second International Colloquim on Grammatical Inference*, pages 222–235. Springer-Verlag, 1994.

Using Domain Information During the Learning of a Subsequential Transducer*

Jose Oncina and Miguel Angel Varó**

Departamento de Lenguajes y Sistemas Informáticos
Universidad de Alicante, E-03071 Alicante (Spain)
e-mail: oncina@dlsi.ua.es

Abstract. The recently proposed OSTI algorithm allows for the identification of subsequential functions from input–output pairs. However, if the target is a partial function the convergence is not guaranteed. In this work, we extend the algorithm in order to allow for the identification of any partial subsequential function provided that either a negative sample or a description of the domain by means of a deterministic finite automaton is available.

1 Introduction

The problem of transducer learning has seldom been studied in the literature. Except for the particular restricted approach in Gold's paper [Gold,78], only very limited or heuristic work seems to have been carried out so far [Vel,78] [LRC,84] [Tak,88] [VGS,90].

In 1991 Oncina and collaborators [OGV,93] [OG,91] [Onc,91] presented a first step towards a formalization of the *transducer learning* (TL) problem from the point of view of its applicability within the *interpretation paradigm*. The framework used was similar to that of *grammatical inference* (GI) [Gold,67] [AS,83], though there are important differences between GI and TL. In particular, the work showed important analogies with the so-called *characterizable* methods in GI [AS,83]. [Ang,82] [GV,90].

In this case, the characterizable class is the set of the *subsequential transductions* which is a subclass of the most general *rational* or *finite-state transductions* but properly contains the class of *sequential transductions* [Ber,79]. A *sequential transduction* is defined as the one that preserves the prefixes of input–output strings. Although this can be considered as a rather natural property of transductions, there are many real-world situations where such a strict sequentiality is inadmissible. The class of *subsequential transductions* makes this restriction milder and may therefore be applied in a wider range of practical situations.

---

* This work has been partially supported by the Spanish CICYT under contract TIC93-0633-C02 & TIC95-0984-C02-01

** Miguel A. Varó is supported by a postgraduate grant from the *Generalitat Valenciana* (local government)

In [OGV,93] only subsequential transductions defined by total functions are considered in order to show the identifiability in the limit. It is not difficult to prove that identification in the limit of partial functions from positive samples is equivalent to identification in the limit of regular languages from only positive data, which is not generally possible. Thus, some additional information is necessary in order to achieve identification. In the following we will explore the use of negative information about the input language (*domain*). Another possibility is that a description of the domain is available. The last approach does not seem to be very useful from a practical point of view but sometimes, a good description of the domain language can be obtained by inferring an automaton from the input part of the training set [GOV,90]. In such a case, we do not have an exact description of the domain as required for identification in the limit but, as shown by some experimental results [Varó,94] [OCVJ,94] [CGV,94], it accelerates learning and, more importantly, it reduces the error rate. Therefore, this may also be seen as a way to introduce heuristic information in the inference algorithm.

2 Mathematical background and notation

Let X be a finite set or *alphabet*, and X^* the set of all strings over X. The *set of prefixes* of a string x is denoted as $\Pr(x)$, and can be extended as $\Pr(L) = \bigcup_{x \in L} \Pr(L)$. The *right quotient* of u and v is $u^{-1}v = w$ such that $v = uw$. The symbol $\oplus$ denotes symmetric difference. A *language* L is any subset of X^*. The *longest common prefix* of a language L is denoted as $\operatorname{lcp}(L)$.

A *finite automaton* (FA) A is defined by a 5-tuple (Q, X, δ, q_0, F) where Q is a finite set of *states*, q_0 is the *initial* state, $F \subseteq Q$ is the set of *accepting* states and $\delta : Q \times X \to 2^Q$ is a partial function. A FA is deterministic (DFA) if $\forall q \in Q$ and $\forall a \in X, \delta(q, a)$ has at most one element. With a DFA this function can be extended as $\delta : Q \times X^* \to Q$, where $\forall q \in Q, \delta(q, \lambda) = q$ and $\delta(q, xa) = \delta(\delta(q, x), a)$.

A *transduction* from X^* to Y^* is a relation $t \subseteq (X^* \times Y^*)$. In what follows, only those transductions which are (partial) *functions* from X^* to Y^* will be considered. It will be assumed that $t(\lambda) = \lambda$. For a partial function $t : X^* \to Y^*$, the *domain* of the function is $\operatorname{Dom}(t) = \{x | (x, y) \in t\}$. The domain function can be extended as $\forall u \in X^*, \operatorname{Dom}_t(u) = \{x | (ux, y) \in t\}$, then $\operatorname{Dom}(t) = \operatorname{Dom}_t(\lambda)$.

A *sequential transducer* is defined as a 5-tuple $\tau = (Q, X, Y, q_0, E)$, where Q is a finite set of *states*, $q_0 \in Q$ is the *initial state*, X is the input alphabet, Y is the output alphabet and E is a finite subset of $(Q \times X \times Y^* \times Q)$ whose elements are called *edges*.

A *path* in a sequential transducer τ is a sequence of edges $\pi = (q_0, x_1, y_1, q_1)$ $(q_1, x_2, y_2, q_2) \ldots (q_{n-1}, x_n, y_n, q_n), q_i \in Q, x_i \in X, y_i \in Y^*, 1 \le i \le n$, denoted also as $\pi = (q_0, x_1 x_2 \ldots x_n, y_1 y_2 \ldots y_n, q_n)$. Let $\prod_\tau$ be the set of all possible paths over τ. The transduction realized by a sequential transducer τ is the partial function $t : X^* \to Y^*$ defined as $t(x) = y$ iff $\exists (q_0, x, y, q) \in \prod_\tau$.

A *subsequential transducer* is defined as a 6-tuple $\tau = (Q, X, Y, q_0, E, \sigma)$, where $\tau' = (Q, X, Y, q_0, E)$ is a sequential transducer and $\sigma : Q \to Y^*$ is a (partial) function assigning output strings to the states of τ'. The partial function $t : X^* \to Y^*$ that is realized by τ is defined as $t(x) = y\sigma(q)$ iff $\sigma(q)$ is defined and $(q_0, x, y, q) \in \prod_{\tau'}$. The class of subsequential functions properly contains the class of sequential functions. It can be easily shown that if t is a subsequential function then $\text{Dom}(t)$ is a regular language.

By using an additional input symbol $\# \notin X$ to mark the end of the input strings, any subsequential transduction $t : X^* \to Y^*$ can be obtained as a restriction to $X^*\#$ of a sequential transduction $t' : (X \cup \{\#\})^* \to Y^*$, so that, $\forall x \in X^*$ $t(x) = t'(x\#)$ [Ber,79]. In what follows the term *subsequential transducer* will be used, at convenience, either to denote a subsequential transducer as defined by $(Q, X, Y, q_0, E, \sigma)$, or a sequential representation.

An *onward subsequential transducer* (OST) is one in which the output strings are assigned to the edges in such a way that they are as *close* to the initial state as possible. Formally, a subsequential transducer $\tau' = (Q, X, Y, q_0, E, \sigma)$ is an OST if $\forall p \in Q - \{q_0\}$ $\text{lcp}(\{y \in Y^* | (p, a, y, q) \in E\} \cup \{\sigma(p)\}) = \lambda$. For any subsequential transduction there exists a *canonical OST* which has a minimum number of states and is unique up to isomorphism [OG,91]. This transducer is obtained through the following construction:

Let $t : X^* \to Y^*$ be a partial function and let $x \in \text{Pr}(\text{Dom}(t))$. The *set of tails* of x in t is $T_t(x) = \{(y, v) | t(xy) = uv, u = \text{lcp}(t(xX^*))\}$ with $T_t(x) = \emptyset$ if $x \notin \text{Pr}(\text{Dom}(t))$.

It can be seen [OG,91] that, if t is subsequential, the number of different sets of tails in t is finite. Therefore, these sets can be used to build a subsequential transducer $\tau(t) = (Q, X, Y, q_0, E, \sigma)$ as follows:

$$Q = \{T_t(x) | x \in \text{Pr}(\text{Dom}(t))\}, \quad q_0 = T_t(\lambda)$$

$$E = \{(T_t(x), a, \text{lcp}(t(xX^*))^{-1}\text{lcp}(t(xaX^*)), T_t(xa) | T_t(x), T_t(xa) \in Q\}$$

$$\sigma(T_t(x)) = \text{lcp}(t(xX^*))^{-1}t(x) \text{ if } x \in \text{Dom}(t), \text{undefined otherwise}$$

Following, [Gold,67] and [AS,83], an appropriate framework for the transducer learning problem can be established as follows: Let $f : X^* \to Y^*$ be a partial recursive function; a transducer learning algorithm A is said to *identify f in the limit* if, for any (positive) presentation of the input–output pairs of f, A converges to a transducer τ that realizes a function $g : X^* \to Y^*$ such that $\forall x \in \text{Dom}(f), g(x) = f(x)$.

3   The transducer learning algorithm

The OSTI algorithm requires a finite sample of input–output pairs $T \subset (X^* \times Y^*)$, which is assumed to be non-ambiguous or *single-valued*; i.e., $(x, y), (x, y') \in T \Rightarrow y = y'$. Such a sample can be properly represented by a *tree subsequential transducer* (TST) $\tau = (Q, X, Y, q_0, E, \sigma)$, with $Q = \cup_{(u,v) \in T} \text{Pr}(u)$, $q_0 = \lambda$, $E = \{(w, a, \lambda, wa) | w, wa \in Q\}$, $\sigma(u) = v$ if $(u, v) \in T$ and being undefined otherwise. This kind of TST is said to be *consistent* with T.

A possible sequential representation, τ', of this TST can be obtained by eliminating σ from τ and extending its set of states and edges as follows:

$$Q' = Q \cup \{u\#|(u,v) \in T\}; E' = E \cup \{(u,\#,v,u\#)|(u,v) \in T\}$$

Whenever such a sequential representation is used, the training pairs (u,v) will be written as $(u\#,v)$.

Given T, an *onward tree subsequential transducer* representing T, OTST(T), can be obtained by building an OST equivalent to the TST of T. This can be accomplished through the following construction (directly given for a sequentially represented TST $\tau' = (Q', X \cup \{\#\}, Y, q_0, E')$): $\forall q \in Q'$, if $w = \mathrm{lcp}\{v \in Y^*|(q,a,v,r) \in E'\} \wedge w \neq \lambda$ **then** : **1:** substitute every outgoing edge of q: (q,a,wz,r) by (q,a,z,r); **2:** substitute every ingoing edge of q: (q,b,y,q) by (p,b,yw,q).

The OSTI algorithm consists of a non-incremental procedure that starts building the OTST(T), $\tau = (Q, X \cup \{\#\}, Y, q_0, E)$, and then proceeds by orderly trying to merge states of τ. This state merging may result in transducers which are not subsequential. In particular they may often violate the condition of *determinism*: $(q,a,u,r),(q,a,v,s) \in E \Rightarrow (u = v \wedge r = s)$. In these cases, we may still insist to preserve the sequential nature of the resulting transducers. For this to be possible, some output (sub)strings associated to the edges of τ often need to be *pushed back* towards the leaves of τ in a process which, to a limited extent, reverses the forward (sub)string displacements carried out to transform the initial TST associated to T into τ. The test as to whether a transducer τ is subsequential is assumed to be supplied by a (hypothetical) procedure *subseq* that takes a transducer and outputs *true* if such a property holds, or *false* otherwise.

The merging process mentioned above requires the states of τ to be successively taken into account in a *lexicographic order* of the names given to these states through the TST construction. Let "$<$" be such an order on Q, with first(τ) and last(τ) being the first and last states with respect to "$<$", and $\forall q \in Q - \{last(\tau)\}$ let next(τ, q) denote the state which immediately follows q in the order "$<$". The merging of any two states $q', q \in Q$, with $q' < q$, results in a new transducer $\tau' = (Q', X \cup \{\#\}, Y, q_0, E')$ in which the state q no longer exists in Q' and all the outgoing edges of q in E are assigned to q' in E'. Let $\tau' = \mathrm{merge}(\tau, q', q)$ represent this merging operation which is quite similar to the merging of states in finite-state automata [Ang,82].

The process of *pushing back* output substrings in a transducer $\tau = (Q, X \cup \{\#\}, Y, q_0, E)$ requires some more detailed explanation. Let $q \in Q$ be a state of τ and $(q', a, w, q) \in E$ (one of) its ingoing edge(s). If $u \in Y^*$ is a prefix of w, then the suffix $v = u^{-1}w$ can be *pushed back* to a state behind q and distributed throughout all the outgoing edges of q to produce another transducer $\tau' = (Q, X \cup \{\#\}, Y, q_0, E')$ as follows:

$$E' = (E - \{(q',a,uv,q)\}) \cup \{(q',a,u,q)\} \cup \{(q,b,vz,r) : (q,b,z,r) \in E\}$$

Let $\tau' = \mathrm{push\_back}(\tau, v, (q', a, uv, q))$ denote this operation, for which the following *equivalence property* can be easily established [OG,91]: if $v = \lambda$ or if

(q', a, w, q) is the *only* edge that enters q, then transduction are preserved and the transducer τ' is *equivalent* to τ.

```
01 Algorithm OSTIA // Onward subsequential transducer algorithm
02       INPUT: Single-valued finite set of input–output pairs T ⊂ (X* # × Y*)
03       OUTPUT: Onward subsequential transducer τ consistent with T
04       τ := OTST(T)
05       q := first(τ)
06       while q < last(τ) do
07          q := next(τ, q); p := first(τ)
08          while p < q do
09             τ' := τ
10             τ := merge(τ, p, q)
11             while ¬ subseq(τ) do
12                let (r, a, v, s), (r, a, w, t) be two edges that violate the subseq condition, with s < t
13                if ((v ≠ w) and (a = #)) or (s < q and v ∉ Pr(w)) then exit while
14                u := lcp(v, w)
15                τ := push_back(τ, u⁻¹v, (r, a, v, s))
16                τ := push_back(τ, u⁻¹v, (r, a, w, t))
17                τ := merge(τ, s, t)
18             end while // ¬ subseq(τ) //
19             if ¬subseq(τ) then τ := τ' else exit while
20             p := next(τ, p)
21          end while // p < q //
22       end while // q < last(τ) //
23 end // OSTIA //
```

Fig. 1. The transducer inference algorithm

The algorithm that performs the procedures outlined above is called *Onward Subsequential Inference Algorithm* (OSTIA) and is formally presented in Figure 1.

4 Identification of partial subsequential functions

The proof that OSTIA can identify the class of the *total* subsequential functions from positive data (input–output pairs) in the limit starts defining a *finite representative sample* T of a total subsequential function t. It can be shown that the transducer $OTST(T)$ contains a subset of states, referred to as *kernel*, which induces a subtree in $OTST(T)$ that contains representations of all the edges of the canonical OST of t, $\tau(t)$, and only these edges. This result allows us to establish that, if a representative sample is contained in the input to OSTIA, then the output will be the canonical OST of the function t. Given that any positive presentation of t will eventually include a representative sample, the property of the *identification in the limit* will result [OG,91].

Definition 1. Let $t : X^* \to Y^*$ be a subsequential function. The string w is a *short prefix* of t iff $w \in \mathrm{Pr}(\mathrm{Dom}(t))$ and $\forall v \in X^*(T_t(w) = T_t(v) \Rightarrow v \geq w)$. The *set of short prefixes* of t, $SP(t)$, includes a short prefix for every different tail in $\{T_t(w) | w \in \mathrm{Pr}(\mathrm{Dom}(t))\}$.

Definition 2. Let $t : X^* \to Y^*$ be a subsequential function. The *kernel* of t is the set: $K(t) = (SP(t)X \cap \mathrm{Pr}(\mathrm{Dom}(t))) \cup \{\lambda\}$.

In other words, $K(t)$ contains the empty string along with the extensions of all of the strings in $SP(t)$ with all symbols in X, as long as these extensions are prefixes of the strings in the domain of t.

Definition 3. Given a *total* subsequential function $t : X^* \to Y^*$, a *sample* T of t is said to be *representative* of t iff:

1. $\forall u \in K(t) \; \exists (uv, w) \in T \mid v \in X^*, w \in Y^*$
2. $\forall u \in SP(t) \; \forall v \in K(t) \; (T_t(u) \neq T_t(v) \Rightarrow \exists (uw, u'w'), (vw, v'w'') \in T \mid (w, w') \in T_t(u), (w, w'') \in T_t(v), w' \neq w'')$
3. $\forall u \in K(t) \exists (uv, u'v'), (uw, u'w') \in T \mid (v, v'), (w, w') \in T_t(u), \mathrm{lcp}(\{v', w'\}) = \lambda$

Condition 1 will guarantee that all the states and *transitions* of the canonical OST $\tau(t)$ are represented in $\mathrm{OTST}(T)$. Condition 2 distinguishes those states of $\mathrm{OTST}(T)$ for which the corresponding states of $\tau(t)$ are different. Finally, condition 3 will make it possible that, for every state of $\mathrm{OTST}(T)$ which is reachable by a string in the *kernel* of t, the edges will be identical to the corresponding edges in $\tau(t)$.

For total functions, a representative set can always be found. In particular, a set that fulfills condition 2 can be found because $\forall u \in X^*$, $\mathrm{Dom}(u) = X^*$ and then, if $T_t(u) \neq T_t(v)$ is because $\exists w \in X^*$ such that $(w, w') \in T_t(u), (w, w'') \in T_t(v)$ but $w' \neq w''$.

For partial functions, a set that fulfills conditions 1 and 3 can always be found. However, there exist transducers for which it is impossible to find a set that fulfills condition 2). For a partial function, $(T_t(u))$ can be different from $T_t(v)$ but $\forall w \in \mathrm{Dom}(u) \cap \mathrm{Dom}(v)(w, w') \in T_t(u) \Leftrightarrow (w, w') \in T_t(v)$, just because $\exists w \in \mathrm{Dom}(u)$ such that $w \notin \mathrm{Dom}(v)$ or vice versa. In such a case, we will say that the two states are not *distinguishable by any transduction*.

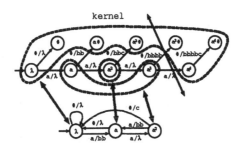

Fig. 2. *Relation between the states of the canonical OST and the OTST of the sample of the example 1.*

Example 1: Let $t : \{a\}^* \to \{b, c\}^*$ be a total subsequential function defined by: $t(a^n) = \lambda$ if $n = 0$, b^{n+1} if n is odd and $b^n c$ if n is even, and let $T = (\lambda, \lambda), (a, bb), (aa, bbc), (aaa, bbbb), (aaaa, bbbbc)$ be a sample drawn from t.

Then, all the different states of the kernel are distinguishable by the training T (fig. 2). In this case the kernel is $K(t) = \{\lambda, a, aa, aaa\}$, as $\{(\lambda, \lambda), (a, bb)\} \subset T_{OTST}(\lambda)$, $\{(a, c)\} \subset T_{OTST}(a)$ and $\{(\lambda, c), (a, bb)\} \subset T_{OTST}(aa)$ these three states are distinguishable. States λ and aaa are not distinguishable, but as they represent the same state, no training set can be found that forces the distinguishability of both. Moreover, all the edges of the canonical OST of t are represented on the OTST made with T.

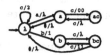

Fig. 3. *Transducer with states (a and b) not distinguishable by any transduction.*

Example 2: Let $t : \{a, b, c\}^* \to \{0, 1, 2\}^*$ the partial subsequential function (fig. 3) defined by: $t(x) = \lambda$ if $x = \lambda$, $2^m 0^{2n}$ if $x = c^m a c^{2n}$, $2^m 1^{2n+1}$ if $x = c^m b x^{2n+1}$, and $\emptyset$ otherwise. Then as $T_t(a) = \{(c^{2n}, 0^{2n})\}$ and $T_t(b) = \{(c^{2n+1}, 1^{2n})\}$ no training pair can exist that allow the distinguibishality of both.

If a method for distinguishing such states can be found then the same technique used for the proof of the convergence in the limit of OSTIA can be used. Obviously, for distinguishing such states additional information must be used. In the following sections we will explore the possibilities offered by the use of negative samples or the knowledge of the domain.

5 Identification using negative information

As we have seen before, on a partial function, $T_t(u)$ can be different from $T_t(v)$ but $\forall w \in \text{Dom}(u) \cap \text{Dom}(v)(w, w') \in T_t(u) \Leftrightarrow (w, w') \in T_t(v)$, just because $\exists w \in \text{Dom}(u)$ such that $w \notin \text{Dom}(v)$ or vice versa.

Such states can be distinguished if we have information about strings not belonging to the domain, i.e. if we know that $vw \notin \text{Dom}(t)$ and $(uw, u'w') \in t$ then the states $T_t(u)$ and $T_t(v)$ must be different.

Definition 4. $S_- \in X^*$ is a negative sample of the partial function $f : X^* \to Y^*$ if $S_- \subset X^* - \text{Dom}(f)$.

Then, for partial subsequential functions the representative sample must be defined as follows.

Definition 5. Given a *partial* subsequential function $t : X^* \to Y^*$, the pair (T, S_-) is said to be *representative* of t iff:

1. $\forall u \in K(t) \, \exists(uv, w) \in T \mid v \in X^*, w \in Y^*$
2. $\forall u \in SP(t) \, \forall v \in K(t)$ such that $T_t(u) \neq T_t(v) \Rightarrow$
   $(\exists(uw, u'w'), (vw, v'w'') \in T | (w, w') \in T_t(u), (w, w'') \in T_t(v), w' \neq w'') \lor$
   $(\exists uw \in S_-, (vw, v'w') \in T | w \in \text{Dom}(v) - \text{Dom}(u), (w, w') \in T_t(v)) \lor$
   $(\exists vw \in S_-, (uw, u'w') \in T | w \in \text{Dom}(u) - \text{Dom}(v), (w, w') \in T_t(u))$

3. $\forall u \in K(t) \exists (uv, u'v'), (uw, u'w') \in T | (v, v'), (w, w') \in T_t(u), \mathrm{lcp}(\{v', w'\}) = \lambda$

This representative sample ensures that all the states of the kernel that represent different states of the (partial) subsequential function can be distinguished.

The original algorithm can be modified in such a way that the rejection of the negative sample is checked every time that a successful block of merges is performed (line 19 in fig. 1). This new **if** condition will be "$\neg subseq(\tau)$ or $S_- \cap \mathrm{Dom}(\tau) \neq \emptyset$", so the new transducer is checked before accepting it. The new transducer adds a new input parameter: a finite set of input strings, S_-, not belonging to the domain.

Example 3: Let t the partial subsequential function defined in example 2. Let $T = \{(a, \lambda), (acc, 00), (acccc, 0000), (bc, 1), (c, 2)\}$ a sample drawn from this function and $S_- = \{ac\}$ a negative sample of the domain.

The algorithm begins building the OTST of the training sample (fig. 4.a). Next, the algorithm, attempts to merge states λ and a (fig. 4.b). This transducer has two edges $(\lambda, c, 2, c)$ and $(\lambda, c, 00, ac)$ which violate the *subseq* condition. Given that $c \neq \#$ and $c > a$ then c is pushed back through the two edges and the states c and ac are merged (fig. 4.c). The rejection of the negative sample must be checked now. As $\tau(ac) = 2$ then $S_- \cap \mathrm{Dom}(\tau) \neq \emptyset$ and the algorithm returns to the fig. 4.a transducer. Next, it tries to merge states λ and b, but then the edges (λ, c, s, c) and $(\lambda, c, \lambda, bc)$ violate the *subseq* condition. Now, the **if** condition does not fulfill, the inner most loop is exited and the algorithm goes back to the transducer of fig. 4.a. After merging the states a and b, (fig. 4.d) and all the subsequent *push_back* and merge operations, the subsequential transducer of fig. 4.e is obtained. As $ac \in \mathrm{Dom}(\tau)$ it must be rejected and the fig. 4.a transducer is recovered. The next two merges (λ with c and λ with $a\#$) can be performed without problems and the fig. 4.f transducer is obtained. Following the algorithm the next successful merges are: λ with $c\#$ (fig. 4.g), a with acc (fig. 4.h), λ with bc (fig. 4.i) and b with bcc (fig. 4.j) which yields the transducer inferred from the training sample.

6   Identification using domain information

In real transductions tasks it is unusual to have negative samples. Instead, sometimes a description of the domain is available or can be inferred from the input strings of the transduction sample.

First, we will show now that if the language that describes the domain is known, then all the different states of the OST that realizes any subsequential function can be distinguished and hence the identification in the limit can be proved. As the domain language of a subsequential function is regular, we can assume that the minimum DFA that describes this language is available (D). Let u, v be two non-distinguishable states from the transduction. If $T_t(u) \neq T_t(v)$ such that $\exists w \in \mathrm{Dom}_t(u) \oplus \mathrm{Dom}_t(v)$, then, as D is the minimum DFA describing the domain language, $T_D(u) \neq T_D(v)$ and $\delta_D(q_0, u) \neq \delta_D(q_0, v)$.

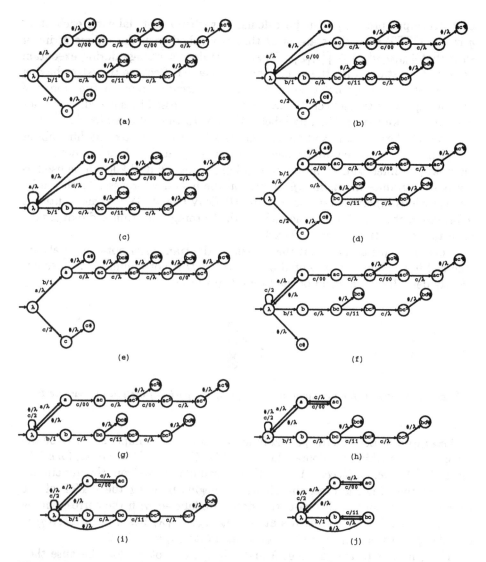

Fig. 4. *Some key steps of the OSTIA-N algorithm as applied to the training set* $T = \{(a, \lambda), (acc, 00), (acccc, 0000), (bc, 1), (bccc, 111), (c, 2)\}$ *and with* $S_- = \{ac\}$

Therefore, if the merge of two states u, v such that $\delta_D(q_0, u) \neq \delta_D(q_0, v)$ is forbidden in the algorithm, the merge of states that are not distinguishable by the transduction can be avoided and then the identification can be reached. The new OSTI algorithm adds a new input parameter (the DFA modeling the domain language, D) and a condition before trying to merge a pair of states (from line 9 to line 19 in fig. 1): "**if** $\delta_D(q_0, \text{input\_prefix}(p)) \neq \delta_D(q_0, \text{input\_prefix}(q))$ **then**".

In this algorithm the function input_prefix$(q) : Q \to X^*$ is introduced, this functions returns the shortest string u such that $(q_0, u, u', q) \in \prod_\tau$. The result of $\delta_D(q_0, \text{input\_prefix}(p))$ can be calculated with no cost, labeling each state q of the OTST with the state of D that is reached with the unique string u such that $(q_0, u, u', q) \in \prod_{\text{OTST}}$. These labels do not change during execution because only states with the same label are merged. Because the edges having $\#$ as input symbol are not true edges but a representation of the function σ of the subsequential transducer, the labels of states accessed by such edges are not relevant and we have arbitrarily labeled them with the initial state of D.

On the other hand, in spite of it is not possible to guarantee anything about the identification in the limit when the language that describes the domain is unknown, an inferred description of it [Mic,80] [Ang,82] [GV,90] can be used as a way to introduce *heuristic information* in the inference process. As shown by some previous experimental results [Varó,94] [OCVJ,94] [CGV,94] this additional information about the domain accelerates the learning algorithm and reduces the error rate of the transducers inferred.

This technique ensures that the domain of the transducer obtained is always included in the language accepted by D, even if D is not minimum or does not exactly describe the domain of the target transducer.

Fig. 5. *Automaton for the domain language of the partial function of example 2.*

Example 4: Let t be the partial function defined in example 2. Let D be the automaton describing the domain language (fig. 5) and let $T = \{(a, \lambda), (acc, 00), (accc, 0000), (bc, 1), (bccc, 111), (c, 2)\}$ be a sample drawn from this function.

As in the previous case, the algorithm begins building the OTST of the training sample, but in this case, the states are labeled with the corresponding state of D (fig 6.a). Then, each state $q \in Q_{\text{OTST}} - \{\lambda\}$ has a label $label(q) = \delta_D(label(p), a)$ where $(p, a, x, q) \in E_{\text{OTST}}$ and $label(\lambda) = \lambda$ (fig 6.a).

Then, it tries to merge states λ and a but it cannot be done because they have different labels. Following lexicographic order, the next pair of states with identical labels is λ and c. They can be merged and the transducer of fig. 6.b is obtained. After merging states λ and $a\#$ the fig. 6.c transducer is obtained. Next, the algorithm, tries to merge the states b and ac (fig. 6.d). As the resulting transducer is not subsequential the inner loop will try to transform it in a subsequential one by pushing back symbols and merging states. At the end the transducer in fig. 6.e is obtained. This transducer does not fulfills the **if** condition in the inner most loop. Therefore, the transducer is rejected and the transducer in fig. 6.c is recovered.

Following the algorithm, the next successful merges are: λ with $c\#$ (fig. 6.f), a with abb (fig. 6.g), λ with bc (fig. 6.h) and b with bcc (fig. 6.i) which yields the transducer inferred from the training sample.

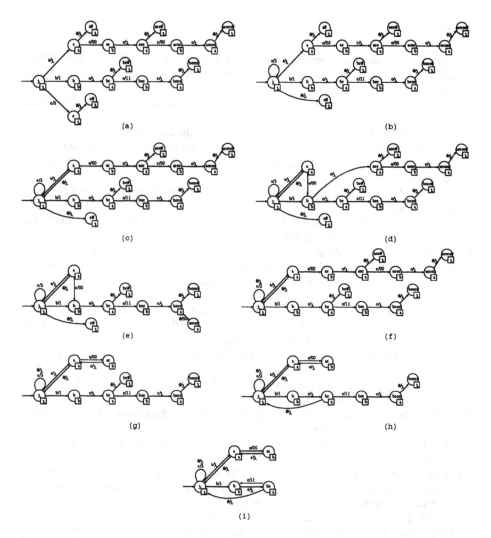

Fig. 6. *Some key step of the OSTIA-D as applied to the training set*
$T = \{(a, \lambda), (acc, 00), (acccc, 0000), (bc, 1), (bccc, 111), (c, 2)\}$

7 Discussions and conclusions

In this work the OSTI algorithm has been extended to allow the identifiability in the limit of any partial subsequential function by using input–output pairs plus some additional information in the form of either negative examples of the domain or a description of the domain by means of a DFA. The techniques presented here are not mutually exclusive and can be used together if necessary.

In addition to the theoretical interest, these methods can be used to introduce heuristic information and help the basic OSTI algorithm even when not enough input–output pairs are available.

References

[Ang,82] D. Angluin, "Inference of Reversible Languages". *J. ACM* 29, 741–765 (1982).

[AS,83] D. Angluin, C. H. Smith. "Inductive inference: theory and methods". *Computing Surveys*, 15, 237–269 (1983).

[Ber,79] J. Berstel. *Transductions and Context-Free Languages*. Teubner, Stuttgart (1979).

[CGV,94] A. Castellanos, I. Galiano, E. Vidal. "Application of OSTIA to Machine translation Tasks". *Grammatical Inference and Applications*. 2nd International Colloquium on Grammatical Inference. R.C. Carrasco and J. Oncina eds. El Campello (Spain) (1994).

[Gold,67] E. M. Gold. "Language identification in the limit". *Information and Control*, 10, 447–474 (1967).

[Gold,78] E. M. Gold. "Complexity of automaton identification from given data". *Information and Control*, 37, 302–320 (1978).

[GOV,90] P. García, E. Vidal, J. Oncina. "Learning Locally Testable Languages in the Strict Sense", *Proceedings of the First International Workshop on Algorithmic Learning Theory*, Japanese Society for Artificial Intelligence, 325–337 (October 1990).

[GV,90] P. García, E. Vidal. "Inference of k-Testable Languages in the Strict Sense and application to Syntactic Pattern Recognition". *IEEE Trans. Pattern Analysis and Machine Intelligence*, 12, 920–925 (1990).

[LRC,84] P. Luneau, M. Richetin, C. Cayla. "Sequential learning from input–output behavior", *Robotica*, 1, 151–159 (1984).

[Mic,80] L. Miclet. "Regular Inference with a Tail-Clustering Method", *IEEE Trans.*, SMC-10, 737–743 (1980).

[Onc,91] J. Oncina. "Aprendizaje de lenguajes regulares y funciones subsecuenciales". Ph. D. dissertation, Universidad Politécnica de Valencia (1991).

[OG,91] J. Oncina, P. García. "Inductive learning of subsequential functions". Univ. Politécnica de Valencia, Tech. Rep. DSIC II 31 (1991).

[OGV,93] J. Oncina, P. García, E. Vidal. "Learning Subsequential Transducers for Pattern Recognition Interpretation Tasks". *IEEE Trans. on Pattern Analysis and Machine Intelligence*, 15, 448–458 (1993).

[OCVJ,94] J. Oncina, A. Castellanos, E. Vidal, V. M. Jiménez. "Corpus based machine translation through subsequential transducers". Proceedings of the *3rd. International Conference on the Cognitive Science of Natural Language Processing*, Dublin (July 1994).

[Tak,88] Y. Takada, "Grammatical inference for even linear languages based on control sets", *Inform. Processing Lett.*, 28, no.4, 193–199 (1988).

[Varó,94] M. A. Varó. "Inferencia de Transductores Subsecuenciales con Información de Dominio y Rango" (in Spanish). Final year project supervised by J. Oncina. Facultad de Informática, Universidad Politécnica de Valencia (1994).

[Vel,78] L. P. J. Velenturf. "Inference of sequential machines from sample computation", *IEEE Trans. Comput.*, 27, 167–170 (1978).

[VGS,90] E. Vidal, P. García, E. Segarra, "Inductive learning of finte-state transducers for the interpretation of unidimensional objects", *Structural Pattern Analysis*. R. Mohr, T.Pavlidis and A. San Feliu eds. New York: World Scientific, 17–35 (1990).

Identification of *DFA*:
Data-Dependent Versus Data-Independent
Algorithms

C. de la Higuera
LIRMM,
161 rue Ada,
34 392 Montpellier
Cedex 5, France.
http://www.lirmm.fr/~cdlh

J. Oncina
Dpto. Lenguajes y
Sistemas Informáticos
Universidad de Alicante,
E-03071 Alicante, Spain.
joncina@dlsi.ua.es

E. Vidal
Dpto. Sistemas Informáticos
y Computación, Universidad
Politécnica de Valencia
46071 Valencia, Spain.
evidal@iti.upv.es

Abstract.

Algorithms that infer deterministic finite automata from given data and that comply with the identification in the limit condition have been thoroughly tested and are in practice often preferred to elaborate heuristics. Even if there is no guarantee of identification from the available data, the existence of associated characteristic sets means that these algorithms converge towards the correct solution. In this paper we construct a framework for algorithms with this property, and consider algorithms that use the quantity of information to direct their strategy. These data dependent algorithms still identify in the limit but may require an exponential characteristic set to do so. Nevertheless preliminary practical evidence suggests that they could perform better.

Keywords: *DFA*, grammatical inference, identification in the limit.

Introduction

Identification of deterministic finite automata (*DFA*) is possible in polynomial time through characteristic sets. The emphasis on deterministic finite automata is justified by the fact that algorithms treating the inference problem for *DFA* can be nicely adapted for larger classes of grammars, for instance even linear grammars [SG94, T88, T94], subsequential transducers [OGV93] or tree grammars. They can even be transposed to solve the inference problem for context-free grammars, when the data is presented as unlabelled trees [S92]. These results are algebraic and do not depend on the algorithms.

The question of identifying a target deterministic finite automaton is the earliest in grammatical inference. In [G67] the problem is studied under the on-line paradigm and in 1978 Gold gives an answer in the given data paradigm [G78]. Other early works on the problem include Trakhenbrot and Barzdin who give a general identification algorithm for this task [TB73]. The algorithmic difficulty of the task is studied in Pitt's 1989 paper [P89]. In this he describes the on-line learning paradigm in which, by using Angluin's results [A87] on oracle learning, it can be proven that for the reasonable definition of polynomial time learning, *DFA* cannot be identified in polynomial time. This result nevertheless must be compared with experimental results (such as [L92] or [D94]) where the performance of Trakhenbrot and Barzdin's [TB73] algorithm or others are analysed. The encouraging results lead to believe that in practical cases an approximate identification of *DFA* is possible.

Other techniques have since been devised to infer *DFA*. Oncina and García [OG92] proposed, along the lines of Trakhenbrot & Barzdin's algorithm, *RPNI*[1], a polynomial algorithm for inference of *DFA*, with the property of identification in the limit. This algorithm has been linked with work on the search space where a correct (inferred) automaton is defined as one obtained through merging states from the Prefix Tree Acceptor, which is the tree-like *DFA* that accepts only the positive data. This leads to exploring the lattice of partitions [DMV94]. Dupont proposed alternative methods based on genetic algorithms to explore this lattice [D94].

RPNI is an optimistic algorithm: at any one step two states are compared and the question is: can they be merged ? No positive evidence can be produced; merging will take place each time that such a merge does not produce inconsistency. Obviously an early mistake can have disastrous effects and we note from Lang [L92] that a breadth-first exploration of the lattice (which corresponds to a breadth wise construction of the automaton) is likely to be better as in such a way more examples will be present to test the proposed merges.

In this paper we aim to compare the different ways this construction can take place. We prove that any data-independent ordering will allow for identification in the limit. We also prove that if we take the heuristic: try to merge those two states for which most evidence is available, the algorithm identifies in the limit, but the characteristic set associated to this heuristic can be exponential. Nevertheless preliminary experimental evidence suggests that the heuristic is interesting.

1) Definitions

An alphabet is a finite non-empty set of distinct symbols. For a given alphabet Σ, the set of all finite strings of symbols from Σ is denoted Σ^*. The empty string is denoted λ. For a string w, $|w|$ denotes the length of w. A language L over Σ is a subset of Σ^*.

A deterministic finite automaton (*DFA*) over Σ is a 5-tuple $A=(Q, \Sigma, \delta, q_0, F)$ where Q is a finite set of states, F a subset of Q, denoting the set of final states of A; δ is the transition function: $Q \times \Sigma \to Q$. δ is recursively extended to a function: $Q \times \Sigma^* \to Q$ as follows:

$$\delta(q, \lambda)=q \text{ and}$$
$$\text{if } w=xw', \text{ with } x \in \Sigma \text{ and } w' \in \Sigma, \delta(q, w)=\delta((\delta(q, x), w')).$$

---

[1]Regular Positive and Negative Inference

A *DFA* *A* accepts a string *w* *iff* $d(q_0, w) \in F$. The language recognized by an automaton is the set of all strings accepted by the automaton. Two automata are equivalent *iff* they recognize the same language. An automaton is complete if its associated transition function δ is total. The size of a *DFA* is the number of its states, which is polynomially related to the number of bits needed to encode it.

Gold presented in 1978 [G78] a model for identification, where a sample of labelled strings <*S*+, *S*->, with *S*+ a set of positive instances, and *S*- a set of negative instances, is presented to the inference algorithm that must return a representation compatible with <*S*+, *S*->. The further conditions are that for each language there exists a characteristic sample with which the algorithm returns a correct representation, and, to avoid collusion (or cheating), this must be monotonous in the sense that if correctly labelled examples are added to the characteristic set, then the algorithm infers the same language. Gold proved that deterministic finite automata were identifiable (in this model) in polynomial time from given data. Further work in this model has contributed the following results: alternative algorithms have been proposed to infer *DFA* [OG92], Even linear grammars have been proven identifiable in polynomial time [T88]&[SG94]; these techniques have been extended to universal linear grammars in [T94]. Following the same idea deterministic even linear grammars are identifiable in polynomial time from positive examples only [KMT95] and the same holds for total subsequential functions [OGV93]. The algorithms provided in these papers have been implemented to deal with practical problems in the fields of speech, pattern recognition or automatic translation.

To take into account the fact that the length of the examples must depend polynomially in the size of the concept to be learnt we use the following definition [H95], which is generalizes Gold's results [G78]. The size of a sample <*S*+, *S*-> (denoted *size*(*S*+∪*S*-)) is the sum of the lengths of all the strings in the sample.

Definition 1 A representation class *R* is polynomially identifiable from given data *iff* there exist two polynomials $p()$ and $q()$ and an algorithm *A* such that:

1) Given any sample <*S*+, *S*->, of size *n*, *A* returns a representation *R* compatible with <*S*+, *S*-> in $O(p(n))$ time.

2) For each representation *R* of size *n*, there exists a characteristic sample <*CS*+, *CS*-> of size less than $q(n)$ for which, if $S+ \supseteq CS+$, $S- \supseteq CS-$, *A* returns a representation *R'* equivalent with *R*.

By this definition algorithm *A* is a polynomial learner. With this definition, Gold's 1978 result can be restated as follows:

Gold's theorem (1978) *DFA* are polynomially identifiable from given data.

In fact his result is even stronger as for any *DFA* a characteristic set can also be computed in polynomial time. The definition above are not trivial: in [H95] is proven that the following classes do not admit polynomial identification from given data:
- Context-free grammars
- Linear grammars
- Simple deterministic grammars
- Non deterministic finite automata.

2 The General Converging Algorithm.

We aim to give a very general class of algorithms that converge in polynomial time. The class is based on merging algorithms as defined by Trakhenbrot & Barzdin [TB73] or Oncina & García [OG92]. For this purpose a general yet abstract data structure is needed. Obviously, for specific instantiations of the algorithm, the data structures need not be so heavy. Moreover research in the direction of finding interesting data structures for grammatical inference is necessary: better structures mean faster algorithms and hence should help produce in the foreseeable future nice results.

The instances will be given by two sets $S+$, $S-$ of strings. For each string in $S+\cup S-$ a mark will enable to know if the string can be read in the automaton, *i.e.* as the automaton may be incomplete, if through reading the string, one ends in a state of the automaton or not.

The initial state will be denoted q_0, and all states will be indexed by positive integers. The transition function δ will consist in an array with two entries, one corresponding to the states, and the other to the alphabet. The value of a cell $\delta(q, x)$ is (the index of) the state reached from q by x. If the edge has not yet been computed, the value will be undefined.

Furthermore a special structure is needed to remember which merges have already been tested: the corresponding array has 2 entries and should be read: $q' \in \text{Tested}(q, x)$ *iff* adding $\delta(q, x)=q'$ has been tested.

Finally given an automaton A, and sets $< S+, S->$ a state in Q can be positive-final if some string in $S+$ terminates in the state, negative-final if some string in $S-$ terminates in the state, or indeterminate if no string in $S+\cup S-$ terminates in the state. Obviously if a state is indeterminate, it can be labelled final or non-final (in the classical sense) without breaking the inconsistency of the automaton towards $< S+, S->$. For this purpose we define two sets of (indices of) states $F+$ and $F-$. In our notations a positive-final state will belong to $F+$, and a negative-final state to $F-$.

For example at some point the data structure could be:

δ	a	b
0	1	0
1		2
2	1	

$F+ = \{1\}$ $F- = \{0\}$
The intended meaning is that:
$\delta(q_0, aba)=q_1$ so $aba \in L$.
$\delta(q_0, bbaa)=$undefined.

We propose an algorithm that uses a function (ϕ) as a parameter:
ϕ can be of any type provided the following specifications are met: given an automaton A, ϕ returns a triple $<q, x, q'>$ such that
        1 $\delta(q, x)$ is undefined and
        2 $q' \notin \text{Tested}(q, x)$.

In such a case ϕ is called *admissible*. Furthermore a function ϕ is called *data-independent* if it does not need information about the data $<S+, S->$ to return its result. Otherwise ϕ is *data-dependent*.

The following algorithm converges:

> **Algorithm** *DFAinfer*(ϕ);
> Input: $S=<S+,S->$
> Output: an automaton (defined by $\delta, F+, F-$)
> {*Initialisations*}
> $n\leftarrow 0$; $\forall x\in \Sigma$, Tested $(q_0, x) \leftarrow \varnothing$; $F+\leftarrow\varnothing$; $F-\leftarrow\varnothing$;
>
> While there are some unmarked strings in $S+\cup S-$ do
> $<q, x, q'>\leftarrow \phi(A)$;
>   If *Possible*($\delta(q, x)=q'$)
>   then $\delta(q, x)\leftarrow q'$;
>   For each unmarked w in $S+$ do
>   if $\delta(q_0, w)=q$
>   then mark(w); $F+\leftarrow F+\cup\{q\}$;
>   For each unmarked w in $S-$ do
>   if $\delta(q_0, w)=q$
>   then mark(w); $F-\leftarrow F-\cup\{q\}$;
>   else   Tested $(q, x)\leftarrow$ Tested $(q, x) \cup \{q'\}$;
>   if $\forall i\leq n$ $q_i\in$ Tested(q, x)
>   then $n\leftarrow n+1$;
> $Q\leftarrow Q \cup \{q_n\}$;
> $\delta(q, x)\leftarrow q_n$;
>   For each unmarked w in $S+$ do
>   if $\delta(q_0, w)=q$ then mark(w);
> $F+\leftarrow F+\cup\{q\}$;
>   For each unmarked w in $S-$ do
>   if $\delta(q_0, w)=q$ then mark(w);
> $F-\leftarrow F-\cup\{q\}$;
> $\forall x\in \Sigma$, Tested $(q_n, x) \leftarrow\varnothing$;
> End-while;

Function *Possible* ($\delta(q, x)=q'$): Boolean;
returns True if adding to δ the rule (q, x, q') does not lead to inconsistency, if not False.

This can be checked easily by testing if in the automaton obtained through adding the transition $\delta(q, x)=q'$ to the current automaton there are two strings uxw and vw such that:
- $\delta(q_0, u)=q$ and $\delta(q_0, v)=q'$ and
- $uxw \in S+$, $vw\in S-$, or $uxw \in S-$, $vw\in S+$.

Before proving that the algorithm converges let us show how it works on an example:

Example 1

Let $\Sigma=\{a, b\}$ $S+=\{\lambda, ab, aaa, aabaa, aaaba\}$ $S-=\{aa, baa, aaab\}$
- $F+\leftarrow\{q_0\}$ $F-\leftarrow\varnothing$ $n\leftarrow 0$

•$\phi(A)$=<q_0, a, q_0> *Possible* returns False, due to the presence of λ in S+, aa in S-. So Tested (q_0, a) ={q_0}. As $\forall i \leq n$ $q_i \in$ Tested(q_0, a), q_1 is created and $\delta(q_0, a) \leftarrow q_1$, $n \leftarrow 1$.

•$\phi(A)$=<q_0, b, q_0> *Possible* returns True, $\delta(q_0, b) \leftarrow q_0$.

•$\phi(A)$=<q_1, a, q_0> *Possible* returns False, due to the presence of λ in S+, aa in S-. So Tested(q_1, a) ={q_0}.

•$\phi(A)$=<q_1, a, q_1> *Possible* returns False, due to the presence of aaa in S+, aa in S-. So Tested(q_1, a) ={q_0, q_1}. As $\forall i \leq n$ $q_i \in$ Tested(q_1, a), q_2 is created and $\delta(q_1, a) \leftarrow q_2$, $n \leftarrow 2$.

•$\phi(A)$=<q_1, b, q_0> *Possible* returns True, $\delta(q_1, b) \leftarrow q_0$.

•$\phi(A)$=<q_2, a, q_0> *Possible* returns False, due to the presence of λ in S+, aaab in S-. So Tested(q_2, a) ={q_0}.

•$\phi(A)$=<q_2, a, q_1> *Possible* returns False, due to the presence of λ in S+, aaab in S-. So Tested(q_2, a) ={q_0, q_1}.

•$\phi(A)$=<q_2, a, q_2> *Possible* returns False, due to the presence of aaa in S+, aa in S-. So Tested(q_2, a) ={q_0, q_1, q_2}. As $\forall i \leq n$ $q_i \in$ Tested(q_2, a), q_3 is created and $\delta(q_2, a) \leftarrow q_3$, $n \leftarrow 3$.

•$\phi(A)$=<q_2, b, q_0> *Possible* returns False, due to the presence of aabaa in S+, aa in S-. So Tested(q_2, b) ={q_0}.

•$\phi(A)$=<q_2, b, q_1> *Possible* returns True, $\delta(q_2, b) \leftarrow q_1$.

•$\phi(A)$=<q_3, a, q_0> *Possible* returns True, $\delta(q_3, a) \leftarrow q_0$.

•$\phi(A)$=<q_3, b, q_0> *Possible* returns False, due to the presence of λ in S+, aaab in S-. So Tested(q_3, b) ={q_0}.

•$\phi(A)$=<q_3, b, q_1> *Possible* returns False, due to the presence of aaaba in S+, aa in S-. So Tested(q_3, b) ={q_0, q_1}.

•$\phi(A)$=<q_3, b, q_2> *Possible* returns True, $\delta(q_3, b) \leftarrow q_2$.

All strings can be read on this automaton, so the algorithm halts, with solution as in Figure 1. Notice that $F+ = \{q_0, q_3\}$, $F- = \{q_2\}$. So state q_1 can be indifferently labelled positive or negative: in both cases the automaton will be consistent with the data.

The function ϕ used in this example will be formally defined later: it corresponds to a classical breadth-wise research based on a total ordering on Σ (here a<b).

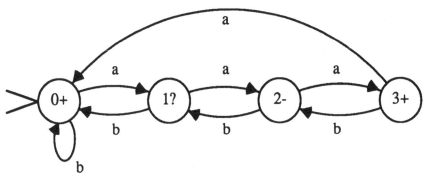

Figure 1

Theorem 1

For any polynomial data-independent function ϕ, $DFAinfer(\phi)$ is a polynomial inference algorithm for DFA.

Proof

Let us first prove that the algorithm is polynomial in $m=size(S+\cup S-)$. Function *Possible* insures us that the solution returned is always consistent with S. The number of states of the inferred automaton is thus at most m. At each pass one of the following quantities increases:

- the number of states
- the number of Tested triplets.

As both are polynomially bounded, so is the overall complexity of the algorithm (provided the specified function ϕ is polynomial).

It remains to be proven that for every regular language L defined by a DFA, there exists a polynomial characteristic set, depending of ϕ, for which, when this set is included in a set of strings compatible with L, an equivalent DFA is inferred.

Let M be the minimum canonical automaton, complete, equivalent to the target automaton A. The characteristic set is computed in the following way: in algorithm *DFAinfer*, after the call to function ϕ ($<q, x, q'>\leftarrow\phi(A)$) increment the characteristic set $<CS+, CS->$ as follows:

If $\delta_M(q, x)\neq q'$ then add w to $CS+$, w' to $CS-$ such that:

either $w=uxv$, $w'=u'v$, and $\delta_A(q_0, u)=q$ $\delta_A(q_0, u')=q'$

or $w=uv$, $w'=u'xv$, and $\delta_A(q_0, u)=q'$ $\delta_A(q_0, u')=q$.

The existence of such a pair $<w, w'>$ is a consequence of Nerode's Theorem: in the minimal DFA, any two different states can be separated by some suffix. Moreover there exists a separating suffix of length at most the number of states of the automaton [H78]. Hence at most as many pairs of strings $<w, w'>$ are needed as there are tests that need to fail. This quantity is bounded by $n^2|\Sigma|$. As ϕ does not depend on $<S+, S->$, adding strings to the learning set cannot modify the behaviour of the algorithm: the strings we have added are compatible with A, hence with M, and any merge that has been accepted beforehand cannot be refused by the added strings. This remains true if a new computation is started with a consistent set of strings including the constructed $<CS+, CS->$ ◊

In [OG92] the authors propose the following function ϕ_α [2]

Let $<_\Sigma$ be a total order on Σ. Consider the following order on $Q\times\Sigma\times Q$:

$<q_i, x, q_j> \ll_\alpha <q_k, x, q_m>$ iff $\qquad$ $i<k$

$\qquad\qquad\qquad\qquad\qquad\qquad$ or $i=k$ and $x<_\Sigma y$

$\qquad\qquad\qquad\qquad\qquad\qquad$ or $i=k$ and $x=y$ and $j<m$.

$\phi_\alpha(A)$ returns the smallest triple $<q_i, x, q_j>$ for $\ll_\alpha$ such that

$\qquad\qquad$ 1 $\delta(q_i, x)$ is undefined

$\qquad$ and $\qquad$ 2 $q_j \notin Tested(q_i, x)$.

---

[2] In this paper we have slightly modified the setting: the natural object under construction in [OG93] (but also in [TP73], [L92], [DMV94]...) is the prefix tree acceptor (*PTA*), which is through successive merges modified into a graph. In the algorithm we propose the *PTA* is not constructed, it is implicit.

Other alternative algorithms are possible and infer in the limit, provided the function ϕ does not depend on the test set. For example, if *a priori* knowledge makes us believe that the letters in the alphabet do not have same probability of appearance a depth-first strategy would be better:

$$<q_i, x, q_j> \ll_\beta <q_k, x, q_m> \text{ iff} \qquad x <_\Sigma y$$
$$\text{or } x=y \text{ and } i<k$$
$$\text{or } x=y \text{ and } i=k \text{ and } j<m.$$

$\phi_\beta(A)$ returns the smallest triple $<q_i, x, q_j>$ for $\ll_\beta$ such that

          1   $\delta(q_i, x)$ is undefined

and   2 $q_j \notin \text{Tested}(q_i, x)$.

The data of example 1 contains more a's than b's. If this was known then for a function ϕ_β constructed upon an order $\ll_\beta$ (with $a <_\Sigma b$), $DFAInfer(\phi_\beta)$ now returns the automaton depicted Figure 2.

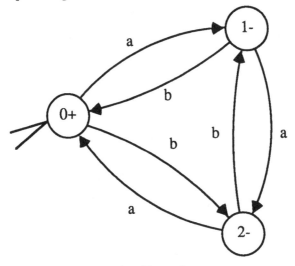

Figure 2

Comparing both automata and considering that alternative orderings could be proposed, a natural question is the following: does there exist for each regular language a universal polynomial characteristic set, one for which, when included in a set $<S+, S->$, any (correct) algorithm would give the same (correct) solution? A general (negative) answer is given in [H95]: for the wide class of all polynomial algorithms, some DFA only admit infinite characteristic sets. But if we consider the algorithms of the family $DFAinfer(\phi)$ we get the following result:

Theorem 2

For any regular language represented by a DFA A with n states, there exists a finite set $<CS+, CS->$ for which, given any superset $<S+, S->$, any admissible function ϕ, $DFAinfer(\phi)$ returns a DFA equivalent to A.

Proof

Let M be the target automaton recognizing language L.

We construct a characteristic set as follows:

For each state q_i let $K(i)=\{w \in \Sigma^*: \delta(q_0, w)=q_i$ and no substring of w is in $K(i)\}$

Now construct $<CS+, CS->$:

For each $<q_i, x, q_j>$ such that $\delta(q_i, x) \neq q_j$ by Nerode's theorem [H78] we have:

$\exists uxw, vw \in \Sigma^*$ with $u \in K(i)$ and $v \in K(j)$ and

either $uxw \in L$ and $vw \notin L$, $uxw \in CS+$, $vw \in CS-$

or $uxw \notin L$ and $vw \in L$, $uxw \in CS-$, $vw \in CS+$.

The construction is obviously finite.

Now let $S+\supseteq CS+$, $S-\supseteq CS-$, ϕ be any function.

DFAinfer(ϕ) identifies L in the limit:

We will only sketch the proof. In the automaton under construction, each state is reachable from q_0. If not this state would not have been created. Thus if at some moment function ϕ proposes as triplet $<q_i, x, q_j>$ then q_i and q_j are reachable through a path without cycles. This path is correct in the target automaton, where it also is cycle-free and thus corresponds to some string in $K(i)$ (and respectively $K(j)$). If $\delta(q_i, x) \neq q_j$ then two strings exist in the characteristic set that distinguish $\delta(q_i, x)$ and q_j. Thus, *DFAinfer(ϕ)* achieves identification in the limit. ◊

Example 2

For the automaton depicted in Figure 2

$K(0)=\{\lambda\}$ $\qquad$ $K(1)=\{a, bb\}$ $\qquad$ $K(2)=\{aa, b\}$

Thus the following set is Characteristic for all ϕs:

$CS+=\{\lambda, aaa, ab, aabb, ba, bbaa, bbb\}$ $\quad$ $CS-=\{a, aa, aab, b, baa, bb, bba\}$

This characteristic set is not overestimated in size: given a class of functions Φ and an automaton A, a pair $<S+, S->$ is characteristic for (Φ, A) if given any function ϕ in Φ, **DFAinfer(ϕ)** identifies A.

Proposition 1

Given any polynomial $p()$, there exists an integer n and a *DFA A* of size n, such that no set $<S+, S->$, with $size(S+\cup S-)\leq p(n)$, is characteristic for (Φ, A), where Φ is the set of all admissible functions.

Proof

Let us consider $\forall w \in \Sigma$ the function $\phi_w(A)$:

If w can be read in A then apply ϕ_α, else return $<q, x, q'>$ such that for $w=uxv$, u is the longest prefix one can read in A, and q' is minimal such that $q' \notin Tested(q, x)$.

Suppose now that the target language is Σ^{n-1}, the set of all strings of length $n-1$. Then consider the run of *DFAinfer(ϕ_w)* on data $<S+, S->$: if no mistake has been done in the first n tests of *possible*, we have at step n the following automaton: $\delta(q_0, x_1)=q_1,... \delta(q_{n-2}, x_{n-1})=q_{n-1}$ with $w=x_1..x_n$. At the next step, $<q_{n-1}, x_n, q>$ must be considered (for some q). For the merge to be avoided, as is necessary, $S+$ or $S-$ must contain at least one string prefixed by w. As this holds for any w, and the number of such strings is exponential, we have established the result. ◊

3 A Data Driven Algorithm

A reasonable idea is that the less information one has before trying to merge two states the more likely an error will appear. This fact has already been noticed by Lang [L92], and been used to justify a breadth-wise exploration. Yet the idea can be enhanced by using a data-dependant function ϕ that would return the triple $<q, x, q'>$ for which most information is available: different measures of this "quantity of information" are possible. We chose here to count the number of strings exiting a given state, or exiting through a given edge.

We propose to adapt algorithm $DFAinfer(\phi)$, in order to maintain the following data structure: given a state q of the automaton A we are constructing,

$\#+strings\_per\_state(q) = |\{w \in \Sigma^*: \exists u \in \Sigma^*\ \delta_A(q_0, u) = q\ \text{and}\ uw \in S+\}|$
$\#-strings\_per\_state(q) = |\{w \in \Sigma^*: \exists u \in \Sigma^*\ \delta_A(q_0, u) = q\ \text{and}\ uw \in S-\}|.$

and given a state q, and a symbol x,

$\#+strings\_per\_edge(<q, x>) = |\{w \in \Sigma^*: \exists u \in \Sigma^*\ \delta_A(q_0, u) = q\ \text{and}\ uxw \in S+\}|.$
$\#-strings\_per\_edge(<q, x>) = |\{w \in \Sigma^*: \exists u \in \Sigma^*\ \delta_A(q_0, u) = q\ \text{and}\ uxw \in S-\}|.$

And ϕ_γ returns the triple $<q, x, q'>$ such that:

- $<q, x, q'>$ is valid: 1 $\delta(q, x)$ is undefined
  $\qquad\qquad\qquad\qquad\qquad$ 2 $q' \notin Tested(q, x)$.
- $\min\{\#+strings\_per\_edge(<q, x>), \#-strings\_per\_state(q')\}$
  $+\ \min\{\#-strings\_per\_edge(<q, x>), \#+strings\_per\_state(q')\}$
  is maximal.

Algorithm $DFAinfer(\phi_\gamma)$ is polynomial and infers an automaton consistent with the data. But does it infer in the limit ?

Proposition 2
$DFAinfer(\phi_\gamma)$ identifies any regular language in the limit.

Proof
A consequence of theorem 2. For the characteristic set as defined in theorem 2 $DFAinfer(\phi_\gamma)$ identifies the automaton in the limit.   ◊

It can be checked that on the data from example 1, $DFAinfer(\phi_\gamma)$ infers the same automaton as with ϕ_β. The algorithm "rediscovers" the fact that the a's are more important than the b's, and thus follows the good order.

Nevertheless the required characteristic set is no longer guaranteed to be polynomial:

Proposition 3
There exists for each n some automata for which $DFAinfer(\phi_\gamma)$ needs a non polynomial characteristic set to identify in the limit.

Proof
A consequence of proposition 1: to a proposed characteristic set one can always add data so that the run of the algorithm will simulate any ϕ_w, for any given string w. ◊

4) Experimental work

The protocol we have followed is proposed in [D94] and based upon previous benchmarks ([T82] and [MG94]). The automata are all relatively small, and thus, the presented results can only give an indication of what to expect in equivalent conditions. Experimentation on larger automata is yet to be done. The 15 following test languages have been defined[3]:

$L_1 : a*$

$L_2 : (ab)*$

L_3 : any string not ending with an odd number of b's followed by an odd number of a's.

L_4 : any string without more than 2 consecutive a's.

L_5 : any string with an even number of a's and an even number of b's.

L_6 : any string such that the number of a's differs of the number of b's by 0 modulo 3.

$L_7 : a* b* a*b*$

$L_8 : a*b$

$L_9 : (a*+c*)b$

$L_{10} : (aa)*(bbb)*$

L_{11} : any string with an even number of a's and an odd number of b's.

$L_{12}: a(aa)*b$

L_{13} : any string with an even number of a's

$L_{14} : (aa)*ba*$

$L_{15} : bc*b+ac*a$

For each language 10 independent learning samples have been randomly created from these DFA, with as a restricting condition that the sample must be structurally complete[4]. The generation of the sample is pursued until the sample size is three times as much as the size of the structurally complete sample. In our case we have used exactly the same data as in [D94].

Our data-dependent method[5] is compared with $RPNI$, which appears in the literature as one of the best methods. Our data-dependent method corresponds to the algorithm from section 2, with function ϕ_γ. The comparison is summarized in table 1. The results are computed as in [D94]. All strings up to length 9 (length 7 for languages L_9 and L_{15}) are presented to each of the inferred automata. Strings present in the training set are not counted. Then the result (appearing in column 2 for $RPNI$, in column 3 for $DDDI$) is the sum of the proportion of correctly classified positive strings, and of the proportion of correctly classified negative strings, divided by 2. Again this formula is given and justified in [D94]. Column 4 gives the size of the canonical complete automaton that is to be identified.

---

[3] Input alphabet is $\{a\}$ for L_1, $\{a, b, c\}$ for L_9 and L_{15}, $\{a, b\}$ for all the others.

[4] A sample is structurally complete if every edge in the automaton is used by some string in the data. For more detail see [MG94], [D94].

[5] We have called it $DDDI$: Data Driven Dfa Inference.

	RPNI	DDDI	Size
L1	100,00	100,00	2
L2	96,60	96,60	3
L3	100,00	100,00	5
L4	100,00	100,00	4
L5	62,90	61,98	5
L6	89,82	89,78	4
L7	92,04	88,67	5
L8	100,00	100,00	3
L9	99,09	99,11	3
L10	97,18	97,18	6
L11	88,31	88,08	5
L12	100,00	100,00	4
L13	89,92	94,99	3
L14	98,78	94,56	4
L15	95,34	95,34	5
Mean	93,87	93,75	

Table 1

The results remain inconclusive. The fact that the data does not have any specificity (same frequency for each letter...) offers no advantage to a data-driven method. Exhaustive tests with training data obtained through other distributions than the uniform one are necessary.

5) Conclusions

"Polynomial identification from given data" is a non trivial condition leading to interesting algorithms in grammatical inference. We have proven that this property could be extended to a wide class of algorithms. The property is lost for data-dependent algorithms but through our preliminary experiments we are convinced that this class of algorithms represents a promising trend of research.

Bibliography

[A87]   Angluin D. (1987). Queries and concept learning. *Machine Learning* 2 , 319-342.

[DMV94] Dupont P., Miclet L. & Vidal E. (1994). What is the search space of the regular inference? *Proceedings of the International Colloquium on Grammatical Inference ICGI*-94 (pp. 25-37). Lecture Notes in Artificial Intelligence **862**, Springer-Verlag. Edited by R. Carrasco and J. Oncina.

[D94] Dupont P. (1994). Regular Grammatical Inference from positive and negative samples by genetic search: the GIG method. *Proceedings of the International Colloquium on Grammatical Inference ICGI*-94 (pp. 236-245).Springer-Verlag Series in Artificial Intelligence **862**. Edited by R. Carasco and J. Oncina.

[G67] Gold E.M. (1967). Language identification in the limit. *Inform.&Control.* **10**, 447-474.

[G78] Gold E.M. (1978). Complexity of Automaton Identification from given Data. *Information and Control* **37**, 302-320.

[H78] Harrison M.A. (1978). Introduction to Formal Language Theory. Reading: Addison-Wesley.

[H95] de la Higuera C. (1995). Characteristic sets for Grammatical Inference. In *Proceedings of the International Colloquium on Grammatical Inference ICGI-96.*

[KMT95] Koshiba, T., Mäkinen, E. & Takada, Y. (1995). Learning Deterministic Even Linear Languages from Positive Examples. *Proceedings of ALT '95,* Lecture Notes in Artificial Intelligence **997**, Springer-Verlag.

[L92] Lang K.J. (1992). Random *DFA*'s can be approximately Learned from Sparse Uniform Examples, *Proceedings of COLT 1992*, pp 45-52.

[MG94] Miclet L. & de Gentile C. Inférence Grammaticale à partir d'Exemples et de Contre-exemples : deux algorithmes optimaux (BIG et RIG) et une version Heuristique (BRIG), *Actes des JFA-94*, Strasbourg, France, pp. F1-F13, 1994.

[OG92] Oncina J. & García P. (1992) Inferring Regular Languages in Polynomial Updated Time. *In Pattern Recognition and Image Analysis, World Scientific* (49-61).

[OGV93] Oncina J., García P. & Vidal E. (1993). Learning subsequential transducers for pattern recognition tasks. *IEEE Transactions on Pattern Analysis and Machine Intelligence* **15**, 448-458.

[P89] Pitt, L. (1989). Inductive inference, *dfas* and computational complexity. *Proceedings of the International Workshop on Analogical and Inductive Inference* (pp. 18-44). Lecture Notes in Artificial Intelligence **397**, Springer-Verlag.

[SG94] Sempere J.M. & García P. (1994). A characterisation of Even Linear Languages and its application to the Learning Problem. *Proceedings of the International Colloquium on Grammatical Inference ICGI-94* (pp. 38-44). Lecture Notes in Artificial Intelligence **862**, Springer-Verlag.

[S92] Sakakibara Y. (1992). Efficient Learning of Context-free Grammars from Positive Structural Examples. *Inf. and Comp.* **97**, 23-60.

[T88] Takada Y. (1988). Grammatical inference for even Linear languages based on control sets. *Information Processing Letters* **28**, 193-199.

[T94] Takada Y. (1994). A Hierarchy of Language Families Learnable by Regular Language Learners. *Proceedings of the International Colloquium on Grammatical Inference ICGI-94* (pp. 16-24). Lecture Notes in Artificial Intelligence **862**, Springer-Verlag.

[T82] Tomita M. (1982). Dynamic construction of Finite Automata from Examples Using Hill Climbing, *Proc. of the 4th annual Cognitive Science Conference*, USA, pp. 105-108, .

[TB73] Trakhenbrot B. & Barzdin Y.(1973). Finite automata: Behavior and Synthesis. North Holland Pub., Amsterdam.

[Y93] Yokomori T. (1993). Learning non deterministic Finite Automata from queries and Counterexamples. *Machine Intelligence* **13**. Furukawa, Michie & Muggleton eds., Oxford Univ. Press.

Author Index

Springer-Verlag
and the Environment

We at Springer-Verlag firmly believe that an international science publisher has a special obligation to the environment, and our corporate policies consistently reflect this conviction.

We also expect our business partners – paper mills, printers, packaging manufacturers, etc. – to commit themselves to using environmentally friendly materials and production processes.

The paper in this book is made from low- or no-chlorine pulp and is acid free, in conformance with international standards for paper permanency.

Lecture Notes in Artificial Intelligence (LNAI)

Lecture Notes in Computer Science